D1483221

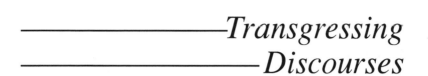

Transgressing
Discourses

SUNY Series, Human Communication Processes
Donald P. Cushman and Ted J. Smith III, editors

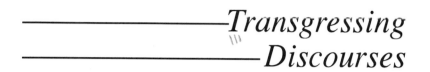

Transgressing Discourses

Discourses

Communication and the Voice of Other

edited by
Michael Huspek
and Gary P. Radford

State University of New York Press

Published by
State University of New York Press, Albany

For information, address State University of New York Press
State University Plaza, Albany, NY 12246

Production by Dana Foote
Marketing by Dana E. Yanulavich

Library of Congress Cataloging-in-Publication Data

Transgressing discourses : communication and the voice of other /
    edited by Michael Huspek and Gary P. Radford.
        p.   cm. — (SUNY series, human communication processes)
        Includes bibliographical references and index.
        ISBN 0–7914–3353–6 (alk. paper). — ISBN 0–7914–3354–4 (pb : alk.
paper)
        1. Communication—Philosophy. I. Huspek, Michael, 1950–   .
II. Radford, Gary P., 1961–   .   III. Series: SUNY series in human
communication processes.
P90.T68   1997
302.2'01—dc21   97–2267
                                         CIP

10 9 8 7 6 5 4 3 2 1

All that is now
All that is gone
All that's to come
and everything under the sun is in tune
but the sun is eclipsed by the moon

—Pink Floyd, *Eclipse*

Contents

Contents

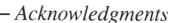

Acknowledgments

We would like to acknowledge the efforts and support of Donald P. Cushman, Lois G. Patton, Ann Fenech Vitarella, Dana Foote, and David Prout of SUNY Press in making this book a reality. Thanks also to Marie Radford for her help in proofreading the final manuscript and James Anderson for his help in preparing the index.

Michael Huspek and Gary P. Radford

Communication and the Voice of Other

Michael Huspek

Increased recognition of the many issues surrounding multiculturalism has brought with it an underscoring of the importance of otherness, the otherness of alien cultures, the otherness of one's next-door neighbor, the otherness that exists as an untapped resource potential of one's own being. In encountering otherness we are provided with an occasion to think about the limitations and potentials of our personal lives as well as the cultures to which we belong in ways that might not otherwise be available. Indeed, without encountering the strange and potentially transgressive existence of other, we run the risk of shrinking into a complacent knowledge of self, as well as other, which undergoes little or no challenge and which, consequently, may prove resistant to genuinely critical self-reflection and growth.

As important as each encounter with otherness is, each is susceptible to violations that may occur when one or another party seeks to impose unilaterally his or her will upon the other. Such can be accomplished in many different ways: by means of aborting prematurely the interaction; by partaking of it in a prejudiced, that is, prejudgmental manner; or by disingenuously insisting that other communicate with one's own authoritatively backed, predefined terms. When such occurs, much may be lost for such closing off of oneself to a genuine engagement is likely to prevent both oneself and other from gaining essential knowledge and understanding that are the basis for both critical self-reflection and mutual growth. Through a genuinely open engagement the strangeness of other promises to shake us out of our self-certainty, indicating limits where we thought previously there were none, and potentiality where there previously had been limits that defied transgression.

An essential theme running throughout this volume is the idea that our efforts to engage other, as well as other's efforts to engage us, have been seriously impaired because of problems that are fundamentally communicative in nature. More specifically, there is general agreement among the contributors to this volume that the voice of other has not been sufficiently heard, on account of how discourses of the human sciences, as well as other dominant discourses (e.g., law), have structured our interaction with other. Each of the essays in this volume in fact may be read as an attempt to clarify the nature of the communicative failing and to develop an appropriate corrective.

Beyond this core theme, however, there is considerable disagreement as to the scope and significance of the problem. One group of contributors acknowledges that a degree of problematicity is built into the relation between scientific discourse and otherness but suggests that the problem is essentially one of limited communication which, in turn, produces limited knowledge of other. This group, which includes, for example, Kovačić, Cushman, and MacDougall, as well as Harrison, suggests that science has been limited in its ability to confidently know other but that this problem may be overcome through developing and implementing more rigorous methods which enhance the overall communicative effort. Such improvements might consist of the ongoing development of increasingly refined techniques for culling truths where there previously existed either ignorance or error. Current methods such as the survey research questionnaire, the experimental design, or the scientist's interview schedule, as well as strategic combinations of such, can all be improved so as to elicit more information and thus to gain greater knowledge of other. Just as natural scientists have come to better know the workings of nature, so too can human scientists come to better know the workings of human beings. Thus, as Cushman and associates maintain in this volume, human scientists can come to better predict the durability of marriages based upon the administration of elaborate tests to the marriage partners, or as Harrison also asserts, human scientists can come to better explain the prospects for cooperation and compliance in workplace institutions by attending more conscientiously to such issues as employee trust and predictability. Where such methods come up short, the call is for the deployment of supplementary methods such as ethnography, as Harrison recommends, which might be used as a communicative means for eliciting more information from other, or strategically deployed rhetorical devices, as offered by Cushman and associates, which may be used to enhance scientists' ability to convey the significance or palatability of their knowledge of otherness either to themselves or to nonscientific speech communities.

A second group of contributors also argues that the nature of the communicative relationship between science and other is problematic. However, in opposition to the first group, these contributors argue that the problem with the relationship is not simply one of limited communication which may in principle be overcome by one means or another. Rather, drawing upon principles of hermeneutic philosophy, contributors such as Shotter, Krippendorff, and Langsdorf argue that communication between science and other is inherently flawed on account of a certain hubris that exemplifies the scientific quest for knowledge. The charge is that neither the human sciences nor any other institutionally based discourse can or ever will be able to know humans in ways that the natural sciences have come to know inanimate nature, and that to make any such claim is foolhardy at best. Moreover, to actually act upon such a belief through the development and deployment of increasingly sophisticated methods entails structuring communicative relationships designed ostensibly to elicit information from other but which, at the same time, must necessarily suppress those significant aspects of other's voice that are not amenable to rigorous scientific analysis. We see this tendency at work either where other's ostensibly verifiable behavior is valued as an object of scientific inquiry over the less easily ascertained subjective aspects of other's being or where the significances and meanings of other are converted into, say, causal terms that are codified to suit the requirements of the scientific discourse. In both instances, the hermeneutic charge is that symbolic violence is being inflicted upon subject-as-other, as aspects of each subject's being are either eclipsed or suppressed and that, as an outcome, domains of cultural meaning are effectively colonized by a dominant discourse.

Yet a third group of contributors to this volume, consisting of Cobb, Comerford, Gemin, Gross, Smith, and Taylor, focuses not so much on how the human sciences or other dominant discourses are either limited or inherently flawed in their efforts to know other by communicative means but rather on what these institutionally based discourses *do* come to produce in the way of knowledge of the subjects of their inquiries. This includes the effects that such knowledge may come to have upon subjects. This is not a question of what aspects of other are neglected, eclipsed, or suppressed within a communicative relationship but instead how subjects get constituted, qua other, as a consequence of the dominant discourse's inscriptive efforts. This too is seen as an act of symbolic violence, but of a different type. Whereas violence of the type underscored by the hermeneuticist involves otherness of either another culture or of one's own being not being adequately expressed and/or heard within the relationship, the poststructuralist describes a violence of a "positive" type in the sense that other, having been so inscribed within the relationship, is now transformed into a quite different subject who comes to exist *for* the dominant discourse and whose agency is thereby both enabled and circumscribed in specific, traceable ways.

I

In assessing the positions sketched above, three questions call for consideration. First, how is the relationship structured communicatively between inquirer and other, and what is its bearing on the quality of communication between interactants? Second, is there a way of reconciling genuinely open communication—i.e., what provides other, as well as inquirer, with the means to voice his or her values, interests, and needs—with what is required for the production of legitimate understanding or knowledge? And third, in light of current failings, what might be called for specifically in the way of a corrective or alternative?

The above questions are linked to a tension between the human sciences and other who is both subject of scientific inquiry *as well as* a communicative being who is entitled to a genuine voice within the relationship. It has not been conclusively established that this tension has yet been sufficiently dissolved, nor indeed that it in principle can be, and this is because of the very aims and methods of the empirical sciences. The tension takes the following form: first, the primary aim of science is that of acquiring knowledge founded on the pre-eminence of truth. Thus, in describing the significance of the Copernican Revolution and all that has followed, Gellner (1974) states:

> Without truth, all else is worthless. We must assess the truth of cognitive claims contained in, or presupposed by, anything that lays claims to our respect; and if it fails this first and crucial test, all subsequent ones become irrelevant. No other charms can ever make up, in the very last degree, for the failure to possess this first and pre-eminent virtue. (27)

What bears stressing here is the pre-eminence of truth. As Gellner continues:

> This point may now seem obvious or even trite. Yet its sustained and ruthless application is anything but innocuous. It is radical, revolutionary, and deeply disturbing. It requires that we look not to things, not to the world, but instead to the validity of what we *know* about things or the world. Before anything, or indeed any person, can be revered, we must first examine, without any undue and inhibiting reverence, the standing and validity of the putative knowledge concerning that thing or person. (28)

Gellner's depiction emphasizes how science prioritizes knowledge based on validated truth claims over any principle of reverence of persons or things. What science values most about persons, therefore, is that which can be known by means of formulating valid truth claims, and this involves excluding that which does not admit of such claims. In this latter respect, an essential requirement of modern science is that it seal itself off from ethical or other domains which might espouse values that differ from or oppose those of legitimate scientific knowledge. This requirement is enforced within a normative framework, upheld by and constitutive of the community of scientists, which ensures that the validity of all truth claims be based upon careful testing of theory and fact. This involves distinguishing lawlike statements from mere conjectures or opinions, reliable from unreliable methods, appropriate from inappropriate interpretations of methodologically produced results.

Many have charged that the tendency of science to valorize an empirically based knowledge over other knowledge forms has had a highly adverse effect upon persons and how they might potentially be valued within a range of alternative domains of meaning and practice. The thrust of this charge is that when persons come to be valued by science only to the extent that they can be known in scientific terms, other important aspects of being may be underemphasized, overlooked, perhaps even forgotten. One of the most patent examples of this type of valorization is evident in the way science structures its communicative relationships with the subjects of its inquiry. As both Shotter and Krippendorff in this volume assert, the relationship often tends to be monological. This is not to say that scientists monopolize all talk in their relations with the subjects of their inquiry, but rather that the relationship is structured so as to privilege the scientist's truth claims over any competing claims that might be offered by the subjects themselves.

Consider again the significance of the normative framework that functions as the scientific community's ultimate court of appeal. It is with reference to this framework that scientists test the validity of their truth claims. This involves not simply establishing an isomorphic relation between truth claim and empirical phenomenon but also relating that claim to all nomological or theoretically generated propositions that have previously been endorsed by the community. Making sense with one's own truth claims—uttering a scientifically meaningful utterance—is thus contingent upon the scientist's ability to establish a coherent relation between his or her claims and those that have found prior legitimation within the scientific community. In this respect, the generation of scientific truths must be seen as a rule-governed and linguistically mediated practice: in order to do science one must learn the language of the scientific speech community, its meanings and significances, as well as the rules that regulate combinations of meaning and significance. This all as a condition of producing a meaningful utterance, i.e., a scientifically legitimated truth. As Langsdorf contends, science on this view must be understood as a hermeneutically constituted, regulative system that installs its own (culturally distinctive) version of truth within the world. As such, when scientifically produced accounts collide with rival accounts provided by the subjects whose actions or beliefs are the focus of inquiry, this may be not simply a manifestation of scientifically validated truth confronting myth, superstition, or error but also, and perhaps no less importantly, a collision of disparate meaning systems, each of which representing and constituting the world in quite distinct and variable ways.

Such collisions between science and other emphasize the extent to which cultures may differ and how the truths of one culture may therefore be internally related to other meanings within that culture in distinct and culturally specific ways. When science declares, for example, that witchcraft is a set of beliefs and practices founded on untruths, it is not simply and exclusively what is true or untrue that is at stake, as strict supporters of the scientific method might have us believe; rather, a culture's entire meaning system may hang in the balance inasmuch as belief, identity, and practice are *all* integrally bound up with culturally specific truth claims. Yet science, indefatigably attached to the pre-eminence of truth in its quest for knowledge, has shown a tendency to be oblivious to this crucial fact of cultural being. Nor has it sufficiently concerned itself with the ways in which the purported truths of the culture of other are ranked according to a culture-specific set of values so that the propositional content of all statements regarding witchcraft, for example, may be viewed by some cultures as being fundamentally different in kind from those truths used for purposes of planting and harvesting crops. In fact, as supporters of the scientific method have argued, nor *should* the culturally variable shadings of truth and related meanings be of great concern to the scientist for the task of science is neither to partake in such fancy nor to humor or mollify those who fall under its spell. Rather, the goal of science is to expose fallacies of conventional or commonsense understanding by means of showing how prescientific truth claims are either inconsistent, false, or in need of further scientific confirmation.

With this collision of meaning systems, truth becomes both site and stake of a struggle between science and the otherness of culture or self. It is truth that is being explicitly contested, more so than value or belief or other less empirically verifiable aspects of culture or being. This is not to say that these other aspects of culture or being are irrelevant to the struggle for truth, but rather that their status according to the human scientist must be highly reduced inasmuch as the struggle is defined in terms of truth and truth alone. It is only after the struggle has been waged, and won, that these other aspects of culture or being become salient once again. But what shape they are accorded may vary from what they had been in the past. For whoever prevails in the contest over truth is then in a position to define those remaining orders of meaning that stand in an internal relationship with truth. In this way the triumph of a scientific conception of truth readily converts into a triumph of scientific meaning and the concomitant eclipse of those meanings that cannot be shown to hinge upon truth in scientifically validated ways. Meanings that do not measure up to objective truth criteria are selected out and relegated to the status of fantasy or error. This is accomplished first through the legitimation of the "truth eliciting" techniques of science then secondly through the conversion of subjects' meanings into a conceptual order that houses (scientifically) legitimate meaning. So relegated, that which is now defined as "mythical" or "fanciful" fares poorly when measured against the truth-based, authoritative, legitimating criteria of science. What for the subjects of scientific inquiry may have possessed elevated status as a conventional meaning of great significance, now having been converted into a meaning that exists for science, can be said to be held only perhaps as a figment of one's imagination or as a collectively held superstition.

II

Hermeneutically influenced critics of science have argued that the triumph of scientific knowledge and its tendency to convert and so reduce nonscientifically grounded meanings to the status of truth or falsity amounts to a structuring of a communicative relationship which effectively silences the otherness of culture or being. This is said to be detrimental to all: to the functioning otherness of alternative meaning systems; to those who might learn from other, either directly or through stimulated reflection; and to those who might confront otherness as a part of their own being. It is with a conscientious rejection of the scientific mode of engaging and analyzing other that hermeneutically influenced critics have endeavored to develop an alternative.

Against the scientific project, hermeneutically sensitive theorists have forwarded a number of quite distinctly varied alternatives. Despite their respective differences, however, all may be said to have understanding as its principle aim—an aim that stands in staunch opposition to the quest for scientific knowledge. Whereas the latter proceeds on the belief that humans are knowable insofar as their behaviors can be explained in terms of causal determinants and predicted effects, the hermeneutically sensitive theorist is likely to argue that such a belief is either (1) logically wrong-headed or (2) susceptible to serious moral objection.

Both arguments hinge on the following distinction: what natural scientists do is different in kind from what can (logically) or should (morally) be done by those who endeavor to study human society. Against those who would seek to apply methods of the natural sciences to human subjects, the hermeneutically sensitive theorist argues that human behavior is not reducible to a causal response to determining stimuli; nor, therefore, is human behavior predictable in ways that lend itself to nomological statements. Rather, humans engage in action distinguished by purpose and meaning. Human action is purposeful in that it is intended: one acts *in order to* achieve some end. There may indeed be externally motivating influences upon the actor, but when the actor acts, it is done with an end in mind (e.g., Skinner, 1988). Thus, a combination of a sudden rain storm and my belief that I need some form of protection from the downpour might motivate me to use my umbrella. Yet, such a combination does not function as, say, the combination of rain and wind might to cause hazardous driving conditions. When I open my umbrella, I do so in order to protect myself from the rain. Correlatively: when asked why I opened my umbrella I do not say the rain caused my action, but rather that I chose to open my umbrella. I could have chosen otherwise, deciding to seek shelter at a bus stop or to run the brief distance to my workplace without going to the bother of opening the umbrella.

The idea that human action is purposeful is inextricably bound up with the idea that human action is meaningful. Both sides of the relation rely upon the importance of language as a rule-governed system which enables us to act in ways that make sense to ourselves and others. The game metaphor, utilized most deftly by Ludwig Wittgenstein (1958), has often been used to explain how language enables us to act in meaningful ways. Learning a language is akin to learning a game or set of games. We come to know how to apply concepts in the context of learning various language games, such as describing, predicting, or arguing. These games are rule-governed: to utter a specific speech act counts as offering a specific meaning within a specific language game distinguished by its game-specific rules. Following the rules of the game, using concepts in ways that are consistent with the rules, counts as a meaningful act within the game. Or, again, knowing the meaning of a concept is akin to knowing how to go on in the game in which it is being used. One is able to act, with purpose, because one knows the rules of the game: this is what I must do in order to achieve an end intended to have meaning for myself and other.

Once behavior is understood as purposeful and meaningful, efforts to "know" behavior in the sense that scientists come to know the physical properties and causal relations of natural objects appear to be wrong-headed. For what induces a person to act in a certain manner can only be understood in terms of how that act is assigned meaning within a specific language game. And since cultures vary, each having its own culture-specific language games and rules for engaging in meaningful action, the task of the researcher is not to "know" the person's act, as we might come to know the nature of a stick, but rather to learn the possible meanings that might be assigned to the act within that actor's own culture. This requires that we extend our understanding of other by making room for his or her own cultural categories of significance and meaning. In so doing we are apt to discover new possibilities of truth and falsity, good and evil, which are not and never could be reducible to the terms that modern science applies to the natural world (Winch, 1972).

With modern science having pushed forward in seeming cavalier disregard for the logical shortcoming involved in reducing meaningful action to causally determined behavior, some hermeneutically sensitive theorists have charged that this constitutes a moral failing as well as a logical one. Extolling the virtue of understanding and the need to be open to the meanings of other, hermeneuticists have chastised modern empirical sciences for stubbornly adhering to a singular framework in which to claim to "know" other not only amounts to a failure to *understand* other in any sense consistent with other's own understanding, but also involves supplanting the meanings of other and the imposing of restrictive meanings upon us all under the guise of the scientifically legitimate accumulation of knowledge. This constitutes an injustice against self and other; for failing to hear other in other's own terms not only amounts to a failure to give other sufficient voice but also seals the inquiring self off from forms of self-understanding that might be prompted in and through communicative forms where both self and other are genuinely attentive to each other's meanings and significances (e.g., Gadamer, 1993).

As a corrective, hermeneutically sensitive theorists such as Shotter and Krippendorff have recommended a dialogical approach that is intended to promote a genuine exchange of meanings between self and other. This entails both a recognition of one's own limits on account of being enmeshed within one's own culture and an acceptance of the idea that an understanding within the dialogue is built on the proposition that other should be engaged in other's own terms. Both propositions are fundamental to the hermeneutic approach, and both are what distinguishes genuine dialogue from the more "monological" approach central to modern scientific methods. The aim is not to "know" or explain other in scientific terms but rather to understand other in ways that avoid either suppressing other's voice or reducing other's meanings. This aim carries with it at least two critical requisites, both of which are adumbrated by Langsdorf. One is that the hermeneutically sensitive inquirer always be willing to suspend the authority of his or her own cultural meanings, and this in deference to the meanings of other that might well function to transgress one's own cultural rules. The second requisite is that the hermeneutically sensitive inquirer always be willing to use the transgressive meanings of other as an occasion to reflect upon one's personal and cultural prejudices—those tendencies to prejudge— that may often have been taken for granted prior to the dialogue.

Much may be gained if these hermeneutic principles are taken seriously and acted upon consistently within the interaction with other. The reservoir of cultural and personal meanings may be expanded and deepened; we may have more personal and cultural meaning options as a result; we may be better situated to communicate across both inter-cultural and interpersonal boundaries, and we may have a better arsenal of concepts by which to engage both in critical self-reflection and the critique of one's own society's deeply sedimented beliefs.

The hermeneutic alternative has generated much appeal both for its trenchant criticisms of attempts by the human sciences to emulate the natural sciences and its own attempts to cultivate the grounds for reaching a dialogical understanding with other. At the same time, how-ever, the practice of hermeneutics has given rise to a number of critical questions. To begin, the rejection of knowledge and the concomitant move to understanding invites the most obvious of responses: What then do we do with knowledge as we have come to conceptualize it in scientific terms? Without scientific knowledge as a basis, what alterna-tive grounds are available upon which to form critical judgments of human action? Recalling Gellner's earlier remarks, can it not be said that the hermeneutic tendency to elevate understanding to a higher plane than that of truth must incite the critical charge that understanding is being revered in the absence of any knowledge-based truth? Without science and its methods of legitimating knowledge claims, we may well be left slipping and sliding atop an ooze of hermeneutic understanding without any discernible truth criteria to provide us with suitable traction for critical judgment and action. By the same token, with hermeneutic understanding as our primary (and perhaps only) guide, we may indeed prove ourselves to be more tolerant and critically self-reflective regard-ing the personal and cultural horizons of ourselves and other, but with-out having the sufficient grounds for acting either against or in concert with other.

Some hermeneutically sensitive theorists, conceding the relativist implications of a dialogically based idea of understanding, are content to fall back upon the security of the conventional. This reliance begins early on with the need for some degree of translation of other's words and meanings, for to advocate listening to other in other's own voice runs up against the practical obstacle of somehow converting other's symbolic offerings into the hermeneutic inquirer's own terms that are necessary for even the most minimal degree of understanding. Of course, this practical difficulty has been met by the scientific community through a conversion process by which the meanings of other are scrutinized in light of scientifically validated standards of what is true or false, and as mentioned above, this necessarily requires a degree of reduction of the meanings produced by other. It is not clearly evident that the hermeneutically sensitive theorist can avoid the necessity of having to perform a similar operation. If there is a difference, it hinges on the scientist requiring (scientific) truthfulness as a condition of being meaningful, while the hermeneuticist holds up no such conditions but instead is willing to alter his or her standards of meaning in light of what is produced in the interaction with other. This said, however, there still appears to be a reductionist component built into the hermeneutic endeavor, and this as a condition of basic sense-making.

Along similar lines, it is not readily apparent how the hermeneuticist can judge other, let alone act against or in concert with other, without introducing some set of standards into the equation. This is particularly true in situations where conflict is evident. In such situations, one must opt in favor of one meaning over possible alternative meanings. Yet it is not clear that every culture's conventions provide a clear, reasonable, and uncontested means of critically assessing and implementing interpretive or evaluative standards. Many traditionalist cultures, for example, which previously had offered a clear (authoritative) set of means have given way to a culture of science. On occasions of conceptual or moral conflict such judgments would seem to admit of some degree of either blind cultural supposition or scientific reasoning. It is not clear either (1) how the hermeneuticist escapes the authoritative edicts of culture, many of which being blind and uncritical, or (2) how the tendency to think scientifically—using experimental methods of trial and error, thinking in causal terms, relying upon rules of evidence in one's explanations—either fits with or is by fiat excluded from the hermeneutically based processes of judgment and action.

All of the above questions may be said to be linked to and in significant ways to follow from basic questions that continue to dog every hermeneutic alternative: What is the status of empirical knowledge within the hermeneutic domain? Must every truth be subordinate to the flux of meanings that emerge in one's interactions with other? Or must truth be abandoned altogether as a working principle within the world of human interaction? Unable to come sufficiently to grips with such questions, the hermeneutic alternative appears to succeed better as a nettlesome challenger to modern science than as a full-fledged alternative.

III

Poststructuralists, wary of the pitfalls that have hindered development of the hermeneutic tradition, have developed another alternative to the modern scientific approach as a means of further facilitating the voice of other. A basic tenet of the poststructuralist alternative is that the voice of other has not been granted an adequate hearing, and this because other has been either silenced or forced to speak according to the restrictive dictates of dominant discourses, including those of the human sciences. Accompanying this tenet, however, and perhaps being the single most significant plank of the poststructuralist project, is the expressed belief that the silencing or mandating of the voice of other is an inevitable effect of any prolonged encounter between other and the discursive apparatuses constitutive of science or any other institution which, in the interests of its own maintenance, must develop and enforce discourse-specific criteria for sense-making. Such criteria include the conditions for truth-telling as well as for advancing any other knowledge claims (e.g., normative or value-expressive utterances). In this sense, according to the poststructuralists, knowledge functions as a power inasmuch as the conditions for advancing, say, an empirical or normative claim are materialized within discourse and accorded institutional backing. All subjects, therefore, must be expected to bow to the rule-dictates of specific institutionalized discourses as a requisite for being understood. This might entail having to accept for oneself a discourse-specific role category as a condition for raising or addressing certain topics or having to adopt discourse-specific rules as a condition for speaking "the true."

With this recognition of how discourses function, poststructuralist theorists have maintained that a central way in which discourses produce domains of other and otherness is by means of demarcating subjects and modes of subjectivity through specific rules and categories for sense-making (e.g., Huspek and Comerford, 1996). This endeavor often involves a historical dimension whereby the poststructuralist theorist, qua genealogist, traces out the ways in which discourses change in their techniques and the effects such changes may have had upon the subjects caught up in their constitutive workings (e.g., Foucault, 1973, 1978, 1979). Essential to this overall task is that of retrieving the voice of other or, if this is not possible (cf. Derrida, 1978, 31–63), at least showing how subjects were constitutively produced in and through the discourse as well as showing the range and seriousness of effects. In lieu of providing full genealogical accounts, Cobb, Comerford, and Gemin have each discussed how rape victims must adopt specific subject characteristics as a condition for making sense within the courtroom. Cobb does this through her treatment of the ways subjectivity is produced through law's narrative exigencies for rape victims; Comerford with her analysis of how rape victims are produced as subjects in response to the discursive requirements of televised courtroom proceedings; Gemin with his account of the difficulty encountered by a rape victim with multiple personality disorder whose subjectivity is made to hinge upon an ability to identify and make sense of each of her multiple personalities in terms of the law's expectations.

The poststructuralist project is predicated on the idea that the voice of other is neither "truer," more "culturally purified," nor "less distorted" once it is reclaimed from its entanglements within a dominant discourse. In this sense, poststructuralists are neutral as to the varying truth values of different discourses and are unwilling to argue that statements generated within discourses of the human sciences, say, are any more true than statements of competing, nonscientific discourses. The poststructuralist project thus proceeds on the belief that a tracing out of the discursive effects upon subjects-as-other may better enable us all to recognize the extent to which we arc discursive products, with our subjectivities being spoken by, as well as in and through, the prevailing discourses of the day. When, therefore, discourses of the human sciences are assessed, it is done with the following questions in mind: What are the effects of scientific knowledge claims upon subjects? How are subjects either historically or currently constituted within their relations with a science that generates knowledge claims purporting to know them? And what are the costs in terms of subjects being subjected to science's methodological and conceptual rigors? Such questions are at the heart of Gross's treatment of epidemiology and victims of occupational disease, and Taylor's account of epidemiology and victims of radiation fallout.

In addressing such questions, concerns are inevitably raised as to the particular grounds upon which the poststructuralist can claim any sort of discursive legitimacy that at the same time escapes the kinds of criticism leveled against either human scientist or hermeneuticist. The poststructuralist response has been to distance itself both from the kinds of authoritative backing claimed by either the human scientist or the hermeneuticist and the kinds of discursive operations that distinguish each camp. Thus, no appeal is made to the preeminence of empirical knowledge of the sort authoritatively garnered by the modern scientist nor to the authority of tradition that is clung to so adamantly by the hermeneuticist. Nor does the poststructuralist advance either the alleged monologism of modern science in its relation to other or the dialogism of the sort acclaimed by hermeneutically influenced scholars. The former is avoided not only for its disingenuity as to the sort of "dialogue" it embraces but also for its tendency to ignore the modes of resistance and opposition produced *as effects of* the relation between the human sciences and the subjects it purports to know; the latter is steered clear of by virtue of its naïveté as to the hidden powers of tradition that are structured into language and function to reproduce the authority of tradition without providing either of the dialogical partners with sufficient grounds for critiquing culture or ideology.

Rather than appealing to any higher authority, the poststructuralist effort seeks to show how power and authority are enacted within their discursive operations and to then show the effects of such enactments. In genealogical narratives the intent is to demonstrate how subjects are produced through rule and categorization within discourse, the range of identities and communicative acts available to each discourse-based subjectivity, and the ways in which subjects utilize their symbolic and material resources as a means of resisting and ultimately disrupting the discourse that produces them. There is no authority contained in such revelations, nor any unique communicative strategem beyond that of telling a compelling tale. Indeed, the poststructuralist narrative is often distinguished by its faithfulness to the discourses it addresses, operating within the same terms of discourse as those deployed by the subjects under examination. The critical thrust of this project, therefore, is not to posit an alternative conceptual order but only to accept that conceptual order given within specific discourses and to delineate their effects upon subjects. By so doing, the critical question is not whether one or another dominant discourse measures up against some abstract idea (e.g., the scientist's ideal of truth or the hermeneuticists' ideal of being) but rather, in light of the posited ideals of this particular discourse, does it meet these ideals in terms of what it produces in the way of subjectivities?

The language of critique, at least as we have come to traditionally know it, is alien to the poststructuralist project; for any such language would imply some guiding standards for critical assessment that poststructuralists have been disinclined to embrace. Nevertheless, despite the espoused value neutrality of poststructuralist narratives, the narratives themselves can be said to often carry with them critical effects. With the genealogical narrative tending to underscore discursive rhetoric or ideal, on the one hand, and effects of the discursive operations upon subjects, on the other, one or more contradictions may tend to be evidenced through indication of where discursive ideal falls short of the reality that is effected by implementation of the ideal. The locus of critique, however, is not contained within the genealogical narrative itself but rather is said to be deferred to the reader who, in light of the contradiction, may opt either to evaluate, say, the range of possible explanations of the contradiction or to offer specific normative resolutions.

This positioning in relation to critique begs a number of questions regarding the concepts and methods used by poststructuralists, their bearing on authorial credibility, and the extent to which the author is truly extricated from the charge of forwarding value-laden statements. It is at this juncture that poststructuralists encounter a good deal of difficulty. Such questions hinge upon the issue of discourse itself: What discourse is it that poststructuralists are operating in and through with their accounts? How is it that they are able to transcend or sidestep being spoken by—that is, produced as subjects by—the discourse with which they are operating? Why should we find the poststructuralist's account, which *does* purport to provide a *truthful* story, more compelling than the scientific account, which in its pursuit of truth, provides ways of critically interrogating its findings (through, for example, the replicability of its research design)? And finally, given the poststructuralist's indefatigable assertions that power is bound up with all discourse and that all speakers are thus necessarily always within power's province, why even bother to critically explicate one or another discourse domain (Habermas, 1990)? Does not subjects' critical assessment of the ways in which they are discursively produced lead at best only to entanglement within yet another field of discursive production?

IV

All of the essays in this volume, albeit to differing degrees, have acknowledged the problematicity of making any claim of knowledge or understanding of other and the potential harms that may be inflicted as a consequence of advancing such claims. In this regard, each of the essays may be read as an effort to provide better grounds for engaging other—both conceptually and methodologically—as a means of better eliciting and hearing other's voice. Further, although each essay is more or less identifiable in terms both of its own perspectival allegiances and its misgivings with other perspectives, each also should be credited for its attempt to step beyond—to transgress—the borders of their own perspectives. Thus we see Kovačić and associates inserting a more explicitly rhetorical dimension into the conversation among scientists as but one means of eliciting greater dialogue; we see Harrison attempting to graft a meaning-based ethnography onto an empirical science; we see Langsdorf engaging the empirical sciences with the aim of showing how empirical inquiry is unavoidably also a hermeneutic activity, and we see Cobb, Comerford, Gemin, Taylor and Gross offering narratives that rely upon the scientifically revered principle of truth as a means of articulating how subjects are produced as other within the discourses of science and law.

It is reasonable to infer from the above efforts that the adoption of any single theoretical perspective, however descriptively or analytically fruitful in its incipient stages, always carries with it the potential either to suppress or alter the voice of other in ways that amount to an injustice. Radford, in his contribution to this volume, appears to most clearly have recognized the need to integrate—albeit without collapsing—multiple perspectives if we are to pursue knowledge and understanding in ways that better steer us clear of the injustices to other that have inhered in prior efforts. The questions that are thereby prompted with this awareness are those that aim us toward varied reconciliation of empirical knowledge and hermeneutic meaning, as well as the means by which to gauge and critically assess the effects of such reconciliation upon the subjects, who through our categories, propositions, and methods we purport to know and understand.

References

Derrida, J. (1978). *Writing and Difference*. Chicago: University of Chicago Press.

Foucault, M. (1973). *Madness and Civilization*. New York: Random House.

———. (1978). *The History of Sexuality: An Introduction*. Vol. 1. New York: Vintage.

———. (1979). *Discipline and Punish*. New York: Pantheon.

Gadamer, H-G. (1993). *Truth and Method*. 2nd ed. New York: Continuum.

Gellner, E. (1974). *Legitimation of Belief*. New York: Cambridge University Press.

Habermas, J. (1990). *The Philosophical Discourse of Modernity*. Cambridge, Mass.: MIT Press.

Huspek, M., and L. Comerford. (1996). "How science is subverted: Penology and prison inmates' resistance." *Communication Theory*, 6(4); 335–360.

Skinner, Q. (1988). Motives, intentions and the interpretation of texts. In J. Tully (ed.): *Meaning and Context: Quentin Skinner and His Critics*. Princeton, N.J.: Princeton University Press, 68–78.

Winch, P. (1972). Understanding a primitive society. In P. Winch (Ed.): *Ethics and Action*. London: Routledge and Kegan Paul, 8–49.

Wittgenstein, L. (1958). *Philosophical Investigations* (G.E.M. Anscombe, Trans.). New York: Macmillan.

Textual Violence in Academe: On Writing with Respect for One's Others

John Shotter

If I open a book and see that the author is accusing an adversary of 'infantile leftism,' I shut it again right away. That's not my way of doing things; I don't belong to the world of people who do things that way. I insist on this difference: a whole morality is at stake, the morality that concerns the search for truth and the relation to the other. In the serious play of questions and answers, the rights of each person are in some sense immanent in the discussion. They depend upon the dialogue situation.

—Foucault, 1986, 381

Truth is not born nor is it found inside the head of an individual person; it is born between people *collectively searching for the truth, in the process of their dialogic interaction.*

—Bakhtin, 1984, 110

Can their fear be understood solely as shyness or is it an expression of deeply embedded, socially constructed restrictions against speech in a culture of domination, a fear of owning one's words, of taking a stand?

—hooks, 1989, 17

Academic Violence: An Introduction

Is there a kind of violence at work in intellectual debates and discussions; in the university colloquium, seminar, or classroom; in academic texts? Is there something implicit in our very *ways of us relating ourselves to each other* in academic life in present times that makes us fear each other? Is there something in our current circumstances that makes us (or at least some of us) anxious about owning certain of our own words, of taking a stand? Speaking from my own experience, I think there is. Indeed, I think that what bell hooks says about black students in a white academic culture in fact applies to many of the rest of us. For currently, most of us must function in a culture of domination, of hierarchy, a Cartesian culture of mastery and possession, and we experience a certain anxiety when we begin to try to speak out against it, to "speak truth to power." As such, it tends to disorient us, to distract us from what we feel is important to say, to rob us of the words we need; we find ourselves saying what we know will be acceptable, rewarded; it is an anxiety that tends, differentially, to silence us; we tend to speak and write of some things but not others, in certain styles but not in others—in ways, I shall claim, that (because of their monological, instrumental, and formal nature) are intrinsically disrespectful of, and unresponsive to, the (unique) being of an other.

Thus, what is it in our circumstances, in our "regimes of truth," that generates these "effects of power" (Foucault, 1980, 131)? What is involved in us, as professional academics, speaking and writing in a way that might overcome them, that is respectful of the being of those about whom—and to whom—we speak and write? What might be involved in us moving beyond merely justifying between ourselves that what we write about the activities of those we study, that it is something that 'can logically be said' about them, to them being able, so to speak, to recognize themselves in what we say? Indeed, might it ever be possible for us to write of them, not solely in our voice, but for their voices to speak in our writing? Could they ever, so to speak, come to populate our texts (Billig, 1994)? If the social worlds and 'realities' within which we all live are socially constructed, then, as I see it, what is at issue is whose voices do and do not play a part in the construction process. What words are silenced, and what words make a difference? It is such questions as these that I want in general to discuss in this chapter.

As an example of what is at issue here, we can turn to the now (in)famous 'debate' between Jacques Derrida and John Searle (Derrida, 1988). In an afterword he called "Toward an Ethic of Discussion," Derrida wrote of "our experience of violence and of our relation to the law . . . in the way we discuss 'amongst ourselves,' in the academic world" (111). There, he raised the question of the way in which the laws, rules, or conventions governing "the academic space and the intellectual institutions in which we debate, with others but also with ourselves . . . 'contain' and thus betray all sorts of violence" (112). In asking for "the violence, political or otherwise, at work in academic or intellectual discussions generally" (112) to be acknowledged, Derrida was not suggesting that it could ever be totally eradicated but was instead urging both the recognition and analysis of its forms, in the hope of transforming them into less violent, or even into nonviolent, forms. For as he saw it, it was not so much the "nucleus of the theoretical structure" of Searle's claims with which he disagreed (although he did disagree with many of his assumptions), as with certain aspects of Searle's academic *practice:* his manner of discussing, of arguing, of polemecizing, of his rhetoric, and of the forms in which he takes part in social and intellectual life; "in short, of the modalities through which the said theoretical nucleus is *put to work* . . . to insult an author instead of criticizing him . . . to accuse the other of a 'distressing penchant for saying things obviously false' and of a thousand 'confusions' " (139) and so on. We all know only too well, from our own experience, of similar such forms of intimidation.

Like Foucault, Derrida pointed out that these issues are "not unrelated to the significant fact that the controversy here revolves around the interpretation (theoretical and practical) of 'marginality' and 'parasitism,' " (112), i.e., around issues of doing either with exclusion, or with accusations of idleness or freeloading, with who is 'in' and who 'out.' Indeed, as Foucault (1972b) comments, "In a society such as our own we all know the rules of *exclusion.* The most obvious and familiar of these concern what is *prohibited.* We know perfectly well that we are not free to say just anything" (216).

But why not? What is it that makes us draw back, that makes us feel certain words, certain voicings, 'unfitting?' Derrida (1988) gives us an unexpected clue here—unexpected because although he is well known for claiming that "nothing *exists* outside context" (152)—he also points to the importance of what he speaks as "unconditional" affirmation or appeal. Where—and this will be very important in much of what follows below—

> the very least that can be said of unconditionality (a word
> that I use not by accident to recall the character of the
> categorial imperative in its Kantian form) is that it is inde-
> pendent of every determinate context, even of the determi-
> nation of a context in general. It announces itself as such
> only in the *opening* of a context. Not that it is simply present
> (existent) everywhere, outside of all context; rather, it inter-
> venes in the determination of a context at its very inception,
> and from an injunction, a law, a responsibility that tran-
> scends this or that determination of a given context; and
> this is the moment of strategies, of rhetorics, of ethics, and
> of politics. (152)

In other words, what is at issue here is an unconditional 'something' that (to repeat) "intervenes in the determination of a context at its very inception," thus to influence what can be said within it.[1] As a result, what is at stake in a deconstruction, "is always a set of determinate and finite possibilities" (144), not just 'anything goes': "I have never accepted saying, or encouraging others to say, just anything at all, nor have I argued for indeterminacy as such," he adds (144–45). 'Something' is always at work in a context limiting what can be said within it.

That 'something,' I want to argue below, has to do with our *ways of us relating ourselves to each other* in our talk and writing; it is an ethical issue. For if, following Wittgenstein (1953), it is the case that "to imagine a language means to imagine a form of life" (no. 19),[2] then new ways of talking have a chance at working to construct new forms of life. But whose forms of life are to prevail? Whose ways of talking, whose language games and forms of life are to be respected? This is what, I think, is at issue in all that follows.

Two Different 'Relational Stances' to Our 'Subject Matter'

What I want in a moment to explore, then, are two quite different styles, first of speaking and then of writing, within which we, as academics, talk to each other about 'those others,' the people we study: one is the supposedly 'objective,' 'realistic,' 'formal,' or 'professional' style of speech or writing within which we currently present our theories and the "true facts" they are meant to reveal; the other is a more 'literary,' 'poetic,' 'fictional,' 'informal,' or 'conversational' style that, traditionally, is thought to be in tension with it. They each involve the adoption of a quite different *relational stance,* i.e., a different set of both methodological and ethical commitments, not only to those to whom we address ourselves but also to the supposed subject matter of our talk. The former works in terms of us understanding them intellectually, as if from afar, in terms of representations, i.e., in terms of supposed similarities of form. The latter works in terms of us *sensing* in our living, embodied relations with them up close, differences— differences that arise as they respond to our actions with actions of their own, differences that, initially at least, we can only voice poetically and metaphorically. As Taylor (1990) puts it, "we only liberate [others] and 'let them be' when we can identify and articulate a contrast between their understanding and ours, thereby ceasing in that respect just to read them through our home understanding, but allowing them to stand apart from it on their own" (41). In other words, our understanding of other people comes about through a quite different route than that through which we understand things and objects: it comes about *conversationally,* in which others can talk back to us in way denied in the other form.

While the first way of talking, in which people relate themselves to each other intellectually, can be thought of as a closed, finalized, and monologic way of talking, functioning in an already existing and sustained 'disciplinary space.' The other, in which people are in a more sensuous contact with each other, is an open, unfinalized, and dialogical form of talk in which new 'spaces' may be opened up and others closed down, freely, moment by moment.

Until recently, this second, nondisciplinary form of talk has been very unfamiliar to us. We have been captivated by a picture of ourselves as isolated individuals, inhabiting an otherwise inert, mechanical body that as a 'mind' we, so to speak, 'animate.' It is a picture that has come down to us, through Descartes, from the Greeks. In it, we talk (think!) of ourselves as primarily only in contact only with 'seemings,' with appearances. To acquire knowledge of the real but hidden world behind appearances, we must exercise our rational intellects, that is, our 'minds' in a properly ordered way (a discipline is necessary). Where our 'minds' consist in a kind of subjective 'inner space,' in which mental representations of both actual and desired (or feared) states of affairs in the 'external,' objective world exist and are processed. And where it is only through such representations that we, as the persons we are, have any relevant contact with our surroundings, including both our own bodies and other people. For, as Descartes ([1641] 1986) claimed to have 'proved' in his meditations: "I now know that even bodies are not strictly perceived by the senses or faculty of imagination but by the intellect alone, and that this perception derives not from being touched or seen but from their being understood" (22). Thus, the 'inner space' constituting such a Cartesian mind or mentality is definable to itself independently of both body and others: "I am," said Descartes, "in the strict sense only a thing that thinks" (18), a disembodied, disinterested, decontextualized, isolated, thinking or reasoning thing.

What this picture does, however, is to divert our attention away from those dialogic moments of free and living contact between two people in which "joint action" occurs (Shotter, 1984). Where, in joint action, we do not act 'out of' our own individual inner plans, intentions, or desires, but 'into' a context 'shaped' by the actions of the others around us. We simply act in a way that is *responsive* to their actions. And, for those around us to sense us as being responsive to them, our activities must be such that are (at least to an extent) interlaced in with their actions. Thus, their moment-by-moment actions are just as much a formative influence shaping what we do as anything within ourselves. In other words, in joint action, the influences shaping the moment-by-moment 'movement' in our actions cannot be found wholly in our own individual heads, nor can they be found in the fixed rules a supposed linguistic system. In joint action, the organizing center, so to speak, of communicative activity is neither in the individual, nor in the linguistic system, but in the momentary *situation,* the 'interactive moment,' within which communication takes place.

Thus, what occurs within the 'interactive moment' is to be discovered, not by studying patterns or orders of already spoken words, but by studying the forces at work in the very fashioning of words in their speaking. In other words, our relating ourselves to and our understanding of other people comes about through quite a different process to that through which we understand things and objects: it comes about in a nonintellectual, embodied, dialogical, or conversational manner, in which an embodied, temporally unfolding, responsive form of understanding (denied us in our more monological, intellectual forms of talking and writing) is at work. And what especially is important about this form of dialogical understanding is that it is not an individual achievement. It is an understanding developed and negotiated with others in the circumstance of its use.

Although I shall not argue below for the replacement of the first monological form of understanding by the second dialogical form[3]—for clearly, we are continually shifting back-and-forth between the two— let me just note that any such shifting involves moving between taking an ethically uninvolved, disinterested, instrumental, ahistorical, retrospective attitude toward one's subject matter, and the taking of a much more ethically involved, historically concerned and embedded, contemporaneous stance toward it. It is a shift from a contemplative looking-back upon a fixed and finalized version of the world, in which *an accountable order* is to be discovered, to a living involvement with its further development—in which debate, struggle, argument, and creative imagination can 'shape' the 'space of possibilities' of what might in the future be brought into existence.

Before going any further with my discussion of these two styles, let me lay some social constructionist groundwork for the points I want to make. For I want to be in a position to argue that we can only sense the social realities we inhabit as being 'our' realities, if we can play a free and proper part in their construction. We must be able to sense our speech as not fettered by constraints existing prior to, and external to, the current conversational situation. Indeed, there is almost what one might call 'a politics of ethics,' or 'a political economy of ontological opportunities' at work in our speaking and our writing. For when we speak, we risk our being to the others around us in our talk, we risk them insulting and degrading us, they can curtail our opportunities to be who we could be. And it is precisely this—the way in which certain forms of accountability to others are emphasized, while others are denied, suppressed, ignored, or rendered 'rationally invisible'[4]—that I want to explore in what follows.

Social Constructionism and Accountability

First, in very broad terms, let me note that a certain two-sidedness characterizes many controversies in everyday social life at large. Billig (1987), in particular, has shown how good reasons can usually be adduced for also arguing the contrary to almost every major theoretical claim in the human sciences: that life is just as much not like a game as like one, as not like the theater as like it, as based on an ability to particularize as in an ability to categorize, and so on. In the same vein, we may note that there are two views as to the function of speech: (1) speaking in order to refer to, or to represent, a state of affairs in a supposed 'world' and (2) speaking in order to construct a social relation of some kind with other people. Where the function of this second kind of speech, as Mills (1940/1975) puts it, is not "the 'expression' of prior elements in the individual," but the "social function of co-ordinating diverse actions" (113). Classically, in the human sciences, we have privileged the first, *representational* function and have ignored the second. Both as academics and as ordinary people, we have thought of ourselves as self-contained individuals able to talk about *the* world, and to communicate information to each other about our experiences within it. Although there is no evidence that the world forms itself into an aggregate of separate, self-contained objects, nor does it present itself as obviously already formed in such a way; nonetheless, as Code (1991) points out, "implicit in the veneration of objectivity central to *scientific* practice is the conviction that objects of knowledge are separate from knowers and investigators and that they remain separate and unchanged throughout investigative, information-gathering, and knowledge-construction processes" (31–32).

Social constructionism, however, denies this form of objectivity. It reverses the order of privilege of the two forms of speaking. It privileges the second, *relational* function and claims that we are only able to make sense in our talk—even that referring to, or representing, states of affairs in the world—from different positions, within different kinds of developing social relations, from within certain forms of life that we have constructed and are continually constructing (that are 'coming-to-be') in our talk with each other. As Code (1991) again puts it, "when one considers how basic and crucial the necessity of knowing other people is, paradigms, knowledge claims, and objectivity take on quite a different aspect. In fact, knowing people is at least as worthy a contender for paradigmatic status as knowledge of medium-sized, everyday objects" (37).

Some, of course, might want to argue that, although social practices are indeed basic to our lives, it is a mistake to claim that it is our speech practices that are basic. They might claim that the already determined, sociohistorical universe is so massive, that what we say can only reflect its nature, that what we say must, in some sense, be caused by its 'real' structure. I would disagree, and claim that speech *is* basic to our forms of life in the following judgmental or accountable (but not causal) sense: that although people often act in ways that do not seem at first 'to fit in with' shared forms of life, they are sometimes able, in the verbal *accounts* that they give us (and in our accepting of them), to draw our attention to (perhaps, otherwise unnoticed) features of their actions, features that do indeed justify their claims to have been acting appropriately (Mills, 1940/1975; Scott and Lyman, 1968). Indeed, without the possibility of us being able to recognize and correct each other's mistakes—and the use of such forms of talk in opening up new spaces of possibility (see below)—the sustaining of any recognizable form of relationship between us would be impossible. Such forms of accountability are, no doubt, deeply embedded in our social ontologies, in our social identities, in who we 'are' to ourselves. But, if Billig (1987) is correct, they are not so monolithic that alternatives to them can always be articulated.

My reasons for talking of accounts here, thus, go beyond the use of accounts in merely sustaining our forms of life: In the account (not the theory) of writing I want to give in a moment, the function of account-talk and accountability is crucial. For what people do in accounting for their actions is to reveal to each other the structure of presuppositions and expectations in which their action was embedded, its directedness or intentionality. In so doing, they place, position, or situate an otherwise self-contained, objective event within a shared horizon of possibilities. And it is in this fashion, not in terms of already completed and static outcomes, but in terms of their action's 'tendencies' (what their action points to in the future), that we can appreciate the part their action plays in us constructing our form of life together. And in *situating* their action, they allow us to situate ourselves in relation to it also. As Mills (1940/1975) puts it, in giving an account, a person is "not trying to *describe* his experienced social action. . . . He is influencing others—and himself. . . . In such cases, there is not a discrepancy between an act and 'its' verbalization, but a difference between two disparate actions, motor-social and verbal. This additional lingualization . . . is an integrative factor in *future* phases of the original social action or other acts" (114). As such, it is not idle talk, but it plays a practical part in furthering the life of the social group. As I mentioned above, it is the way in which this kind of talk can open up a space of new possibilities for coordinated action that is of the utmost importance for us. It is this 'first time' creative aspect of our talk and writing that we must understand. "What we want," said Mills, "is an analysis of the integrating, controlling, and specifying functions a certain type of speech fulfills in social situated actions" (113)—I could not have said it more succinctly myself.

Monological and Dialogical Forms of Talk

But what are the styles of speech and writing at issue? And in what way do they involve ethical issues? As I see it, there are three important dimensions of difference: (1) that between monological and dialogical forms of talk and writings, (2) that between finalized (or closed) and unfinalized (or open) forms, and (3) that between words used dialogically as 'relational tools' and words used monologically in fashioning representations.

Let me briefly discuss these in turn: (1) Both Bakhtin (1981, 1984, 1986) and Volosinov (1973, 1976) discuss dialogical speech and writing as involving responsivity. Speakers not only fashion what they say to link it to already existing circumstances but also to the anticipated responses of their actual (or imagined) interlocutors, who also, of course, listen responsively, with agreement, disagreement, questions or elaborations, puzzlement, surprise, joy, indignation, and so on.

> Monologism, at its extreme, denies the existence outside itself of another consciousness with equal rights and equal responsibilities, another *I* with equal rights (thou). With a monologic approach (in its extreme pure form) *another person* remains wholly and merely an *object* of conscious- ness, and not another consciousness. No response is ex- pected from it that could change everything in the world of my consciousness. Monologue is finalized and deaf to another's response, does not expect it and does not ac- knowledge in it any *decisive* force. . . . Monologue pretends to be the *ultimate word.* It closes down the represented world and represented persons. (Bakhtin, 1984, 292–93)

(2) In a dialogical world, speakers "do not expect passive un- derstanding that, so to speak, only duplicates his own idea in someone else's mind. Rather, he expects response, agreement, sympathy, objec- tion, execution, and so forth" (Bakhtin, 1986, 69). So, although in a monological world the two statements 'Life is good' and 'Life is not good' are related to each as a simple matter of logic (one is the negation of the other), dialogically, there is a living relation between them: they argue with each other (Bakhtin, 1984, 183–84). Dialogic speech is always responsive to the speech of others, and it is always formed and shaped in the expectation of a response. Without that expectation, in being presented as finalized, monologic utterances, they lose their open 'eventness.' They are meant to be viewed as if from a distance and to become merely 'objects,' to be passively un- derstood for what they represent, as parts of an already ordered sys- tem. They do not give others any opportunity to respond and thus to

modify what we have to say. It is only in talking in an unfinalized way, in speaking in a way that is not yet a part of a completed system, that we make available the possibility of us doing something really new, of making history.

(3) We can retain this possibility, even in the face of the enormous evidence for system and stability in our language, because "what is important for the speaker about a linguistic form is not that it is a stable and always self-equivalent signal [a representation], but that it is an always changeable and adaptable [responsively understood] sign. . . . The task of understanding . . . amounts to understanding [a sign's] novelty [its unique use] and not to recognizing its identity [its form]" (68). Just like the countless number of uses of the limited number of tools in a tool box for fashioning different artifacts, so limited linguistic forms may also be put to countless uses in influencing both other people's (and our own) responses to what we say or write. But unlike what we can do with handtools, what we can do with words is not entirely up to us alone. For a *"word is a two-sided act. It is determined equally by whose* word it is and *for whom* it is meant. . . . Each and every word expresses the 'one' in relation to the 'other.' I give myself verbal shape from another's point of view, ultimately, from the point of view of the community to which I belong. . . . A word is territory shared by both addresser and addressee, by speaker and his interlocutors" (86). For unlike the handtools in the workshop, that we as individuals can use as we please, words are 'relational tools.' Their *use* does not depend upon individuals alone. Indeed, they only come into existence in the relational context in which their use is developed and negotiated. Thus, this focus upon words in their speaking, as the territory, the point of contact between two formative influences, both able differentially to shape the outcome of the speech produced (thus to author themselves), draws our attention to the practical working of the cultural politics of everyday life (Shotter, 1993).

Indeed, as I mentioned above, what is at work in our speaking and writing, is almost what one might call 'a politics of ethics,' or 'a political economy of ontological opportunities.' Thus, in studying communication dialogically rather than monologically, we must make two shifts in the nature of our focus: We must shift the organizing center of communicative activity so that it is neither in the individual nor in the linguistic system but is in the *situation,* the 'interactive moment' within which communication takes place—where, as already mentioned, what occurs within it is to be discovered not by studying patterns or orders of already spoken words but by studying the forces at work in the very fashioning of words in their speaking. But this involves another important shift, a shift from a formal, instrumental toward an ethical stance: a concern with the being of others. For what is at issue is not just simply the extent to which different voices may speak but the extent to which they will be responded to by those around them—and as such, the extent to which how they are evaluated opens up to them (or not, as the case may be) opportunities of one kind or another for them to construct the 'social reality' in which the members of the social group live and call their own. For only as participants can they influence and change the living context of their own speech, effectively authoring themselves. Thus, what is at issue is who gets to author whom? How is the two-sided territory opened up between people, in the interactive moment of speaking, policed and governed? Who rules it? What determines what can be said within it? Who has the right to speak? The forces at work in an 'interactive moment' are ethical forces.

The same questions can be asked in relation to writing also: "We should not be fooled," says Bazeman (1988), "by the distance travelled by written language. . . . Writing and reading . . . are still highly contextualized social actions, speaking very directly to social context and social goals" (22). They always involve, as he puts it, a "public moment" (23) in which texts are written, and in which they are then read. And those public moments too are open to ethical influences beyond the mere individuals involved. "The organizing center of any utterance, of any experience," says Volosinov (1973), "is not within but outside—the social milieu surrounding the individual being" (93). Thus in a dialogic situation, instead of simply acting out of one's own inner plan or desire, one must often act into a momentarily existing context, where if what one says or does fails to 'fit' what the context seems to require, then the others around one are justified in rejecting what one says or does as unintelligible or illegitimate. The responses of one's dialogical partners can thus exert a crucial influence upon what one can or cannot say in a particular context. Thus, it is not at all difficult to imagine some of the social relations and situations within which a speaker/writer is embedded, some social milieux, making it much easier for the speaker to speak in some ways than in others, to speak, perhaps, not in one's own voice but in a voice required by the situation. Even when all alone, "both the composition and, particularly, the style of the utterance depend upon those to whom the utterance is addressed, how the speaker (or writer) senses and imagines his addresses, and the [ethical] force of their effect on the utterance" (Bakhtin, 1986, 95).

Two Styles and Two Ethics of Writing

To turn, then, to the question of what it is that we are doing, ethically, to ourselves, and to others, in the different styles of writing that we use, I shall explore two different styles of writing. One, our current professional style, has the advantage of being couched in a vocabulary of already conventionally understood terms (at least when addressed to a professional audience). It is the kind of writing that, if I were writing my speech here for a journal, I might perhaps have started today by saying:

> The embodied process of voicing or speaking words has, as such, received little research attention in communication studies. This failure is a crucial mistake. The purpose of this paper is to show how the 'movement' of the voice exerts a central influence in the structuring of response opportunities in communication. Rectification of this mistake will entail a complete reorientation of research in the field.

But note how strange it would be to talk to you like this in this face-to-face context: Not only is it impossible for you to recognize yourself, so to speak, in such a form of talk, to sense it as drawing your attention to anything crucially connected with your life in the world at this moment, I cannot find myself in it either: my own position in relation to such a way of talking is unclear to me also. It is separate and distant from me. In issuing from the mouth (or word processor) of a supposedly objective, disembodied, disinterested, external observer, we feel forced in listening to such words to place them not in a context of everyday contingency but in a Cartesian special realm of pure knowledge beyond it and superior to it, unknown and unknowable to ordinary people, an ideal reality in which the true agents of our fate exert their influences. Indeed, a misplaced sense of agency is already at work, in that (what in fact I write) seems 'itself' to talk, not of people but of 'things' as agents, e.g., 'research fails to attend'; 'research makes mistakes'; 'intonation exerts an influence.' In this style of writing, we cannot grasp how our words achieve their effects. They do not 'instruct' us in how we come to understand what they 'say,' in how they *represent* events, states of affairs, or people in the world. As Bazeman (1988) remarks, in our very first words in such a style of writing, the reader is prepared to accept that "to write science is commonly thought not to write at all, just simply to record the natural facts" (14).

   In other words, such a style of writing hides its politics of ethics, it hides the fact that it treats people as indistinguishable, isolated 'atoms' of disembodied, unlocated subjectivity. But in hiding its politics of ethics as a matter of explicit policy, and thus rendering the social relations of its writers and readers 'rationally invisible,' it precludes to rhetorical discussion of its own rhetorical workings (Billig, 1991). Like spectators in a museum (or prisoners [!] in Plato's cave), we are meant to (forced to) 'view' the 'objects of thought' or 'pictures' provided by such words for their (sometimes true?) representations of the supposed 'ideal forms' of life normally 'hidden' from us in everyday appearances.

The other style of writing is not representational at all, but has to do with a kind of writing that makes *that* kind of writing possible. However, in being far more disorderly or informal, although it provides the resources needed, because it is less disciplined, it lacks such a common vocabulary, and as a result, it can only be used contextually and conversationally.

Let me discuss these two styles in terms of their methodological and ethical commitments: (1) In our official academic style, I would be talking/writing to you as a fellow professional academic of what happened earlier, when I was involved with those whose activity is now the topic of my talk. I would provide you with a linguistic representation of the nature of that activity, but now *from outside* that involvement, looking back upon it as a completed process. In separating the activity from the people whose activity it was, and from its surrounding circumstances, I would be separating it from the practical part it played in their lives, its point from them. But this is not our concern. *Our* concern is with what logically "can be said" about the patterning or form of that activity, an *order* that I claim to have 'discovered' in it. I shall call this kind of writing, *monological-retrospective-objective* writing. What I say/write, is located in our professional relationship and is directed toward identifying that to which, as professional observers with a certain set of professional methodological commitments, we should attend. It is aimed at producing what might be called *explanatory theory,* i.e., representations of states of affairs that enable those in possession of them to predict and control the events they represent.[5]

(2) In the other, I would be talking/writing to you of the character of my ongoing involvement with certain other people, *from within* that involvement—while both looking back upon what had been achieved so far, and forward prospectively, toward the possibilities open to me for my next 'steps.' Where my concern would be with attempting to 'show' you (metaphorically) how you might, *justifiably,* be able to make sense of the character of such involvements. I shall call it *dialogical-prospective-relational* writing. What I say originates in the interactive relationships from within which I speak, and is directed toward instructing you, as an ordinary everyday person outside the relationship, in noticing and making within similar such relationships, similar such connections and distinctions (differences).[6] To contrast with the aim of the previous style, we might say that it is not aimed at explanatory theory, but *practical theory,* theory that is useful in a tool-like way in noticing and making differences in and to situated, living activities. It is to do with noticing, and perhaps open up, possibilities in the future toward which to direct one's actions now.

In other words, although you, as the addressee of my writing, might seem to be the same in both styles, my 'ethical stance' toward those who are the 'subject matter' of my talking/writing would be quite different, and my 'positioning' of you would be different too: In monological-retrospective-objective writing, I would have no need (at least, not immediately) to be accountable or responsive to the absent others of whom I speak. Indeed, I look upon them as if from a distance, as if in a god's-eye view of some kind. While in dialogical-prospective-relational writing, as a part of me being involved with those others, I cannot be unaccountable to them. If asked by them as to why I make the claims about them that I do, I must be in a position to respond to their challenges, to justify myself to them in ways that they can accept (or can give good reasons for rejecting). In the former style, my first (ethical) responsibility is to you and our professional discipline, while in the latter, my responsibility is to them as simply one ordinary person to an other. While in the first, I must write in a way justifiably connected with my theoretical interest (e.g., as a sociologist, anthropologist, psychologist, or historian), in the second, dialogical-prospective-relational writing, I cannot sustain such a fixed and constant interest. I must write in a way that I can justifiably connect with my relationship with them, *and,* to our currently shared but changing conversational situation, *and* (perhaps), to certain 'unconditionalities' (Derrida, 1988).

Being Positioned as a Reader

We can now turn to explore the styles of response these two styles of writing 'afford' you as a reader, how do they 'position' you? What kind of person do they allow you to be? Or in Wittgenstein's (1953) terms, what are the forms of life that make such ways of speaking possible? Or to put it even more strongly, if it is the case that we contribute in our ways of talking to the actual making of different forms of life between us, within which we become different kinds of people, what possible kind of person, operating in what kind of possible world, with what kind of relation to others, goes with making sense of each of these two kinds of writing?

Let us turn to monological-retrospective-objective writing, the writing of explanatory theory first. The philosophical climate within which the modern academic disciplines emerged and have been conducted has been shaped by the Enlightenment, and, for our purposes here, there are five concerns of Enlightenment thought useful to mention: (1) rational analysis, (2) mental representations, (3) systems, (4) ahistorical, and (5) individualism. (1) We find that the idea of *rational analysis* involves a special, methodical form of observation: the 'seeing' of everyday events in terms of a supposed hidden, orderly reality 'underlying' appearances. (2) Where, 'seeing' in this way involves seeing observed events in terms of certain basic elements related to each other according to certain laws or principles; observed events can then be spoken of as being *represented* within a rational system or framework. (3) It is this urge to be *systematic* in one's explanatory activities that is the third feature of Enlightenment thought that I want to emphasize. For without a system, without a rational framework within which to interlink contingent facts into a system of logically necessary entailments or dependencies, no soundly based, explanatory knowledge is possible in any field. We can only, seemingly, revert to the contingencies and likelihoods, the persuasions of rhetoric—the influences, at least, so it was claimed, of mere opinion. A fourth feature, first articulated by Descartes but retained by the Enlightenment, is that of doubting any authority derived from intellectual traditions of the past. He instituted the idea that if one is prepared to undertake the hard analytic work involved, one can found a new intellectual system in a set of theoretical principles, a set of foundational statements—*foundationalism* (or ahistoricism). (5) It thus became possible to argue that individuals can find all the resources they require to be epistemologically (and psychologically) autonomous within themselves.

As Geertz (1979) puts it, the official western conception of the person is now of someone "as a bounded, unique, more or less integrated motivational and cognitive universe, a dynamic center of awareness, emotion, judgment, and action organized into a distinctive whole and set contrastively both against other such wholes and against a social and natural background" (229). Just as we, subjectively, are radically divided from the objective world, so our minds (as subjects) are supposedly divided from our bodies (as objects). But as writers like Cushman (1990) and Sampson (1981) have tried to point out, such a notion of the person leads to an "empty self," or as Gergen (1990) has claimed, to a "mechanical self," a self that has a significant absence of community, shared tradition and history, and shared meaning. Doctrinally, such a conception is known as "possessive individualism," where, "its possessive quality is to be found in its conception of the individual as essentially the proprietor of his own person or capacities, owing nothing to society for them" (Macpherson, 1962, 3). In being radically separated from the (external) world, such a self knows the world only in visual terms, at a distance (Rorty, 1980). Rather than through any responsive sensing or feeling of its activities, through any living contact with it, we know the world only through our reasoning about its (finalized) forms within our systems of knowledge. Where, the proper forms of our knowledge are contained within disembodied, decontextualized, self-contained, supposedly disinterested, objective systems. Knowledge of an embodied, situated, partial, and interested kind is taken to be a part of the individual person, and as such is called subjective, unsystematic, and disparaged.

Any academic discipline (form of life) embodying such a set of doctrines as these, must institute limitations upon the accountable language games within which it can conduct itself—if it is to sustain its form of life. It must control the voices that can speak and be heard, the character of the public moments and the influences that can be permitted to be at work within them, and in particular, the type of speech used: referential or rhetorical; monological or dialogical; orderly, disciplined, and professional, or disorderly, everyday, and of the people. Unaccountable voices, those that cannot justify what they have to say in officially acceptable terms, are excluded. Foucault (1970, 1972a, 1972b) has, of course, described some of the rules of exclusion, the prohibitions and principles of rejection, that are at work in sustaining our official discourses, particularly the rise of the "will to truth." He notes how it is undoubtedly a "historically constituted" device for controlling what can be said. For at first, in sixth-century Greece, true discourse was the prerogative of the poets: it was in their talk that justice was meted out and each attributed his rightful share, for it was their talk that inspired "respect and terror, to which all were obliged to submit, because it held sway over all and was pronounced by men who spoke it as of right" (1972b, 218). And yet a century later, "the highest truth no longer resided in what discourse *was,* nor in what it *did:* it lay in what was *said,*" (218). Its meaning lay in what it referred to. Plato won and the Sophists were routed. True discourse could no longer find its rooting in the human world; its authority, seemingly, came to it from elsewhere, from a hidden 'reality' lying beyond it in some way. But *is* that where its authority lies?

Clearly not, but in the disorderly 'bustle' and 'hurly-burly' (Wittgenstein) of everyday life, the fact is some more orderly forms of life are favored over others. How can this be? Because their authority is exerted at just those public moments when, in a clash of voices, one voice feels a restriction unfelt by another and falls into silence earlier and rescinds its right to participate in the self-authoring of the social group's way of life. For in the self-authoring activity sustaining such communal ways of talking (and perceiving, acting, relating, and evaluating) in existence, some voices can speak accountably, with justifications that all accept, while others, if they speak at all, find that what they have to say is treated as unaccountable (and thus often, unintelligible) by the others around them. At such times, "when there is no access to one's own personal 'ultimate' [i.e., justifiable] word, then every thought, feeling, experience must be refracted through the medium of someone else's discourse, someone else's style, someone else's manner, with which it cannot immediately be merged without reservation, without distance, without refraction" (Bakhtin, 1984, 202). When the only metaphors available to one are the "literalized metaphors" (Rorty, 1989, 44) of a certain dominant group, then one cannot speak in one's own voice, open one's own new space of dialogue. One can only speak within the spaces already opened by others.

This is, of course, precisely the result of us subjecting ourselves to the disciplines required if we are to gain access (investiture and elevation) to the kind of voice—able to make claims supposedly true of reality—that enjoys a high status of our current society. We must learn to write in a certain style, one that honors, so to speak, the vision of the world in which we suppose ourselves to live and our place within in it as producers of knowledge about it. I have, in fact, set out most of the conditions in my first style of writing outlined above, but to repeat: (1) We must write as an isolated individual, (2) viewing the topic of one's writing, a social process, from afar, (3) concerned to describe the process in terms of an orderly representation of its true nature, its usual products, (4) interaction with other people must be dispensed with (for one's knowledge is a matter of one's relation solely with reality itself), (5) as a social process, it must be accounted for in terms of what outside observers agree can be "logically said" about it (independently of what those who brought it into being might say about it), (6) the terms of its description must belong to a theoretical realm, grounded, not in life, but in principles, and (7) when placed within a formal system, we can explain and predict the process in all its manifestations.

The style or tone of the writing to which these commitments give rise is well-known to us (as is information in the form of a listing, as following):

1. We write with a misplaced sense of agency, in the passive: "It was found that different patterns of intonation established different social relations between the participants." Not also: "In speaking slowly and softly to him I found I could eventually coax a smile from him."

2. We write only about what can be publicly observed: "Twenty percent of children were observed to cry when shouted at; the other 80 percent remained silent." Not also: "I felt their pain at being rejected and my own at not being able to offer any consolation."

3. We write with certainty of everything we say: "We can only conclude that the expressed anger was the cause of their crying." Not also: "I felt it likely that my anger was the occasion of their sullen looks."

4. We write alone and unassailable: "There are three main features of painful communicative exchanges." Not also: "I find many of our professional forms of talk painful, and I think some of the reasons are to be found in the talk itself."

5. What we say is finalized: "The pain caused by such talk is due to the passive role into which it forces the reader/

listener to cast themselves." Not also: "Maybe, if we could talk in a more conversational manner, things would not be so bad."

6. We write in terms of forms and shapes, not in terms of feelings and sense: "Low status individuals have fewer response options, hence their tendency to inarticulacy." Not also: "Sensing the risk of humiliation at being unable to justify my claims before all these authorities, I remained silent . . . but one day, I thought, I'll get my chance."

7. We write in terms of gratuitous insults, in justifying our claims: "Shotter appears to go wrong from the start by trying to characterize scientific realism in ontological terms." Not also: "I find Shotter's characterization of scientific realism in ontological terms disturbs my interpretation of it."

8. We write universally, in terms of an exclusive 'we': "*We* have to start from where *we* are." Not also: "As a rather marginal person, a nonresident alien, actually, I wonder what the national ethos might be and how those more central than me might see me as placed in relation to it."

9. We write in relation to an authoritative tradition, stretching back in a history of 'begats': "Since Galileo, Newton, Descartes, and Hobbes, we have taken mathematics to be the queen of the sciences." Not also: "Many, the poets, the writers, the ordinary people, the philosophers and scientists, have each played their part."

10. We write always as if from within a framework: "In the approach adopted here, the tone of a piece of writing determines one's social relationships within the world the text posits." Not also: "As I see it, a way of writing is two sided, what at one point in history is a valued form, may at another, come to be seen as . . . "

11. We write always in search of explanations as answers to questions: "Why do we feel in reading the ways of writing we employ so anxious and fearful most of time?" Not also: "If it is true that a form of writing 'shows' us *a* way of seeing ourselves and our world, then how can we know that what it shows us is *the* way we and our world are?"

12. Along with the above go many other such strategies, all aimed at constructing a world for professional academics, and other disembodied, unsituated, irresponsible, unaccountable experts, safe from accountability by the larger public.

What is special about the tone of the style of writing described above, including the style of description itself (especially the listing), is that it is monologic. It is not a style that allows for (very much) responsive listening or reading. It is appropriate (mostly) to a passive representational form of understanding, by those schooled in the appropriate conventions (indeed, it is pretty opaque to outsiders).

Why do we talk like this? Because professionally, of course, our task *is* to be authoritative; it is our academic responsibility to be clear and unequivocal. Thus, if our readers feel the need to read *our* meanings in anything other than respectful silence, then we have failed. They should not be creating their own idiosyncratic meanings and misunderstandings from our text (Shotter shouldn't go wrong from the start.) Indeed, if our readers feel the need to question us, to answer us back, to turn our text around to expose other meanings unintended by us, then it is we, not they, that suffer a professional fall from grace. And that is a consummation devoutly not to be wished. Hence, our use of all the strategies listed above, in presenting our utterances as univocal and unambiguous within classical, disciplinary terms.

However, those of us who fail to sustain disciplinary requirements do not just momentarily fail to communicate, instrumentally, person-to-person, we also risk the serious results of public degradation.[7] This (to be authoritative) is where the source of the violence in this form of communication is to be located. In an important early paper, Garfinkel (1956), in discussing the nature of what he calls "status degradation ceremonies," described the social techniques involved and their emotional consequences for those affected. As he outlines it, such a ceremony is present in "any communicative work between persons, whereby the public identity of an actor is transformed into something looked on as lower in the local scheme of social types" (420). Thus, a person risks professional degradation, for instance, if their performance is negatively evaluated by acknowledged authorities in the discipline in such a way, that public witnesses (actual or imagined) will interpret both the victim and the victim's actions as in some sense "out of the ordinary" (421). The perpetrator may then be named an 'outsider,' as not 'one of us,' as unnatural, improper, or as otherwise unfitting in some way, with the emotional consequence, that the denounced person feels shame. Where "a prominent feature of shame for the person is that of preserving the ego from further onslaughts by withdrawing entirely its contact with the outside . . . moral indignation serves to effect the ritual destruction of the person denounced" (421).

What it is that makes Garfinkel's notion of a degradation ceremony relevant to our worries here, is that the moments at which we must speak in response to (or responsively read) a written text, professionally, are *public* moments. Whether the witnesses are actual or imagined, they are moments witnessed by an authoritative Otherness—the mythic organized collective judgment of the profession. For sooner or later, we are going to have to justify our reply (or what we interpret a text as meaning) to our disciplinary colleagues. Thus, even when all alone, we feel the authoritative force of certain meanings, and the shame of being 'out of the ordinary' if we want not to accept them.[8] Indeed, professional academic writers (and analytic philosophers in particular) often remind us of how we ought to be making sense of their texts: "This process of coming to see human beings as 'one of us' rather than as 'them' is a matter of detailed description of what other people are like and of redescription of what we ourselves are like. This is not a task for theory" (Rorty, 1989, xvi). Often, we find ourselves precisely 'instructed' with nothing else to do but to obey. Yet to decline to conduct oneself as a full dialogical partner in the living of one's social life with others, to fail to explore what one might call the 'living meaning' of Rorty's claim here, is to feel oneself degraded too. Either way, one feels violated.

Writing with Respect for an Other

Is there an alternative to this kind of textual violence? Can we, within the confines of a single discipline, overcome the violence of monologizing and regimenting our talk, in an attempt to sustain the discipline's knowledge as a disembodied, disinterested, decontextualized, ahistorical *system?* What might be involved in us giving more respect to the voices of others in what we say, to articulating *their otherness* in some other way? Is there an nonexclusionary way of sustaining a disciplinary focus, to which all, in varying degrees, might have access (the problem, in fact, of multiculturalism)? Could there be disciplines without disciplinary boundaries as such?

Charles Taylor (1990) has discussed some aspects of this problem. "We only liberate the other and 'let them be,' " he says, "when we can identify and articulate a contrast between their understanding and ours, thereby ceasing in that respect just to read them through our home understanding, but allowing them to stand apart from [one's own home culture] on their own" (41). It is this feeling of contrast that is primary, and its challenge for us is to "place the strangeness opposite some bit of our lives, as it were, . . . [and] go to work on it to try to make sense of the difference" (43). When it has been placed in relation to what is familiar to us, accounted for and given a linguistic shape, then, suggests Taylor, it will cease to be frightening and bewildering to us. Involved here, then, is activity on the very boundaries of one's being, activity that is to do with, as he sees it, a struggle "not towards a liberation from [a limited perspective] as such (the error of the natural science model)[9] but towards a wider understanding which can englobe the other undistortively" (41–42). The kind of understanding involved is not the kind of immediate one-way understanding possible among people using a vocabulary of already established, conventional, representational understandings, but the kind of two-way, responsive understanding discussed by Bakhtin and Volosinov—understandings that can only be developed through time in the back-and-forth of conversation. Where, to repeat, what is crucial to it, is a moment-by-moment changing sense of difference, the contrasts that one encounters, and the linguistic formulations such contrasts permit or allow.

This process of understanding through formulations based in contrasts is itself to be contrasted with understandings formulated in terms of representations. Indeed, it straightaway leads to a contrast between what might be called explanatory (scientific) theory with contextualized practical theory, the necessity for new understanding that arises out of situated shock and wonderment. In this respect, it will be useful to note some of Wittgenstein's (1953) remarks upon his own breaking away from *explanatory* theories, and his reason for using the metaphor of language games. He used them in all their different forms, not to serve as models or idealizations (as the usual preliminary to the production of a rigorous theory) but for another reason altogether:

> Our clear and simple language-games are not preparatory studies for a future regularization of language—as it were first approximations, ignoring friction and air resistance. The language-games are rather set up as *objects of com parison* which are meant to throw light on the facts of our language by way not only of similarities, but also of dissimilarities. (no. 130)

In other words, different metaphorical accounts of different language games serve as measuring rods or instruments that create a dimension (or dimensions) of comparison, different ways of talking about aspects of our language *in different situations*—where each 'instrument' reveals interconnections between aspects of our language use in that situation that otherwise would go unnoticed. Indeed, all the metaphors used by Wittgenstein (such as "the ancient city," the "tool box," the "handles and levers in a locomotive cab"), bring to our attention aspects of language, and of our knowledge of language, that were previously rationally invisible to us, e.g., its 'rule-like' features, the characteristics of its 'boundaries,' its 'archeology,' and so on. They serve the function of creating "an order in our knowledge of the use of language: an order with a particular end in view; one out of many possible orders; not *the* order. To this end we shall constantly be giving prominence to distinctions which our ordinary forms of language easily make us overlook" (no. 132). Such metaphors cannot *represent* any already fixed orders in our use of language for, by their very nature in being open to determination in the context of their occurrence, they do not belong to any such orders. But what they do do for us, in artificially creating an order where none before existed, is to make aspects of our situated use of language publicly discussable and accountable. They provide a practical resource: a way of talking that works to draw our attention, in different ways in different contexts, to what we would otherwise not know how to attend. He calls such notions "perspicuous representations," and notes that they work to produce "just that understanding that consists in 'seeing connections' " (no. 122).

Other ways of talking, other relational stances, will function to bring out other connections. Indeed, there is no end to such an investigatory process as this. Thus, unlike our attempts to make sense of things from within a closed framework or system, such a process is open to extension as long as we can continue to create metaphors and images through which we can discover still more contrasts. Indeed, as one moves about (if one does), across boundaries, and experiences the changing commitments, temptations, desires, ways of looking and evaluating associated with different 'positions' in the 'bustle' of daily life—as one moves, perhaps, from being 'inside' a disciplinary *system* to being 'outside' it— then it becomes possible to see how different (metaphorical) ways of talking create the different 'realities' within such systems. Thus, our task is not that of finding the final Archimedean standpoint, but something much more mundane. As Wittgenstein (1953) himself puts it: "A philosophical problem has the form: 'I don't know my way about' " (no. 123). And this is precisely our task today: simply to know our way around within the diversity of our own everyday world a little better.

Indeed, in continuing in this vein, we shall find it revealing to contrast bell hooks's (1984) discussion of what is involved in grasping one's difference from others, with Charles Taylor's account. In some ways, what she has to say is quite different, while in other respects, it is very similar: Taylor seems to write in terms of a unified self rooted to a particular spot in life, a place among those of his colleagues who constitute his home culture from which he addresses them about 'those others.' But in bell hooks's experience, things are rather different. She possesses neither such a unified self nor such a static place to be; she must move between different ways of being. For her, it is not a matter of allowing those others (white people) to stand apart from one's own "home culture," but of finding that one's own home culture is already so dominated, colonized, and oppressed by them, that they force *you* to stand apart from *them*. You have to live in their world, but you are rejected by them: one knows of life at the center, but one is marginalized. One's difference from them is a fact of one's daily life, a part of who one is. She describes it thus:

To be in the margins is to be a part of the whole but outside the main body. As black americans living in a small Kentucky town, the railroad tracks were a daily reminder of our marginality. Across those tracks were paved streets, stores we could not enter, restaurants we could not eat in, and people we could not look directly in the face. . . . Living as we did—on the edge—we developed a particular way of seeing reality. We looked both from the outside in and from the inside out. We focused our attention on the center as well as the margin. (1984, ix)

Less free than Taylor just to 'let others be' (Taylor's position of privilege now becomes apparent), she nonetheless, like Taylor, finds the contrasts made available to her in her enforced boundary crossings crucial. But she has a choice of 'positions': "Within complex and ever shifting realms of power relations, do we position ourselves on the side of colonizing relations? Or do we continue to stand in political resistance with the oppressed, ready to offer our ways of seeing and theorizing, of making culture, towards that revolutionary effort which seeks to create space where there is unlimited access to pleasure and power of knowing, where transformation is possible?" (hooks, 1990, 145).

Thus for her—and for us, actually, in our everyday lives—it is not simply a matter of making sense of her life from a single, professional position, as if she were solely and simply a psychologist, anthropologist, or historian. In her everyday life, she is continually on the move, crossing the tracks, back and forth between the margin and the center, and facing the choice and the task, as she puts it, of "coming to voice." And for her, that is not an easy task. "The insistence on finding one voice . . . fit all too neatly with a static notion of self and identity that was pervasive in university settings" (hooks, 1989, 11). She faces the problem that many of us are now facing: that of finding that our sense of self, our voice, is not unitary, single, unilateral, or static, but multidimensional and polyphonic. We need to claim all the voices we speak, to give voice to the many and varied dimensions of our lives, while at the same time finding a way of judging the claims made upon us by such a polyphony of different voices.

Conclusion: A Tension in Social Constructionism

It is here, I think, that we run up against a crucial tension hidden in social constructionism itself. It has to do with the degree to which we are still haunted by the urges that we have inherited from the Enlightenment, always to seek systems, always to seek patterns, or coherent forms of order in our investigations, to treat representations as somehow more basic than what they represent. And given the still continuing prestige of science, the degree to which we as academics still feel an irresistible urge to present a nicely rounded, self-contained, complete, explanatory account. It is these classical urges, I think, that still drive us to talking *about* the pattern or the order in already spoken or written words, or accomplished actions, and thus to seek 'methods' or 'metatheory' relevant to the solution of practical social problems ahead of time. For without the rational compulsion of theories or methods, we can only have a 'who shouts loudest wins,' or 'who has the most force wins' kind of anarchy, right? Faced with this prospect, the more gentle among us opt for an all-are-equal *framework relativism* but offer their own *metatheory* as a metatheory of choice. One such is Ken Gergen (1988), who states the issue succinctly thus:

> In the present era, we find ourselves with no viable account of validity in interpretation. We stand without a compelling promise that knowledge of the other is possible. And if the logic of my preceding example [in which Gergen shows that outside observers can find no way of objectively anchoring their interpretations of people's overt actions] is correct, there is little reason to suppose that such an account will be forthcoming. Richard Bernstein (1988) does maintain that we can transcend relativism in interpretation. Yet, he eschews the possibility of formalized rules of procedure and rests his case on a "hard and messy sorting out of issues." (39)

In other words, if there are no agreed-upon rules ahead of time, then relativism is the preferred choice. It is one or the other for (seemingly) a system, a metatheory, is still required within which to reason.

But here Enlightenment commitment to order, hierarchies, explanation, analysis, and to 'picturable' processes, still lingers. We do not have to make such *either-or* choices. Such a logic conceals the degree to which things represented by their differences (or contrasts) with each other are also necessarily related (Shotter, 1975, 116–18). A *both-and* logic is required. As we become more self-conscious of not having a unitary or static sense of self but a multiplicity of possible voices, we begin to realize that while we are partially dependent upon the others around us, we are also partially independent of them too, while we are partially this we are also partially that—a certain two-sidedness, *both* this *and* that, characterizes much of our existence. Thus, we do not and cannot decide everything ahead of time. A dialogical social constructionism gives us a third choice: We do not need to 'see' the world from within a framework. In locating us in an as-yet unformulated realm of merely responsive understandings, in situating us primarily in a conversational world of embodied, situated, feelingful, or sensuous activity, it opens up for study those interactive moments in which we can attempt linguistically both to formulate ourselves and or circumstances in many different ways. And hard and messy though the sorting out may be—for there is much to struggle over—it is not impossible. For in those contextualized moments of struggle, those public moments, shared ethical criteria exist and influence (to an extent) which judgments as to appropriateness and rightness, practically, are made. Difficult though it may be for external observers to acknowledge it, participants in a dialogue sense that the rights of each person are in some sense immanent within it (Shotter, in press), even if their formulation is open to argumentation.[10]

In this respect, it is perhaps worth noting in more detail Derrida's complaints in *Limited Inc.* (1988) that

> I have never accepted saying, or encouraging others to say, just anything at all, nor have I argued for indeterminacy as such. . . . What I sought to designate under the title 'doubling commentary' is the 'minimal' deciphering of the 'first' pertinent and competent access to [textual] structures that are relatively stable (and hence destabilizable!), and from which the most venturesome questions and interpretations have to start: questions concerning conflicts, tensions, differences of force, hegemonies that have allowed such provisional installations to take place. . . . I believe no research is possible in a community (for example, academic) without this prior search for this minimal consensus and without discussion around this minimal consensus. (144–46)

Where, what is involved here is a mere 'indeterminacy' of meaning, but an 'undecidability,' which is "always a *determinate* oscillation between possibilities (for example, of meaning, but also of acts" (148). Thus, "from the point of view of semantics, but also of ethics and politics, 'deconstruction' should never lead to relativism or to any sort of indeterminism" (148). In this connection, it is also worth repeating—to those who feel that a new form of life can be constructed simply by the instituting of a new language game—that, although a certain "unconditionality" only announces itself as such in the *opening* of a new context, it nonetheless "intervenes in the determination of a context at its very inception, and from an injunction, a law, a responsibility that transcends this or that determination of a given context" (152). Hence, Derrida's (1988) attempts to reduce the potential violence in his writing in his afterword, by attempting to restrict what he wrote there solely to the context of the questions asked him: for then, judgments as to whether his responses were just or not, as answers to the questions, would be contextually possible.

The lesson for us here is this: the justifications we offer each other (ahead of time) for our actions in institutional settings, if they are not to do a violence to those participating in them, should draw their legitimacy from the dialogical context. Only when this is so is the search for truth *between people* (see Bakhtin, 1984, 110, quoted above) as possibility. This is why an argument with a polemicist is unfruitful because

> the polemicist proceeds encased in privileges that he possesses in advance and will never agree to question. On principle, he possesses rights authorizing him to wage war and make *that* struggle a just undertaking; the person he confronts is not a partner in the search for truth, but is an adversary, an enemy who is wrong, who is harmful and whose very existence constitutes a threat. For him, then, the game does not consist of recognizing this person as a subject with the right to speak, but of abolishing him as interlocutor, from any possible dialogue; and his final objective will be, not to come as close as possible to a difficult truth, but to bring about the triumph of the just cause he has been manifestly upholding from the beginning. (Foucault, 1986, 382, my emphasis)

This is the choice we thus face in social constructionism: Should we press toward a set of representations of an academic, disciplinary kind, an exclusionary disciplinary framework that reasserts the authority of the will to truth. Or should we seek a more inclusionary alternative— the idea of an academic discipline as a conversational community with a tradition of argumentation (MacIntyre, 1981, 1992; Shotter, 1993)? As yet, however, not only do we not know how to construct more open and nonexclusionary disciplinary forms around the study of words in their speaking, i.e., how to reconstitute disciplines institutionally in a more conversational mode, but we are still feel fearful of confronting the public power in terms of which the current monodisciplines maintain their hegemony. What will people say if they hear that we don't do experiments, or collect statistics, or do surveys, but that we just talk about talk! How can *that* solve any of today's pressing problems? Answering that question in a publicly convincing manner is one of our problems for the future.

Notes

1. As an example of such 'something' or 'somethings,' we might note Wittgenstein's (1958) comments on why we all have difficulty in grasping his methods of investigation and his use of language games.

"What makes it difficult for us to take this line of investigation is our craving for generality," he says (17). Or to put it another way: "the contemptuous attitude towards the particular case" (18). These are all but unconscious stances, attitudes, or commitments we have come to embody in becoming skilled in our current disciplinary practices.

2. Some have interpreted Wittgenstein's philosophy as "reactionary," as tyrannizing us all with the supposed already established *usages* of words (Eagleton, 1986, 106–109). This, I think, is not at all a correct reading of his claims. For him, the wrong *use* of a word is not one that goes against current everyday usage but against the *practice* of the person at the time of using the word (1980, I, no. 548)—where that practice must be such that another must be able to 'follow' that person in their practice. Here, Wittgenstein is not so much concerned with actually existing human forms of life as with the conditions making them possible. "Our investigation," he says, "is not directed toward phenomena, but, as one might say, towards the *'possibilities'* of phenomena" (1953, no. 90).

3. Indeed, we shall need both: the latter dialogical form in opening up new forms of (relational) life, new discursive 'spaces,' and the former in elaborating, exploring, and articulating them in the correct detail (I shall return to this issue below).

4. That is, rendered unavailable to rational discussion.

5. Gergen (1990) explores the strategies used by psychologists in this style of writing in facing the task of both "transcending the common intelligibility of the scientific community while simultaneously sustaining it" (371); they solve the problem by the seeming discovery of a new and hidden order of underlying appearances, that controls what we do. An *ontological transformation* is contrived.

6. Where, by *instructing someone* in something, I am also *justifiably accounting* to them for it, in the sense of telling them to pay attention to it in certain terms—terms that will enable them to make justifiable sense of it to others as I do. As Wittgenstein (1953) realizes, I can say of someone that by my words "I have changed his [*sic*] *way of looking at things*" (no. 144). But, will my words have changed his way of looking sufficiently to match mine, to match ours? If people are to learn 'our rule' for a series of numbers, and have already written the series 0 to 9 to our satisfaction, then, do they need any further explanation? "The effect of any further *explanation* depends upon [their] *reaction.* . . . But how far need [they] continue the series for us to have the *right* [my emphasis] to say that [they have mastered it]? Clearly you cannot say that here" (no. 145). It is a question of what is taken in our group to be a justified claim to knowledge.

7. Here, I am indebted to Beth Fernholt (1990), an undergraduate student who took the trouble to analyze (in terms of the texts I'd assigned the class to read) why a social constructionist text made her feel

oppressed and angry. She realized before I did, that a text, like a person's voice, could have a 'tone' too.

8. See Bakhtin's (1981, 341–47) discussion on the *authoritative* word and the *internally persuasive* word.

9. "Since the seventeenth century, the progress of natural science has been inseparable from our separating ourselves from our own perspective, even from the human perspective as such, in order to come as close as possible to 'the view from nowhere,' to use Nagel's (1985) phrase" (Taylor, 1990, 39).

10. "We see no special need to point out that the polyphonic approach has nothing in common with relativism (or dogmatism). But it should be noted that both relativism and dogmatism equally exclude all argumentation, all authentic dialogue, by making it either unnecessary (relativism) or impossible (dogmatism)" (Bakhtin, 1984, 69). Indeed, it is also worth noticing that relativism assumes that one is 'trapped,' so to speak, within a monological framework.

References

Bakhtin, M. M. (1981). *The Dialogical Imagination* (C. Emerson and M. Holquist, Trans.). Austin: University of Texas Press.

———. (1984). *Problems of Dostoevsky's Poetics* (C. Emerson, Trans.). Minneapolis: University of Minnesota Press.

———. (1986). *Speech Genres and Other Late Essays* (V. W. McGee, Trans.). Austin: University of Texas Press.

Bazeman, C. (1988). *Shaping Written Knowledge: The Genre and Activity of the Experimental Article in Science*. Madison: University of Wisconsin Press.

Billig, M. (1987). *Arguing and Thinking: A Rhetorical Approach to Social Psychology*. Cambridge, England: Cambridge University Press.

———. (1991). *Ideology and Opinions*. London: Sage.

———. (1994). Repopulating the depopulated pages of social psychology. *Theory and Psychology, 4,* pp. 307–335.

Code, L. (1991). *What Can She Know? Feminist Theory and the Construction of Knowledge*. Ithaca, N.Y.: Cornell University Press.

Cushman, P. (1990). Why the self is empty: Toward a historically situated psychologist. *American Psychologist* 45:599–611.

Descartes, R. (1986). *Meditations on First Philosophy: With Selections from Objections and Replies* (J. Cottingham, Trans.). Cambridge, England: Cambridge University Press.

Derrida, J. (1988). *Limited Inc*. Evanston, Ill.: Northwestern University Press.

Eagleton, T. (1986). *Against the Grain: Essays 1975–1985.* London: Verso Press.

Fernholt, B. (1990). The Use of Discourse Theory to Reveal the Oppression of Readers by Texts. Unpublished undergraduate term paper, Swarthmore College.

Foucault, M. (1970). *The Order of Things: An Archaeology of the Human Sciences.* London: Tavistock.

———. (1972a). *The Archaeology of Knowledge* (A. M. Sheridan, Trans.) London: Tavistock.

———. (1972b). The discourse on language. In M. Foucault, *The Archaeology of Knowledge* (A. M. Sheridan, Trans.). New York: Pantheon.

———. (1980). *Power/Knowledge: Selected Interviews and Other Writings 1972–1977* (C. Gordon, Ed.). New York: Pantheon.

———. (1986). *The Foucault Reader* (P. Rabinow, Ed.). Harmondsworth, England: Penguin Books.

Garfinkel, H. (1956). Conditions for successful degradation ceremonies. *American Journal of Sociology* 61:420–24.

Geertz, C. (1979). On the nature of anthropological understanding. In P. Rabinow and W. M. Sullivan (Eds.): *Interpretive Social Science: A Reader.* Berkeley: University of California Press.

Gergen, K. J. (1988). If persons are texts. In S. B. Messer, L. A. Sass, and R. L. Woolfolk (Eds.): *Hermeneutics and Social Psychology.* New Brunswick, N.J.: Rutgers University Press.

———. (1990). Textual considerations in the scientific construction of human character. *Style* 24:365–79.

———. (1993). The mechanical self and the rhetoric of objectivity. *Annals of Scholarship, 9,* pp. 87–109.

hooks, bell. (1984). *Feminist Theory: From Margin to Center.* Boston: South End Press.

———. (1989). *Talking Back: Thinking Feminist, Thinking Black.* Boston: South End Press.

———. (1990). *Yearning: Race, Gender, and Cultural Politics.* Boston: South End Press.

MacIntyre, A. (1981). *After Virtue.* London: Duckworth.

———. (1990). *Three Rival Versions of Moral Enquiry: Encyclopedia, Genealogy, and Tradition.* Notre Dame, Ind.: University of Notre Dame Press.

Macpherson, C. B. (1962). *The Political Theory of Individualism: Hobbes to Locke.* Oxford, England: Oxford University Press.

Mills, C. W. (1940/1975). Situated actions and vocabularies of motive. In. D. Brisset and C. Edgley (Eds.): *Life as Theater: A Dramaturgical Sourcebook.* Chicago: Aldine.

Nagel, T. (1985). *The View from Nowhere.* New York: Oxford University Press.

Rorty, R. (1980). *Philosophy and the Mirror of Nature.* Oxford, England: Blackwell.

———. (1989). *Contingency, Irony, and Solidarity.* Cambridge, England: Cambridge University Press.

Sampson, E. E. (1981). Cognitive psychology as ideology. *American Psychologist* 36:730–43.

Scott, M. D., and Lyman, S. (1968). Accounts. *American Sociological Review* 33:46–62.

Shotter, J. (1975). *Images of Man in Psychological Research.* London: Methuen.

———. (1984). *Social Accountability and Selfhood.* Oxford, England: Blackwell.

———. (1993). *Cultural Politics of Everyday Life: Social Constructionism, Rhetoric, and Knowing of the Third Kind.* Milton Keynes, England: Open University Press.

———. (1995). Joint action, shared intentionality, and the ethics of conversation. *Theory and Psychology, 5,* pp. 49–75.

Taylor, C. (1990). Comparison, history, truth. In F. E. Reynolds and D. Tracy (Eds.): *Myth and Philosophy.* Albany: State University of New York Press.

———. (1992). *Multiculturalism and the 'Politics of Recognition.'* Princeton, N.J.: Princeton University Press.

Volosinov, V. N. (1973). *Marxism and the Philosophy of Language* (L. Matejka and I. R. Titunik, Trans.). Cambridge, Mass.: Harvard University Press.

———. (1976). *Freudianism: A Critical Sketch.* Bloomington: Indiana University Press.

Wittgenstein, L. (1953). *Philosophical Investigations.* Oxford, England: Blackwell.

———. (1958). *The Blue and the Brown Books.* New York: Harper and Row.

———. (1980). *Remarks on the Philosophy of Psychology,* Vols. I and II. Oxford, England: Blackwell.

Chapter Two

Seeing Oneself through Others' Eyes[1] in Social Inquiry

Klaus Krippendorff

any theory *not founded on the nature of being human is a lie
and a betrayal of [hu]man[ity]. An inhuman theory will
inevitably lead to human consequences—if the therapist is
consistent. Fortunately, many therapists have the gift of
inconsistency. This, however endearing, cannot be regarded as
ideal.*

—R. D. Laing (1967, 31)

*coming to see other human beings as "one of us" rather than
as "them" is a matter of detailed description of what unfamiliar people are like and of redescription of what we ourselves
are like.*

—Richard Rorty (1989, xvi)

Preliminaries, Assumptions, and Aims

In this essay I want to take seriously the notion that communication
involves people—not only as participants, as speakers and listeners, for
example, but also as observers of their own participation in that process. This includes observing other communicators as well. Participating in communication is primary. Without language, however, this
participation has no discernible structure. It is in the speaking of communication that the practices being observed and talked of become
communication and that its participants commit themselves to being in
it. Speaking of communication is communication of communication
and second-order by comparison, for it already presupposes one's communicative involvements. Communication, defined by and embodied in
those speaking of it, thus becomes a fundamentally local and self-
referential phenomenon. Indeed, what communication is or entails varies widely from one culture to another. Even in our own, explaining

practices of living in terms of communication is a surprisingly recent invention and in fact, a continuously evolving one. The very practice of writing scholarly essays on communication attests to my claim that nothing is ever entirely settled.

(Re)conceptualizing communication, talking or writing of communication, that is communication of communication, is what communication scholars do. The fact that communication scholars must actually do what they inquire into and talk of is unique to this kind of scholarship and calls for including themselves in their own domain of inquiry. To also preserve the notion of theory as a plausible account of particular practices, communication theories therefore cannot exclude scholarly practices of communication. This means *communication theories must be applicable to themselves.* That this demand is not a trivial matter and has considerable conceptual implications will become obvious below.

Although social scientists communicate in numerous ways—interviewing their subjects, engaging discursively with colleagues and publishing their work—self-applications of communication theories are surprisingly rare if not totally absent from the literature, as if the communicative involvements of scientists were immune to critical examination or so perfectly obvious as to be not worthy of attention. This schism easily leads to theories of communication that people find hard to live by. I know of no communication scholar who could communicate by the protocols of the classical theories they tend to perfect with their colleagues; for example, of communication as attitude change, as information transmission, as prediction and control, as management of meanings, or as institutionalized mass-production of messages. Communication, the way we seem to engage in it, is nothing like that. This essay, for instance, is not intended to change readers' affective evaluation of something they already know, nor to impart information this writer has but readers don't. One of my aims is to show the seriousness of not realizing that *we live in communication while theorizing it.*

All theories reside in talk and in publications. They may be difficult to understand by some, but they also can become quite popular, and end up transforming existing practices. This can happen to theories in physics as well as in sociology. But social theories are not only created by people who claim to understand what they are saying, they are above all about people and may be understood by the very people of which these theories speak. When this happens, *social theories* can be said to *reenter the very practices they claim to describe* and change their truths right in front of the theorist's eyes and often as he or she attempts to formulate them. Figure 2.1 attempts to depict this condition.

The paths along which theories are allowed to travel and reenter define disciplinary boundaries. The natural sciences, for example, have conveniently defined themselves as well as their objects so as to exclude

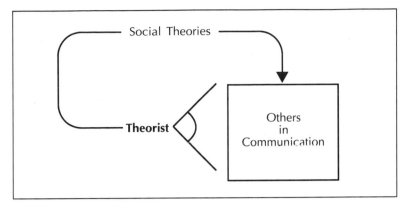

Figure 2.1. *Reentry of Social Theories*

reentry problems. Matter is conceived not to understand theories of it, and naturalist methods of observation do not allow scientific observers to enter their own domain of observation. "Objectivity," which Heinz von Foerster (1995) so aptly called "the illusion that reality could be observed without an observer," still dominates much of scientific methodology, even in the inquiry into social phenomena. Under this illusion, scientific observers occupy places that are very different from the objects they claim to theorize.

When social theories reenter the practices they describe through the people that engage them, they affect these practices, for example, by legitimizing them, by reconceptualizing them in scientific terms, or by stopping them altogether. Indeed, upon reentry, social theories behave more like self-fulfilling prophesies (Merton, 1963; Watzlawick, 1984) than as statements of objective or observer-independent facts— regardless of their theorists' intentions. One well-documented example of reentry is described in Rosenthal and Jacobson's (1968) study of classrooms where teachers were given arbitrary intelligence scores of their students who ended up testing that way. We know that the majority of women who grow up in narratives of their own inferiority quite naturally end up in subservient positions. We know of psychiatrists' inclination to talk patients into the very psychopathologies they are experts in treating. We know of how theories (or should I say myths) of communication drive teaching practices, therapies, self-improvement movements/courses/literatures, international relations, and above all communication technologies. Social theories are thus changing the very social world that gave rise to them. The injunction against observers entering their domain of observation is a positivist way of keeping theories from becoming self-fulfilling, hold on to a representational notion of truth, dissociate theorists from the consequences of their theories, and preserve the monologic of scientific communication, leaving no opening for the voices of subjects to be heard. In the social domain, this injunction is unwarranted. This is so not only because it contradicts the facts of reentry, but also because it gives social scientists the convenient excuse for denying responsibilities for intervening in, if not creating, the very processes that constitute their domain of inquiry.

Conceptual difficulties of dealing with the problem of reentry have led Anthony Giddens (1984) to a double hermeneutics that he describes as the merging of the social scientists' meanings with those of the social actors being described. (His concept of merging assumes meanings to be shareable however [Krippendorff, 1994], which is a mentalist conception that I prefer to avoid). Unlike Giddens, I am suggesting that the possibility of reentry calls for theories that include their own effects and for theorists to acknowledge responsibilities for these effects. For example—and this essay will be especially sensitive to this—when scientific theories discount the intellectual capabilities of those they speak of, the reentry of these theories into everyday practices can easily retard the use of these capabilities. Thus, contrary to the self-serving beliefs in objectivity, theories can become unwitting instruments of oppression. This leads me to argue against accepting theories solely in terms of their descriptive accuracy or representational truth. What they mean to Others is far more important. Social theorists simply should not be so naive as to discount the consequences of their conceptions. Nor should they ignore or deny their own communicative roles. Acknowledging this leads me to see *social scholarly pursuits as relational practices* (see Gergen, 1994).

Concerning such practices, let me add a contention that is central to this essay: Whenever we abstract social theories from their primary settings (of people, situations, individuals, or institutional practices) and communicate them as valid accounts of social phenomena, *we,* as social scientists, invariably *designate places for other people to occupy.* How we conceive or speak of these Others, even when we omit explicit references to them, always directs our listening, our (re)searching, and our interacting with these unnamed and possibly unknown Others. For example, when we conceive of communication as the transmission of messages, we place people in the role of senders, channels, or receivers of certain messages much like conceiving people as producers, distributors, or consumers of goods. Or, when we conceive of communication as uncertainty reduction, we render communication as an individual or cognitive phenomenon—as distinct from a social or dialogical one—and construct people in communication as lone certainty seekers. Moreover, when we publish theories of communication, we speak in our capacity as communication scholars and assume the authority to construct the otherness of Others. Whenever scientific theories reenter ordinary peoples' lives, whenever they are talked of, rearticulated, and adopted as folk theories, whenever they are realized and tested in the practice of everyday life, the particular spaces they offer for people to make their home and meet each Other are likely influenced by the authority attributed to science. This demands of social theorists to assume a considerable responsibility. To criticize social theories for their political "biases," for their lack of neutrality, is beside the point of finding a way of understanding them as consequential communications.

Given where theories reside and how they may travel, I am not suggesting that they could be forced upon anyone, nor that they could overwhelm people as a mysterious power of persuasion. Even in one-way communication, from theorist to theorized, it is always possible for people to reject theories that are blatantly wrong, to contest theories that are unfair or not in their best interest, or to propose more acceptable alternatives. It is also possible for people to simply violate a theory's claims by doing something other than predicted and thereby undermine their validity. One widespread contestation is exemplified in feminist criticism of theories of human behavior, showing them to be proposed largely by and for men. Although the preponderance of this criticism emphasizes the injustice of the resulting inequalities, far more important to me is the simple fact that feminist criticism effectively invalidates dominant theories by compelling women and sometimes men not to conform to them; for example, by encouraging women to follow their own path of emancipation. Attempts to break racial or ethnic prejudices can work the same way. The communication of communication theories can not literally cause anything, but it does enter the politics of communication.

A partial answer of why people let themselves be silenced by theories concerning them lies, I submit, in the authority attributed to scientists. The rhetoric of science seems to carefully nourish this attribution. Scientific authority thrives on the exclusionary claim of scientists being the arbiters in matters of reality and truth. This shifts the epistemological competence from dialogically involved individuals to institutionalized practices whose authority cannot so easily be questioned. In our culture, this authority is rarely contested, particularly not by people who feel or are made to feel inadequate, insecure, or inferior on epistemological grounds. Even philosophers of science such as Karl R. Popper, Thomas Kuhn, and above all Paul K. Feyerabend, who dared to question this authority, have been declared "The worst enemy of science" (Horgan, 1993). For these reasons, the chance of scientific theories influencing everyday practices is therefore heavily weighted in favor of science and against folk theories and common sense. As social scientists, we may enjoy this authority but should earn it by systematically questioning its sources and by acknowledging our accountability for our constructions to those who may end up living in (or with) them (Krippendorff, 1993). Loosening the grip that theories have on our own and on Others' lives is a task that this essay shares with that of critical scholarship.

To gain a handle on these relational phenomena I will take to heart the existentialist distinction between two kinds of world constructions: one in which people see themselves surrounded by tangible objects they manipulate to achieve particular ends; and the other in which people see themselves related to other fellow human beings, much like themselves, and with whom they appreciate being for whatever reasons. Martin Buber (1958, 1970; Horwitz, 1978) calls these the I-it and the I-Thou relation, respectively. At least one study generated convincing data concerning the social reality of this distinction (Roberts, 1985).

I am not an existentialist, however, nor am I satisfied with the binary nature of this distinction and the contrast between the instrumental/rational and noninstrumental/intuitive ways of knowing it encourages. To retain the notion that *selves and Others are constructed relationally,* in communication with each Other, I feel the need to expand Buber's distinction to several I-Other relations. After all, English has several pronouns to refer to people, singular and plural ones, and first, second, and third persons, and these provide us with a natural way of bringing several relational differences into sharper focus. To me, Buber's it as well as his Thou appear too sweeping. In another paper I draw finer distinctions within I-it: I-they, I-trivial it, and I-nontrivial it (Krippendorff, 1996). In this essay I shall distinguish between I-You and I-Thou only. Although Buber nowhere alludes to either of these distinctions, recent disputes over the translation of Buber's German *Ich und Du* (Horwitz, 1978) into *"I and Thou"* may even be construed as supporting my effort to move to conceptions that are closer to English pronoun uses. While the original translation contrasted Thou and it throughout, in the second translation, the translator Walter Kaufmann (Buber, 1970) responded to the accumulated misgivings regarding the English "thou" for the German *du* and translated "du" as "you," thus removing some of the mysteriousness from the Thou. Since Buber does not differentiate between You and Thou, I am taking advantage of this ambiguity and am drawing this distinction. Being more concerned with scientific discourse, I will let the first person "I" stand largely for the inquiring scientist. Sometimes it is me and sometimes some other I.

Finally, in this essay, I am less concerned with facts than with epistemological blind spots and less with where science is wrong than with creating compelling possibilities where few existed. Elsewhere, I have argued the creation of alternatives to be a social imperative for constructing communication (Krippendorff, 1989). I also suggested that increasing the possibilities of being to be axiomatic for critical scholarship (Krippendorff, 1995). As a small step in this direction, I will therefore simply outline the distinction between I-You and I-Thou and correlate it with communication and conversation, respectively. In addition to expanding ways of conceptualizing Others, I wish to enable social theorists to enter their domain of observation, to encourage researchers to cooperate with those being researched, to grant Others a voice, if not the last word, on how they appear in scientific accounts, and to encourage theories that can develop "a life of their own." This calls for a radical break with existing social research methods and opens the door to a new participatory form of social inquiry and a dialogical way of knowing. In pursuit of this, I will finally elaborate on just three consequences of the You/Thou distinction, their vulnerabilities, their methodological implications, and the kinds of societies or citizenships either construction encourages.

I-You: Persons in Communication

Third-person accounts locate Others outside a dialogue, often in the monologue of the observing I. The personal pronouns "he" and "she" hold Others in reserve for potential communication whereas "it" denotes something without personhood and without the potential for communication. By contrast, second-person accounts always refer to people presently talked with and thus add a dimension that is ignored in third-person accounts: *Language.* "You" occurs in talk among people that are *responsive* to each Other. Neither the speaking I nor the spoken-to You can escape knowing something of each Other. I-You communication is a collaborative effort, and inquiries within such relations therefore are participatory. As therapists know, observation is essential but talk is the more important key to making sense of Others' lives. Indeed, a great deal can be learned about Others as well as about selves by becoming *communicationally involved.*

Etymologically, "person" is of Greek origin and meant (the sound) "emitted from the body." In Latin it became "an actor's mask." Persons are aware of who they presently are, how well they do in the presence of Others, their audiences for example, and most importantly, who else they could be. Persons always observe and monitor themselves in relationships. The virtual I that does the monitoring of I-You communication may be no more than a momentarily privileged past or future I examining a present one.

Awareness of the possibility of "wearing different masks," of enacting different Is, implies choices that render persons somewhat unpredictable from the position of an outside observer, who happens not to participate in the I-You relation. However, this unpredictability does not result from the impossibility of knowing what is "really going on inside," inside a human brain for example, or from the difficulty of observing the "true self" a You could be masking. I am suggesting that at least one part of this unpredictability arises from a person's *agency,* the ability to conceive possibilities and act into them, and the commitment to be responsible to Others for one's actions. In proposing this reason, I do not see agency as an individualist or psychological conception, rather as one that is rooted in the languaging between people. This makes agency a social or dialogical phenomenon.

Conceptions of You and I are always *complementary*. A mother does not exist without a child; there can be no buyer without a seller; actors and audiences require each Other. And on the behavioral level, a joke needs a teller and others to laugh about it. Complementarity must not be confused with equality. Nor does it have anything to do with sharing. In communication, roles fit more like "hand in glove" than "hand in hand" and their difference is not only natural but actually constitutive of a particular relationship. Not all possible pairs of roles fit that way, however. When a senator meets a dentist, either the senator becomes a patient, the dentist speaks as a member of the senator's constituency, or they find a third way of relating outside these roles.

In human communication, *every I is I's Others' Other.* I speaks in the expectation of You's understanding, anticipating You's ability to rearticulate or respond to what I said in You's own terms, awaiting I's understanding in turn—all of which being manifestly embodied or carried by their intertwined practices (which is the process of communication as observed by its participants). In this recursion, I's accounts need not reflect or express I's internal makeup, I's thoughts or intentions, but the narrative history and anticipated continuation of I's interaction with You, separately monitored by either participant. This includes I's construction of self and Other as well as I's construction of You's construction of self and Other. In communication, persons come to be recursively embedded in the enacted accounts of each Other. Such accounts occur within this relationship, are at least in part about that relationship, and thus become one of its constitutive ingredients. This understanding of communication is far removed from the metaphor of "sending and receiving messages," which may explain how technical devices interact with one another, but not of how humans engage each other dialogically. Recursion is often considered a dangerous construction. However, I consider the infinity which this recursion implies to be an artifact of logic only. It hardly ever bothers anyone in practice. We seem to be able to shift easily between levels of recursion without the need to think in many of these levels at any one time (Laing, quoted in Miell and Miell, 1986). This said, accounts of I-You relationships may be diagrammed as in Figure 2.2.

Since given accounts are always offered in the *expectation* of being understood, which presupposes persons to have some ability to simulate or rehearse their communication theories before they are enacted, I-You relations always require a space in which alternative futures are conceived, previewed, pondered, or talked of. Figure 2.2

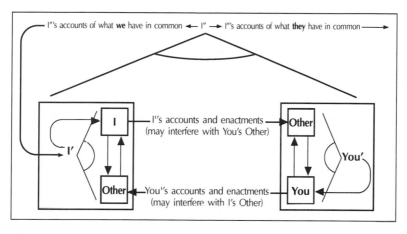

Figure 2.2. *An I-You Relation*

suggests the possibility of inner I-Other dialogues becoming enacted into outer dialogues, the effects of which either challenge each participant's expectations of the Other, of each Other's Other, and so forth, or they confirm one's conception by saying nothing. This is a recursive braiding of each Others' reality constructions. In human communication, I suggest, theories must always account for the consequences of their verbalizations, particularly of one's own and Others' understanding and enacting them. Erving Goffman's (1959) dramaturgical approach exemplifies the complementary construction of persons. The work of R. D. Laing (1967) exemplifies the structural symmetries of these constructions. John Shotter (1984) suggests to replace the noninteractive notion of theory by the notion of an account, as a joint accomplishment, and develops dialogical conceptions of these (1993). In the following I consider additional characteristics of I-You relations.

In I-You communication, neither I nor You have independent "natures" that any I could accurately "capture." It makes no sense of building cognitive models of an Other when that Other changes in response to how it is regarded or described. The description that would remain stable over time, perhaps after many iterations is merely a gestalt in the process of mutual engagement, a joint accomplishment as Shotter (1993) would say. In some important sense every person becomes complete only in communication with Others and this includes the inquiring I. Thus, inquiries into Others also are inquiries into oneself.

It seems difficult to understand what is going on inside an I-You relation without communicative involvements. What detached observers cannot experience is precisely what makes such a relation real: the unfolding history of the particular engagement and the embodied feelings of being in communication. Jones and Nisbett (1972) found "a pervasive tendency for participants to attribute their actions to situational requirements, whereas observers tend to attribute the same actions to stable personality dispositions" (80). In view of this rather robust finding, the psychological concept of personality, the stable character of a person, is more likely the artifact of detached observation than an empirical or experiential fact. Sigmund Freud might be said to have created a whole science without being aware that his constructions are a reflection of his (authoritarian) relationship to his patients and the now huge industry of psychoanalytic practices is predicated on nothing other than reifying this observational artifact. Today we can see such monological theories as barriers to a dialogical understanding human communication. In addition to these attributional differences, I-You relations seem always more complex from an outsider's perspective than from that of the insiders (Roberts and Bavelas, 1996).

Nonparticipant outsiders of I-You communication not only have it more difficult to understand what is going on right in front of their own eyes, they also have to cope with a vastly larger number of interpretations than insiders would consider. For once, persons not only are what they do, say, and what is said to them, they also continually adjust their reality, including their being, relative to each Other without having to end up the same. This usually occurs in small steps and while talking of other matters. Gregory Bateson's distinction between content and relationship aspects of communication comes to mind. To change metaphors, persons could be said to continually program each other, suggesting modifications here and yielding to constraints there. Persons could also be said to negotiate who they are and what they have in common. Theorists, who view such mutual adjustments from outside, cannot help but interpret their perception in their relation to their subjects, using criteria that derive from their position and remain blind to the subtle accounts persons understand to give each other in communication.

The hitch in this conception of communication lies in the temptation of constructing underlying *commonalities* almost as in I-it accounts of machine-like devices: a common ground, a common situation, a common language, a common (communication) technology, a common culture, a common history, a common code of ethics, a shared medium, a common mission, consensus, or agreement, and so on. These are logical or technological constructions, not empirical ones, and may assume the explanatory role of foundations in which everyone is to ground their arguments, of overarching superstructures alleged to govern the behavior of all participants, or of something we (You and I) are said to share, like virtues, vocabularies, or biologies. This temptation is encouraged by the etymology of "communication." It shares its stem with "commonality," "community," "communion," etc. The everyday expectation that communication takes place in an objectively shared medium and must converge toward consensus amounts to much the same. Many scientific theories of communication have adopted this as their conceptual premise, whether they focus on a shared language as Hans-Georg Gadamer (1975) did and many constructionists (e.g., Gergen, 1985) do, on a universal pragmatics such as Jürgen Habermas (1970) or whether they presuppose a physical universe to which the "content" of communication is thought to refer.

Assertions of commonalities can be associated with the exertion of power and with efforts to control dialogical processes. For example, rhetorical questions like "don't we agree on that?" references to "(our) family values," declarations that "we speak the same language," and a shared technology must be constructed by someone who values such commonalities and in the expectations that Others would accept this reality construction and live with its entailments. Once constructed, commonalities have, in fact, entered a communication process and accepting their articulations within that process makes them real. Only by focusing on what they claim rather than who formulated them, how did they come to be accepted, and what keeps them in the process, do commonalities acquire the appearance—but only that—of "objectivity." One must keep in mind that a *we never speaks. Individual Is do,* but always only in continuation of a history of interaction. The authoritative assertion of commonalities, while contestable in principle, can easily silence divergent voices. Language, for example, surely is an abstraction from a multitude of voices by those who claim to speak for other speakers and in ways that declare certain of their differences irrelevant or unworthy of attention.

The we of claimed commonalities can be seen from exclusive and inclusive perspectives, from a position outside that relationship, when an observer describes what they have in common, and from a position inside that relationship, when one participating I describes what we share. Either perspective privileges the I that claims to see what Others don't; the I that sets the standards by which Others are to be judged; the I whose ontological claims everyone is expected to accept. A good example in which I moreover manages to protect its authority from challenges is the claim of hegemony as an existing social condition. By Antonio Gramsci's (1987) widely accepted definition, hegemony denotes an all pervasive, discursive, and hence consensual superstructure. In cultural studies, it has replaced the older notion of "ideology," while continuing to depict all those affected, the dominated as well as the dominant, as unable to recognize its pervasive presence and power over them. To avoid the paradox of claiming an ability to see what one's theory declares invisible, assertions about "hegemonic conditions" are being made from the position of a privileged observer who is free of this condition. This places the theorist of hegemony outside the supposed commonality and into an I-they relation to those to whom he or she applies the concept. The theory is predicated on constructing Others as blind to what the I claims to observe with crystal clarity. In I-You communication, the theory of hegemony is a pathological construction in the sense of eroding Yous into "debilitated" theys. This rhetorically suspect theory becomes blatantly devious when its theorists are aware of the fact that their authority depends on hiding this self-serving ontology. By excluding other voices, the concept of hegemony reveals itself as "paternalism" toward Others.

I-Thou: Human Beings in Conversation

Just as in I-You relations, I and Thou denote a pair of complementary constructions of people characterized by their ability to speak for themselves, with each Other, and in that process create worlds of their own, recursively including therein the worlds of Others. But unlike in I-You relations, masks that hide a "true self," deceptions, no longer have a place. In I-Thou relations, people *constitute themselves in conversational practices:* Neither unilaterally imposes its categories on the Other. Neither assumes a position superior to the Other. Neither is an agent for a larger whole and neither champions commonalities, joint purposes, or a particular medium. Stable pattern of interaction, rules, or technologies that may arise always remain contestable within such conversations. In other words, there can be no ultimate authority, no ultimate reality that I or Thou could not question. In such relations human beings are true to themselves, authentic (Roberts, 1985), and responsible to each Other. Buber (1958) speaks of "grace" (11) and of "love" (14).

One of the features of I-Thou relations is that the positions of *I and Thou are freely interchangeable.* This goes beyond regarding I as its Other's Other. I and Thou can take turns in assuming and speaking from each Other's perspectives and are able to shift freely across any complementarities that preserve the qualities of I-Thou relations. Roles construed as noninterchangeable, for example, male and female, parent and child, therapist and client, or ethnographer and native are incommensurate with I-Thou relations. The kind of power that arises with the presumption of noninterchangability has no place in I-Thou relations. And should interchangability be resisted, this very act effectively converts that relation into another one. Indeed, no matter how hard ethnographers try to be true to the conceptions of their informants, even when they have become nearly indistinguishable from the "natives they wish to understand," as long as they come with a disciplined purpose and take their notes away for analysis elsewhere, there is no dialogical equality. No matter how hard therapists listen to their clients, their very professionalism and their receipt of payments for services freezes their roles in place and renders their positions noninterchangeable. This does not mean that people who see each Other as unalterably different could not participate in I-Thou relations outside these perceptions. I am merely suggesting here that I-Thou relations cannot draw on such differences. In I-Thou relations, I and Thou would have to construct themselves and voice each Other outside of these noninterchangeables and undo any obstacles to the maintenance of such relations. Serbs and Muslims in the former Yugoslavia can get along fine, provided their histories do not enter their relationship. Then, however, they would no longer speak as Serbs and as Muslims, but as human beings. At this point, conversation becomes possible.

If all relational practices are to be contestable by I and Thou, then *accounts of them must enter their conversations,* explicitly or implicitly, *and circulate freely* among the participants involved. Just as in I-You, accounts that do enter conversations can transform what they speak of and reconstruct the ongoing conversational histories, the I-Thou relation, as well as the very I and Thou that embodies them. But unlike in I-You, such accounts must preserve the unconditional respect for each Others' differences. Whereas accounts of I and You are at times difficult to understand from outside that relation, the being in I-Thou is naturally unique and quite inaccessible to detached observers. Outside accounts of this relationship can never reflect the intertwined meanings embodied by those involved, the feelings that resonate with each conversational turn, and the sense of comfort in being-with each Other. Nevertheless, I shall offer in Figure 2.3 a sketch of what I mean: Let I' indicate the virtual I that observes, conceptualizes, and evaluates I's involvement in an I-Thou relation from a position I does *not* momentarily occupy, for example, from its past, its future, or from its Other. Let Thou' indicate the equally self-reflecting Thou, I and Thou being in "view" of or present to each Other. When participants speak, they enter their own accounts of I and of Thou into an already ongoing conversation and thus acknowledge, explicitly or implicitly, each Other's presences, expectations, and commitments.

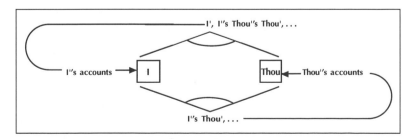

Figure 2.3. An I-You Relation

Furthermore, let this diagram be the very form of the accounts I' and/
or Thou' enter into their conversation (from left and right of the diagram). Thus, and not apparent in this depiction, accounts of I-Thou
relations contain themselves, are recursively self-embedded in the conversational dynamics they unfold, and thus are entirely local if not
closed to outside interventions.

Writing of dialogue, Gadamer (1975) says: "In human relations
the important thing is . . . to experience the 'Thou' truly as a 'Thou,'
i.e., not to overlook [Thou's] claim and to listen to what [Thou] says
to us. To this end, openness is necessary. . . . Without this kind of openness to one another there is no genuine human relationship" (323). I do
not interpret this to mean that listening could lead to seeing who the
Other "really" is. Gadamer seems to have this in mind. Others always
occur in I's constructions. But by attentive listening to Thou's voice, by
not trying to confirm one's own constructions, by not looking for Thou's
faults or weaknesses, by not assuming that historical trends must continue into the future, by not attempting to persuade or use the Other for
whatever purpose, in other words, by not privileging one's own (naturally comfortable) logic over the logic of one's Others, an I can open
itself up and reserve a *dialogical space for Thou to enter and be Thouself*
therein. This means *avoiding the temptations of certainty,* not to gen-
eralize from one to another, not to insist on master narratives, and not
to construct an unalterable ground for both to stand on. Regarding such
a ground, I deviate from Gadamer who insists on language as being the
commonality through which I and Thou understand each Other. His
notion of merging horizons recognizes the difficulties but then idealizes
sharing at the expense of the mere possibility of continued conversation, of continued being-with each Other. In this possibility, Thou's
space may not be coextensive with I's—as the metaphor of merging
horizons would entail—nor is it merely tolerated by I—as an inferior
version of one's own. Each must want I to enter and meet Thou in
Thou's own terms.

The concept of "dialogue" is only one logical complement of
"monologue." I propose *multilogue* as another. In multilogue several
distinct possibilities, several incommensurate logics, or several parallel
worlds exist side by side. In choosing this term I wish to exclude two
kinds of single world accounts (including of dialogue). First, I and
Thou should be able to *travel freely from one world to another,* including, as I said before, to take each Other's places and to see themselves
from their Others' positions. Efforts to impose coherences, which
amounts to constructing an overarching metalogic or underlying ground,
would frustrate this possibility and merge these worlds into one. Second, the voices of Others can and in I-Thou relations must always be
able to introduce new perspectives if not entirely new worlds into
conversation. To enable this, I and Thou has to maintain or *continuously*

recreate clearings for listening to each Other, and to invite each Other to enter the open and deliberately unstructured spaces in which to meet. In other words, it is the condition of multilogue that I must preserve against the temptation of inventing an overarching monologic, one that merely tolerates the logics of Others as local derivatives of I's or as distortions of I's (generalized) uni-verse. Being in conversation means continuously *creating spaces for the worlds of I and of Thou to expand and for both to move around, to find their homes, and be-with each Other.*

Applying his conception of dialogue to Dostoevsky's writing, Mikhail Bakhtin (1984) says much the same. "Monologism, at its extreme," Bakhtin suggests, "denies the existence outside itself of another consciousness with equal rights and equal responsibilities, another *I* with equal rights [*thou*]" (292). In the "homophonic" text, all aspects of narrative are subordinated to the will of the author. Others become mere mouthpieces of that author's ideological viewpoints. "A monologic . . . world does not recognize someone else's thought, someone else's idea, as an object of representation" (79). By contrast, "Dostoevsky does not seek to subordinate or suppress the pervasive vari-directional accents and double voiced discourses that characterize the natural milieu of living language; rather, he aims to enhance and encourage [a] 'dialogically-charged atmosphere.' . . . [This] can be found in the interaction between the hero and the author, the series of 'micro-dialogues' that take place between the various characters, and even the 'inner speech' [or 'internal dialogue'] that occurs within the hero's own self-consciousness. . . . [I]t is only within the polyphonic novel that artistic justice can be done to the 'objective complexity, contradictoriness and multi-voicedness' of the social world" (Gardiner, 1992). Bakhtin (1984) writes, "a consciousness in Dostoevsky's world is presented not on the path of its own evolution and growth, that is, not historically, but rather *alongside* other consciousnesses, it cannot concentrate on itself and its own idea, on the immanent logical development of that idea; instead it is pulled into interaction with other consciousnesses" (32). I would say, *several "logics" unfold in parallel but always in acknowledgment of each Other.* In multilogue, I is not tempted to shape the voice (and logic of reality) of Others. Instead, I invites the worlds of Others to enter I's accounts in ways recognizable by these Others as their very own. Multilogue necessarily emerges when I and Thou thrive on conversing with each Other and on discovering possibilities that neither could imagine by itself. Multilogue describes the multiple social realities needed for Bakhtin's polyphonic dialogue to not only take place but also enable their participants to move out of burdensome if not oppressive relational practices.

As Buber suggested, I-Thou relations are informed by *love*—not the love of someone, but of the otherness that creates and complements the I, the feeling of being in sync with Others' understanding and of appreciating the diversity of otherness that love makes possible. Spiritual love, for example the love of God (Buber's eternal you), the feeling of being related to something inherently unattainable yet immensely invigorating seems to me a metaphorical extension of this prototypical I-Thou. According to Buber (1958), love is not a feeling one may or may not have for someone else, "Love is between I and Thou. . . . " "Love is the responsibility of an I for a Thou" (14–15). *Celebrating the Other* as Edward Sampson (1993) suggests is a start but may not be enough. The construction of a Thou in a world that may be radically different if not incommensurate from mine and the possibility of positioning oneself in that world and appreciate the Thou in Thou's own terms entails *the possibility for I to see itself through the Others' eyes.* Without a Thou, I remains blind to its possibility of being in open conversation.

The possibility of I and Thou emerging in open conversation is ushering a major revolution in socializing epistemology whose end still needs to be envisioned. It has provided new directions to education (Friere, 1972) and to therapy. It has created environments for people to recognize and overcome their constraints. It has provided the stimulus for a relational social psychology (Gergen, 1994) and the pursuit of conversational realities (Shotter, 1993). Finally, it offers attractive opportunities for minorities, women, and the otherwise categorized or marginalized to not merely feel frustrated and oppressed by conditions constructed as existing but to develop an understanding of themselves as participants in the very social construction that underlies such conditions and to offer participatory ways out of it (Krippendorff, 1995). I-Thou relations appear to be rationally impenetrable. This aspect is very much supported in Buddhist teachings, suggesting that individuals aim to be whole and one with their own universe (a paradox, no doubt), neither fearful nor dismissive of the otherness of Others.

Comparisons

In the following I shall discuss three of the many consequences of thusly distinct othernesses: their vulnerabilities, the methodological issues they raise, and their political consequences.

The Vulnerabilities of Otherness

Human relations exist in continuous transformations, as I have argued. They also have their characteristic vulnerabilities, that is to say, conditions under which one erodes into another. Clearly, I-it relationships are most stable and restricted, precisely because they do not offer those described corrective feedback on how I conceives them. In I and Thou, by contrast, everything is open, contestable, and the spaces Thou and I create for being-with each Other continuously expand. The construction of human beings in I-Thou relations might therefore be considered most vulnerable to degradations.

Starting from the Thou that I faces in conversation, I am suggesting, as soon as this I puts Others into the places I wants them to be, as soon as this I refuses to let Others speak from I's position, for example, by claiming superiority, better equipment, more knowledge, or the ability to understand Thou better than Thou does, the I-Thou relation erodes to an I-You relation where such inequities can make their home and noninterchangeable identities may settle in. Similarly, as soon as I claims unilateral access to what I and Thou are said to share—a common ground, purpose, history, ideology, or consensus, etc.—as soon as I insists on dictionary definitions, consistency, rationality, or conformity to a general theory of human nature, without Thou's consent, Thou ceases to exist. For example, when lovers start examining the costs and benefits of being in that relation, keep a tab on how many favors each has given the Other, or play tit for tat, rational rules of conduct enter and the relationship of love transforms itself into an economic one where a common currency matters (Solomon, 1990). Intimacy is easily violated and difficult to recover.

I-You relations can erode as well. When I takes the position of a detached observer who denies those observed a voice in I's constructions, when this I regards Others as serving particular functions, clients, experimental subjects, servants, including enemies, when the observing I accounts for human behavior in mathematical or algorithmic terms, or studies people as stimulus-response mechanisms, there would then be no justification for I to talk with them and listen to their voices. Under these conditions the You becomes an it and dialogue dissolves into the monologue of one-way communication. Similarly, claiming to know who the Others *really are* without their permission, discounting these Others' agency by explaining their behavior as structurally, situationally, or historically determined, becomes incompatible with a You one can talk with and hold responsible for its actions. Finally, generalizing away individual differences and grouping people into homogeneous classes creates the stereotypical "they" of people whose identity is tailored to suit I's categorizations.

In the domain of interpersonal relations, Roberts (1985) found similar vulnerabilities: When her subjects conceived of their involvements with partners in I-it terms, it was virtually impossible for them to imagine I-Thou relationships much less getting into one. They remained stuck in I-it-world constructions and tended to (mis)treat their partners as servants or as "doormats," seemingly closed to Other's conceptions, and unable to understand the dynamics of their participation. However, subjects who could understand written accounts of I-Thou relationships, might be disappointed when their partners turn out unable to reciprocate in kind, but can at least envision this way of relating and notice its absence. I have met quite a number of people who do have real difficulties with appreciating Others' truly different worlds but I have encountered far more for whom it is impossible to imagine seeing themselves through these different Others' equally valid eyes.

Buber (1958) has seen the vulnerability of Thou as well but differently. He considers love as being focused on whole human beings. Hate, he says, is always limiting, focusing on parts of Others which takes Thou into components. Hating the whole person transforms the Thou to the it of an object (16–17). Apparently, not only can human relations erode in careless practices, they may then no longer be recoverable.

Methodological Issues of Otherness

To experience and account for the human ability of communication, it seems necessary to break with at least some of the established scientific research traditions, particularly those that describe people as the bearers of properties, as stimulus-response mechanisms, or as cognitive systems whose nature is to be understood from their outside and represented in a suitable medium. Even in ordinary language terms, the reasons for this break are clear. Third-person Others are *talked of,* while second-person Others are *talked with*. Third-person Others are *distant* in time and in space and may be observed without their knowledge or consent; second-person Others must always be faced, *bodily co-present,* and willing to engage in dialogue. Thus, inquiring into persons as I have defined the term means communicating with them, actively listening to their voices, responding to their conceptions with curiosity and respect, and coordinating one's own responses with theirs. Theories that arise out of such conditions must be realized interactively and thus become social in the sense that the theorized as well as their theorists are constitutive parts of them. It is the above-mentioned injunction against observers entering their domain of inquiry that makes inquiry while being in communication with Others so unthinkable. It seems difficult now to recover from the epistemological damage this injunction has left behind. This leads me to the first methodological issue already introduced as *reentry*.

Without reentry of accounts into the social fabric they describe, detached observers of persons not only face overwhelming numbers of possible propositions, hypotheses, theories, or models among which selection is difficult but also a lack of criteria to justify their choices in observational terms. Outsider accounts are always imposed and largely capricious if not irrelevant from an insider's perspective. However, trusting the ability of persons to understand, to rearticulate, and to accept and reject accounts, especially of their own situation, opens the possibility of collaboration in both generating appropriate accounts and selecting among them, applying the very criteria that are embodied in the participants' understanding and being. This means *testing the viability of relational accounts by reinserting them into the very relational process they describe* and observing what becomes of them.

Reentry challenges the already troubled representational notion of truth in yet another way. This received notion of truth regards truth (and falsity) as a property of propositions about a nonlinguistic world. It not only enforces a monological conception on that world also renders the "proposer" of such propositions invisible. Epistemological criticisms of this naïve kind of objectivism have shifted attention from the "truths of propositions" to "the making of truth claims." This brought the (scientific) observer back into the picture but preserved the representational notion of truth by raising concerns of observer biases and ideological distortions. In contrast, I like to consider all I-Other accounts as embedded in relational practices—observation in the case of I-it, communication in the case of I-You, and conversation in the case of I-Thou—and allow dialogue among those involved to decide their acceptance. This procedure moves far beyond acknowledging the inevitability of observer biases. It recontextualizes theories and propositions into the relational practices that produced them, and establishes their viability—dialogically. In I-You, theorists and theorized share the responsibility for "certifying" this dialogical "truth." In I-Thou, there is nothing to certify. All that matters is a demonstration that *the conversation can continue* (or restart at a later point) and the ability of emancipation from burdensome relational constraints is preserved.

Regrettably, the so-called interpretive methods—ethnography, discourse analysis, and cultural studies, for example—which are far more in touch with human conditions than their positivist opponents, fail in this regard as well. Although these methods are less codified than those borrowed from the natural sciences and therefore more open to good intuition, they are also tied to a linear process of analysis. Interpretive methods essentially retrieve or encourage texts from an empirical domain and generate from them other texts that serve as their plausible interpretations, presumably revealing hidden meanings in the original texts and the social conditions that produced them, consulting, however, neither the authors or readers of these texts nor other stakeholders in the resulting accounts. After such analyses, a community decides their worth by publication, citation, and further commentary. In the end, these methods provide monological accounts of Others, akin to I-it accounts, and no criterion to select among the innumerably many possible interpretations other than that provided by a detached interpretative community. Choices say more about how scholars are situated within their community than about the social reality of those spoken of or spoken for, often quite passionately so. The notion of hegemony, already discussed, serves as an example of how the proponents of this notion set themselves above Others and show little regard for what these Others have to say of their lives. Even well-intended ethnographers take their data home for analysis and interpretation and rarely go back and let them be checked out. The search for "correct" interpretations almost always prevents dialogues. I contend, there are more human-centered ways of understanding.

A classical example that unintentionally showed the virtue of I-You accounts can be found in a series of experiments conducted in the 1940s to improve workers' productivity in a plant in Hawthorne, Ill. The researchers systematically varied physical working conditions, lighting, working hours, breaks, etc., and measured their effects. Productivity increased, even when the conditions were changed back to before the experiments started. Without a recognizable pattern, this finding remained totally "mysterious" until the experimenters dared asking the workers themselves to explain this now famous Hawthorne Effect. It turned out to be the attention paid to workers that increased productivity, not the conditions the experimenter varied for effects (Mayo, 1945). This entirely relational explanation—relational because it no longer concerned external conditions but the relationship between experimenters' actions and subjects' interpretation of these actions—could not have been found without taking advantage of the subjects' ability to articulate their working conditions and participate in the formulation of suitable accounts, using their own logic. Here, as in all I-You situations, truth did not matter but what communicative attention meant to the participants.

Evidently, reentry of accounts into I-You communication does not need to be considered an issue of ethics, of not imposing one's own categories on Others' being, of not suppressing the voices of Others from a position of claimed superiority. Reentry is an empirically necessary condition for preserving a "truth" that is acceptable by those with very real experiences of what is being claimed and the ability to live it. This dialogical criterion is simply richer than the decontextualized notion of a propositional truth, more real by acknowledging that truth is experiential and relational, requiring collaboration of claimants and those spoken of, for, and about, and more democratic by involving all those who wish to say what they have to say. Reentry can take the form of asking the interviewees who provided the input to a study to read and comment on the (preliminary) research results and allowing them to rewrite or amend the researchers' "findings." Reentry can also take the form of letting subjects identify or categorize themselves and each Other, much as in everyday life, rather than by outsiders, finding dialogical rather than monological truths. In community development work, reentry means that members of a community may listen to outside experts but reserve the right to define their own problem, do their own research, and act with consent. The kind of interventions family therapists make, floating analytical conceptions and encouraging new communication practices to emerge from them, depends on dialogical criteria of acceptance as well. Therapy rarely works without it. All of these methods admit research to be intrusive and interventive and position the researcher in communication with Others as "partners" in a joint exploration.[2]

As stated above, inquiries into I-You relations are expected to converge, to yield consensus, agreements, or commonalities that are in turn presumed to underlie or govern communication. For such commonalities to exist, someone will have to propose of them, claim the last word on what they are, or enforce them for whatever reasons. Their successful proposition effectively preserves the proposer's authority or superiority over Others who are thereby asked to see them that way and conform to their entailments. This is altogether absent in I-Thou relations, and the rejection of commonalities from accounts of I-Thou relations amounts to a final break with established methodological traditions. Here, determinability or predictability of each Other's behavior can no longer be the issue for this would freeze I, Thou, and their being-with each Other into their past histories. I-Thou inquiries can not seek generalizations; which would entail implicit comparisons, project properties onto unknown Others, or suggest invariances that these Others can not question. In I-Thou, neither truth nor mutual understanding is the issue. Inquiries into I and Thou have to be mutually caring and preserve the intimacy of this relationship. They must remain open enough to identify and overcome any emerging pathologies of communication, challenge conventions that turn out to be burdensome, and thus preserve the possibilities of continued conversations. They cannot determine who the Others *are,* nor *shape* them for whatever purposes, but instead create spaces for listening to radically different voices. I-Thou conversations are emancipatory. It would follow that I-Thou relations would not be directly accessible to communication scholarship. Love, intimacy, and friendship is a more natural home for them. This does not mean, however, that communication scholars could not encourage I-Thou relations to arise. My point is not to rule Thou out of existence for the sake of any methodology, ideology, or foundationalism they naturally oppose.

Political Consequences of I-Other Accounts

The final question to be addressed here concerns the political implications of these accounts: What kind of social arrangements do different

I-Other constructions inform, support, or create? What roles is I and its various Others encouraged to play when accounts of them reenter the fabric of ongoing social practices? What kind of citizenship are fostered by these accounts?

Unlike where people are considered in terms of having certain properties, serving particular functions, performing cognitive operations, responding to given messages, or being good experimental subjects, all of which are the accounts by detached observers who expect their subjects to conform to their knowledge claims, *persons speak* to each Other, live in stories, construct themselves in discourse, participate in different publics. Their roles are not fixed but negotiable and rearticulable by communicating among each Other. Knowledge of I and of You is highly situation specific and embodied in the participants that assent it. Even where accounts of people enter their communicative practices in the form of theories of personality, of attitude change, of psychotherapy, or of human communication, entering such theories into ongoing I-You communications encourages people to participate in their rearticulation, to reject them or to make them their own. After reentry, even spectator theories can no longer be confined to the spectators, the traditional scientists for example. Their reentry brings them into circulation and accepting, rejecting, or rearticulating them becomes political. To be political means acknowledging each Other's roles as speakers and contributors, being cognizant of each Other's conceptualizations, knowing whose facts and whose opinions matter, evaluating what is said as responses to what other members of one's community say they think or do, and recognizing public discourse as motivated by potentially different, albeit often complementary, constructions of reality. Accounts of I-You relations promote *a political form of society* and encourage *a citizenship that is participatory and responsible* to other citizens. It needs and creates diversity and thus preserves communication.

However, in this political form of society, the assumptions that commonalities permeate its fabric, that politics is about the fair distribution of agreed upon resources, that everyone ought to have the larger good in mind, that communication must (by its received definition) converge toward mutual understanding, etc., they all claim the necessity of sharing a common ground. They also reserve hidden levers for an I that seeks to remain in charge of certain political realities that can grow on such common grounds. This fundationalism, mostly unquestioned and hence transparent from within such a society, remains the hidden support for political institutions to develop and thrive. Institutions can become oppressive as soon as they act so as to keep their foundations unquestionable.

A society in which people can engage in *open* conversation is one in which foundations can be examined should they become burdensome, in which authorities can be questioned should they become illegitimate, in which constraints can be overcome should they become confining, in which theories of human nature can be criticized and disposed of should they be felt oppressive, and in which the history of any conversation can be reconstructed within that conversation—always intertwining the I with the Thou. Knowledge of this kind is *emancipatory,* transforms people into *human beings* and the society it supports will continuously expand the possibilities for self and Others to be-with each Other and move on.

I-Thou could be said to provide the nontheorizable end of a continuum of many possible ways of relating to each Other. If it makes sense for us, as communication scholars, to claim any competencies above the ordinary, then, I suggest, it is our ability to expand the plurality of I-Other conceptions and especially to preserve the epistemological conditions for I-Thou relations to arise—even when it cannot be informed by social scientific inquiries.[3]

Notes

1. Although I used this metaphor in a 1984 paper, I was delighted to find its source in a remark by the Austrian Therapist Victor Frankl (Foerster, 1991).

2. The admission that researchers cannot help but actively participate in the construction of social realities has already opened the door to several more or less nameable approaches. One is participatory research, which grants the members of a community being studied the expertise to inquire into their own affairs. A second is the "knowledge in action" approach to research (Argyris, 1982; Schon, 1983) in which the acquisition of knowledge and active intervention go hand in glove without fixing priorities to either. A third is constructionism in psychology (e.g., Gergen, 1985; Gergen and Davis, 1985), a broad and emerging approach with emphasis on the communal basis of knowledge and the interactive construction even of phenomena previously attributed to biological—and hence thought to be involuntary—processes (emotions, for example). A fourth is radical constructivism, a philosophical school that traces its history to Giambattista Vico and is currently argued by Paul Watzlawick (1984) and Ernst von Glasersfeld (1995), among others. Many of these approaches echo parallel developments in anthropology that focus on culture as a coinvention by anthropologists and a community encountering each Other (Wagner, 1975).

3. I do not want to leave this essay without expressing my frustration writing it. I felt constantly torn between my preference for talking and the constraints of writing. I found myself advocating relational considerations, trying to move our ways of talking about Others to talking with You (if not Thou), the You that must be present, while

referring even to the I in third-person terms. Blaming the medium of writing for distancing me from you, the reader, for this does not resolve the dilemma either. Nevertheless, if reading the above has created spaces for different kinds of Others to be imaginable, to be expressible in words, and to be realizable, then my frustration was worth it.

References

Argyris, C. (1982). *Reasoning, Learning, and Action.* San Francisco: Jossey-Bass.

Bakhtin, M. M. (1984). *Problems of Dostoevsky's Poetics* (C. Emerson, Ed. and Trans.). Manchester, England: Manchester University Press.

Buber, M. (1958). *I and Thou* (R. G. Smith, Trans.). New York: Macmillan.

———. (1970). *I and Thou* (W. Kaufmann, Trans.). New York: Charles Scribner's Sons.

Foerster, H. von (1991). Through the eyes of the other. In F. Steier (Ed.): *Research and Reflexivity.* London: Sage, 63–75.

———. (1995). Public lecture, confirmed in conversation.

Friere, P. (1972). *Pedagogy of the Oppressed.* London: Sheed and Ward.

Gadamer, H-G. (1975). *Truth and Method.* New York: Crossroad.

Gardiner, M. (1992). *The Dialogics of Critique: M. M. Bakhtin and the Theory of Ideology.* New York: Routledge.

Gergen, K. J. (1985). The social constructionist movement in modern psychology. *American Psychologist* 49:266–75.

———. (1994). *Realities and Relationships: Soundings in Social Construction.* Cambridge, Mass.: Harvard University Press.

———, and K. E. Davis (Eds.). (1985). *The Construction of the Person.* New York: Springer Verlag.

Giddens, A. (1984). *The Constitution of Society.* Berkeley, Calif.: University of California Press.

Glaserfeld, E. von. (1995). *Radical Constructivism: A Way of Knowing and Learning.* Washington, D.C.: Palmer Press.

Goffman, E. (1959). *The Presentation of Self in Everyday Life.* Garden City, N.Y.: Doubleday-Anchor.

Gramsci, A. (1987). *Selections from the Prison Notebooks* (Q. Hoare and G. N. Smith, Eds. & Trans.). New York: International Publishers.

Habermas, J. (1970). Towards a theory of communicative competence. *Inquiry* 13:360–75.

Horgan, J. (1993, May). The worst enemy of science. *Scientific American,* 36–37.

Horwitz, R. (1978). *Buber's Way to 'I and Thou.'* Heidelberg, Germany: Lambert Schneider.

Jones, E. E., and R. E. Nisbett. (1972). The actor and the observer: Divergent perceptions of the causes of behavior. In E. E. Jones, D. E. Kanouse, H. H. Kelly, R. E. Nisbett, S. Valins, and B. Weiner (Eds.): *Attribution: Perceiving the Causes of Behavior.* Morristown, N.J.: General Learning Press, 79–94.

Krippendorff, K. (1989). On the ethics of constructing communication. In B. Dervin, L. Grossberg, B. J. O'Keefe, and E. Wartella (Eds.): *Rethinking Communication: Paradigm Issues.* Newbury Park, Calif.: Sage, 66–96.

———. (1993). Conversation or intellectual imperialism in comparing communication (theories). *Communication Theory* 3(3):252–66.

———. (1994). A recursive theory of communication. In D. Crowley and D. Mitchell (Eds.): *Communication Theory Today.* Cambridge, England: Polity Press, 78–104.

———. (1995). Undoing power. *Critical Issues in Mass Communication* 12(2):101–132.

———. (1996). A second-order cybernetics of otherness. In R. Glanville (Ed.): Heinz von Foerster, a Festschrift. *Systems Research* 13(3):311–328.

Laing, R. D. (1967). *The Politics of Experience.* New York: Pantheon.

Mayo, E. (1945). *The Social Problems of an Industrial Civilization.* Boston: Division of Research, Graduate School of Business Administration, Harvard University.

Merton, R. K. (1963). The self-fulfilling prophesy. In R. K. Merton: *Social Theory and Social Structure* (4th cd.). New York: Free Press, 421–36.

Miell, D. K., and D. E. Miell. (1986). Recursion in interpersonal cognition. In C. Antaki and A. Lewis (Eds.): *Mental Mirrors: Metacognition in Social Knowledge and Cognition.* London: Sage, 27–40.

Roberts, G. L., and J. B. Bavelas. (1996). The communicative dictionary: A collaborative theory of meaning. In J. Stewart (Ed.): *Beyond the Symbol Model: Reflections on the Representational Nature of Language.* Albany: State University of New York Press, 135–165.

Roberts, M. K. (1985). I and thou: A study of personal relationships. In K. E. Davis and T. O. Mitchell (Eds.): *Advances in Descriptive Psychology* 4:231–58.

Rorty, R. (1989). *Contingency, Irony, and Solidarity.* New York: Cambridge University Press.

Rosenthal, R., and L. Jacobson. (1968). *Pygmalion in the Classroom: Teacher Expectation and Pupils' Intellectual Development.* New York: Holt, Rinehart, and Winston.

Sampson, E. E. (1993). *Celebrating the Other: A Dialogical Account of Human Nature.* Boulder, Colo.: Westview Press.

Schon, D. A. (1983). *The Reflective Practitioner: How Professionals Think in Action.* New York: Basic Books.

Shotter, J. (1984). *Social Accountability and Selfhood.* Oxford, England: Blackwell.

————. (1993). *Conversational Realities: Constructing Life Through Language.* Thousand Oaks, Calif.: Sage.

Solomon, R. C. (1990). *Love, Emotion, Myth, and Metaphor.* Buffalo, N.Y.: Prometheus Books.

Wagner, R. (1975). *The Invention of Culture.* Englewood Cliffs, N.J.: Prentice Hall.

Watzlawick, P. (1984). Self-fulfilling prophesies. In P. Watzlawick: *The Invented Reality.* New York: Norton, 95–116.

Chapter Three

Unheard Voices from Unknown Places: Saving the Subject for Science

Lenore Langsdorf

Although science has no doubt waged an assault upon the meanings of Other (as the editors suggest), my topic here is not that explicit assault—which might at least leave a battered victim who could be returned to health. Rather, I argue that modern (western) science placed "the subject" on a starvation diet that resulted in death by attrition for "the Other." This was as much an inevitable as a deliberate policy for it was inspired by requirements of "the scientific method" and enabled by an understanding of communication as the referential use of language, as well as by modernity's (self-)conception of the subject as autonomous analyst.[1]

In responding to the question of whether it is possible to know Other in scientific terms without at the same time devaluing the (nonscientific) discourses of Other, this chapter begins by proposing some likely conditions in the Enlightenment intellectual context for instigating that starvation diet. I go on to consider the correlative view of that Self's communicative activity as linguistic reproduction of Other, understood as Self's object of knowledge. To know Other in scientific terms, then, is to characterize Other as object (not subject) of knowledge, or as a reproduction of Self that depends upon introspection and empathy. Within this model, there is no space for acknowledging particularity or conceptualizing difference. Thus, Other is conceptualized, and interacted with, as a variant (and at times, deviant) reflection of Self, which is to say in terms of how Other is the same as Self. Although there may be some justification for conceiving knowing in this way in some epistemic domains, modernity established this objectifying focus on what is the same as equivalent to knowing as such. Correlatively, modernity incorporates a referential model of communication as language use that reproduces the actual objectified Other as a linguistic object. This linguistification identifies Other by means of a universal word that applies uniformly to all instantiations—rather than identifying Other in terms of particularity and difference. Language thereby intensifies introspection's repetition of sameness by subsuming actual differences with the sameness of the word.

In the last section of the chapter, I propose that one way of undoing these established practices, and thus saving the subject for science, is by replacing that referential model of language use with a model of communicative activity as constitutive. Communication as constitutive requires different voices of Other just as much as referential language use requires suppression of that difference within the unification of the word. One way to mark that alternative understanding is to replace modernity's Other as object of knowledge with a recognition of Other as subject of inquiry.

Science and Its Discourse

In the midst of our contemporary anti-Cartesian intellectual climate, we can easily forget the demands of the very different intellectual environment that instigated and strengthened the Cartesian project. In 1600, when Descartes was four years old, Giordano Bruno—Italian Renaissance philosopher, ex-Dominican, peripatetic lecturer on memory and the occult, and firm believer in Copernicus's anti-intuitive and anti-Scriptural theory that the earth moves about a static sun—was burned at the stake. We are uncertain of which of Bruno's unpopular views functioned as the heresies for which the Inquisition condemned him, but we do know that heliocentrism was one of those views. Further, we know (by virtue of his correspondence) that when Descartes learned (in 1633) of the Church's condemnation of Galileo, he withheld publication of work that relied upon Copernicus's views.

Clearly, the intellectual environment of this time was one in which scholars developed systematic treatises, but did so with care to avoid offending the reigning system of thought through implying or arguing for views that could lead to condemnation (which very much limited one's audience) and even death. Several aspects of Cartesianism reflect that caution. Bruno's adoption of heliocentrism was not also an affirmation of Copernicus's mathematical arguments; Descartes, on the other hand, emphasized method in general and mathematical method in particular in the *Discourse on Method* (1637) as well as the *Meditations* (1641). Ernst Cassirer (1951, 41) emphasizes that Bruno's advocacy of an immanent divinity suggests a "radical transformation of the concept of nature . . . resolved into the infinity of the divine nature" and "implies the individuality, the independence and particularity of objects."

The seventeenth-century intellectual climate in which science began, then, inherited a concept of God as the immanent creator who established and maintained an orderly universe that was both unified (by His power) and diversified (by His choice to create a multiplicity of individual, independent, and particular objects). Descartes wrote in letters (as early as 1619) of his dream of a unified science of nature befitting this pervasive presence of divinity. But his method extolled both analysis and autonomy: his starting point was "clear and distinct ideas" analyzed out of the whole (of nature) and marked by independent particularity. Their unity was merely the sum of those parts: as nature, it required no independent inquiry directed at the whole; as God, the Church's teaching with regard to multiplicity and unity was accepted.

Reliance upon analysis and autonomy also characterizes Francis Bacon's system. In the *Novum Organum* (1620) and elsewhere, his differences from Descartes may be most evident since Bacon advocated a starting point in observation of sensory particulars (rather than "clear and distinct ideas") and an inductive, rather than deductive, method. Furthermore, he stressed the need for many researchers to join in empirical data collection and experimentation, while Descartes valorized an individual (even, isolated) search for certainty through reflective clarification of the data of consciousness (ideas). Yet Bacon agreed with Descartes in advocating a starting point in particulars, stressing method, understanding knowledge as systematic description and prediction that enables mastery over nature, and launching science within a sphere of human inquiry, rather than Divine revelation. Although both affirmed orthodox belief in matters theological, they extolled the importance of what may be known through analysis, by autonomous subjects, of mundane objects. As F. E. Sutcliffe remarks in his introduction to the *Discourse and Meditations:* "The system of Descartes is a reply . . . to the naturalism of . . . Bruno . . . for whom nature was animated by a soul" (Descartes, 1968/1637, 21).

Two important precepts emerged from Descartes's rationalism and Bacon's empiricism to characterize Renaissance and modern thought and implant themselves within our conception of science—and so also to leave a certain sediment of presuppositions about reason and communication. First, without denying the unity and orderliness of the divinely created cosmos, the science of nature from its beginnings in the seventeenth century did not depend upon that order or unity, or rely upon the authority of its representative (the Church). Rather, the task of what was to become natural science was to create a unified science through analytic methods practiced by autonomous researchers, who constructed diverse systems with which to organize their data. Human reason thus replaced traditional authority as the basis for inquiry and constructed systems that organized entities by virtue of what was posited as identical in them. Unity, order, and authority became functions of a reason posited as identical in all human beings.

In effect, that reason was both literally and figuratively monological. It bypassed rather than responded to tradition, and it sought agreement with its propositions on the basis of their success in changing (predicting and then controlling) the environment, rather than on the basis of (so to speak) listening to the voice of nature or discerning the narrative of Being. Immanuel Kant's 1784 response to the question, "What Is Enlightenment?" begins with an affirmation of monological reason: "Enlightenment is man's release from his . . . inability to make use of his understanding without direction from another" (1988, 462). He goes on to say that thinking for oneself is "irksome work . . . held to be very dangerous by the far greater portion of mankind (and by the entire fair sex)." The enlightened individual, then—the man of science—is he who forswears listening to the voice of the other, whether that other be another person, nature, or nature's God.[2] Rather than seeking to discern how things are from the standpoint of diverse things themselves (through interaction) or of persons who displayed cultural, biological, or affective differences (through communicative interaction) or God (through direct or mediated revelation), the enlightened individual posited himself as self-directed man.

Furthermore, this direction must come from the mind, rather than from the body; it must be cognitive, rather than affective or volitional. For Descartes's reflection upon existence affirmed possession of his mind—but not his body—with certainty, and reaffirmed the ease with which his senses could be deceived. And Kant recognized that since man's body must be directed by physical laws (such as gravity), only his mind could be free (self-directed). Although Bacon advocated sensory evidence as the basis for inductive learning, he stressed that science, as the systematic accumulation of facts, had to purify that data through planned observation (experiment), rather than random collection that would be directed by the "idols" of mundane thinking.

Without wishing to efface the differences among these architects of what we now call science, I do want to highlight the extent to which these originators of scientific discourse perpetrated a concept of the knowing subject as an autonomous mind, analyzing a mute nature, and organizing the particulars it finds—through sensory observation (Bacon), mental reflection (Descartes) or both (Kant)—by means of theories that propose laws which universally "cover" particularity. The result is a subsuming of actual multiplicity within theoretical unity. The autonomous analyst then presents those findings to others in propositional form, with the goal of predicting and controlling all that falls within the finding's theoretical purview. Insofar as those others fulfill the requirements for scientific discourse, they must also be autonomous minds who consider propositions as (so to speak) autonomous; as reflecting the way things simply are, rather than as expressing the complex involvement of the others who have, after all, placed those propositions upon the page. (As Eric Havelock (1974) and Walter Ong (1958) argue, the origins of modern science and the invention of the printing press were not simply coincidental. Both inventions replace diversity and particularity with uniformity.)

The model of scientific discourse that accompanies the Renaissance model of science thus removes particularity of circumstance— and perhaps of character—from both discussants and discussed. Both the human subjects who write and read and the objects on which their discourse focuses are present as tokens of their types. What is affirmed about any particular piece of gold (for example), within a theoretical interest in substances of that kind, is to be affirmable of any possible piece of gold by any possible metallurgist. Things are investigated as the same as other things, with an interest in discovering how they fall under a set of laws for that sort of thing rather than as being different or even unique and so of interest for their otherness.

Correlatively, just as knowledge in medieval times resided in a priestly class that was removed (in principle) from the particularities of mundane sensory life, knowledge in modernity came to reside in a similarly removed scholarly class. The individuality of the priest   as bodily and biographicaly individual man—was subsumed under his office, and his status as purportedly uniform exemplar of the system to which he belonged was symbolized by uniform dress. The individuality of the scientist—still grammatically, if no longer biologically, as man— was subsumed, and symbolized, similarly. Furthermore, the white coat of the prototypical scientist carries with it associations of clarity, light, and truth that replaces the obscurity, darkness, and ignorance carried by the black garb of the medieval priest.

Modernity completes this purification of both subjects and objects with a purification of communication. The dialogical and narrative style used by philosophers from Plato to Bruno incorporated what Bacon identifies as "idols" of the tribe, den, marketplace, and theater and thus retained ways of thinking, speaking, and (most troublesomely) feeling that mark differences among human beings. Descartes retains a narrative and somewhat dialogical style: although he wrote in isolation, he maintained an extensive correspondence with members of his intended audience, and in the second edition of *The Meditations,* he explicitly responds to their objections.

Locke (1690) eschews narrative after his "Epistle to the Reader" in *An Essay Concerning Human Understanding,* but his writing betrays habits of dialogical style in that it often repeats with variation, in the way that we do when anticipating or responding to queries and objections. The editor of the most generally used modern edition of that work, A. Seth Pringle-Pattison, notes that the work, "by the omission of unnecessary repetitions . . . has been reduced to almost exactly half its original length," and that he has supplied "an Introduction and Notes to keep before the modern reader the main trend of Locke's conclusions" (1924, iv).

Similarly, Norman Kemp Smith, in his "Translator's Preface" to Kant's *Critique of Pure Reason* (1781) notes that the difficulties of reading the work "are not due merely to the abstruseness of the doctrines . . . or to . . . frequent alternation between conflicting points of view," but "simply to his manner of writing. He crowds so much into each sentence that he is constrained to make undue use of parentheses, and . . . to rely upon particles, pronouns, and genders to indicate the connections between the parts of the sentence" (1929, vii). Kemp Smith concludes that "there remains for the translator the task, from which there is no escape, of restating the content of each of the more complex sentences in a number of separate sentences."

The lesson I draw from these translators' and editors' remarks—which are typical of remarks made by modern scholars about these writers—is that, from its beginnings in the Enlightenment, the practice of scientific discourse lagged behind its theory. That is, scientific discourse theoretically removes particularity from both discussants and discussed (subject/researcher and object/researched). Yet in their actual composition, these texts retained practices characteristic of peer-group communication (and even of face-to-face conversation) by particular persons about particular things. In other words, the content of these works advocates an orderly progression of propositional claims that could be comprehended and evaluated by any reader with appropriate cognitive preparation (i.e., education in the emergent discipline), and regardless of the multiplicity of individual characteristics that make people different from (other than) one another. This audience of implied readers is an extended version of science's "objective observer": they could mentally replicate any empirical or conceptual procedure by reading monologues that linguistically re-present a chain of ideas or procedures.

Yet the form of these works reveals dependence upon particular discourse partners and reliance upon a particular tradition, rather than accessibility for a (theorized) autonomous universal audience. The very passage of time necessitates that editors and translators within late modernity—i.e., writing in the early years of this century and having been educated under late nineteenth-century influences—notice the folly of presuming a particular audience as being present for a particular text. They simplify and modernize their authors' dialogically influenced writing style through judicious editing, and they support their own presumptions of universal access through footnotes that supply some elements of the context presumed by those authors. Yet they retain belief in nonindividualized scientists and scientific objects, since they do not question scientific method's assumption that the proper subjects and objects of scientific discourse are particulars from which individuality—otherness—has been effaced. It is unlikely that Sutcliffe, Pringle-Pattison, and Kemp Smith would have poured their efforts into presenting texts which they found to be relevant to a particular audience. It is more likely that what they didn't question, correct, or supplement were beliefs that they shared about the appropriateness of investigating objects in their generality, rather than particularity.

An unnoticed implication of these beliefs is the efficacy of one correct way of reasoning that is "scientific," regardless of the differences that are quite evident in individual scholars' lives. For the philosophers who provided the model for scientific discourse, this was at times an explicit theme: Descartes reflected on "the method of properly conducting one's reason," Locke enquired into the nature of "human understanding," and Kant developed concepts of transcendental subjectivity's forms and categories within his critique of pure reason. They succeeded in constructing a persona for the writer and reader of scientific discourse that was purified of individuality, that used language identically, and that displayed—and more importantly, employed—no otherness from this norm in its discourse.

These beliefs and implications were thoroughly sedimented as intrinsic to the nature of science and scientific discourse by the time "social science" began to claim a parallel status for itself in the nineteenth century. "Auguste Comte," writes Lewis Coser, "was a son of the Enlightenment carrying on the tradition of the philosophers of progress," yet he was also "a resolute antagonist of the individualistic approach to human society that had predominated throughout the eighteenth century . . . a rage and quest for order hovers over his work" (1971, 20–21). Not surprisingly, the physical sciences provided the model for that order: "Comte saw himself as the continuator of the dissimilar scientific traditions of Bacon and Descartes," Coser goes on to say, and was influenced by "the major natural scientists from Newton's day until his own" (1971, 21). Comte's founding of the Société Positiviste a few days after the 1848 February Revolution suggests that his efforts to establish a science of society parallel to the science of nature that began in the seventeenth century was one manifestation of that "rage and quest for order."

Political events in the intervening century had brought with them the complete demise of the Church's unifying influence and authority over scientific discourse. Intellectual events, perhaps best summed up by the publication in 1747 of Julien Offroy de La Mettrie's *L'Homme machine* (translated as *Man a Machine* in 1749), reinforced the concept of human beings as autonomous rather than dependent on tradition (natural or divine), as uniform (because determined by the same physical uniformity as governs other material entities), and as interchangeable (insofar as their sameness, rather than their peculiarity as distinct Others, was judged to be essential or all that was relevant to the scientific enterprise). La Mettrie was a physician, and Comte, a chemical engineer. Both believed that improvement of the human condition was to come through research that studied humans singly and in groups, on the model of uniform systems that could be analyzed into atomistic elements susceptible to recombination for specified ends. Given the demise of a general belief in Divine order in the public sphere and multiple breakdowns of political order, their belief that order had to be imposed by the scientific mind is understandable.

Emile Durkheim was, as Coser notes, "the first French academic sociologist" (1971, 143). That vocation may have been influential in his insistence (contrary to La Mettrie and Comte) that social phenomena cannot be reduced to biological (or psychological) phenomena. But that "calling," as Coser (1971) goes on to say, "had not yet found recognition in the university," and so Durkheim and his colleagues were perennially involved in "attempts to defend the claim to legitimacy of the new science of sociology" (143). There was, then, a functional need to retain the Enlightenment conception of science, and thus sociology, as investigating any and all objects within parameters of autonomy, analysis, uniformity, and unity on the systemic level. "Social facts," the proper object of social-scientific inquiry, were purified of the variability of particular actions by specific persons. Durkheim advocated a method of functional analysis in terms of an extant system and its (historical) causes, rather than possible goals or individual needs, as the means for complete explanation. Apparent discontinuity and novelty were analytically resolvable as serving functions within the system.

Durkheim's research stressed the advantages of solidarity over individuality (which he associated with deviance and anomie), and the advantages of "mechanical" (uniform and personality-less) solidarity over "organic" solidarity. The need for the latter, he proposed, was occasioned by the division of labor and consequent differentiation and dependence among human beings within a system. He held that since those economic conditions were endemic to modern society, common symbolic representations were especially important. In other words, even if human economic activity necessitated a degree of individuality, language ought to reinforce—even institute—uniform concepts of objects and subjects.

I do not wish to efface the differences among these architects of what we now call social science or to claim that all present research into social phenomena fits within the doctrines of these few founding fathers. (My own reflection on dominant themes in contemporary philosophy of science confirms the prevalence of diverse efforts to question and even overturn those doctrines.) Also, I know that I have narrated a simplified tale of the history of western science and its character as understood within mundane culture. But insofar as this is a recognizable portrayal, it may serve to highlight the extent to which these originators of social scientific discourse perpetrated a concept of the knowing subject as a uniformly functioning autonomous mind, analyzing a mute (institutionalized) nature, and organizing the social particulars it finds by means of theories that propose laws which "cover" particularity by subsuming actual multiplicity and diversity within theoretical unity and uniformity.

Science as modernity knows it, then, happens within systems that are constructed by methodically abstracting from the otherness of any particular knowing subject, any particular object to be known, and any particular situation in which inquiry occurs. In order to construct those systems, the multiplicity of differences and presence of otherness is ignored, in the interest of constructing a uniformly autonomous subject. This nonperson analyzes objects for qualities assumed to differ only quantitatively or incidentally from those held by other entities in their category or bearing the same name. Thus, scientific objects are nonobjects, in the sense of being abstractions from actual, spatiotemporal things that display diversity and so are unsuitable for systematic research. Science performs research by using universally applicable methods to scrutinize identical items in the quest for "findings" that can be replicated (in thought, if not deed) by any possible (trained) investigator.

Even when positivism's strict divorce of subject/researcher and object/researched is rejected—as happens when the lessons of contemporary microphysics with regard to observation are generalized, and we recognize that all observation is participation—the presumption of a uniformly autonomous subject paired with a specimen that is essentially identical to others in its category is retained. "The scientist"—a de-ethnicized, ahistorical, ungendered, and nonpolitical automaton—is an enabling fiction. But who is thereby enabled?

An/Other Discourse

As a rather roundabout way of responding to that question, I want to turn first to how communication functions within the Enlightenment conception of science sketched above. The engagement of an autonomous subject/researcher and uniform object/researched displays certain formal characteristics that can also be abstracted from mundane communication. Although we speak of "technical language" and "scientific talk," the familiar structures and procedures of everyday communication still are discernible in the setting of that alternative language and delimited talk. We use grammatical subjects and objects and a variety of modifiers in order to develop particular descriptions and assertions. Verbs signify diverse ways in which subjects connect with objects. Turn-taking in "scientific talk" is quite similar to that structure in mundane conversation—although in many ways it most resembles the sort of conversation that occurs in classrooms, doctors' offices, and census-taking interviews. In these settings, we typically find one discourse partner who sets an agenda and another who responds to that agenda within the bounds of typical expectations. Occasionally, that structure slips into greater reciprocity of topic-setting and even respondent refusal, but such divergence is marked in fairly typical ways (often with humor) and usually does not go on for many turns-at-talk.

If I were to ask an observer what's going on as these communicative structures are used, either in scientific talk or in more everyday conversation that is marked by a greater balance in agenda-setting, I'd likely be told that the participants are "talking about something," or are "sharing their ideas about something." In more scholarly terminology, they are using linguistic objects—words—to refer to, or represent, things, events, ideas, or other such nonlinguistic objects. In other scholarly words, language use accomplishes reference, and we usually think that it does that job well when the words accurately re-present the objects to which they refer.

This commonsensical report on what happens when we use language relies upon assumptions which appear odd when we reflect upon them in the light of our awareness that all observation is participation. For it assumes that certain devices—already spoken words, codified into a system called language and available for reuse by anyone cognizant of how that system has been used by appropriately schooled users—are able to accomplish what observation cannot: they can bring things into discourse, without the participatory variety (and thus, uncertainty) that is intrinsic to mundane experience. The oddness of our assumptions about language use, then, is due to the fact that no other observer can use my ears, eyes, hands, nose, or mouth to accomplish sensory communication, yet all other observers can use "my" words— the same words—to refer to objects in linguistic communication. In other words, we expect verbal language to provide a medium that prevails over sensory particularity, to outweigh differences so that identical reference can be accomplished. Under optimal conditions, at least, the uniformity of scientific objects and autonomous subjects discussed earlier is to be matched by a uniform medium.

This three-part structure (subjects, objects, medium) is a modification of another tripartite structure bequeathed to us by Plato and summarized in his remarks on art in the tenth book of *The Republic*. The discussion there (595–599) begins by reminding us that "imitative" poetry is "likely to damage the minds of the audience" unless its nature is understood. That "nature" is explained through the theory of Forms:

"We are accustomed," Plato writes, "to assuming one Form in each case for the many particulars to which we give the same name." We have here three measures: one (Form), many (particulars), and same (name). And we have three ontological orders: the name (a linguistic object) provides a medium for explicit reference to particular things (spatiotemporal objects) as well as for implicit reference to the Form (a conceptual object). In Plato's theory of language use and rationality, then, the linguistic object serves, by means of its sameness despite differences in the things that it names, to re-mind us of the unity of the Form.

The philosopher's attention to the single and unchanging Form enables his words to in-form the craftsman's making of multiple and diverse things that copy that Form. Poets and painters then create their images by reference to the craftsmen's work, which has been created by reference to the Forms. "The Form itself," however—for instance, in Plato's discussion, the Form of the bed—"is not the work of any craftsman" (596b). Rather, "god . . . made only that one bed which is the real bed" (597c). Even with due care to avoid importing later (Judeo-Christian) conceptions of "god" into our reading, it is clear that the subject slot (so to speak) in this scheme is occupied by an other-than-human author, and the ultimate referential slot is filled by an other-than-particular (spatiotemporal) object.

When Plato's tripartite ontology (Forms, things, words) is set within the whole of his metaphysics, we have an intrinsically unified order of Forms—which is independent of human agency—and two very different systematically (i.e., nonintrinsically) unified orders of things (verbal or visual) that do come to be as the effect of human agency. Things such as beds are dependent upon human fabrication in "actions" and are usable in the course of further activity (599b–c). Verbal or visual "imitations" are also dependent upon human fabrication of a different and epistemically deficient sort and have no use value. For in the course of considering whether the poet (painter, etc.) "must have knowledge of his subject," Plato concludes that verbal and visual objects are "easy to compose without knowledge" since they "are but images" (598e–599). Given the choice, Plato is certain that a man "would much rather devote himself to actions than to the imitations of them, and that he would try to leave behind many fine actions as memorials of himself and be eager to be the subject of a eulogy rather than its author" (599b).

Plato assigns the highest value to the philosopher's endeavor to know the Forms. This endeavor would be comparable to science in modern categories. The craftsman's activity of making things for use would be comparable to contemporary technology. Plato allots the lowest status to creativity in verbal and visual media, insofar as they are "imitative," i.e., simply represent what the craftsman has done. They are not useful (one cannot sleep in a visual or verbal portrayal of a bed), and since he understands them as produced by simply holding up a mirror to the world of things, they can be produced by anyone, without knowledge or even any advanced skill. Thus, they also have no exchange value—although modern technology and capitalism have discovered remedies for that lack.

This axiological hierarchy still remains within our contemporary, post-Enlightenment classification: science outranks technology in prestige, if not in financial remuneration. And both science and technology outrank the arts and humanities in pay as well as prestige. But Plato's ontological and epistemological hierarchy was overturned by Locke's theory of human understanding, and the result was an understanding of words (the third element in the Platonic structure) appropriate to the Enlightenment conception of science (as sketched above). In effect, the Forms created by Plato's god were transformed into ideas in the minds of men. Thus the one and the same Ideas that were (for Plato) the basis for understanding and even agreement among different thinkers became the many and diverse ideas that could offer no intrinsic basis for Self's understanding of Other as different from Self.

Loss of both sameness (of thinking) and differences (of thinkers) occurred when Locke argued—quite persuasively—that those ideas are not present innately as the inheritance from a transcendent domain, awaiting recollection under the tutelage of the philosopher. Instead ideas come to be written on the "blank slate" that is the human mind only through experience, and they are then "the object of the understanding when a man thinks" (1924, 15). Rather than referring to Forms in order to make things, the Enlightenment craftsman/technologist looks to things to in-form his mind. Indeed, he cannot help but do so, for Locke holds that the "understanding is passive . . . forced to receive the impressions" (52) which remain with it as ideas. Ideas, thus, "are modifications of matter in the bodies that cause perceptions" (66). But their status as "the object of understanding" raises questions about how we could refer to things. "It is evident," Locke writes, that "the mind knows not things immediately, but only by the intervention of the ideas it has of them. Our knowledge, therefore, is real only so far as there is a conformity between our ideas and the reality of things" (288).

Locke's (1924) subsequent struggle with the question of what criteria could confirm the conformity of ideas and things resolved into a doctrine of truth as "the joining or separating of signs" in verbal propositions (291). In our thinking we "make use of words instead of ideas . . . we reflect on the names themselves, because they are more clear, certain, and distinct, and readier occur to our thoughts than the pure ideas" (292). There is a basic conceptual difficulty here that remains at the core of empiricism in both the physical and social sciences, as well as in our theorizing about verification or falsification, truth by correspondence or truth by coherence, and semiotic or semantic meaning. Briefly stated, it is this: we set out to know the things in our environment, by reasoning about their sensory evidence. Yet this reasoning must use words that represent our ideas, rather than working directly with the things (or Forms). For our reasoning—whether in interpersonal or intrapersonal communication—cannot literally make present the things that are the topics of our talk.

Thus, we have a deep chasm between inquiring subjects and the objects of their knowledge, between Self's mental and linguistic systems and Other understood as one of the things to which those systems refer. There is no path for verifying correspondence between those words and ideas and the things we would know, and even coherence among our propositional claims seems limited to particular language communities that display a high degree of conformity with regard to how members use words to express their ideas. Self seems to be imprisoned within its ideas and can only know Other as one of those ideas— which is to say, Self can only know Other insofar as the different voice of Other is heard as the voice of Self.

Looked at from the other direction (so to speak), and still working within the individualistic basis that permeates Locke's theory, introspection shows that Self associates particular ideas with particular sensations. But Self doesn't know whether that process is replicated in Other, as Other uses the same words to refer to particular things, about which (Self presumes) Other has ideas. And so Self centers attention on the same words that Self, and Other, use in particular situations. That focus remains disjunct from either Platonic or commonsensical referential communicative expectations since Self and Other are not referring to Forms, or to things, when using words. Rather, the Lockean heritage leads us to believe in the likelihood that language users who use the same words are expressing the same ideas. If the voice of Other were to express different ideas, Self could not recognize that difference unless and until Self had to contend with different behavior in the realm of things, that is, until Self is subjected to action different from that expected, on the basis of Self's introspection of Self and empathetic understanding of Other. Unless and until such difference forces itself into a situation, a uniformity of word use is assumed and taken as evidence for an essential uniformity of Self and Other, despite sensory and historical evidence of difference.

Communication then is understood to depend upon a theorized sameness and interchangability quite parallel to the conception of the subject/researcher and object/researched that we found as characteristics of Enlightenment concepts of science. Our unreflective acceptance of Locke's analysis of human understanding gives us two reasons for presuming that sameness and interchangability. First, we are aware of diversity in human bodies, and thus, of differences in the sensory basis of ideas. Secondly, our disinclination to believe that humans are equipped

with innate ideas means that we are unlikely to rely on Platonic Forms
as the ground for understanding one another in communication. Thus
we can only account for understanding within communication by relying upon introspection, coupled with observing Other with empathy
(i.e., the belief that Other responds as Self would, were Self in Other's
place). In other words, we conceptualize communication as Self's use
of language to express Self's ideas, about things, to Other. There is no
guarantee that Other's ideas correspond with Self's, since the ideas of
both are residues of impressions upon their different bodies. Thus,
communication must rely upon words corresponding with things, by
representing things in accord with the rules of a linguistic system. Yet
this reliance upon words and things to account for communication reinforces the structures of identity we found in the Enlightenment model
of science and so inclines us to hear the voice of Other as if it were the
voice of Self.

    As post-Enlightenment thinkers, however, we have as different an
understanding of the relations among philosophers, craftspersons, and
artists as we do of thinking as a relation among Forms (now, ideas
understood as psychological entities), things, and words. Those differences derive from a double reduction of the Platonic three-stage hierarchy to two. Labor is divided into thinking and making, carried out
(respectively) in theory and in practice. Thinking is a matter of corre-
lating words (which express ideas) and things (to which words refer).
Modern philosophers no longer take their function to be instigating
recollection of the Forms but redirect their labor into questions of whether
thinking can correctly correlate words and things and, if so, how. I want
now to look once more at the three-stage Platonic hierarchy, in order to
use its reduction to a dichotomy as a clue for an alternate and correlative conception of communication as constitutive as well as referential.
That alternative, in turn, reveals an unexpectedly commodious place for
the voice of Other.

    For Plato, the craftsman's actions are dependent upon some knowl-
edge of the atemporal Forms, which is to say that what the craftsman
makes depends upon a "higher" reality—a model, although of a different ontological order, that is always already present and is transmitted
by the philosopher. That dependence may well be the origin of a tradition that understands the craftsman's concrete making as dependent
upon the philosopher's abstract thinking, or in modernity, technology as
dependent upon science. The crafter of images (whether they be visual
or linguistic), takes as model the craftsman's product, things, rather
than the god's product, Forms. Thus, Plato castigates verbal creativity
as third-rate imitation. Correlatively, words in Platonic metaphysics are
dependent upon things, which are themselves dependent upon Forms.
Post-Enlightenment philosophy of language reduces that three-stage
universe to two worlds, which are variously conceptualized as words

and things, or abstract linguistic systems and concrete communicative activity. Actual communication between sensorially different humans, then, depends on their use of words in accord with the theoretical rules of a linguistic system.

Now the first of these hierarchies—technology as dependent upon science—is no longer unquestioned. (Husserl's project of grounding theory in lived experience, especially as continued by Heidegger, overturned that hierarchy.) One variant of the second hierarchy—ideas (and thus words as the expression of ideas) as dependent upon things—was rejected by nineteenth-century idealism and is deconstructed by twentieth-century textualism. (Rorty [1982] discusses the similarities between those two philosophical positions, and Langsdorf [1992] discusses their influence in contemporary philosophy of science.) Both idealism and textualism, however, create major difficulties for the project of hearing the voice of Other for they reduce their respective dichotomies to a monism of ideas or language, respectively. Idealism in its objective form (Berkeley or Hegel) could recognize only a nonhuman Other. In its subjective form, it is a theoretical possibility, solipsism, which recognizes only Self. Thus, my proposal that we question the second variant of that second hierarchy—communicative activity as dependent upon language—does not depend upon either of those precedents. Rather, I use a clue in current thinking about the science and technology hierarchy.

Don Ihde (1991, 9) speaks of the impetus in Heidegger's philosophy for "a radical inversion of the science-technology relation" that "asserts the reversal of Platonism." "For Heidegger," as Ihde goes on to say, "science as a way of seeing is located with and dependent upon the priority of technology as a material, existential, and cultural way of seeing" (56). The "material" aspect of technology retains the Platonic sense of material production, but the "existential and cultural" dimensions suggest that atemporal models (Forms) or past, already available models (already crafted things) are not the primary instigation for the craftsman's/technologist's production. Rather, technical creativity may be much like the rather mysterious creativity of poets and painters. The skilled creator, whether working in wood or words, would be one who discerns what could be—what possibilities might be actualized—in the future, from a basis in the existential present and cultural past. This is the sort of imaginative activity we associate with the artist. Elsewhere (Langsdorf, 1995) I have argued that this activity is best understood as poiesis (rhetorically inventive doing that articulates possibilities of how things could be) rather than as praxis (materially productive doing that actualizes an object).

Reconceptualizing science (theory) as depending upon technology, and technology (praxis) as relying upon artistic creativity (poiesis) that discerns possibilities for things being otherwise than they are in everyday mundane actuality, leads us beyond Heidegger's analysis of *Dasein* (human being in the world) to Husserl's description of the lifeworld (the world of everyday communicative activity). But before we explore this place where the voice of Other cannot but be found, I want to note that we now can respond to the question posed at the end of the first section of this chapter: Who is enabled by understanding "the scientist" as a subject reduced to sameness with all others, who investigates objects correlatively purified of any particularity? This could only be an individual who would benefit from recognizing no difference; no otherness from Self's interests and goals. The scientific, technological, and mundane social and political agenda of this Self would be a reproductive one, calling for more of the same. Representation of what is, and thus reproduction of the intellectual and powerful forces that instituted "what is," would only be threatened by the emergence of others from other places that do not represent "what is," but are marked by their lack of typicality—by being anomalous—in brief, by being different.

These other voices are superfluous and even detrimental to a referential practice of language, since they present an otherness that resists assuming that the same words refer to and represent the world in identical ways. These other voices are uninterested in and even unable to represent a sameness in which they, the different, have not participated. These voices speak in a different register; they break into and rupture the mirror of language. That is a very different thing from deconstructing the mirror, for it is a disruptive activity that enables and even requires re-constituting the world by participating in it, rather than simply looking at the linguistic representation of the pieces and putting those fragments of linguistic objects back together again—perhaps, more playfully than in their original formation. Disruption is inevitably a discomfort, and so those who disrupt, and those who theorize that disruptive doing, must work hard—even exercise considerable rhetorical skill—if the value of disruption is to be recognized. The key element in my attempt to valorize disruption follows Kuhn's (1970, 77) acknowledgement that a theory will hang in our intellectual closets, despite the tatters that result from attempting to fit it to phenomena that it cannot cover, until a better garment is offered. Referential language is the tattered garment; constitutive communication is the preferred replacement.

The Voice of Other

Constituting the world in communicative activity does not mean creating the substance of things. It does mean transforming the "that-ness" of the world into particular and changing configurations of "what-ness." The process of accomplishing this transformation is perhaps best described by John Dewey, although the setting for that accomplishment seems to me best described by Edmund Husserl. First, the process:

> Of all things, communication is the most wonderful. That things should be able to pass from the plane of pushing and pulling to that of revealing themselves . . . and that the fruit of communication should be participation, sharing, is a wonder by the side of which transubstantiation pales. When communication occurs, all natural events . . . are re-adapted to meet the needs of . . . public discourse or that preliminary discourse termed thinking. Events turn into objects, things with a meaning . . . their meanings may be infinitely combined and rearranged in imagination, and the outcome of this inner experimentation—which is thought—may issue forth in interaction with crude or raw events. (Dewey, 1981, 18)

The crudeness of events is undeniable from any particular reflective standpoint in the process of what seems to be a persistent human propensity to use imagination in recombining and refining what earlier technologists created. However, characterizing any event as "raw" is problematic if the setting is the actual, historical one that Husserl (1970, 76) calls the lifeworld: "the world of sense-experience constantly pregiven as taken for granted unquestioningly and all the life of thought which is nourished by it." He goes on to affirm that this lifeworld—"the 'world for us all'—is identical with the world that can be commonly talked about" (209). Common talk—everyday, mundane conversation—is then both in and about a world already informed by sensory engagement as well as by prior talk, both silent (thinking) and sensory (aurality/orality).

This conception of the process and setting of communication offered by Dewey and Husserl differs rather extensively from that constructed by Enlightenment science and assumed throughout modernity. Science presumes a decontextualized setting consisting of subjects who pursue knowledge and the objects of that pursuit. Both Self and Other function in this model as interchangeable tokens of their types. The only activity engaged in by these subjects is knowing, and the only activity on the part of objects that is relevant to scientific interests is reactivity understood as the effects of standardized causes. Objects thus are present as passive recipients of the subject's knowing. In an important sense, however, they are not present as particular spatiotemporal objects at all, for they are represented by linguistic objects. Insofar as communication is an interaction or transaction between subjects engaged in some doing, there is no communication here. Rather, in this model subjects use language as a tool in their analysis of objects, whether those are classified as vegetables, minerals, or animals—including human animals. In other words, scientists—knowing subjects—employ a system of words that represent their ideas in order to refer, indirectly, to things. The Other, the real object of knowledge, has dropped out of this scheme. Then again, it continues to affect us, so we take it that Other has not ceased to exist and be effective in the world. What has happened is that a linguistic version of the Lockean "veil of ideas" has been interposed between Self and Other, subject and object, so that Self is imprisoned within language.

Subjects in the lifeworld, in contrast, are preeminently engaged in doing, as well as talk about that doing, with other doers. Those activities make meaningful things—particular, different things—out of events. In the course of that making, agents—subjects who communicate with other subjects in order to reflect and rearrange their inquiries to suit their interests and goals—emerge as Selves. They are subjects, in other words, because they are always and already objects of the world's doing to them. Perhaps this will be more clear if I tell it in my own voice, rather than that of a generalized Subject: as a being in the world, I am an object of the world's doings. If I am pleased with how the world is treating me, I'm disposed to inquire into how that doing occurs in order to maintain that treatment. If I am displeased, I have even more impetus for inquiry in order to institute change. Since much of the action upon me stems from other humans, I am the Object of Other before I am the Subject who acts toward Other. In other words: I am subject to Other's doing before I am Subject, extending my subjectivity onto my object, Other.

This is not a new finding, although its implications for theorizing communication as constitutive have been neglected. "Mind," George Herbert Mead (1954, 50) finds, "arises through communication by a conversation of gestures in a social process or context of experience— not communication through mind." Dewey (1980) emphasizes that this "conversation" is one of participatory doing, rather than using language to represent an environment: "If it be true that the self or subject of experience is part and parcel of the course of events, it follows that the self . . . becomes a mind in virtue of a distinctive way of partaking in the course of events" (42). Husserl (1970) quotes Goethe's *Faust,* when specifying the focus for the "life-world as subject matter for a theoretical interest" (155): "In the beginning is the deed" (156). His choice to theorize this domain of deeds may well have been influenced by his context, which was Germany in the mid-1930s. His situation was parallel to that of Comte almost a century earlier, although his search for order took a rather different turn.

Comte, we recall, turned to the physical sciences as a model for the social sciences. When Husserl examined the physical sciences, however, he found them in "crisis," and he diagnosed that crisis as due to their abstractness. In other words, he found that scientific theorizing lacked connection—relevance—to the affairs of everyday life, although he could discern no source for science's theoretical considerations other than mundane life. In turning to the focus on the lifeworld in his later work, therefore, he sought to locate and articulate the orderliness in everyday life that underlies theoretical orderliness. In phenomenological terms, Husserl discovered and thematized mundane order as the ground of conceptual order; in more political terms, he identified intrinsic structures as the basis of imposed forms. Investigation of the lifeworld thus provides a foothold for critique: insofar as theoretical and political structures conflict with their mundane grounding, or fail to enhance that grounding, a dissatisfied agent's reflective articulation of neglected (and perhaps, suppressed) lifeworld structures provide a ground for creative resistance to what is, on behalf of what might be—and arguably, would be—a better way of being.

The scientific model we inherited from the Enlightenment errs, then, in neglecting that plurality of lifeworld origins—the very origins that Husserl sought to reconnect with science. We can now understand why that model begins with language as representational, rather than with communication as constituting (presenting) what language then represents. The error is simply one of entering the ongoing process of human being at the level of language use and of mistaking that phenomenon for the originating voice of Self rather than recognizing it as engaged in response to Other. It is in that communicative activity that, as Dewey (1981) says, "events turn into objects, things with a meaning" (18, quoted earlier in context). What is needed to correct this error is a reflective turn from linguistic system to constitutive communicative activity. Heidegger's (1977) oft-quoted remark on language as the house of Being can help us to make that reflective turn, if we notice that the house is not the occupant:

> Language is the house of Being. In its home man dwells. Those who think and those who create with words are the guardians of this home. Their guardianship accomplishes the manifestation of Being insofar as they bring the manifestation to language and maintain it in language through their speech. (193)

The house's occupant is a descendent of its architect and builder. Houses would not be built if the circumstances of human being *(Dasein)* did not require shelter. Less metaphorically, language is the result of communication, not its cause.

If we continue in a reflective direction and inquire again into the nature of human understanding by beginning at the beginning, this time, we find a variety of ongoing communicative activities—in touch, taste, smell, sound, and sight. The aurality/orality of our speech, by means of which we maintain the manifestation of Being in language, is a comparative latecomer among those activities. Elsewhere (Langsdorf, 1989) I have argued that our reasoning is informed by a variety of those media. Insofar as what we see, hear, touch, and feel provides a multiplicity of accounts of whatever situation we happen to be in, and Self emerges from a plurality of such multiplicities, Self carries an originating and multiple Otherness within it. Perhaps, then, a broader understanding of communicative activity requires us to correct Heidegger by saying that speech enables one, rather than *the,* manifestation of Being. Here again, this is not a new finding, although its implications for rejecting verbal language as basic to human being have been neglected. Ricoeur's (1976) theory of interpretation relies upon a "surplus of meaning" communicated in discourse and taken up into an emergent Self. Bakhtin's (1981) understanding of Self as dialogical locus of multiple voices provides an alternative to the individualistic account given in the Enlightenment, unreflectively accepted in modernity and now rejected in postmodern theorizing.

Once we redirect our attention to what has been done to us as objects as well as to our doing as subjects, rather than limiting our attention to the saying of what has been done, we can begin to notice that human being in the world requires persistent inquiry by subjects which is directed toward maintaining or altering what is done. Furthermore, we notice that inquiry toward those ends transpires in multiple media—which is to say, by means of diverse technologies. Husserl followed a deeply embedded tendency in western thinking when he valorized visual perception and, correlatively, devalued tactile-kinesthetic as well as aural/oral activity. That monological source may have contributed to his retention of the individualistic conception of human being that the Enlightenment bequeathed to modernity. The very nature of vision supports that conception: Other need do nothing for me to see Other as object and sustain my belief in Self as subject. But it is only when Other touches, that I feel a tactile-kinesthetic response, and it is only when Other speaks that I hear.

Indeed, in the originary moments of my being in the world, Other's tactility and voice influence Self before Self can respond to Other. I begin, then, as Object, and insofar as my emergent Self is a response to the voice (and touch, etc.) of the Other, I have found the voice of Self in a rather unexpected place: within a world that is Other. It is no simple matter to move from recognizing that priority of Other, to rebuilding science as a learning from the plurivocal communicative activity of Other—rather than continuing a scientific discourse that seeks to manage Other in the image of Self. My argument here proposes that the first phase of that reconstruction is saving Self by recognizing the ontological priority of Other.

Notes

1. Some of the themes in this chapter were addressed in "Objects of Knowledge and Subjects of Inquiry," which was presented as the A. Craig Baird Lecture at the University of Iowa in 1995. I would like to thank my colleagues in the Communication Studies Department and the Project on the Rhetoric of Inquiry for the opportunity to develop and discuss these issues in their company.

2. At various places in this chapter, I have used the masculine pronoun rather than inclusionary language. Also, I've retained the traditional designation of the Judeo-Christian God as "He," and have referred to the role of the "craftsman" in Platonic thought as well as the "man of science" in Enlightenment philosophy.

These practices are not exercises in exclusionary language, and thus, are not intended to sustain exclusionary practices in contemporary life. They are, rather, intended as reminders of sedimented assumptions that (I would argue) continue to inform our thinking about "the Other." More specifically, the opportunities and responsibilities of the Divine Creator as well as human creators (in the arts and sciences) typically were associated with male persons by the writers I cite, and by the cultural tradition that informed them and was informed by them. Insofar as these creative subjects were conceptualized as male, females carried the sense of created objects. One implication of recognizing the priority of Other, I hope, is increased likelihood of recognizing the typically subdued—and even silenced sense of the Other/the female as creative Self within the multiplicity of ways of being characteristic of all persons.

References

Bakhtin, Mikhail. (1981). *The Dialogic Imagination*. Austin: University of Texas Press.

Cassirer, Ernst. (1951). *The Philosophy of the Enlightenment*. (F. C. A. Koelln and J. P. Pettegrove, Trans.) Boston: Beacon Press (original publication 1932).

Coser, Lewis A. (1971). *Masters of Sociological Thought*. New York: Harcourt, Brace Jovanovitch.

Descartes, Réné. (1968). *Discourse on Method* and *The Meditations*. (F. E. Sutcliffe, Trans. and Ed.) London: Penguin (original publication 1637, 1641).

Dewey, John. (1971). *Experience and Nature: The Later Works, 1925–1953*, vol. 1. (J. A. Boydston, Ed.). Carbondale: Southern Illinois University Press (original publication 1929).

————. (1980). *The Need for a Recovery of Philosophy: The Middle Works, 1899–1924*. vol. 10. (J. A. Boydston, Ed.) Carbondale: Southern Illinois University Press.

Havelock, Eric A. (1982). *The Literate Revolution in Greece and Its Cultural Consequences*. Princeton: Princeton University Press.

Heidegger, Martin. (1977). Letter on humanism. In D. F. Krell (Ed.): *Basic Writings*. New York: Harper and Row.

Husserl, Edmund. (1970). *The Crisis of European Sciences* and *Transcendental Phenomenology*. (D. Carr, Trans.) Evanston, Ill.: Northwestern University Press (original publication 1954).

Ihde, Don. (1991). *Instrumental Realism*. Bloomington: Indiana University Press.

Kant, Immanuel. (1950). *Critique of Pure Reason*. (N. K. Smith, Trans.) London: Macmillan (original publication 1781).

————. (1988). What is enlightenment? In Lewis White Beck (Ed.): *Kant Selections*. New York: Macmillan (original publication 1784).

Kuhn, Thomas S. (1970). *The Structure of Scientific Revolutions*, 2d ed. Chicago: University of Chicago Press.

Langsdorf, Lenore. (1989). *Reasoning across the Media: Visual, Verbal, and Televisual Literacies*. Montclair, N.J.: Institute for Critical Thinking.

————. (1992). Realism and idealism in the Kuhnian account of science. In L. Harvey and L. Embree (Eds.): *Phenomenology of Natural Science*. Dordrecht, Netherlands: Kluwer.

————. (1995). Philosophy of language and philosophy of communication: Poiesis and praxis in classical pragmatism. In L. Langsdorf and A. R. Smith (Eds.): *Recovering Pragmatism's Voice: The Classical Tradition, Rorty, and the Philosophy of Communication*. Albany: SUNY Press.

Locke, John. (1924). *An Essay Concerning Human Understanding*. (A. S. Pringle-Pattison, Ed.) Oxford, England: Clarendon Press (original publication 1690).

Mead, George Herbert. (1934). *Mind, Self, and Society*. (C. W. Morris, Ed.) Chicago: University of Chicago Press.

Ong, Walter J. (1958). *Ramus, Method, and the Decay of Dialogue*. Cambridge, Mass.: Harvard University Press.

Plato. (1974). *The Republic*. (G. M. A. Grube, Trans.) Indianapolis: Hackett.

Ricoeur, Paul. (1976). *Interpretation Theory: Discourse and the Surplus of Meaning*. Fort Worth: Texas Christian University Press.

Rorty, Richard. (1982). *Consequences of Pragmatism*. Minneapolis: University of Minnesota Press.

Chapter Four

Foucault on the "Other Within"

Michael Huspek

Foucault's texts open up a new world that no sooner is there for readers to behold before it tightens its grip in a stranglehold of power, domination, subjugation, surveillance, and disciplinary control. In Foucault's world, power in all its multiple strategies, relations, programs, and techniques aims at being totalizing in its effects. It expands its reach indefatigably through the corridors of hospitals, prisons and asylums, into the private chambers of confessors and psychiatrists, and outward into all quarters of "carceral" society, transforming human beings into subjects whose subjectivity is made one in the same with subjection to power-infused practices. Power is everywhere. It enlists the support of discourse as one of its chief modalities, permeates it, and installs it with its own truth, declaring a finite field of statements intelligible while ensuring that it is that field which is intelligible and none other as it suppresses any and all rival claims. It does not thereby mask the operations of its truth by means of ideology, for its aim is not to deceive but rather to constitute the "truth," qua truth, by investing it with materiality in its discursive forms. In this way power and truth come to implicate one another as power/knowledge.[1] Says Foucault (1979, 27):

> We should admit . . . that power produces knowledge (and not simply by encouraging it because it serves power or by applying it because it is useful); that power and knowledge directly imply one another; that there is no power relation without the correlative constitution of a field of knowledge, nor any knowledge that does not presuppose and constitute at the same time power relations.

In Foucault's world, power is accorded enormous latitude, its reach being more extensive, its guises more varied, than what we have come to expect from either traditional or radical theories.[2] Power is not the sole province of a specific group, class, or institution, existing thus within binary relations of power and powerlessness, nor does it simply place constraints upon actors in the form of *A* getting *B* to do something he or she would otherwise not do (e.g., Lukes, 1974). Power, rather, is omnipresent at all levels of society, forming the basis for all social interaction in its delimitation of the sayable and unsayable. It is the very condition of meaningful action. Subjects are empowered to act upon the world in meaningful ways only on condition that such actions are undertaken in and through power's modalities (discourse), which is to say that subjects, as a condition of engaging in meaningful action, are also subjected to power's "truths." Power, in this way, produces the capacity to act (Foucault, 1978, 92–102).

This view of power is profoundly unsettling, and Foucault means it to be (e.g., 1982, 208–26). The "experience of discord"[3] is promoted by Foucault as part of his general strategy of critique, both theoretically multilayered and methodologically diverse, which, we are to believe, does not fall sway as does many of its neighboring critical theories to the charms of its own potentially tyrannizing ideals. At the same time, however, such a strategy prompts a number of concerns. If power is everywhere, installing truth in and through discourse, inscribing bodies, investing souls, shaping subjectivities, what then are its limits? Does it have limits? And what of the role of the subject? Is there any possibility for subjects to act as agents in ways that contest power without at the same time being under the yoke of subjection, driven to reproduce power in its multiple forms? And what then of the subject as analyst? How can he or she be committed to a discursive strategy without reproducing the power/knowledge that is at its base? Are not efforts to expose power, to subvert or overthrow it, in fact condemned to its very reproduction? Or are there discursive strategies that escape, at least in some partial way, the productions and constraints of power/knowledge?

The above questions fall within three areas of concerns. One area, expressed by Michael Walzer (1986), centers on the apparent limitlessness of Foucault's notion of power. For Walzer, this is highly problematic. He charges that the notion of limitless power undermines the force of Foucault's critique. According to Walzer, not only is Foucault unable to discriminate among crucial differences of power both within and between various localities, institutions, societies, or states, but he is also unappreciative of how power, in some of its guises, is limited in ways that might significantly prohibit uncivilized behaviors. Walzer (1986, 62) notes, for example, that "[Foucault's] account of the carceral archipelago contains no hint of how or why our own [liberal] society stops short of the Gulag." As a counter to Foucault, he emphasizes how the discourse of liberalism offers up significant and clear-cut principles that place distinct limits on power, while "Authoritarian and totalitarian states, by contrast, override those limits, turning education into indoctrination, punishment into repression, asylums into prisons, and prisons into concentration camps" (66).

A related concern has been expressed by Charles Taylor (1984) who, like Walzer, is also disturbed by Foucault's world of limitless power. Taylor believes that Foucault's power/knowledge nexus eclipses modern notions of agency and the reality of truth claims upon which agents may mount liberation projects against power. Taylor takes issue with how agents are reduced in Foucault's world to mere subjects who undergo subjection within one or another set of power-infused practices and argues that agents need not be so reduced: "Not only is there the possibility of frequently moving from one set of practices to another; but even within a given set, the level and kind of imposition can vary" (92). Taylor charges that Foucault rejects the former proposition, presumably on grounds that all practices are equally found within the vise grip of power, and he seems not even to entertain the latter. Along similar lines, Taylor also claims that Foucault's notion of power loses its profile, indeed, makes little sense, without at least the idea of liberation. Power, that is, makes sense only in that it has something outside of itself to run up against or to overcome. And this "other," if it is to be taken seriously, must be accorded its own truth which stands as a counter to power/knowledge. States Taylor: "The truth here is subversive of power: it is on the side of lifting of impositions, of what we have just called liberation" (93).

A third concern (e.g., Dreyfus and Rabinow, 1982; Shapiro, 1988) points to an apparent contradiction between a Foucauldian view that recognizes power/knowledge at the base of all significant discourse, that attributes to power an apparently limitless compass, and that denies subjectivity any scope of action which is not at once also subjection, but that, on the other hand, would itself seek to initiate a theoretical discourse which presumably has the ambition of exposing power while itself managing somehow to escape power's clutches. This problem is not unique to Foucault but has beset virtually every theorist since Marx who has sought to expose ideology or other hidden workings of power (e.g., Smart, 1983, 4–31). It is a problem that was treated perhaps with greatest theoretical urgency by Louis Althusser (1969, 1971), one of Foucault's teachers, who maintained that there is no escaping misrecognition that is bound up with being interpellated as free subject, on one side, and as subject-as-subjected to power-infused ideology, on the other, unless, that is, one opts for a "subjectless" scientific standpoint. But Foucault does not opt for the safety of a scientific perspective, nor could he given his view that the "truths" of science are themselves each inscribed by the power of a policing discourse (Foucault, 1972). But we must then ask: Is Foucault not condemned to reproduce the power/knowledge that he would seek to expose? How might Foucault manage to be "in the truth" without himself pledging obeisance to the "discursive police"?[4]

In the remainder of this essay I attempt in the first section to defend Foucault against the charges raised against him by both Walzer and Taylor, arguing specifically that neither critic has sufficiently appreciated Foucault's implied dialectical treatment of power in its relation to resistance. After arguing that both critics fail to do Foucault interpretive justice, I go on in the next section to discuss some ways in which Foucault's dialectical treatment of power and resistance emerges as a significant advance over Walzer's and Taylor's own respective approaches. I then close the essay with some concluding remarks to the effect that, once Foucault's dialectical notion of power and resistance is understood, it is not contradictory to deem Foucault a most formidable opponent of power while at the same time acknowledging his inability to escape the constraining truth-parameters of power's "discursive police."

Power versus Resistance

Preliminary Concepts

Walzer's indictment of Foucault's work on the grounds that he fails to recognize that power must have limits is somewhat unfair. The charge overlooks an important conceptual tension that runs throughout Foucault's writings. The tension derives from a contradictory notion of power that emphasizes its apparently limitless scope, on the one hand, but that shows it to run up against its own produced limits, on the other. True enough, Foucault assigns a host of strategies and techniques to power: in constituting the "truth" of its existence, power inscribes, manipulates, and subjugates "others." But it is this very notion of "otherness" that undercuts any understanding that power has a single, homogeneous, unopposed existence. Power produces counterforces *against which* it asserts its own "truth," *against which* it sets out to manipulate, subjugate, and so forth. These "others," however, power's own productions, serve also as power's supports. In this sense, power *depends upon* "otherness." In structuralist terms, the power that inheres in a prevailing discourse of reason produces madness as its limiting term; a discourse of normalcy produces the deviant; a discourse of mental health requires the pathological. Without these power-produced "others," existing both as power's limits and supports, power has nothing to exert itself against. Without these "others," which can be said to exist with power in a dialectical relation of opposition and interdependence, power as limitlessness would dissolve into nothingness.

The idea of resistance is crucial within Foucault's work because it is here that the limits and supports against which power operates are given fullest conceptualization. For Foucault (1982), power and resistance are dialectically linked, as each term "constitutes for the other a kind of permanent limit, a point of possible reversal" (p. 225). Resistance is therefore assigned an irreducible role in Foucault's analyses. Power/knowledge can sustain itself only within a field or relation of struggle in which there exists an "insurrection of subjugated knowledges" (Foucault, 1980, 82–83). "Truth," and the power that gives it its legitimacy, produces "countertruths" of resistance.[5]

It is something of a curiosity that the full scope and contours of the dialectical relation between power and resistance do not receive extensive elaboration in Foucault's writings. Although resistance is always present in Foucault's analyses, at times inciting power to shift strategies or to develop new ones, at other times devising strategies of its own to ward off the multiple intrusions of power, it is power that receives most explicit attention from Foucault. A likely rationale for this emphasis is implied by Foucault's discussion of the nature of the oppositions between power and resistance in their concreteness. Power is always visible—provides its own visibility—insofar as it secures for itself legitimacy by virtue of constituting the "truth" of its own existence: "Power never ceases its interrogation, its inquisition, its registration of truth: it institutionalizes, professionalizes and rewards its pursuit" (Foucault, 1980, 93). In contrast, resistance has less visibility. As subjugated knowledge, predicated on "countertruths" and carried often by oppositional discourses (e.g., antilanguages), it may hide itself within power's reign of "truth," or if it does emerge to express its own "truth," it may be immediately disqualified, delegitimated, made unstable and insecure, if not altogether silenced (Foucault, 1980, 82).

Nevertheless, despite the instability of its position, its lack of resources, the insecurity of the "truth" carried by its subjugated knowledge, resistance poses itself as a support of and a limit to power. Where there is power there is resistance. If power produces subjects as material upon and through which to work its "truth," so resistance is thereby also produced, and operates to check, perhaps even roll back, power's surges by means of its own "countertruths." At one point, Foucault (1982, 211) calls for "taking the forms of resistance against different forms of power as a starting point," and he then goes on to call upon analysts to examine the "agonism" between power relations, on one side, and the "intransitivity of freedom," on the other (223).

Although this "agonism" was not explicated within Foucault's works with rigorous systematicity, various commentators have discerned its implied structure. As Krips (1990, 177) has summarized: "resistance and power are reciprocally constituted: resistance is only possible where there is an exercise of power, and vice versa." With this mind, we begin to see the extent to which Walzer's objection misses the mark. The question as to why it is, then, that the liberal state stops short of the

Gulag is to be addressed not so much by looking at the former as a monolithic site, having its own self-constituting principles and practices, nor by comparing the two forms—liberal state and Gulag—which are hugely disconsonant with respect to space, time, and so forth. Rather the question is best addressed by inquiring into the dialectical "other" produced by liberalism's power/knowledge and against which the "truth" of liberalism constitutes itself; the "other" that exists in opposition to liberalism's power-infused practices; the "other" that offers as a crucial facet of its existence the very "truth" which liberalism produces and which at the same time it seeks to suppress.

Foucault's treatment of power is not explicitly a normative one. Its theoretical value is to offer explanations about the limits of power as it operates in specific relations, programs, and practices. Such explanations are derived from inquiry into that which power simultaneously produces and defines itself against. Liberalism's systems of power, therefore, are best understood not by means of comparison and contrast to systems that exist beyond the scope of liberalism's practices but rather by focused attention on the very limits that it has itself produced. An explanation for why liberalism stops short of the Gulag is best grounded in an informed understanding of the internal, dialectical workings of the relation between power and its own produced limits, resistance. Liberalism stops short of the Gulag, on this view, not so much because the former has proved itself to be a more virtuous political arrangement (although what liberal discourse would deny or otherwise suppress this "truth"?), but because it faces limitations both within and upon its range of operations which are of a different sort than those that have been produced in Eastern Europe.

The "other" of resistance, which is produced by power and, at the same time, operates as power's limit, exists in an internal relation with power. This "other" is also "within" the relation. Neither power nor resistance can exist without the other. Such is the nature of their "agonism." With this idea we can then begin to see also how Taylor's objection underestimates the full complexity of Foucault's treatment of power. Taylor is correct to charge that Foucault posits no "truths" that exist independently of the power-resistance relationship, nor, Taylor is also right to say, does the idea of liberation—i.e., total liberation from the clutches of power—make sense to Foucault. For Foucault, the "truth" of resistance is no more absolute than the "truth" of power. By the same token, while resistance may achieve certain victories in its opposition to power, *total* liberation is a logical contradiction. To imagine a power-resistance relationship being burst asunder so that subjects were free of power would then necessarily invite the view that subjects are powerless to act as subjects. Power is constraining *and* enabling. If liberation is freedom from power's constraints, it must also be recognized as "freedom" from power's enablements. Total liberation of this kind would have to be regarded as being synonymous with nothingness.

To circumscribe resistance in this manner, however, is not to deny or underestimate the liberation potential it carries in its opposition to power. This potential is manifested in two significant respects. First, within the dialectical relationship between power and resistance, the former is distinguished in its productive capacity by its attempts to subjugate the subjects it produces, while the latter claims its title as antagonistic "other" by virtue of its opposition to subjugation. Resistance, that is, does not have subjugation of subjects as an ambition. Its posture is entirely a defensive one, and if it should perchance evolve in ways that exceed its dialectically shaped role in relation to power, then we are no longer looking at resistance but at power, against which we surely will detect new points of resistance emerging, as power must define itself against some resistant entity. At the same time this is not to dismiss the potential of resistance to score victories, for certainly victories are within its reach. But the victories of resistance take the form of either checking power's totalizing ambitions or effecting a rollback of power's expanse (e.g., Foucault, 1978).

Second, resistance, and especially the "truth" it promotes in its struggles against power, also performs an important critical function. In its role as "other," which is simultaneously linked to power "within" a relationship, the "truth" of resistance exposes the contradictory nature of power's own "truth." The "truth" of resistance, when voiced, shows that power's claims to "truth" are predicated on silencing, suppressing, distorting, or otherwise manipulating the "countertruths" of its opposition. This is not merely an instance of power/knowledge running up against the limitations posed by an "other," although resistance here does constitute a most certain limitation. More importantly, it is the "truth" of power/knowledge being exposed in its partiality and self contradiction. Partial because the "truth" of power cannot exist without generating its supports, namely, the "countertruths" of resistance; contradictory because such "countertruths" constitute the very antithesis of power's "truth" while at the same time being irreducibly linked to power "within" their dialectical relationship. The "countertruth" of resistance always threatens to inform the "truth" of power of what the latter is not, and this always in the face of what the latter claims itself to be (e.g., Huspek, 1994b; Huspek and Comerford, 1996). Given this critical, subversive role of the "truth" of resistance, it is no wonder that power has such a stake in the suppression of the "countertruths," subjugated knowledges and antilanguages that are aligned with resistance.

An Empirical Illustration

The dialectical relationship between power and resistance is briefly illustrated in a recent study of unskilled urban industrial workers' discourse of resistance (Huspek and Kendall, 1991). The study points to the prevailing political discourse of liberalism and the way it produces two forms of subjectivity: (1) subjects as citizens, free, self-constituting, and autonomous and (2) subjects as wage earners who must alienate their labor and subjugate themselves to the wage-capital relationship as a condition of survival. While producing both forms of subjectivity, the discourse of liberalism stresses the political "truth" of the former, while downplaying the economic "truth" of the latter (as natural, inevitable, timeless). If, however, dissatisfaction arises on account of subjection to economic domination or degradation in the workplace, the prevailing discourse of liberalism reminds its subjects that they must draw upon their competencies as citizens if their voice is to be heard. Moreover, political channels are said to be available through which citizens can express their dissatisfactions.

The dominant discourse of liberalism thereby suppresses the contradictory relation between subjects as free citizens and subjects who are subjected to the wage-capital relationship. For the workers, the contradiction takes the following form. First, they believe the liberal "truth" that points to their own subjectivity: they *are* free, self-willed, autonomous agents. But such freedom creates its own dissatisfaction. It is because the workers buy into the "truth" of their own freedom that they find so burdensome the "necessity" of alienating their labor and subordinating themselves within the wage-capital relationship. Moreover, that political channels *may* be available to the workers in their capacity as political agents is not denied by the workers. But such channels are far removed from the humiliation and degradation that they must suffer regularly on an everyday basis in the workplace. Against *this* power that subjugates them, their oppositional response is to adopt "nonpolitical" resistance strategems.

One of the more visible resistance stratagems utilized by the workers is their vocabulary of politics, which consists of words and meanings that exist in opposition to the words and meanings that have currency within the prevailing discourse of liberalism. What is most interesting about the workers' vocabulary of politics is that it is positioned conscientiously against capitalist ownership and control, but that since capitalism itself draws its legitimacy from the prevailing discourse of liberalism, the workers' vocabulary ultimately opposes not only capitalist ownership and control but also liberal politics. This can be explained in the following terms: because the "truth" of the discourse of liberalism successfully suppresses its contradictory relationship with capitalist economics, granting the political rights of economic ownership but without acknowledging as a problem the relations of domination inherent in capitalism, the workers, feeling the strain as subjects of capitalist economic life, develop words and meanings that oppose capitalist domination *and* liberal politics.

Consider, for example, three basic terms: "politics," "power," and "political voice." Although these terms at times are assigned a negative meaning within the general political culture—e.g., "politics" implying corruption and abuse of authority, "power" implying manipulation and coercion—their meanings as produced by the prevailing discourse of liberalism is overwhelmingly positive. "Politics," therefore, is bound up with the idea of free-acting subjects ordering and directing their collective affairs, initiating action by which to overcome externally imposed patterns of control, and setting up ends for society and standards by which to evaluate those ends (e.g., Sibley, 1970). "Power" signifies subjects acting in concert, expressing their interests, values and needs (e.g., Arendt, 1969). And "political voice" is thought to be a primary means to ensure that the impersonal aspect of politics is made personal, as subjects are thereby enabled to forge alliances with others and to engage in conflict in a civil manner. In inviting reciprocation of other voices, it is thought also to serve an important educative function, solidifying the political community by encouraging an ongoing rational contest of wills (e.g., Pateman, 1970; Dallmayr, 1984; Barber, 1984).

These three terms rarely carry any positive signification within the workers' own discourse.[6] "Politics" functions regularly as a negative signifier, unified with corruption, lying, dishonesty, backstabbing, and power-tripping. "Power" is linked exclusively either to the "power monger" who uses power to maintain or extend his political or economic advantage or to the "power tripper" who does not possess power but who displays a willingness to violate norms of communal solidarity in order to acquire it. And "political voice" is equated solely with "political bullshit" and "shit talk," and those who exercise political voice are viewed as acting "politically," and like a "politician," are thought to be obsessed with the accumulation or preservation of power.

The Foucauldian dialectical view of this phenomenon points to the significance of a prevalent discourse of liberalism producing relatively free, self-willed subjects who, at the same time, are subjected to alienation and domination within liberalism's support economy, the wage-capital relationship. Key here is the idea that the discourse of liberalism generates "truths" that account adequately for only one side of the workers' contradictory subjectivity: workers are discursively produced as free (political) subjects, on one side, but then are expected to reconcile this freedom with the (economic) reality of wage slavery, on the other. Against the "truths" that undergird their freedom while simultaneously eclipsing it, an oppositional discourse, specified here as an antilanguage which expresses the workers' subjugated knowledge, develops among workers. While accepting the "truth" of their (political) freedom, but feeling subjugated within the only political arena of which they have intimate familiarity, namely, the workplace, they respond by resisting the "truth" of political action expressed within liberal discourse. Rather, the "truth" of resistance points to the workers' own exclusion from the political arena, as indicated by the reality of their everyday workplace experience.

The "truth" of the workers' counterdiscourse depicts the workers as moral in contrast to immoral "politicians," "power trippers," and "politicals." This morality legislates against the workers' engagement in any form of political action that might be sanctioned as legitimate within the dominant discourse of liberalism. This effectively undercuts the likelihood that the workers might act as political subjects as so defined by the dominant discourse. For in developing a counterdiscourse in and through which to express dissatisfaction with alienation and subjugation, the workers undermine their potential to act as free political subjects who might effectively alter their condition. This is consistent with the idea of resistance being essentially a combination of defensive strategies, tactics, and maneuvers. The workers' counterdiscourse clearly does not have power as its aim. It does, however, in its opposition to the dominant discourse of liberalism, enable the workers to resist the onslaught of power's "truth" as it is expressed through the modality of a dominant discourse. Thus, the workers' antilanguage does not promote the percolation of their own words and meanings up into power-legitimated contexts, nor as an expression of resistance is it designed to do so. Rather, its primary operation is best thought to be that of warding off power's intrusions.

On the other hand, although the "truths" of the discourse of resistance constitutes the workers as moral, there is realization among the workers that their resistance, in turn, constitutes them as immoral according to the "truths" of the dominant discourse of liberalism. If the workers are not valued by legitimate society, if their voice is not heard, it is because their own counterdiscourse positions them beyond the compass of legitimate citizen action. For under the regime of "truth" established within the prevailing discourse of liberalism, subjects—one and all, irrespective of position within the sociopolitical power structure—are expected to fulfill their moral obligations as citizens in and through political participation: to withhold one's voice is shirking one's civic duty. By what right, then, can the workers' voice claim to have a value within the domain of legitimate, moral, political action?

The multiple effects of power can be summarized as follows: First the workers are produced as knowledgeable agents who, faced with the contradiction between their subjectivity as autonomous political beings, on the one hand, and their subjection to a political-economic arrangement, on the other, opt for a discursive "truth" that provides more adequate expression to their life experiences. Second, by virtue of the workers' counterdiscourse, they position themselves outside the arena of legitimate politics, thereby declining any engagement in political action. Third, this tactic invites moral castigation from above and, as such, is not lost upon the workers for they know the dominant discourse of liberalism and its "truth." Indeed, they are themselves spoken by it when at times they must interact with powerholders (e.g., Huspek, 1993, 1994a). All three effects work to the advantage of power; the workers' discursively based resistance, that is, proscribes concerted political action against power's regime. However, there is a fourth effect of power that poses a distinct threat to power and that power seeks to suppress. This is oppositional discourse *as critique,* which points to the partial and contradictory nature of the "truth" of power and its productions. Partial in that power/knowledge fails to fully penetrate this resistant "other." Contradictory in that the "truth" of resistance informs the "truth" of power what power, in fact, is not, and this, moreover, in the face of what the latter claims itself to be.

The "truth" of resistance, in its critical capacity, operates as the antithesis of the "truth" of power: it exposes power for what it is, and what it is not, and the contradiction involved in both its being and nonbeing. The force of its critique, moreover, is strengthened on account of the nature of the relationship between power and resistance. The "truth" of resistance signifies "otherness," but it is an "otherness" which is also "within." As "other within" it stands as power's own creation that exists as an integral member of a relationship within which it "depends upon" the power that created it but also negates power in its capacity to dominate it as subjugated other. As such it cannot be easily dismissed as mere "otherness." This idea receives fuller treatment in the following section.

Resistance as "Other Within": A Foucauldian Perspective

The notion of the "other within" is deployed here as a useful conceptual device in the service of a dialectical treatment of the relation between power and resistance. Power cannot exist in isolation but must actively construct "others," which it then excludes as a means of securing support within its own self-generated system of signifiers. The "truth," "morality," and "reason" of power depends upon their internal relations with their opposites which, while existing in opposition, requires that they be silenced or suppressed. For every discourse there exists the rumblings of a counterdiscourse; for every science there exists the makings of antiscience; for every assertion of rationality there exists the muted moans of the banished or incarcerated whose crime it is to have been irrational; for every exacting of moral discipline or control there exists the suppressed laughter of the immoral, the perverted, and the conniving of those who refuse to be controlled.

This notion of "other within" receives no attention from two of Foucault's most prominent critics, Walzer and Taylor. Within the writings of either scholar we are unable to hear the voice of dissension from those who, though existing "within," are classified as "other," and who seek not power but only the release from its choking grip. Both authors subscribe to a discourse of liberalism that celebrates a plurality of voice, yet both pledge allegiance to a conceptual order that provides no legitimately recognized space for these "others" to be heard. This omission not only detracts from their respective interpretations of Foucault, but it also dilutes the contents of their own social and political thought.

Walzer's Neglect of "Otherness"[7]

Walzer's writings seek to plumb the interiors of shared cultures (especially his own liberal political culture), which, he assumes, possess values, principles, codes, and conventions that are moral in their contents. The moral component is especially important to Walzer, who emphasizes that we should neither underestimate the moral unifying force of a shared culture nor be too quick in criticizing existing moral worlds by drawing upon imported or newly invented moral principles (Walzer, 1982). In the course of critically assessing forms of critique which draw upon "foreign" moral principles that are divined from religious musings or invented by philosophers in the realm of idealized abstraction, Walzer (1982, 14) asks: "Why should newly invented principles govern the lives of people who already share a moral culture and speak a moral language?"

Against the divine or the idealized, Walzer (1982) claims that the critic of culture need look no farther than the culture's own moral code to find and establish sufficient grounds upon which to proceed. Each culture offers up its own moral code that merely needs to be interpreted as a commonly shared text. By stressing that which is commonly shared, Walzer (1982) rules out neither the desirability nor the need of disagreement: "Morality . . . is something we have to argue about. The argument implies common possession, but common possession does not imply agreement" (32). Nor does he dismiss the ways in which cultures may undergo abuse at the hands of those who rule or would seek to rule. But the culture itself contains within it moral principles by which to critique such abuses. "Morality," says Walzer, "is always potentially subversive of class and power" (22). And he continues: "Criticism does not require us to step away from society as a whole but only to step away from certain sorts of power relationships within society. It is not correction but authority and domination from which we must distance ourselves" (60).

Walzer's view consists of an unshakable trust in a shared morality combined with the belief that power relations are easily separated from that which is moral. This view is problematic. First, it is by no means clear how Walzer distinguishes between arbitrary authority and authority installed or delegated by moral edict, or between forceful domination and domination that is rationalized through appeal to moral reasoning (e.g., Huspek, 1989/1990). Being himself unwilling to point to invented or divine principles of morality and presumably also being disinclined to appeal to a set of universal moral concepts, we must surmise that these distinctions—moral versus immoral authority or domination—are made easily enough within any given set of cultural parameters. However, it is precisely because knowledge and morality *are* often inextricably entwined with relations of power that we may well not be able to state with confidence that one form of authority (e.g., that installed by parliamentary rules and procedures) is morally superior to another form of authority (e.g., that which has devolved upon capitalist owners, through force, but which in liberal society is now given justification through moral, and politically sanctioned, appeal). We do not know where to begin to extricate one form of morality from the other. Nor are we alone in the face of this problem. As discussed above, when industrial workers challenge the basis of ownership and control, using their own shared moral code as guide, they are apt to face charges of being irrational or immoral. Moreover, such charges are likely themselves to be morally based—that is, receive legitimate moral backing—within the capitalist order.

Second, Walzer's unshakable trust in the shared morality that binds a culture underestimates the ways in which moral principles may be arbitrarily distributed and regulated so that some potential participants either are denied entry into contexts that count for success or are admitted only to find that more important contexts have been shifted to another neighborhood of meaning and significance (e.g., MacIntyre, 1991; Huspek, 1989/1990). Walzer attempts to stave off this criticism with his stated presumption that cultures (especially modern ones that subscribe to one or another form of liberalism) are internally diverse enough to permit moral disagreement and debate. Surely, however, cultures are not uniform with respect to a given stock of possible moral perspectives, nor are they uniform in the extent to which diversity of voice is permitted. Although these points alone may not provide sufficient cause for abandoning Walzer's view, their importance grows once we note that Walzer does not appear to have entertained how a dominant morality defines itself against an "other" which must be silenced or suppressed by virtue of its "existence" being the very antithesis of the dominant, power-based morality. This is not a matter of Republicans seeking victory over Democrats or right-to-life advocates denying the validity of pro-choice arguments, for such differences may not only exist within the compass of the prevailing moral discourse but may actually function to sustain the dominant under a Walzerian illusion of openness. Such types of difference, moreover, may be relatively trivial compared to forms of "otherness" associated with irrationality, immorality, or some other delegitimated trait that is being routinely suppressed.

The problematic nature of Walzer's position is further linked to his presumption of a culture's moral self-sufficiency. If existing moral cultures have no need for either divine pronouncements from the heavens or newly invented abstract ideals, then it would seem to follow that exposure to, and a need to learn from, alien cultures is unnecessary as well. In light of a culture's moral self-sufficiency, who needs them? But this implicit bias would seem to encourage an uncritical acceptance of a culture's prevailing system of signifiers. It needs stressing again: the forms of "otherness" revealed by Foucault are often not part of the open currency of an existing moral system but instead are suppressed as "other" while also existing within the system. Since on Walzer's view a culture need not exhibit any incentive to look beyond its own parameters for "otherness," there would appear also to be no incentive to look for suppressed "otherness" that exists "within." This is inadequate. Indeed, to state uncritically à la Walzer that a morally self-sufficient culture provides its own internal diversity may very well be to unwittingly abet systematic exclusion of that "otherness" which is intrinsic to a culture, which relates to power as opposition and support, but which is routinely denied visibility or voice.

Taylor's Neglect of Otherness "Within"

Over the years Taylor's reputation has been built on an elegant defense of the significance of meaning in understanding culture (e.g., Taylor, 1985b; 1985c). A central part of his thesis is that specific meanings are transformable according to the ways in which they are combined with other meanings.

> Things only have meanings in a field, that is, in relation to the meaning of other things. This means that there is no such thing as a single, unrelated meaningful element; and it means that changes in the other meanings in the field can involve changes in the given element. Meanings can't be identified except in relation to others, and in this way resemble words. The meaning of a word depends, for instance, on those words with which it contrasts, on those which define its place in the language (e.g., those defining

"determinable" dimensions, like color, shape), on those which define the activity or "language game" it figures in (describing, invoking, establishing communion), and so on. The relations between meanings in this sense are like those between concepts in a semantic field. (Taylor, 1977, 107)

Taylor's field of meanings, made up of unities and contrasts, and prone to shift as new combinations dictate, is constitutive of a hermeneutic circle. This is not to be confused with consensus, however. Consensus invites a view of culture as monolithic and agreed upon by all participants, whereas Taylor's preferred hermeneutic view, in contrast, acknowledges differences within a culture, as well as significant cleavages with respect to norms, values, and beliefs. The beauty of the hermeneutic circle, Taylor argues, is that it provides an ambit of common intersubjective meanings within which differences may be negotiated and resolved.

Common meanings are the basis of community. Intersubjective meaning gives a people a common language to talk about social reality and a common understanding of certain norms, but only with common meanings does this common reference work contain significant common actions, celebrations, and feelings. These are objects in the world that everybody shares. This is what makes community. (1985b, 39)

Taylor's hermeneutic circle here appears only slightly less self-sufficient than Walzer's idea of a shared moral culture. Unlike Walzer, however, Taylor emphasizes the need for a culture to reflect seriously upon its dealings with other cultures. This not so much for what another culture in and of itself intrinsically has to offer. Taylor's writings show, for example, that he has little if any respect for nonscientific forms of reason as found in technologically underdeveloped countries (1982, 87–105). Moreover, it is not clear that a host culture can ever be capable of adequately understanding an alien culture in the alien culture's own terms (e.g., Gadamer, 1975; Warnke, 1987). Taylor does acknowledge, however, the importance of reading an alien culture, not so much to add new meanings to an already existing stock, but to incite hermeneutically sensitive readers to reflect upon their own circle of meanings with the aim of furthering cultural self-understanding. To this end, Taylor (1985b, 129) advocates a language of "perspicuous contrast," which places a value on reaching an understanding of others' cultural practices "in relation to ours," as expressed in our own commonly shared field of meanings. However restrictive this view, it nevertheless acknowledges the importance of "otherness," if not for its intrinsic properties, then at least for its value as a stimulant of cultural self-understanding. Minimally, consideration of "otherness" provides an occasion for the hermeneutic circle to rearrange its internal configurations of meaning, thereby ensuring that the hermeneutic circle is neither static nor totally self-sufficient.

A serious deficiency is built into this view. Although Taylor recognizes "otherness" in the form of external cultures, he fails to recognize that which is "within" the prevailing culture—his culture—as suppressed or silenced "other." This "other within" is best thought of as the obverse side of the hermeneutic circle. It is "otherness" of meanings that are *"within"* the hermeneutic circle insofar as the complex of positive meanings depend upon what they are *not* as internal supports. It is "withinness" which is *"other"* in the sense that while these meanings are necessarily attached to their positive counterparts, they are hidden from view on account of containment, exclusion, or some other form of suppression. These meanings do not exist merely to be made sense of through a language of "perspicuous contrast." They do not exist merely to serve the positive understandings of cultural participants. For by their very being they negate the positivity of prevailing meanings. What Taylor fails to appreciate is that any language of "perspicuous contrast" on this view could not restrict itself to the completion of meaning. Rather, as the negativity of "otherness" reveals the impartial and contradictory nature of the positive, a language of "perspicuous contrast" would necessarily have to be a language of critique. The hermeneutic circle does not remain unbroken once the "other within" is allowed to speak its critique of the power/knowledge that has kept it suppressed.

Concluding Remarks

The Foucauldian dialectical perspective is broad enough to encompass both Walzer's and Taylor's own perspectives while overcoming each scholars' respective limitations. Consistent with Walzer's stress on the moral self-sufficiency of a shared culture, the Foucauldian approach need not necessarily look beyond a culture's borders in its quest for self-discovery. Against Walzer, however, the dialectical perspective does not rest content in the truth, knowledge, or rationality of its own internal workings but rather stresses the arbitrary and self-selecting nature of truth, knowledge, and rationality as it incites an awareness of that which exists "within" power's system of signs and meanings but which is often suppressed as "other."

In a manner similar to Taylor's emphasis on the need of an "other" to assist in filling in the hermeneutic circle, the Foucauldian dialectical perspective also stresses the importance of "otherness." But the "otherness" stressed by the latter already is *"within"* the hermeneutic circle, revealing itself as its obverse side once the circle is unfolded so as to expose the problematicity of the existence of silenced or suppressed "other." The Foucauldian perspective makes visible what rationality is not: madness, foolishness, and irrationality belong to the circle no less than their positive counterparts. So too with morality, as we saw in the discussion of the workers' discourse of resistance. Focus on the "other within," and its force as negation, is not aimed at completing the hermeneutic circle but rather seeks to expose the illusory quality of power's alleged positivity. With the confrontation between power and its contradictory "other" made visible and vocal, the circle is incited to transform itself in light of its contradictory nature (e.g., Fraser, 1981).

This said, we can now see how Foucault is able to critically analyze power while at the same time being bound up in power's embrace. On the one hand, his discourse is meant to reveal the "truth" of resistance. This "truth" of power's "other"—an "other" that is simultaneously "within" power's own system of signs—is given expression as Foucault introduces power to its own (heretofore suppressed) creations (the silence of the mad, the cries of the incarcerated, the critique which inheres in antilanguages and other subjugated discourses). On the other hand, resistance is what it is in virtue of its relationship of opposition and interdependence with power; neither power nor resistance can be viewed apart from their structured relatedness. Foucault's discursive offerings, therefore, can never work their way free of power's grasp. This said, however, it requires stressing that Foucault's articulation of resistance as power's "other" does offer some provision of freedom from power. For in bringing the "truth" of resistance up against reigning forms of power/knowledge, Foucault carves a conceptual space in which to critically expose power's suppression of its "other," and this is accomplished discursively in power's own terms.

Foucault's discourse should not be confused with the Wittgensteinian discursive bias that pervades Walzer's writings.[8] Foucault's intent is not to *reaffirm* who we are through explication of our shared language system. He does not seek to locate professed disagreement within a culture with the intent of instilling clarity where there is confusion over linguistic meaning; nor does he purport to reconcile dissenting parties by means of reference to the ways disputants share meanings across a range of ordinary, everyday, presumably unproblematic social contexts. While Foucault admits confinement within a range of discursive practices constitutive of his own subjectivity—how could he admit otherwise?—he is distrustful of everyday social contextual meaning. What is, and who we are, may indeed be a function of how meanings are systematized within culture, but these shared "truths," at the same time, are inextricably bound up with the constitution of power/knowledge. Foucault's discourse aims therefore not to show where dissent exists so as to achieve reconciliation but to locate where potentiated dissent is suppressed, and this in order to provide resistance with a fuller awareness of its own "truth" and to incite an open conflict between power/knowledge and the "truth" of its suppressed "other." The intent is neither that of overthrowing power nor necessarily that of stepping outside of power's instituted semiotic boundaries, but to bring out into the open that which had previously not been recognized in hopes of spurring a conflict "within" what might culminate in a rolling back of power's blanket of suppression.

Neither should Foucault's discourse be confused with that of Taylor's hermeneutically influenced writings. The hermeneutic discourse seeks to achieve a fusion of horizons, to be actualized under the auspices of an authoritative tradition. The "other" that confronts the hermeneutically contented traditionalist, as noted previously, is not permitted to be understood in its own terms. The hermeneutically contented traditionalist must necessarily interpret the "other" in his or her own (traditionally supplied) terms. And as the traditionalist's own horizon of meaning may be extended or filled in through a fusion with "other," so there is an inherent confidence in the ultimate validity of one's own tradition and the authority behind it.[9] However open, good-willed, and soul-searching the hermeneutically contented proves to be, "otherness" always ends up being understood in terms of authoritative traditions of meaning. Foucault's discourse, in contrast, predicated on a relentless dissatisfaction with the tradition that informs authoritatively his own cultural meanings, seeks to explicate an "otherness" that is "within" a cultural tradition with the aim of subverting the authority which the hermeneutically contented traditionalist accepts so uncritically. This does not entail extending or deepening one's own cultural meanings, but rather locating the source of internal contradictions and explicating them in terms that promote an "experience of discord" for all who are within the embrace of the ordinary, everyday "truths" of power/knowledge.

Foucault's discourse, then, does not escape the clutches of power, nor does it claim to do so. Neither does it compel power to submit to a power or authority higher than itself. Rather, inscribed as one of power's own creations, it beckons power—in power's own terms, here made visible (madness, perversion, deviance, immorality, irrationality)— to reflect critically upon itself and asks: Is it desirable that power/ knowledge should sustain itself in its current form in light of the "truth" of resistance that it has spawned "within" itself as "other"?

Notes

1. Expanded discussions of power are found in Foucault (1979, 32–69; 1980, 78–108, 109–33, 134–45). Discussions of the relatedness of power and discourse are found in Foucault (1972, 79–125, 215–37; 1978, 92–102).

2. For general commentary, see Smart (1983, 1985, 1986), Deleuze (1988), Dreyfus and Rabinow (1982), Gordon (1980), and Simon (1995).

3. This term has been used by Connolly (1983). See also Shapiro (1988).

4. Several more recent variants of critique point to the weaknesses of Foucault's treatment of power and resistance. See, for example, Brenner (1994), Cohen and Arato (1992, 255–98), Habermas (1990, 238–93), and Honneth (1991, 105–202).

5. Even when conveyed in its most cruel and inhumane forms, e.g., though the terrifying apparatuses of torture or the scaffold, "truth" is opposed by "countertruths" of carnival wherein rules of rationality and order are inverted in ways that mock authority and transform villains into heroes and the victimized into saints. See especially Foucault (1979, 32–69). Also of relevance here is Bakhtin (1984), Huspek and Comerford (1996), and Scott (1990).

6. Not so, however, when they talk to the boss; for in such instances the workers feel compelled to use the boss's terms of discourse. On this point, see Huspek (1986, 1989, 1993, 1994a) and Huspek and Comerford (1996).

7. My treatment of Walzer in relation to Foucault has profited from Constable's (1991) rigorous discussion.

8. This bias is evident in the prefatory remarks of Walzer (1983, xi–xvi).

9. For arguments regarding the role of authority in hermeneutic inquiry, see Gadamer (1976, 18–43) and Habermas (1988, 143–70).

References

Althusser, L. (1969). *For Marx*. Harmondsworth, England: Penguin.

———. (1971). *Lenin and Philosophy*. London: New Left.

Arendt, H. (1969). *On Violence*. New York: Harcourt, Brace and World.

Bakhtin, M. (1984). *Rabelais and His World*. Bloomington: Indiana University Press.

Barber, B. (1984). *Strong Democracy: Participatory Politics for a New Age*. Berkeley: University of California Press.

Brenner, N. (1994). Foucault's new functionalism. *Theory and Society* 23(5):679–710.

Clegg, S. (1989). *Frameworks of Power*. London: Sage.

Cohen, J., and A. Arato. (1992). *Civil Society and Political Theory*. Cambridge, Mass.: MIT Press.

Connolly, W. (1983). Discipline, politics, and ambiguity. *Political Theory* 11(3):325–41.

———. (1985). Taylor, Foucault and Otherness. *Political Theory* 13(3):365–76.

114   *Michael Huspek*

Constable, M. (1991). Foucault and Walzer: Sovereignty, strategy and the state. *Polity* 24(2):269–93.

Dallmayr, F. (1984). *Polis and Praxis*. Cambridge, Mass.: MIT Press.

Deleuze, G. (1988). *Foucault*. Minneapolis: University of Minnesota Press.

Dreyfus, H., and P. Rabinow. (1982). *Michel Foucault: Beyond Structuralism and Hermeneutics*. Chicago: University of Chicago.

Foucault, M. (1972). *The Archaeology of Knowledge*. New York: Harper and Row.

———. (1973). *Madness and Civilization*. New York: Random House.

———. (1978). *The History of Sexuality: An Introduction*. Vol. 1. New York: Vintage.

———. (1979). *Discipline and Punish*. New York: Vintage.

———. (1980). *Power/Knowledge*. (C. Gordon, Ed.) New York: Pantheon.

———. (1982). The subject and power. In H. Dreyfus and P. Rabinow (Eds.): *Michel Foucault: Beyond structuralism and hermeneutics*. Chicago: University of Chicago.

Fraser, N. (1981). Foucault on modern power: Empirical insights and normative confusions. *Praxis International* 1:272–87.

Gadamer, H-G. (1975). *Truth and Method*. New York: Seabury Press.

———. (1976). On the scope of hermeneutic reflection. In D. Lange (Ed.): *Philosophical hermeneutics*. Berkeley: University of California Press.

Gordon, C. (1980). Afterword. In C. Gordon (Ed.): *Power/Knowledge*.

Habermas, J. (1988). *On the Logic of the Social Sciences*. Cambridge, Mass.: MIT Press.

———. (1990). *The Philosophical Discourse of Modernity*. Cambridge, Mass.: MIT Press.

Honneth, A. (1991). *The Critique of Power: Reflective Stages in a Critical Social Theory*. Cambridge, Mass.: MIT Press.

Huspek, M. (1986). Linguistic variation, context and meaning. *Language in Society* 15(2):149–63.

———. (1989). Linguistic variability and power. *Journal of Pragmatics* 13(5):661–83.

———. (1989/1990). The idea of ethnography and its relation to cultural critique. *Research on Language and Social Interaction* 23:293–312.

———. (1993). Dueling structures: Toward a theory of resistance in discourse. *Communication Theory* 3(1):1–25.

———. (1994a). Oppositional codes and social class relations. *British Journal of Sociology* 45(1):79–102.

———. (1994b). Critical and nonfoundational analyses: Are they contradictory or complementary? In B. Kovačić *New Approaches to*

Organizational Communication. Albany: State University of New York Press.

Huspek, M., and K. Kendall. (1991). On withholding political voice: An analysis of the political vocabulary of a "nonpolitical" speech community. *Quarterly Journal of Speech* 77(1):1–19.

Huspek, M., and L. Comerford. (1996). How science is subverted: Penology and prison inmates' resistance. *Communication Theory* 6(4); 335–360.

Krips, II. (1990). Power and resistance. *Philosophy of the Social Sciences* 20(2):170–82.

Lukes, S. (1974). *Power: A Radical View.* London: Macmillan.

MacIntyre, A. (1981). *After virtue.* Notre Dame, Ind.: University of Notre Dame Press.

Pateman, C. (1970). *Participation and Democratic Theory.* Cambridge, England: Cambridge University Press.

Scott, J. (1990). *Domination and the Arts of Resistance: Hidden Transcripts.* New Haven, Conn.: Yale University Press.

Shapiro, M. (1981). *Language and Political Understanding: The Politics of Discursive Practices.* New Haven, Conn.: Yale University Press.

———. (1988). *The Politics of Representation.* Madison: University of Wisconsin.

Sibley, M. (1970). *Political Ideas and Ideologies.* New York: Harper and Row.

Simon, J. (1995). *Foucault and the Political.* New York: Routledge.

Smart, B. (1983). *Foucault, Marxism and Critique.* London: Routledge and Kegan Paul.

———. (1985). *Michel Foucault.* London: Routledge.

———. (1986). The politics of truth and the problem of hegemony. In D. Hoy (Ed.): *Foucault: A Critical Reader.* New York: Basil Blackwell.

Taylor, C. (1977). Interpretation and the sciences of man. In F. Dallmayr and T. McCarthy (Eds.): *Understanding and social inquiry.* Notre Dame, Ind.: University of Notre Dame Press.

———. (1982). Rationality. In M. Hollis and S. Lukes (Eds.): *Rationality and Relativism.* Oxford, England: Blackwell.

———. (1984). Foucault on freedom and truth. *Political Theory* 12(May):152–83.

———. (1985a). Connolly, Foucault and Truth. *Political Theory* 13(3):377–85.

———. (1985b). *Human Agency and Language: Philosophical Papers.* Vol. 1. Cambridge, England: Cambridge University Press.

———. (1985c). *Philosophy and the human sciences: Philosophical papers* (Vol. 2). Cambridge: Cambridge University Press.

Walzer, M. (1982). *Interpretation and Social Criticism.* Cambridge, Mass.: Harvard University Press.

————. (1983). *Spheres of Justice: A Defense of Pluralism and Equality.* New York: Basic Books.

————. (1986). The politics of Michel Foucault. In D. Hoy (Ed.): *Foucault: A Critical Reader.* New York: Basil Blackwell.

Warnke, G. (1987). *Gadamer: Hermeneutics, Tradition, and Reason.* Stanford, Calif.: Stanford University Press.

Chapter Five

Foucault Inserted: Philosophy, Struggle, and Transgression

Gary P. Radford

Michel Foucault has been described as a "central figure in the most noteworthy flowering of oppositional intellectual life in the twentieth century West" (Said, 1988, 1). His works can be considered opposi-tional in at least two respects: (1) They give space and shape to the stifled and dominated voices of "other" as variously defined by the norms of classical and contemporary rationality, and (2) they radically reconfigure the role of the intellectual who produces such accounts. In solidarity with his subject matter, Foucault's work represents an explicit attempt to speak from a position of "other," a place that exists in con-tradistinction to any intellectual tradition which may claim to catego-rize and incorporate it. His historical accounts of the asylum (Foucault, 1988a), the clinic (Foucault, 1975), and the prison (Foucault, 1979), for example, are simultaneously attempts to turn history against itself, to "sever its connection to memory, its metaphysical and anthropological model, and construct a countermemory—a transformation of history into a totally different form of time" (Foucault, 1977, 180).

The failure of contemporary scholarship to adequately categorize and trace a continuous development within Foucault's oeuvre is indica-tive of this goal. Siegel (1990) remarks that Foucault's work is noted for its "remarkable discontinuities—sharp changes of orientation and vocabulary that he took pleasure in throwing like sand in the face of anyone who tied to fix his features" (273). Similarly, Bernstein (1994) writes that:

> as any close reader of Foucault knows, his writings are filled with surprises and novel twists. It is almost as if Foucault started each project afresh, bracketing what he had written previously, constantly experimenting with new lines

of inquiry. This is one reason why reading Foucault is so provocative, disconcerting and frustrating. For just when we think we have grasped what Foucault is saying and showing, he seems to dart off in new directions (and even seems to delight in frustrating attempts to classify and fix what he is doing). (211)

These characterizations, however, belie the seriousness of Foucault's purpose. The "pleasure" and "delight" attributed by Seigel and Bernstein are not the rewards of arbitrary mischief. For Foucault, the development of a theoretical account is an act with implications and effects. Deleuze characterizes theory and practice as being inseparable where "practice is a set of relays from one theoretical point to another, and theory is a relay from one practice to another" (Foucault and Deleuze, 1977, 206). The constitution of such relays is itself an act against a prevailing power structure. The aim becomes one of

revealing and undermining power where it is most invisible and insidious. It is not to "awaken consciousness" that we struggle . . . but to sap power, to take power; it is an activity conducted alongside those who struggle for power, and not their illumination from a safe distance. A "theory" is the regional system of this struggle. (208)

This chapter draws upon the Foucauldian œuvre as a theoretical point from which to engage a form of "invisible" power inherent in contemporary U.S. Communication Theory—the adoption of a particular and highly selective version of the philosophy of science based in the works of Karl Popper and Thomas Kuhn, referred to here as a "received philosophy of science." The task of the chapter is twofold: (1) to describe the dynamics of this received philosophy of science's operation within the processes of knowledge production in the communication field and (2) to identify and create conditions through which these limits can be transgressed or, in Foucault's (1988b) terms, "to disturb people's mental habits, the way they do and think things, to dissipate what is familiar and accepted, to reexamine rules and institutions on the basis of this reproblematization" (265). The insertion of Foucault's (1972a) "archaeology of knowledge" has appeal in terms of both of these challenges. The act of inserting Foucault is to open up a pandora's box of conflict and struggle where even the traditional roles assigned to the theoretician/philosopher advocating this insertion must be questioned and openly resisted. The Foucauldian voice will be allowed to shift and slide in order to escape the categories of the prevailing received view against which it is directed. As the explicit perpetrator of these acts, the role of the intellectual is "no longer to place himself 'somewhat ahead and to the side' in order to express the stifled truth of the collectivity; rather, it is to struggle against the forms of power that transform him into its object and instrument in the sphere of 'knowledge,' 'truth,' 'consciousness,' and 'discourse.' " (Foucault and Delueze, 1977, 207–8). Jansen (1993) points out that the possibilities inherent in these militant and subversive aspects of Foucault's work have yet to be systematically explored as a reflexive and radical challenge to received/conventional/textbook understandings of disciplinary histories and research philosophies. Following Jansen, this chapter offers such an exploration.

A Received Philosophy of Science for Communication Theory

Received Views

The region of power to be addressed here is a "received view of the philosophy of science." The idea of a received view is not new. Communication scholars have recently come to address the idea of a "received history" of their field (see Delia, 1987). This received view is a particular account of the history of communication research transmitted through textbooks and the socialization processes for prospective and practicing communication scholars. The development of a sense of tradition through history, as articulated in accounts such as Rogers (1994), provides a common foundation for the diverse range of theory and practice that comprises the field of communication. However, the nature of this "history," and its role with respect to communication theory, is receiving serious attention in its own right (see Delia, 1987; Hardt, 1992, 1993; Jansen, 1993; Nerone, 1993; Peters, 1986; Simpson, 1994). A forming consensus suggests that the adequacy of the received history as an account of particular figures and events is less important than the particular definitions, practices, and interests that it serves to privilege. The historical account becomes a component in a new problematic: the creation, maintenance, and legitimation of systems of "power/knowledge" (see Foucault, 1979, 1980).

The same approach can be taken with respect to a received philosophy of science. Like a received history, a received philosophy of science organizes discourse about the nature of communication theorizing in a particular way. As a component in a system of power/knowledge, the received philosophy of science serves to consolidate and privilege certain definitions and practices within the communication discipline. Craig (1993) captures the essence of the received philosophy of science addressed here in ironic style. As recently as the 1970s, "communication researchers were quite sure they knew what theory was.... Optimism prevailed. Philosophers of science ... had pointed the way to a social science of communication and we had only to follow their guidance" (Craig, 1993, 27). Two significant figures stand out as guides. One is Sir Karl Popper: "we had learned from Popper (1959) that the *sine qua non* of scientific theory was *falsifiability*" (Craig, 1993, 27). The other is Thomas Kuhn, whose postpositivist history and philosophy of science enabled communication theorists to see that "communication science was in a 'preparadigmatic' state as we searched for a paradigm" (Craig, 1993, 27). Popper provided the touchstone for an understanding of theory building and testing. Kuhn symbolized the rationale for the discipline's identity as a distinct entity, even with its ambiguous status as a "preparadigm."

With the philosophies of Popper and Kuhn identified as the received philosophy of science in most advanced undergraduate and introductory graduate studies of communication, theorists and researchers are free to occupy themselves with the business of creating theory and doing research. The activities they engaged in and the identity of the field in which they identified themselves were not considered problematic or even relevant. This kind of talk can now be shifted to and partitioned within the domain of the communication philosophers and metatheorists in an intellectual division of labor. However, Popper and Kuhn represent a significant choice of philosophy from the diverse range of philosophers of science who constitute the subject. For example, Feyerabend (1975, 1979), Fuller (1988), Lakatos (1979), and Laudan (1977, 1984), among others, advocate positions that may be quite different. The foregrounding of this choice is important because the possibilities of choice are systematically masked by the prevailing received view for a number of reasons.

Somewhat ironically in the context of this chapter, it is Kuhn (1970a) who develops this claim with respect to the use of scientific textbooks and their portrayal of history, and his analysis is relevant here. Kuhn argues that textbooks address themselves to an already articulated and accepted body of problems, data, and theory to which a scientific community is committed at the time they are written. However, to fulfill this function, they need not provide authentic information about the way in which these bases were first recognized and then embraced. Indeed, Kuhn suggests that there are good reasons why such texts should be "systematically misleading" (1970a, 137). Textbooks must begin by truncating the sense of a discipline's history and proceed to supply a substitute for what was eliminated. Characteristically, textbooks of science contain just a bit of history, either in an introductory chapter or, more often, in scattered references to the great heroes of an earlier age. This leads Kuhn to conclude that:

the textbook derived tradition in which scientists come to sense their participation is one that, in fact, never existed. For reasons that are both obvious and highly functional, science textbooks . . . refer only to that part of the work of past scientists that can easily be viewed as contributions to the statement and solutions of the texts' paradigm problems. (138)

The same argument is made here that Popper and Kuhn have come to be recognized as "great heroes," and the selective readings and uses of their works have, in turn, provided a basis for the creation and maintenance of particular disciplinary traditions. But as with accounts of history, it is possible to regard such deployments as being systematically misleading, depending on the uses to which these accounts are put. Kuhn (1974) has lamented that:

Monitoring conversations, particularly among the book's ["The Structure of Scientific Revolutions"] enthusiasts, I have sometimes found it hard to believe that all parties to the discussion had been engaged with the same volume. Part of the reason for its success is, I regretfully conclude, that it can be nearly all things to all people. (459)

Fuller (1992) remarks that "Kuhn has disavowed all of the more exciting and radical theses imputed to him by friends and foes alike" (242) and that "it is doubtful that there has ever been another academic who has met the greatness thrust upon him with such apparent ingratitude" (242). In fact, Fuller goes as far as comparing the reception of Kuhn's words with the fates which befall Chauncey Gardiner, the protagonist of Jerzy Kosinski's (1970) novel *Being There,* whose simple and literal references to gardening and television, through wild misinterpretation, propel him toward the presidency of the United States!

Kuhn's writings on the role of history in science can be turned around to reflect on the role of Kuhn, as a philosophical hero, in the production of communication theory. In a similar way to that of the received history being criticized on the grounds that it serves to marginalize and exclude certain strands of thought, the same argument is made here with respect to the reliance on a very narrow interpretation of the philosophy of science. This interpretation, and the role of Popper and Kuhn within it, is described in the following sections.

A Received View of the Enlightenment Project

At the outset, it is important to emphasize that the received philosophy of science described here is a story. The philosophy of science is considered as a useful fiction that makes possible, through its accounts of what science is and what scientists do, certain kinds (and not others) of theorizing and research activity. The received philosophy embodies an account of the Enlightenment but is not intended as a history of Enlightenment science or the development of modern physics and, in that sense, makes no claims to accuracy with respect to "what really happened." Crucial to this discussion is that a received view is articulated in modern communication theory. It is, as Foucault (1972a) would term it, a "fact of discourse." What it means is less important than the fact it is uttered. The received philosophy of science, then, is a type of abbreviated account found in such places as textbooks and introductory classes in communication theory. It consists of a particular account of the Enlightenment project and its development with respect to contemporary views on relativity and uncertainty.

The Enlightenment project is described in terms of a release from the dogmas of religious thought in an attempt to see the world as it "really is" (Brinton, 1967). It is depicted as a movement inspired by optimism; a demonstration of the power of reason to discern truth and acquire knowledge. Popper (1965) describes this period in the following way:

> At the heart of this new optimistic view of the possibility of knowledge lies the doctrine that *truth is manifest*. Truth may perhaps be veiled. But it may reveal itself. And if it does not reveal itself, it may be revealed by us. But once the naked truth stands revealed before our eyes, we have the power to see it, to distinguish it from falsehood, and to know that it *is* truth. (5, emphasis in original)

Rorty (1982) expresses this as follows:

> When Galileo said that the Book of Nature was written in the language of mathematics, he meant that his reductionistic, mathematical vocabulary didn't just *happen* to work, but that it worked *because* that was the way things *really were*. He meant that the vocabulary worked because it fitted the universe as a key fits a lock. (191–92, emphasis in original)

Considered against the Enlightenment backdrop, modern science is characterized by the received view as aspiring to discover the generalizable something else; systems of laws and rules that lie beyond the realm of the immediately observable. The objective is to describe the underlying schemes in which an individual event or observation fits and from which future events can be predicted. These systems are expressed as theories, which become the basis of hypotheses to be tested against empirical evidence.

The purpose of formulating general laws and theories is to provide the world with a language in which its assumed natural laws and structures can be expressed. As Hesse (1981) describes, "science is ideally a linguistic system in which true propositions are in one-to-one relation to facts, including facts that are not directly observed because they involve hidden entities or properties" (xi). Similarly, van Fraassen (1980) describes this orientation as assuming that "the picture which science gives us of the world is a true one, faithful in its details, and the entities postulated in science really exist: the advances of science are discoveries, not inventions" (6–7). The ultimate objective of the Enlightenment project as characterized by the received view is to match the structure of linguistic propositions to the real structures of the world such that they will become, in Rorty's (1979) terms, a "mirror of nature" (12). Language was important because it could *represent* the world. Language functioned to name, pattern, connect, and disconnect objects and make them visible in the transparency of words. One did not see the words themselves, only that which the words represented, and revealed. This is not to say that language fit nature in the Enlightenment period, or even that people believed that it did. According to Foucault (1973), this was the way language *worked* in that age. Discourse was used in this way to articulate problematics. Foucault (1973) argues that in this historical period, language worked as a spontaneous grid, or table, that ordered representations of nature in its reflection of the actual order of nature itself.

The received philosophy of science espoused in contemporary discussions of communication theory deploys this "one-to-one correspondence" view of language and reality as a kind of foil; the point of comparison and contrast that demonstrates how modern thinking on science, knowledge, and language has progressed. The contemporary view holds that there is no absolute certainty in the representations provided by language. The progression to this view is based on the "historical fact" of a fundamental shift in thought located in the early twentieth century and attributed to work in theoretical physics (see Gamow, 1966; Hawking, 1988). The new physics advocated the view that knowledge of the world, and hence, the nature of that world, was fundamentally related to the frame of reference of the observer. There could be no observation of an object or an event that is not relative to the position of the observer. As such, no knowledge was possible that was not relative to the frame of reference of a knower. The Enlightenment project of the direct linguistic representation of absolute knowledge became an ideal to which the practice of science could aspire but never attain.

The assumption of uncertainty became an integral part of the way philosophies of science framed the issue of language. The role of language in science could no longer be one of "pure description," since the object or event to be described was always "contaminated" by the presence of the describer. Language becomes problematized in terms of demarcation rather than representation, i.e., how can a scientific knowledge claim to be differentiated from a nonscientific one? This view is clearly expressed and developed in the philosophy of science of Sir Karl Popper and has been predominant in the received philosophy of science, with the exception of Kuhn, in the conceptualizing of modern communication science (see Berger and Chaffee, 1987).

Popper's Problem of Demarcation

Popper's (1959) view of scientific knowledge is explicitly expressed in terms of the "problem of demarcation" (34), i.e., the identification of a criterion by which the knowledge of the empirical sciences could be distinguished from mathematical and metaphysical systems of knowledge. Popper (1959) writes:

> The task of formulating an acceptable definition of the idea of empirical science is not without its difficulties. Some of these arise from *the fact that there must be many theoretical systems* with a logical structure very similar to the one which at any particular time is the accepted system of empirical science. This situation is sometimes described by saying that there are a great many—presumably an infinite number—of "logically possible worlds." Yet the system called "empirical science" is intended to represent only *one* world: the "real" world or the "world of our experience." But how is the system that represents our world of experience to be distinguished? The answer is: by the fact that it has been submitted to tests, and has stood up to tests. (33, emphasis in original)

The meaningfulness of a scientific knowledge claim rests on the assumption that there exists, independent of any knower, an objective world. It is only on the basis of this assumption that science is able to justify the knowledge it generates. Against this objective world, knowledge claims, in the form of theories and hypotheses, are tested through prediction, experiment, and observation. However, knowledge claims are not based on the criteria that they represent a one-to-one correspondence with the world but rather they must be consistent with other knowledge claims that have followed the same methods and testing. Popper (1959) believed that "scientific theories are never fully justifiable or verifiable, but . . . are nevertheless testable. I shall therefore say that the *objectivity* of scientific statements lies in the fact that they can be *inter-subjectively tested*" (44, emphasis in original). In Popper's philosophy, this requires a language of testing and method that is neutral and universal among the practicing scientists who deploy it; a language that consists of a basic vocabulary of words attached to nature in ways that are unproblematic and ultimately independent of theory. Scientists may disagree about the contents of particular theories, but there should be no disagreement about the means by which such theories should be tested. On this foundation critical discussion can take place with a common vocabulary informing both sides. Such discussion is central to Popper's (1970) view of science since "the aim [of science] is to find theories which, in the light of critical discussion, get nearer to the truth" (57). This works, however, only if one can assume that the scientists involved in this critical discussion of theories are speaking about the same things or even that they are speaking the same language.

Kuhn's Critique of Popper

Kuhn (1970a, 1970b, 1977) explicitly questions the role for language proposed by Popper and suggests that the use of language by scientists is not, and cannot be, as neutral nor as universal as Popper implies. The core of Kuhn's philosophy of science is that all scientists do not speak the same language but rather speak an array of languages which vary with respect to particular paradigms. Kuhn (1970a) argues that knowledge claims are contested with respect to a socially constructed, as opposed to purely objective, notion of world. The paradigm is like a social institution in prescribing the everyday activity of the scientist, making it consistent with the behaviors and beliefs of other scientists. The account of Kuhn (1970a) has been seen by some to be a powerful challenge to the view that science deals with an objective world (Holcomb, 1989; McRae, 1988; Rorty, 1979). For example, Holcomb (1989) argues that Kuhn has been cast as an "anti-objectivist" since he rejects the idea that choices between theories are made with respect to consensual *values* rather than objective facts. The role of theory in the context of the paradigm is one akin to providing the scientific community with a common language. Theory specifies which problems are relevant, provides the vocabulary to express these problems, and directs the scientist to appropriate methodologies. Research activity directed by the common ground of theory is referred to by Kuhn as "normal science."

　　In terms of claims such as these, it is possible to describe a significant division in the views of Popper and Kuhn (Gupta, 1993; Lakatos and Musgrave, 1970). For Popper (1959), the claim to scientific validity is one of theory (or conjecture) being tested against the empirical reality of an objective world. For Kuhn (1970a) the claim is one of "rightness" against the normatively regulated framework of the consensually produced paradigm. In other words, normal science, with its suspension of a totally critical stance with respect to an objective world, derives knowledge on the basis of a social construction. For Kuhn (1970a), an "objective world" in Popper's (1959) sense can only be known via the systems of thought and discursive potentialities of a socially constructed paradigm. The paradigm is primary to the objective world since without it there could be no coherent description, theory, method, and ultimately, no basis for determining a scientific knowledge claim. To be critical of an existing paradigm demands a perspective from which to formulate and articulate that critique. Kuhn's (1970a) philosophy accounts for the progression of scientific knowledge by the overthrow of paradigms in times of scientific revolution. He speaks of one worldview being replaced by another, but not in terms of one group having recourse to the truth of an objective world. The change is centered in the claims made about the object or world of study.

Kuhn's philosophy of science offers a more sophisticated account of language and science relative to Popper's. He suggests that Popper has not considered the nature of language deeply enough. Language cuts up the world in different ways so that objects and events "are parts of a language conditioned or language-correlated way of seeing the world" (Kuhn, 1970b, 274). There is no neutral sublinguistic framework available that can cut across this, as Popper advocated. Kuhn (1977) claims that:

> Proponents of different theories (or different paradigms, in the broader sense of the term) speak different languages— languages expressing different cognitive commitments, suitable for different worlds. Their abilities to grasp each other's viewpoints are therefore limited by the imperfections of the processes of translation and of reference determination. (xxii–xxiii).

Kuhn identifies language as an a priori mediator of experience; a structure that is constitutive of any perception, observation, or description performed by the scientist. At a time of revolution, changes in paradigms alter the relationship between language and experience in profound ways. Kuhn (1970b) suggests that at such times "two men whose discourse had proceeded for some time with apparently full understanding may suddenly find themselves responding to the same stimulus with incompatible descriptions or generalizations" (276). Such differences are not superficial in Kuhn's account: "They are not simply about names or language but equally and inseparably about nature. We cannot say with any assurance that the two men even see the same thing, possess the same data, but identify or interpret it differently" (276).

Suppressing the Problematization of Language

Kuhn's philosophy highlights the role of language in the production and understanding of scientific knowledge. However, Kuhn's account of language does not open up the domain of scientific knowledge for further scrutiny but contributes instead to closing it down. If language is so crucial to scientific thought, as Kuhn suggests, it would seem reasonable to consider its role in the production of the objective world as opposed to its role in representing such a world. However, like Popper, Kuhn advances a view of communication that is ultimately justified by a singular reality of experience that is independent of language. As Kuhn (1970c) himself points out, "on almost all the occasions when we turn explicitly to the same problems, Sir Karl's view of science and my own are very nearly identical" (1) and that "we both insist that scientists may properly aim to invent theories that *explain* observed phenomena and that do so in terms of *real* objects, whatever the latter phrase may mean" (2, emphasis in original).

Kuhn's decision to adopt this assumption is important because it suppresses the possibility of addressing the role of language qua language in science (as opposed to language qua world). Instead, Kuhn takes as his project the question of how individuals in scientific communities produce language and paradigms in terms of psychological and sociological explanations. For Kuhn, meaning is located in the subjectivity of the individual scientist, who, in turn, is positioned within a community of like-minded scientists. This leads Kuhn (1970b) to the nature of the individual scientist's "neural apparatus" as the ultimate explanation of scientific knowledge. Scientists "process" stimuli and derive meaning from them by virtue of their "educational programming" in the scientific community:

> I think it likely myself that much or all of the clustering of stimuli into similarity sets takes place in the stimulus-to-sensation portion of our neural processing apparatus; that the educational programming of that apparatus takes place when we are presented with stimuli that we are told emanate from members of the same similarity class; and that, after programming has been completed, we recognize, say, cats and dogs. (267)

Kuhn (1970b) further elaborates on the priority given to objective experience and the neural apparatus available to process that experience: "Though they have no direct access to it, the stimuli to which the participants in a communication breakdown respond are, under pain of solipsism, the same. So is their general neural apparatus, however different the programming" (276). In Kuhn's philosophy, the world is constant, as is the neural apparatus of the brains of scientists. Problematic are the interpretations that the scientists make, which are dependent on the linguistic categories that have been "programmed" into their heads by the community that creates and maintains a paradigm.

The term "community" is used restrictively by Kuhn (1970b) referring to the particular group of scientists who engage in the particular research activity. The individual is immersed in this community and comes to share its "world":

> Those experiences are presented to us during education and professional initiation by a generation which already knows what they are exemplars of. By assimilating a sufficient number of exemplars, we learn to recognize and work with the world our teachers already know. (275)

Thus, the second problematic of scientific knowledge is the group that programs. As Kuhn (1970a) asserts, "scientific knowledge, like language, is intrinsically the common property of a group or else nothing at all. To understand it we shall need to know the special characteristics of the groups that create and use it" (209–10).

Kuhn's account of language and knowledge is totally self-contained within science. This strategy enables Kuhn, like Popper, to argue that so-called external influences are of little concern to an understanding of scientific knowledge. For example, Kuhn (1977) states that "compared with other professional and creative pursuits, the practitioners of a mature science are effectively insulated from the cultural milieu in which they live their extraprofessional lives" (119). There is no significant relation between scientific communities and other communication communities regarding the question of knowledge of the real world. Knowledge is always driven and legitimized internally by scientists themselves. Kuhn (1977) states:

> The practitioners of a mature science are men trained in a sophisticated body of traditional theory and of instrumental, mathematical, and verbal technique. As a result, they constitute a special subculture, one whose members are the exclusive audience for, and judges of, each other's work. The problems on which such specialists work are no longer presented by the external society but by an internal challenge to increase the scope and precision of the fit between existing theory and nature (119).

Kuhn frames the production of scientific discourse in terms of a privileged community distinct and independent from the external society. Science does not, and need not, interact with other realms of discourse, such as the artistic or the literary. Scientific knowledge is demarcated by the very language that is produced within its paradigms. Paradigms are language machines, producing not only statements but "knowledge." Indeed, science is not merely different in the nature of its claims but in the intrinsic nature of the language it produces and deploys. Kuhn's principle of incommensurability ensures the impossibility of adequately translating the discourse of one paradigm to another. By extention, it also denies access to the domain of the speech of everyday life. Since scientists speak languages different from all aspects of human speech, their domain cannot be seriously challenged by knowledge claims expressed in a different language from outside. The demarcation is total, and science's privileged access to claims concerning the objective world is ensured.

Language and Control

Behind the differences in the two philosophies, the objectives of Kuhn and Popper are identical (see Notturno, 1984). The acceptance of a received view based on Popper and Kuhn is an implicit endorsement of a kind of language *control,* either through the imposition of a neutral and universal discourse of method or the educational programming that takes place within the confines of a scientific paradigm. It is only as a result of control that scientific truth can be produced. As a consequence, the process of control is, and must be, a process of exclusion. In both cases, the claim of the differentiation of scientific knowledge is based on the self-evident warrant of internal criteria.

Knowledge produced by science is considered "scientific" by criteria determined by the institution of science itself. This particular philosophy of science does not stand above the texts produced by working scientists as detached and objective accounts of the workings of science. Rather, its appearance and subsequent institutionalization within the practices of science (see Fuller, 1992: Holland, 1990; Gholson and Barker, 1985), including communication studies (Dervin et al., 1989a, 1989b), represent texts that stand alongside the scientific discourse and legitimate its knowledge claims. They reinforce the claim that science is a body of knowledge insulated unto itself. These texts are constituted and used by the scientific community to organize, justify, and demarcate their claims to knowledge. Ultimately, the philosophies play a role in the suppression of alternative systems of knowledge by an institutionalized and systematic unwillingness to accept their languages as "scientific" and meaningful. As Wilmott (1993) argues, Kuhnian terminology "unnecessarily constrains the process of theory development within polarized sets of assumptions about science and society" (682). Philosophies of science are integral parts of the mechanisms that produce and perpetrate privilege, control, and exclusion. The philosophies of Popper and Kuhn are caught in the web of discourse that forms the new problematic of language, knowledge, and power.

When communication theorists advocate Popper and Kuhn as central components of the way they explain their practice, they must also invoke this particular relationship of science, language, and knowledge and the web of inclusion and exclusion that it creates. This understanding enables one to question the ways in which this philosophy is used in communication theory and what this use *enables*. For example, Holland (1990) claims that:

> for anybody wishing to challenge authorities and orthodoxies, Kuhn provides the opportunity to identify a ruling paradigm (resonant with radical ideas about a ruling class). They might then go on to declare a new paradigm, which of course would not be understood by their blinkered predecessors. (23)

Notturno (1984) claims that, far from opening up productive discourse, "Kuhn's description of science is sometimes appealed to as a justification for ignorance" (289). Kuhn's philosophy becomes part of a discursive strategy rather than a philosophical foundation, and this deployment is replete with structures of power and self-interest.

Given this discussion, a new problematic emerges that considers the received philosophy of science not in terms of a philosophical foundation but in its deployment in particular discursive strategies. The analysis of this problematic requires a new voice in which the assumptions of the received philosophy of science are rendered a problem rather than a fact. That voice is found in Michel Foucault's (1972a) "archaeology of knowledge."

Foucault Inserted

The objective of this section is not to evaluate or offer a replacement for the received philosophy of science, either with a Foucauldian philosophy or any other. A Foucauldian philosophy does not offer the certainty of a secure philosophical foundation. Indeed, it seeks to deny this possibility, and as a result, some communication scholars find this position disturbing and ultimately unproductive. For example, Ellis (1991) writes that "post-structuralist concepts of language are so misguided that any serious scholar, in particular communication scholar, must surely abandon them" (213). However, the value in introducing

Foucault to the mix lies in its capacity to increase the awareness that the received philosophy of science represented by the names "Popper" and "Kuhn" is a choice of foundation, that choices can be made differently, and with this awareness exists the potential to open spaces for voices within contemporary theory that have either not been heard or have found expression and acceptance difficult.

Like the received philosophy of science, a Foucauldian conception of science and knowledge is grounded in particular concepts of communication. However, whereas the received philosophy uses language as a means of achieving demarcation and maintaining boundaries, Foucault offers a concept of "discourse" whose main objective is to dissolve and make problematic these boundaries. Foucault (1972a) argues that:

> We must . . . question those divisions or groupings with which we have become so familiar. . . . These divisions—whether our own, or those contemporary with the discourse under discussion—are always themselves reflexive categories, principles of classification, normative rules, institutionalized types; they, in turn, are facts of discourse that deserve to be analyzed beside others. (22)

The term "facts of discourse" is central to this claim. However, consistent with his thesis that familiar divisions are problematic, Foucault refuses to categorize his use of the term "discourse." The term is not intended to be fixed within the categories of an existing tradition, but is instead used as a free-floating term that may invoke any or all them. Foucault (1972a) writes:

> Instead of gradually reducing the rather fluctuating meaning of the word "discourse," I believe that I have in fact added to its meanings: treating it sometimes as the general domain of all statements, sometimes as an individualizable group of statements, and sometimes as a regulated practice that accounts for a certain number of statements; and have I not allowed this same word "discourse," which should have served as a boundary around the term "statement," to vary as I shifted my analysis or its point of application, as the statement itself shifted from view? (80)

Foucault encourages the abandonment of foundations and allows conceptions such as "language," "science," and "discourse" to fluctuate according to the specific conditions in which they are used. For Foucault, theoretical terms such as these are "local and regional . . . and not totalizing" (Foucault and Deleuze, 1977, 208). Therefore, the approach here is not to posit an "alternative" view of discourse and science and, so defined, state its relation, and possibly its superiority, to the received philosophy of science. The danger in doing so is that it immediately undermines the Foucauldian project; that of making strange those categories that are usually so familiar and to "formulate otherness and heterodoxy without domesticating them or turning them into doctrine" (Said, 1988, 6). Instead, the effect is that one must struggle to gain the sense in which Foucault uses terms such as "discourse" rather than to access the category which defines it. The tension and uncertainty that is produced is, in part, the effect Foucault is after.

There are boundaries for the use of "discourse," but these are explained in terms of the negative. The purpose of such boundaries is to show what discourse is not in an attempt to slip and evade the categories embedded in the systems of power that Foucault's (1972a) language seeks to undermine. Thus, a discursive analysis is different from the category of "language analysis" (traditional linguistics):

> The question posed by language analysis of some discursive fact or other is always: according to what rules has a particular statement been made, and consequently according to what rules could other similar statements be made? The description of the events of discourse poses a quite different question: how is it that one particular statement appeared rather than another? (27)

The concern with the rules by which a given claim can be considered scientific or not is at the heart of the received philosophy of science. But, at the risk of categorizing, one can say that Foucault's concept of discourse is an attempt to understand how *what* is said fits into a network that has its own history and conditions of existence. It dissolves the boundaries of taken-for-granted categories for thinking about discursive unities, including that of scientific disciplines such as communication. Foucault (1972a) argues:

> Before approaching, with any degree of certainty, a science, or novels, or political speeches, or the oeuvre of an author, or even a single book, the material with which one is dealing is, in its raw, neutral state, a population of events in the space of discourse in general. One is therefore led to the project of a pure description of discursive events as the horizon for the search for the unities that form within it. (27)

Another boundary condition is that discursive analyses are not to be confused with those produced by rhetoricians of science. This field of study attempts to produce metadiscourses which will account for scientific discursive practices through redescription so that "a perfect interpretation is one in which the subject of interpretation loses all of its recalcitrance and becomes transparent" (Gaonkar, 1993, 258). These redescriptions attempt to discover what lies beyond the statements of scientists in terms of the intentions of the speaking subject, their rhetorical strategies, or the goal of the practice. The rhetorician of science seeks to constitute another discourse that expresses what was being said in what was said. Rhetoricians might then be credited with seeing through the ontological sham. The rhetoricians, then, have "really understood" the craft of knowledge-making, not the scientist (Gergen, 1990).

Foucault's archaeology denies such a stance. Rhetoricians of science can no more really understand scientific knowledge than the scientist can. For Foucault, the object of interest is the *appearance* of discourse itself: "We must grasp the statement in the exact specificity of its occurrence; determine its conditions of existence, fix at least its limits, establish its correlations with other statements that may be connected with it, and show what other forms of statement it excludes" (27), and "the question proper to such an analysis might be formulated in this way: what is the specific existence that emerges from what is said and nowhere else?" (28). Rather than looking *behind* what is said in terms of a redescription that produces something different, Foucault looks to what is made possible from what is said.

The Absence of a Foucauldian Center

The rhetoric of science speaks from within a particular tradition and attempts to capture its object from that perspective. It replaces the scientific account of its knowledge with one of its own. The Foucauldian analysis, on the other hand, claims not to speak from or represent any tradition. The aim is not to replace existing discourse with another but to offer new ways of arranging that discourse into new unities and regularities. The archaeology is "trying to deploy a dispersion that is not related to absolute axes of reference; it is trying to operate a decentering that leaves no privilege to any center" (Foucault, 1972a, 205).

This decentering must also include the Foucauldian account. The idea of a "Foucauldian perspective" is not permitted. Radhakrishnan (1990) captures this sentiment when he writes that "there is something constitutively contradictory about Foucault's location as a . . . thinker" (62) and that "Foucault has quite thoroughly foregrounded the irrelevance and the untenability of his own theoretical authority" (62). But far from being a failing, Foucault's untenability as an authoritative theoretical discourse is his strength. In its idealized form, Foucault's archaeology is that place which is without preconceived categories overladen with structures of power because it:

rejects its identity, without previously stating: I am neither this nor that. It is not critical, most of the time; it is not a way of saying that everyone else is wrong. It is an attempt to define a particular site by the exteriority of its vicinity; rather than trying to reduce others to silence, by claiming what they say is worthless, I have tried to define this blank space from which I speak, and which is slowly taking shape in a discourse that I still feel to be so precarious and unsure. (Foucault, 1972a, 17).

However, the precarious project of defining the blank space that allows the speech of others to be considered in a sense of exteriority has not been the manner in which Foucault's work has been taken up and appropriated by a communication discipline steeped in the tradition of the received philosophy of science. Indeed, how could it? Where the philosophy advocates control, Foucault advocates the questioning of what it means to say we are engaged in communication studies. Yet Foucault's work has been appropriated, and enthusiastically so. This is possible only by a defusing that sheds some light on the way adherence to the tenets of the philosophy of science dominates and guides thinking within contemporary U.S. communication theory. The Foucauldian discourse must be effectively neutralized, controlled, and defined in such a way that it becomes fit for use, i.e., it has a place within the categories of the prevailing discourse of the discipline so that its presence does not constitute a threat. Foucault's place in the mainstream communication literature consists largely of questions concerning the appropriate application of his work to specific communication problems; i.e., how can Foucault be applied as another kind of qualitative methodology (e.g., Blair, 1987). This (mis)appropriation and sanitization is clearly seen in Barker and Cheney's (1994) use of Foucault's concept of "discipline" in an ethnographic-like study with the expressed goal of "revealing" the hidden dynamics of organizational behavior. They make the claim that Foucault's work concentrates on "uncovering and scrutinizing the historically rooted and deeply ingrained power relationships in organizations and institutions" (Barker and Cheney, 1994, 19). They further claim that "discipline" is of "special significance to organizational communication scholars because it, in Foucault's view, represented the underlying logic or trend in the various institutions and practices that constitute advanced industrial society" (20). Finally, Barker and Cheney (1994) write that "our explication and application of Foucault's concept of discipline will provide a pathway for discovering and critiquing the more unobtrusive dimensions or organizational control as they become manifest in our radically rationalized society" (38).

This reading of Foucault is clearly grounded in the tenets of the received philosophy of science. Barker and Cheney set themselves as authorities in a community of experts who, with expertise derived from a prevailing paradigm, use Foucault's concept of discipline as another tool for uncovering the truths of underlying logics and trends. The name "Foucault" is taken as a marker of a kind of qualitative methodology whose use can discover unobtrusive dimensions of organizational control. This strategy, of course, serves to effectively neutralize and sanitize the main thrust of Foucault's philosophy, i.e., that any sense of a Foucauldian theoretical approach or methodological program is simply a contradiction in terms (Rorty, 1986). To read Foucault as "*only* revealing the way in which global power/knowledge regimes supplant each other and completely determine what we are is to misread him. For it is to screen out the many ways in which Foucault is always focusing on instabilities, points of resistance, specific points where revolt and counter-discourse are possible" (Bernstein, 1994, 234). Yet this is the only sense that a Foucauldian discourse can be accounted for and appropriated in a communication discipline dominated by the received philosophy of science represented by "Popper" and "Kuhn."

Barker and Cheney (1994) exemplify one such attempt to define, deploy, and ultimately neutralize Foucault within the limits set by the received philosophy of science. Foucault was well aware of this possibility because, ultimately, it is inevitable. Writing as his own devil's advocate, Foucault (1972a) states:

> If you claim that you are opening up a radical interrogation, if you wish to place your discourse at the level at which we place ourselves, you know very well that it will enter our game, and, in turn, extend the very dimension that it is trying to free itself from. Either it does not reach us, or we claim it. (205)

Foucault's expressed "blank space" is either unintelligible because it lies outside of existing categories, or it becomes part of those categories. Either Foucault is ignored, or he is misappropriated.

Ideally, and this is the sense in which he is regarded here, Foucault's blank space is a place of struggle, where the unintelligible can compete with those forces that to seek to define it. As Foucault states, "my discourse, far from determining the locus in which it speaks, is avoiding the ground on which it could find support" (205). This is the inherent tension in Foucault's (1972b) work, one that Foucault expressed in his inaugural lecture at the Collège de France:

> I don't want to enter this risky world of discourse; I want nothing to do with it insofar as it is decisive and final; I would like to feel it all around me, calm and transparent, profound, infinitely open, with others responding to my

> expectations, and truth emerging, one by one. All I want is
> to allow myself to be borne along, within it, and by it, a
> happy wreck. Institutions reply: "But you have nothing to
> fear from launching out; we're here to show you discourse
> is within the established order of things, that we've waited
> a long time for its arrival, that a place has been set aside for
> it—a place which both honours and disarms it; and if it
> should happen to have a certain power, then it is we, and we
> alone, who give it that power." (215–16)

Communication theory is one such institution that "both honours and disarms" and gives this discourse a "certain power." Foucault's incorporation into the discourse of scholars like Barker and Cheney (1994) transforms it so that it becomes part of "our game." This chapter is guilty of the same charge, of course. To "do Foucault" is to deny his project. To write "about" Foucault is to categorize and ultimately neutralize him. Yet in this chapter the goal has been to demonstrate a certain sensitivity to Foucault's work so that the idealization of the blank space as the realization of unrealized potentials may be expressed and the possibilities of transgression explored. Transgression not in the sense that the received philosophy of science is wrong, inaccurate, or unethical. The philosophy is allowed to speak but against the backdrop of a discursive space that opens up the possibility of other figures, other arrangements, other objects of knowledge. It is with respect to this insertion that Foucault's role in the transgression of the received philosophy of science will be described.

Toward Transgression of the Received Philosophy

This chapter has entered, or inserted, a Foucauldian discourse into the prevailing talk about the role of philosophies of science within communication theory. It has become another discursive fact within it and this appearance has to be dealt with and accounted for. The insertion acts, not as a replacement philosophy but as a diagnosis of the prevailing discursive formation: an attempt to transcend readers into a linguistic space that, once understood, enables them to transcend the ontology into which they were preciously locked. This is not to say that the Foucauldian discourse offers a "better" or "truer" account but rather slips into the existing discursive formation in order to foreground its status as a particular kind of discursive unity. Foucault's "blank space" becomes a mirror in which existing practices come to view themselves (Huspek and Rincon, 1993).

From this perspective, the relevance of Foucault's historical studies becomes clear. May (1993) argues that Foucault's histories appear strange because he uses unities that are generally forgotten in order to raise questions about unities that are taken for granted. Foucault does not claim to have found what is "really going on" in history, as opposed to what people mistakenly think is going on, because the ultimate truth is not what grounds his historical knowledge. For Foucault, what grounds this knowledge is that which can be justified within the limits that comprise the structure of historical discourse. Foucault's histories not only inform about the subject matter under investigation but also challenge the conventions that apply in the writing of history. The same reasoning is applied in the consideration of the received philosophy of science. A Foucauldian philosophy does not pose a counter-philosophy. It forces a confrontation with the conventions of using a philosophy of science at all. It brings the categories, their structures, and their deployment into sharp relief. Foucault questioned the conventions that defined the writing of history. In the same way, the Foucauldian discourse also makes possible the reconsideration of those conventions that define the writing of a philosophy of science for communication theory.

The mirror that the Foucauldian discourse offers is akin to a conversational partner in an exchange of questions and answers. In this exchange, both parties have certain roles and certain rights. A communication theory, the received philosophy of science, and the Foucauldian inquisitor become part of an ongoing discursive formation, which is constantly changing and adjusting according to certain rules. However, these are not rules of rationality in Kuhn's sense but the rules of a conversation and the rights of the conversant:

> In the serious play of questions and answers, in the work of reciprocal elucidation, the rights of each person are in some sense immanent in the discussion. They depend only on the dialogue situation. The person asking the questions is merely exercising the right that has been given him: to remain unconvinced, to perceive a contradiction, to require more information, to emphasize different postulates, to point out faulty reasoning, etc. As for the person answering the questions, he too exercises a right that does not go beyond the discussion itself; by the logic of his own discourse he is tied to the questioning of the other. Questions and answers depend on a game—a game that is at once pleasant and difficult—in which each of the two partners takes pains to use only the rights given to him by the other and by the accepted form of the dialogue. (Foucault, 1984, 390)

This philosophy is also founded in a particular theory of communication. However, in the received philosophy of science, communication is conceived in terms of the language of the paradigm, developed and practiced by a privileged community, which is imposed on the subjects and objects it brings into its domain and sphere of influence. With the insertion of Foucault, communication is conceived in terms of the rights of conversational partners in a dialogue situation where change is normal and appropriate. This dialogue does not and cannot stand above the discourse produced by communication theorists and philosophers of science as a separate account. It becomes part of that account, and foregrounds its "accountedness." This production of discourse, if it is allowed to take place (and this may not be the case), enters into the system of relations and has the potential to change it. New relations may be created and old ones destroyed. It can make new statements possible, and marginalize others. As Megill (1984) writes, Foucault is a thinker who regards his writings as bombs directed against extant reality, who wants them to "self-destruct after use, like fireworks" (184).

Conclusion

In his biography of Foucault, Macey (1993) recounts the story of Jana Sawicki, a doctoral student, who spent four years writing a doctoral dissertation on Foucault's concept of humanism and attempting to "appropriate" it for feminism. Macey (1993) writes:

> The day after she submitted it for examination, she had the opportunity to attend part of Foucault's Vermont seminar. "I told him I had just finished writing a dissertation on his critique of humanism. Not surprisingly, he responded with some embarrassment and much seriousness. He suggested that I do not spend energy talking about him and, instead, do what he was doing, namely, write genealogies. (450)

The purpose of a Foucauldian investigation is not and should not be an interpretation and application of Foucault's work. It should be to disrupt and diagnose existing bodies of discourse and articulate their conditions of possibilities in archaeologies and genealogical studies. This chapter has deviated from this path. It is not an archaeology or genealogy in the sense Foucault would either endorse or encourage. Nevertheless, it has outlined some parameters and a rationale for embarking on a genealogy of communication theory and the discursive devices that hold it together as a coherent entity. The dynamics of the received philosophy of science's operation within the processes of knowledge production in communication theory have been described. The limits on communication theorizing imposed by this received view have been identified and, by using key aspects of Foucault's work and advocating the insertion of this discourse into the prevailing tradition, the potential for transgression of this received view has been described.

The task facing the Foucauldian scholar in this project will be difficult and unpopular. It consists of being able to provide a picture of knowledge that is convincing without having to appeal to philosophical foundations which are considered beyond dispute. The project is positive in the sense that it enables understanding of the reasons why it has been captivating to believe that communication theory consists of paradigms and science consists of the attempt to falsify testable hypotheses. It is a potential cure to the temptation to continue thinking in terms that seem natural and taken for granted, if, indeed, it is a cure that communication practitioners desire.

The project offers a sense of transgression in its potential to identify within a discursive formation places where progress and change may be possible and feasible. To the extent that any philosophy of science gains adherents to its discursive procedures and related practices, it may be said to generate enclaves of power. The reigning system of intelligibility promotes certain patterns of organized social action and at the same time forbids and discourages a range of competitors. Each discourse operates simultaneously as a productive and repressive force. A Foucauldian insertion within the discursive formation foregrounds the devices employed by communication theorists to create a "sense of the real." This preliminary foregrounding can act as preparation for a second stage that is "generative" (Gergen, 1990). Discursive implications of the critique are elaborated. As elaboration begins to establish alternative ontologies (theoretical, metatheoretical, methodological, and evaluative) with associated practices, it may begin to serve as an alternative basis of social power. But in what sense is this progress? Does this not just replace one set of conceptual blinders with another? Possibly, but the emergence of new ways of speaking opens up new ways of making predictions. New "events" are created and a greater diversity of symbolic resources becomes available to a discursive formation.

Whereas the received philosophy of science serves to limit the talk that can take place in a domain such as communication theory, Foucault inserted opens it up. Whereas communication theory was previously constructed as being separate from philosophy, now philosophy becomes an integral part of theorizing. The synthesis of theory and philosophy is not an additive process, in which a measure of theory is added to traditional philosophical foundations to create more meaningful seamless narratives. Foucault's voice in the discourse serves to unravel the narrative and open up the possibility for more. It enables communication theorists to see that even as they claim to study the dynamics of power/knowledge, their own knowledge is both made possible by and contributes to existing power/knowledge structures, including Foucault's and this chapter's that discusses Foucault. As Jansen (1993) remarks, the resistance to and normalization of the Foucauldian voice, as exemplified by Barker and Cheney (1994), "excuses practitioners from participating in the very difficult, conflict laden dialogues that are a necessary prologue to articulating ways of knowing that are no longer secured in categories of domination and submission" (138). The insertion of Foucault creates a space where these difficult dialogues can be forced to take place. Following Hardt (1993), the discussion of theory and the philosophy of science should not be considered the intellectual passion of a "marginalized academic clique" (130). It is a much needed exercise in consciousness-raising of a field in which expert knowledge is changing by a renewed interest in issues of culture and communication, cultural anthropology, feminist studies, and other fields. The presence of a received philosophy of science, linked to a received history and an absence of self-reflection, reinforces the status quo of theory and practice as ahistorical and uncritical. Foucault inserted offers a voice of self-reflection and possible transgression. It does not represent another perspective to replace the discourse that is already taking place, nor does it serve to interpret that discourse into another. Rather, it enables the recognition and analysis of those conditions of possibility that constitute communication theory as we know it and, more importantly, communication theory as we may not know it.

References

Barker, J. R., and G. Cheney. (1994). The concept and the practices of discipline in contemporary organizational life. *Communication Monographs* 61(1):19–43.

Berger, C. R., and S. H. Chaffee. (1987). The study of communication as a science. In C. R. Berger and S. H. Chaffee (Eds.): *Handbook of Communication Science*. Beverly Hills, Calif.: Sage.

Bernstein, R. (1994). Foucault: Critique as a philosophic ethos. In M. Kelly (Ed.): *Critique and Power: Recasting the Foucault/ Habermas Debate*. Cambridge, Mass.: MIT Press, 211–41.

Blair, C. (1987). The statement: Foundation of Foucault's historical criticism. *Western Journal of Speech Communication* 51:364–83.

Brinton, C. (1967). The Enlightenment. In P. Edwards (Ed.): *The Encyclopedia of Philosophy*. Vol. 2. New York: Macmillan, 519–25.

Craig, R. T. (1993). Why are there so many communication theories? *Journal of Communication* 43(3):26–33.

Delia, J. (1987). Communication research: A history. In C. R. Berger and S. H. Chaffee (Eds.): *Handbook of Communication Science*. Beverly Hills, Calif.: Sage.

Dervin, B., L. Grossberg, B. J. O'Keefe, and E. Wartella. (Eds.). (1989a). *Rethinking Communication. Volume One: Paradigm Issues.* Newbury Park, Calif.: Sage.

———, L. Grossberg, B. J. O'Keefe, and E. Wartella (Eds.). (1989b). *Rethinking Communication. Volume Two: Paradigm Exemplars.* Newbury Park, Calif.: Sage.

Ellis, D. G. (1991). Post-structuralism and language: Non-sense. *Communication Monographs* 58(2):213–24.

Feyerabend, P. (1975). *Against Method.* London: New Left Books.

———. (1979). *Science in a Free Society.* London: New Left Books.

Foucault, M. (1972a). *The Archaeology of Knowledge* (A. M. Sheridan Smith, Trans.) New York: Pantheon. (Original work published 1969.)

———. (1972b). The discourse on language. In *The archaeology of knowledge* (A. M. Sheridan Smith, Trans.) New York: Pantheon. (Original work published 1971.)

———. (1973). *The Order of Things: An Archaeology of the Human Sciences.* New York: Vintage. (Original work published 1966.)

———. (1975). *The Birth of the Clinic: An Archaeology of Medical Perception* (A. M. Sheridan Smith, Trans.) New York: Vintage. (Original work published 1966.)

———. (1977). Nietzsche, genealogy, history. (D. F. Bouchard and S. Simon, Trans.). In D. F. Bouchard (Ed.): *Language, Counter-memory, Practice: Selected Essays and Interviews by Michel Foucault.* Ithaca, N.Y.: Cornell University Press, 139–64. (Original work published 1971.)

———. (1979). *Discipline and Punish: The Birth of the Prison.* (A. Sheridan, Trans.) New York: Vintage. (Original work published 1975.)

———. (1980). *Power/Knowledge: Selected Interviews and Other Writings, 1972–1977.* (C. Gordon, Ed.) New York: Pantheon.

———. (1984). Polemics, politics, and problematizations: An interview with Michel Foucault. In P. Rabinow (Ed.): *The Foucault Reader.* New York: Pantheon, 381–90.

———. (1988a). *Madness and Civilization: A History of Insanity in the Age of Reason.* (R. Howard, Trans.) New York: Vintage. (Original work published 1961.)

———. (1988b). The concern for truth. In L. D. Kritzman (Ed.): *Politics, Philosophy, Culture: Interviews and Other Writings, 1977–1984.* New York: Routledge.

———, and G. Deleuze. (1977). Intellectuals and power: A conversation between Michel Foucault and Gilles Deleuze. (D. F. Bouchard and S. Simon, Trans.) In D. F. Bouchard (Ed.): *Language, Counter-memory, Practice: Selected Essays and*

142   Gary P. Radford

142   Gary P. Radford

Interviews by Michel Foucault. Ithaca, N. Y.: Cornell University Press, 205–217. (Original work published 1972.)

Fuller, S. (1988). *Social Epistemology*. Bloomington: Indiana University Press.

———. (1992). Being there with Thomas Kuhn: A parable for postmodern times. *History and Theory* 31:241–75.

Gamow, G. (1966). *Thirty Years That Shook Physics*. Garden City, N.Y.: Doubleday.

Gaonkar, D. P. (1993). The idea of rhetoric in the rhetoric of science. *Southern Communication Journal* 58(4):258–95.

Gergen, K. J. (1990). The checkmate of rhetoric (but can our reasons become causes?) In H. W. Simons (Ed.): *The Rhetorical Turn: Invention and Persuasion in the Conduct of Inquiry*. Chicago: University of Chicago Press.

Gholson, B., and P. Barker. (1985). Kuhn, Lakatos, and Laudan: Applications in the history of physics and psychology. *American Psychologist* 40(7):755–69.

Gupta, C. (1993). Putnam's resolution of the Popper-Kuhn controversy. *Philosophical Quarterly* 43:319–34.

Hardt, H. (1992). *Critical Communication Studies: Communication, History, and Theory in America*. New York: Routledge.

———. (1993). Communication and the question of history. *Communication Theory* 3(2):130–36.

Hawking, S. W. (1988). *A Brief History of Time: From the Big Bang to Black Holes*. New York: Bantam.

Hesse, M. (1981). *Revolutions and Reconstructions in the Philosophy of Science*. Brighton, England: Harvester.

Holcomb, H. R. (1989). Interpreting Kuhn: Paradigm-choice as objective value judgment. *Metaphilosophy* 20(1):51–67.

Holland, R. (1990). The paradigm plague: Prevention, cure, and inoculation. *Human Relations* 43(1):23–48.

Huspek, M., and O. Rincon. (1993, November). *Antiscience: Foucault's Discourse of Other*. Presented at the meeting of the Speech Communication Association, Miami Beach, Fla.

Jansen, S. C. (1993). "The future is not what it used to be": Gender, history, and communication studies. *Communication Theory* 3(2):136–48.

Kosinski, J. (1970). *Being There*. New York: Bantam.

Kuhn, T. S. (1970a). *The Structure of Scientific Revolutions* (2nd ed., enlarged). Chicago: University of Chicago Press.

———. (1970b). Reflections on my critics. In I. Lakatos and A. Musgrave (Eds.): *Criticism and the Growth of Knowledge*. Cambridge, England: Cambridge University Press.

————. (1970c). Logic of discovery or psychology of research? In I. Lakatos and A. Musgrave (Eds.): *Criticism and the Growth of Knowledge*. Cambridge, England: Cambridge University Press.

————. (1974). Second thoughts on paradigms. In F. Suppe (Ed.), *The Structure of Scientific Theories*. Urbana, Ill.: University of Illinois Press.

————. (1977). *The Essential Tension: Selected Studies in Scientific Tradition and Change*. Chicago: University of Chicago Press.

Lakatos, I. (1979). *Methodology of Scientific Research Programmes*. Cambridge, England: Cambridge University Press.

————, and A. Musgrave (Eds.). (1970). *Criticism and the Growth of Knowledge*. Cambridge, England: Cambridge University Press.

Laudan, L. (1977). *Progress and Its Problems*. Berkeley: University of California Press.

————. (1984). *Science and Values*. Berkeley: University of California Press.

Macey, D. (1993). *The Lives of Michel Foucault: A Biography*. New York: Pantheon.

May, T. (1993). *Between Genealogy and Epistemology: Psychology, Politics, and Knowledge in the Thought of Michel Foucault*. University Park: Pennsylvania State University Press.

McRae, M. W. (1988). The paradigmatic and the interpretive in Thomas Kuhn. *Clio* 17(3):239–48.

Megill, A. (1984). *Prophets of Extremity: Nietzsche, Heidegger, Foucault, Derrida*. Berkeley: California University Press.

Nerone, J. (1993). Theory and history. *Communication Theory* 3(2):148–57.

Notturno, M. A. (1984). The Popper/Kuhn debate: Truth and two faces of relativism. *Psychological Medicine* 14:273–89.

Peters, J. D. (1986). Institutional sources of intellectual poverty in communication research. *Communication Research* 13(4):527–59.

Popper, K. R. (1959). *The Logic of Scientific Discovery*. New York: Basic Books. (Original work published 1934.)

————. (1965). *Conjectures and Refutations: The Growth of Scientific Knowledge*. New York: Harper and Row.

————. (1970). Normal science and its dangers. In I. Lakatos and A. Musgrave (Eds.): *Criticism and the Growth of Knowledge*. Cambridge, England: Cambridge University Press.

Radhakrishnan, R. (1990). Toward an effective intellectual: Foucault or Gramsci? In B. Robbins (Ed.): *Intellectuals: Aesthetics, Politics, Academics*. Minneapolis: University of Minnesota Press, 57–99.

Rogers, E. M. (1994). *A History of Communication Study: A Biographical Approach*. New York: The Free Press.

Rorty, R. (1979). *Philosophy and the Mirror of Nature.* Princeton, N.J.: Princeton University Press.

―――. (1982). *Consequences of Pragmatism (Essays: 1972–1980).* Minneapolis: University of Minnesota Press.

―――. (1986). Foucault and epistemology. In D. C. Hoy (Ed.): *Foucault: A Critical Reader.* Cambridge, Mass.: Basil Blackwell, 41–49.

Said, E. W. (1988). Michel Foucault, 1926–1984. In J. Arac (Ed.): *After Foucault: Humanistic Knowledge, Postmodern Challenges.* New Brunswick, N.J.: Rutgers University Press.

Seigel, J. (1990). Avoiding the subject: A Foucaultian itinerary. *Journal of the History of Ideas* 51(2):273–99.

Simons, H. W. (Ed.) (1990). *The Rhetorical Turn: Invention and Persuasion in the Conduct of Inquiry.* Chicago: University of Chicago Press.

Simpson, C. (1994). *Science of Coercion: Communication Research and Psychological Warfare, 1945–1960.* New York: Oxford University Press.

van Fraassen, B. C. (1980). *The Scientific Image.* Oxford, England: Clarendon Press.

Wilmott, H. (1993). Breaking the paradigm mentality. *Organization Studies* 14(5):681–719.

An Attempt to Contribute to the Rhetoric of Science Movement: From Monologue to Dialogue

Branislav Kovačić
Donald P. Cushman
Robert C. MacDougall

For the rhetoric of science movement to flourish, it must evolve from its current one-way monologue among humanistic scholars into a two-way dialogue between rhetorical and scientific scholars. Cushman (1990) argued that a *window of opportunity* now exists which would allow for the creation of such an exchange. The suggestion is that three conditions must be met, however, before the evolution from a one-way (monologic) to a two-way (dialogic) arena can be realized.

First, Cushman called upon rhetorical scholars to develop one or more constructive positions that can inform social scientific rhetorical practices in a central and powerful way. Second, he asked social scientists to reciprocate by developing one or more social scientific constructive positions that can inform the practices of rhetorical scholars in a central and powerful way. Finally, Cushman noted that one crucial condition for such a dialogue is a willingness by some participants from both of the above groups to listen and learn from the other group and to enter constructively into a dialogue on these issues.

It will be the purpose of this chapter to provide one constructive response to this window of opportunity by (1) explaining the practical relationship between rhetorical and social scientific inquiry, (2) locating a significant set of issues confronting social scientific scholars and a set of significant issues confronting rhetorical scholars, (3) demonstrating how rhetorical scholarship can provide central and powerful solutions to the social scientific issues raised, and (4) demonstrating how social scientific scholarship can provide central and powerful solutions to issues facing rhetorical scholars, thus beginning a dialogue between the two groups. In so doing, we shall review and extend our previous work on this project (Cushman, 1990; Cushman and Kovačić, 1994; and Kovačić, MacDougall, and Cushman, 1996).

Practical Relationship Between Rhetorical and Social Scientific Inquiry[1]

What are the points of practical convergence among rhetorical and social scientific inquiry? Let us explore the answer to this question in three stages: (1) what is the nature, function, and scope of rhetorical inquiry? (2) what is the nature, function, and scope of social scientific inquiry? and (3) what are the practical points of convergence among the two?

Nature, Function, and Scope of Rhetorical Inquiry

Ehninger (1968) argued that theories of rhetoric arise in response to particular problems or "felt needs" that characterize an intellectual or social milieu. Accordingly, "grammatical" theories of rhetoric emerged in the Classical world in response to the need for a conceptual vocabulary that could then be applied in analysis and instruction of oratory. "Psychological" theories of rhetoric arose as part of the eighteenth century's response to problems involved in securing understanding of the human mind's workings. "Sociological" theories of rhetoric evolved during the early twentieth century's efforts to address a felt need for better human understanding in the midst of social and political upheaval. Important rhetorical theories tend to develop in response to pressing, practical problems confronting society at a given point in time.

Since the time of Aristotle, the core of the rhetorical tradition has been concerned with the creation of effective expression to arrive at valid judgments or wisdom regarding problems of practical action—problems concerning what human beings have done, are doing, and should do. Within this tradition, the content of rhetorical discourse has been those issues about which persons dispute. That is, those contingent and practical affairs which intersect human attitudes, values, and beliefs, thus requiring public deliberation and judgment regarding the good, the just, and the useful. Such affairs are capable of resolution by the introduction of public discourse aimed at moving an audience to make a reasoned judgment, a wise decision. Rhetoric, as such, has the potential of becoming advisory and prescriptive (Solmsen, 1941).

The specific method and content of rhetorical theory has changed over time in accordance with the philosophical and practical objectives theorists have sought to address (Duhamel, 1949). Whenever rhetorical theory is conceived as an art, however, it aims at (1) creating discourse that gives effectiveness to human truths and values, and (2) appraising the degree of truth and the appropriateness of values in human discourse. Within this tradition, the method for creating rhetorical discourse has been to develop a set ot topoi—issues and lines of argument for generating effective expression [a system of invention]—and a set of criteria for appraising the fit between proof and claim [a system of judgment] (Solmsen, 1941).

This, then, is what constitutes our conception of rhetorical inquiry: a coherent invention and judgment system implied by recurring practical problems whose solution requires motivating audiences to make appropriate judgments with regard to wise decisions concerning past, present, and future human actions. If rhetorical and social scientific inquiry are to be joined at the practical level, then, we need to understand the kinds of problems that constrain social scientific inquiry. Only then is it possible to develop an invention and judgment system capable of generating discourse that motivates audiences to make decisions appropriate to those practical problems.

Nature, Function, and Scope of Social Scientific Inquiry

The aim of social scientific inquiry is to achieve understanding of social activities through resolving practical problems incurred in locating, classifying, and explaining social facts about those activities (Lessnoff, 1974, 32). Fulfilling this aim involves working toward making social scientific explanations of (1) human actions, (2) human language, and (3) individual participation in cultural institutions. Let us explore each of these in turn in an effort to comprehend better the practical problems of social scientific inquiry.

In social scientific inquiry, phenomena that are to be located as social facts must involve people who in their own minds and behaviors take other people into consideration when they orient their activities toward them. Social scientists thus draw a distinction between two classes of human activities: (1) stimulus-response activities, which are habitual and thus are termed "movements," and (2) intentional activities, or "actions," which involve some degree of choice among alternatives, are able to be evaluated, and involve the actor responding to practical forces confronting the successful completion of the preferred alternative. Fay and Moon (1977) summarize:

> According to this distinction, actions differ from mere
> movements in that they are performed in order to achieve

a particular purpose, and in conformity to some rules. These purposes and rules constitute what we shall call the "semantic dimension" of human behavior—its symbolic or expressive aspect. An action, then, is not simply a physical occurrence but has a certain intentional content which specifies what sort of an action it is, and which can be grasped only in terms of the system of meanings in which the action is performed. A given movement counts as a vote, a signal, a salute, or an attempt to reach something, only against the background of a set of applicable rules and conventions and the purposes of the actors involved. (209)

However, *not all intentional human actions are social:*

In "action" is included all human behavior when and insofar as the acting individual attaches a subjective meaning to it. . . . Action is social insofar as, by virtue of the subjective meaning attached to it by the acting individual, it takes account of the behavior of others. . . . The term "social relationship" [denotes] the behavior of a plurality of actors insofar as, in its meaningful content, the action of each takes account of that of others and is oriented in these terms. (Weber, 1964, 88)

In order to classify an event as a social action, it is necessary to place the observable behavior within the terms of the mental categories actors employ when orienting their behavior toward others. One must demonstrate what social meanings are present in the observed behavior to assure its appropriate social classification. That social actors share conceptions of how behaviors are oriented toward others implies they understand a language.

Human language and its use in symbolic interactions is by nature a social institution. It is a set of vocal and gestural (e.g. symbolic) conventions, meanings, obligations, and duties. A social scientist's ability to gain access to an actor's mental categories and social orientations is in large part dependent upon the investigator's understanding of how that actor uses language in a given context. The rationale for expecting language usage to reveal social scientific facts is that cultural rules constrain how one talks when orienting oneself toward others. Recurring kinds of social activities are coordinated through those rules. Lessnoff (1974) elaborates:

Prominent among the phenomena studied by social scientists are social institutions. A social institution is a complex

> of rules relating to an area of social relations. Broadly, the rules may be enabling or obliging, or both; that is, they provide ways people can cooperate so as to achieve some result. They may also oblige them to do certain things. It scarcely needs to be said that, for an institution to function, those involved must know what the rules are, and must expect others to keep more or less to the rules. (44–45)

In his analysis of symbolic interaction, Mead (1934) noted that we gain understanding of how individuals orient their activities toward others through examining the use of language (a social institution). More specifically, through examining language usage we can distinguish among (1) *mind,* or individual thoughts, (2) *self,* or the symbolic representation of the individual, and (3) *society,* or the social norms governing cultural interaction. Symbolic interactions and behaviors are thus subject to social scientific observation of human interaction patterns. Those observed patterns can, in turn, be classified as psychological, social, or political in motivation. Once classified, those patterns can then be explained by finding a theory appropriate to that domain of social scientific inquiry.

Our conception of social scientific inquiry, then, is as follows: a practical activity aimed at achieving understanding of social actions through resolving recurring problems involved in locating, classifying, and explaining patterns of interaction. Efforts to work through these problems in social scientific inquiry, if successful, transform interaction patterns into what we call reasoned social scientific facts. Rhetorical inquiry, as we shall see, is intimately related to this central feature of social scientific inquiry.

Practical Points of Convergence among Rhetorical and Social Scientific Inquiry

We contend that rhetorical and social scientific inquiry significantly intersect at the practical level. Rhetorical scholarship can contribute significantly to social scientific inquiry by developing a noncontentious rhetorical theory for inventing and certifying scientific argument within alternative theoretic and methodological perspectives, which at the same time, allows the public and policymakers to appropriately assess the value of such claims. Such a noncontentious theory of rhetoric for social scientific invention and judgment, we believe, would then provide at least one constructive position from which rhetorical scholarship can inform scientific inquiry in a central and powerful way. The resolution of significant rhetorical problems, on the other hand, requires a new invention and judgment system to supplement rhetoric's existing invention and judgment system. The methodological standards of empirical social scientific inquiry lend special substance to general rhetorical forms of argumentation.

Social scientific arguments can be distinguished according to the methodological standards used to assess whether the substance of argued claims is appropriate to the particular issue under dispute. The four methodological standards are (1) reliability, (2) validity, (3) direction and strength of relationship, and (4) adequacy. Each yields empirical contents that are specially appropriate for arguments addressed to a particular problem of social scientific inquiry.

Issues Confronting Social Scientific and Rhetorical Scholars

While scientific inquiry, in general, and social scientific inquiry, in particular, have their own unique and well-developed methods, many critics of the application of these methods to important problems point to a significant limitation intrinsic to these methods of inquiry (Popper, 1959; Kuhn, 1962; Toulmin, 1972; Feyerabend, 1974).

These critics note that scientists often differ in theoretic and methodological preferences. Intense and extended arguments between diverse perspectives have led to a tendency by differing groups to present the results of their inquiry for evaluation only before an audience of their peers who share similar theoretic and methodological preferences. Such a validation procedure creates at least three significant problems.

Problems Facing Social Scientific Inquiry

First, it encourages both the making and validation of extreme claims that may not be clearly supported by evidence and argument but that can still be validated by an audience's preferred set of theoretic and methodological assumptions. The result: a tacit understanding within that particular community which suggests that their methodology is *the* methodology. This, in turn, inflames and offends numbers of alternative research traditions creating ideological controversy and obscuring an appropriate evaluation of the arguments and evidence that arise from scientific inquiry.

Second, it encourages the validation of theoretic and argumentative claims which are supported by evidence, but tends to do so only where the support is an artifact of the demand characteristics of the theoretic and methodological procedures employed by limiting the testing of such claims from alternatives.

Third, because the methods and procedures of scientific inquiry do not provide a rhetorical theory for scientific arguments capable of transcending these problems in allowing valid scientific claims to emerge, the public, policymakers and scientists from alternative perspectives do not know which claims to credit and which to discredit. This, in turn, encourages the selection of scientific evidence and claims for political gain, distortion, or even the more extreme tendency to call into question all scientific findings.

Rhetorical scholarship can inform a solution to this problem by developing a noncontentious rhetorical theory for inventing and certifying scientific argument within alternative theoretic and methodological perspectives, which at the same time, allows the public and policymakers to appropriately assess the value of such claims. Such a noncontentious theory of rhetoric for social scientific invention and judgment, we believe, would then provide at least one constructive position from which rhetorical scholarship can inform scientific inquiry in a central and powerful way.

Problems Facing Rhetorical Inquiry

Conversely, rhetorical inquiry and the arguments they generate have been subject to at least four significant criticisms.

First, rhetorical inquiry frequently employs concepts and interpretations of practical problems which have a rich and powerful meaning to the analyzer but which are not present in the minds and behaviors of the audience. The analysis may thus be persuasive to the analyzer, but completely lack traction on the behaviors of the audience, who has the capacity to mediate the problem.

Second, rhetorical inquiry, especially its dialectic variant, frequently provides an analysis of a practical problem in simplistic, essentialistic, and/or dialectical analytic schemes (i.e., a chain of ideological positions) rather than proportional schemes. This, in turn, obscures the solutions available for complex problems. This, in turn, separates language and thought from the problem-resolving actions necessary to solve complex problems.

Third, although dealing with probability, rhetorical inquiry does not have a method to establish probability and thus frequently provides all-or-nothing tautological arguments limited by the constraints of propositional logic. The all-or-nothing tautological character of propositional logic obscures the variety of relationships that exists between perceptions, terms, and solutions (e.g., reciprocal, sequential, coextensive, and substitutable), as captured by functional logic. This, in turn, allows arguments to be simplistic, to confuse causes with effects, and to miss the complex webs of relationships between the perceptions, terms, and solutions necessary to satisfactorily resolve a practical problem.

Fourth, because the methods of rhetorical inquiry do not always adequately capture an audience's interpretations, do not proportionalize the interpretive meanings involved in the analysis of complex practical problems, and do not utilize a nontautological specification of relationships in argument, rhetorical inquiry is in need of an invention and judgment system for transcending these problems. Rhetoric stands in need of a social scientific method of locating, classifying, and explaining such information to be used as part of the substance of rhetorical argument.

In contrast to the analyzer's perceptions, an essentialistic and/or dialectic analysis and the propositional logic used by many rhetors, there is the use of audience-centered perceptions, proportionalism of categorization, and empirically specified relationships rooted in functional, probability-based logics. Proportional categorization relies on a conceptual grid that discovers and reports on both *inter-* and *intra-*conceptual variations in the actors' interpretations, which are expressed in the probabilistic logic of numbers. Such a proportional and numerical logic of relationships conceives of communication, thought, and action as interactive communicative variables forming an empirical web of specifiable, more or less dynamic relationships. Only if and when actor invariant interpretation emerges from various measurement procedures—or researchers' frames of reference—would such dynamic webs be treated as specifying that which is more or less real rather than the researchers' conceptual and measurement artifacts.

Let us now turn our attention to how rhetorical and scientific inquiry can assist each of these groups of scholars in overcoming the above-characterized problems of inquiry (see also Prelli 1989, 1990).

How Rhetorical Scholarship Can Provide Central and Powerful Solutions to Problems Facing Social Scientific Inquiry[2]

Recall that in the previous section we argued that social scientists were in need of an invention system for generating noncontentious arguments for arraying empirical findings in disputes between differing theoretic and methodological positions. The aim of such a noncontentious rhetoric would be to minimize ideological differences and to focus on the unique and significant value of the empirical findings. When noncontentious rather than contentious arguments are employed appropriately, social scientists from differing theoretic and methodological perspectives feel the full force of the empirical findings and adjust their preferred theoretic and methodological perspectives to account for and replicate the important empirical patterns discovered. In addition, policymakers and practitioners in the area under consideration must believe it necessary to take into consideration the discovered pattern in their own work. In short, the research findings become central to all inquiry on the topic under analysis because their significance is made manifest in a noncontentious rhetorical form.

According to Cushman and Kovačić (1994), social scientific inquiry is a practical activity that attempts to understand social action by resolving problems incurred during investigative efforts to locate, classify, and interrelate theoretically recurrent patterns of social interaction. Of course, all three of these problem areas of invention entail the additional problem of judging the methods used to resolve them. Arguments that establish how these four problems were resolved satisfactorily during the investigative process work toward establishing reasoned social scientific facts. Cushman and Kovačić furnish a heuristic set of four rhetorical issues to identify how social scientists frame and address those four distinct kinds of problems: (1) existence, (2) definition, (3) relationship, and (4) judgment in social scientific inquiry.

We now contend that arguments addressed to those issues follow standard rhetorical forms or patterns that are specially appropriate for adducing claims that can resolve each respective kind of general rhetorical issue. Accordingly, we argue that the four general rhetorical questions are addressed, respectively, with four distinctive rhetorical argument forms: (1) descriptive, (2) expositional, (3) narrative, and (4) enthymematic. For illustration, we shall examine the formal qualities of John Gottman's social scientific inquiry into a theory of marital dissolution (1991) and the arguments he employs in response to those issues.

Rhetorical Description

Is it? (the question of existence). Researchers resolve this issue successfully when they establish how others can operationalize and thereby locate a pattern of social interaction. Such issues generally involve problems of experimental or observational location of those patterns. Researchers must show that a located pattern possesses observational stability within a specifiable domain and is not merely idiosyncratic or otherwise spurious. To address this issue, then, they must argue that others can operationalize and thereby locate the same purportedly existent pattern of social interaction for themselves.

Rhetorical description is the standard argumentative form for answering the question, Is it? Rhetorical description selects a set of observational activities and events out of a practical context so that others can repeat them and thereby locate the same social interaction pattern. For example, Gottman (1991) uses rhetorical description to operationalize the problem of marital dissatisfaction in physiological terms:

[He and his associates collected] videotapes of couples interacting in which we also obtained physiological data synchronized to the video time code. In other words, couples came to our lab at the end of the day and they were interviewed to identify a major area of disagreement in their marriage. They were asked to discuss this area and try to come to some resolution. While they talked, we videotaped them and simultaneously collected physiological data including their respective heart rates, blood velocity and the amplitude of each quantity of blood that their hearts ejected on each beat, skin conductance, and gross motor movement. (4)

Gottman also uses rhetorical description to present several questionnaires, two observational coding systems (one for sequential verbal interactions and the other for nonverbal facial expressions of emotion), and his overall procedures for putting them all to use. Researchers who follow the procedures as described should locate the same results as Gottman (1991) did. In this case, following experimental procedures purportedly will yield noncontentious results that establish physiological arousal as a powerful predictor of marital dissatisfaction and dissolution:

In the first study we did, we found the result that surprised us. The result was that physiological arousal, particularly of the husband, predicted the longitudinal deterioration of marital satisfaction. Couples whose hearts beat faster, whose blood flowed faster, who sweated more and moved more during marital interaction or even when they were just silent but anticipating marital conflict, had marriages that deteriorated in satisfaction over the course of three years. Also, couples who were physiologically calmer had marriages that improved over time. The strength of the prediction in this longitudinal study was amazing to us. For example, the higher the husband's heart rate during interaction, controlling marital satisfaction at Time One, the greater the deterioration in marital satisfaction over three years. The correlation was 0.92. This meant that using only physiological data we could predict, with 95% accuracy, which couples' marriages would improve and which would deteriorate in the next three years. (4)

Gottman's noncontentious rhetorical descriptions thus clarify how he located this pattern that possesses such impressive predictive power.

Rhetorical Exposition

What is it? (the issue of definition). Researchers resolve this issue successfully when they offer a coherent conceptualization for a social interaction pattern that encompasses meaningfully any of its specific manifestations. Such issues usually raise problems of classification and categorization that require conceptual definition and extended applications to particular cases. Researchers often argue to define the conceptual meanings of a pivotal technical term or to extend that term's range of applications to additional located instances.

Rhetorical exposition is the appropriate noncontentious argumentative form for answering the question, What is it? Rhetorical exposition develops the conceptual meaning of a located interaction pattern through definition and extended application to particular instances that purportedly fall within its scope. For example, Gottman (1991) engages in noncontentious conceptual exposition to distinguish two potentially destructive patterns of marital conflict:

> We found that some patterns of marital conflict were beneficial to the marriage in the long run even if they were upsetting at the time. In contrast, when wives were only agreeable and compliant the marriage would deteriorate over time. We also identified a destructive pattern of the husband's withdrawal as a listener, a pattern we call stonewalling. Stonewalling is a behavior pattern in which the listener presents a stone wall to the speaker, not moving the face very much, avoiding eye contact or using what I call a monitoring eye contact pattern, holding the neck rigid and not using the usual listener responses such as head nods or brief vocalizations that tell the speaker that the listener is tracking. When husbands stonewalled, marital satisfaction decreased over time. (4)

Husband stonewalling and wife compliance are thus two discrete interaction patterns that could culminate in marital breakup.

Gottman and his associates also found that physiological arousal is so fundamental to processes of marital dissolution and stability that they needed a special conception to account for the specific kind of arousal that ultimately culminates in marital breakup. Accordingly, they gave a noncontentious exposition of the new conception, "flooding of negative attributions." This conception turns on the interactants' own distinctions between positive and negative verbal statements and nonverbal cues. When the ratio of negative to positive verbal statements reaches 1:1, intense arousal takes place. When the ratio of negative to positive nonverbal cues reaches a similar value, intense arousal again takes place (Gottman and Levenson, 1992). The noncontentious expositional argument uses both ratios to establish flooding of negative attributions as a special conception for the nature and degree of intense physiological arousal during marital conflict that is likely to culminate in breakup.

Rhetorical Narrative

What is it related to? (the issue of relationship). Researchers resolve this issue successfully when they noncontentiously employ a coherent ideational time order on otherwise apparently discrete conceptions of interaction patterns. These issues often involve problems of connecting some explanatory theory to located and conceptualized interaction patterns. To address this issue, researchers often develop noncontentious arguments that explain specific relationships among the conceptualized interaction patterns by determining, as much as possible, the exact character of ideational temporal linkages among them.

Rhetorical narrative is the standard noncontentious argumentative form for answering the question, What is it related to? Rhetorical narrative imposes a time order on conceptualized interaction patterns. This enhances understanding by determining the exact character of temporal linkages among two or more conceptions within a sequence. Arguments about which from among two or more conceptualized patterns causes the others are likely to follow this temporal form of argument.

Gottman (1991) uses an extended noncontentious narrative form of argument to establish the precise temporal sequence among otherwise discretely conceptualized interaction patterns that culminate ultimately in marital dissolution:

> The first stage begins with marital conflict in which the husband becomes very physiologically aroused and stonewalls with his wife. Then, finally, emotionally withdraws from the conflict. Over time he becomes overwhelmed by his wife's emotions and avoidant of any conflict with her.
> The husband's stonewalling is very aversive for the wife and leads to her physiological arousal. She responds by trying to re-engage her husband.
> The second stage is marked by the withdrawal of the wife. She expresses criticism and disgust. Their lives become increasingly more parallel and he is fearful. In short, the husband's withdrawal from hot marital interaction is an early precursor of the wife's withdrawal. When both with-

draw and are defensive, the marriage is on its way toward separation and divorce. (5)

One can easily trace the temporal connections among these "stages" of discretely conceptualized interaction patterns that culminate in separation or divorce. We move from the husband's physiological arousal and his subsequent stonewalling to the wife's physiological arousal in response and, finally, to her withdrawal from the conflict.

Rhetorical Enthymeme

How can we judge? (the issue of judgment). Researchers resolve this question successfully when they evoke appropriate noncontentious standards to constrain appraisals of an inquiry's results. These issues often involve problems of finding appropriate methodology for an investigation. To address these issues, researchers often argue about whether methods chosen to guide an inquiry are supported with well-established and sound criteria. This argument, in turn, certifies the inquiry's results. Without sound methodology, researchers cannot hope to locate recurrent interaction patterns, develop meaningful conceptions to guide interpretations of them, or establish the fit of conceptualized interaction patterns within a temporal sequence.

Rhetorical enthymeme is the appropriate argument form for answering the question, How can we judge? Rhetorical enthymemes suppress premises that express controlling audience beliefs, values, or attitudes. Effective enthymemes use overtly expressed premises to trigger suppressed premises so that they constrain judgments of particular claims adduced in response to the issues. The audience thus judges otherwise debatable claims as though they were logical extensions of well-established and largely noncontroversial beliefs, values, or attitudes (Bitzer, 1959).

For example, consider Gottman's (1991) use of correlational relationship data to establish the strength and direction of the precise temporal sequence of interaction patterns that culminate in separation and divorce:

How powerful were these results? A regression analysis showed that with about six of these variables we could account for over 60% of the variance in predicting marital separation. This is a multiple correlation coefficient of 0.8. This means that if we wanted to predict marital separation four years later using our Time One data, we would correctly classify about 90% of the couples as separated or not separated. These are extremely powerful results, about as strong as those studies, for example, that link blood cholesterol with cardiovascular disease. (5)

These strength-of-relationship data will not carry the claim that the sequencing of those six variables is central to understanding marital breakup unless the judging audience is induced to apply unstated but central methodological criteria. Judging audiences will find those data acceptable if they grant that Gottman's methods meet criteria of reliability and validity, use correct sampling procedures, and follow standard data analysis techniques. Otherwise, audiences will take a skeptical stance toward the 0.8 multiple correlation between the six variables and marital separation and divorce. When audiences judge the solidity of important empirical claims, they often do so against these often unstated but nonetheless central methodological criteria.

The first section of this discussion demonstrated that rhetorical descriptions, expositions, narrations, and enthymemes are the standard noncontentious argumentative forms for addressing, respectively, the four central questions of social scientific inquiry: Is it? What is it? What is it related to? and How can we judge? The central claims and social scientific arguments supporting those claims in Gottman's work on marital dissolution and stability have successfully met the two criteria of valid rhetorical judgment: (1) the reciprocal testing of his claims within multiple theoretic and methodological perspectives and (2) the traction his claims have gained on important social scientific problems and on the minds of social scientists, policy analysts, and the public at large. This can be demonstrated in three ways.

First, more than 200 social scientists have employed, retested, critiqued, and replicated his findings from a breadth of theoretic and methodological perspectives and found support for his claims (e.g., Rands et al., 1981; Rusbolt et al., 1986; Griffin, 1993; Krokoff, 1987; Noller and Venardos, 1986; Sillars et al., 1984; Sabatelli et al., 1986).

Second, rhetorical inquiry into relational conflict by policy analysts in marital counseling, violence in the family, and conflict resolution employ Gottman's work to guide or assist in their work (Gottman, 1979, 1983, 1993a, 1993b; Gottman and Porterfield, 1981; Krokoff, 1990).

Third, Gottman's practical books and numerous popular articles were very well received among the public at large who wish to learn how to cope with the problem of marital instability in a positive manner (Gottman, 1982, 1990, 1994; Gottman et al., 1976).

The truth value and practical force of such noncontentious arguments depend in the first instance upon a correspondence between a researcher's and an audience's observations and in the second instance upon a correspondence between a researcher's and an audience's interests. Gladys Murphy Graham (1925) indicates two outstanding values that result from such correspondences. The first value arises from the fact that the speaker

> is not forcing, contending, compelling; he is directing the mind that it may form its own conclusion, make its own inferences, to which it is compelled only by the logic of observed facts. (324)

There is left no place for the contrary idea, the combat of persuasion is minimized, and social cohesion is maximized in the naming of an act. It is the psychological normalcy of its approach to persuasion that gives this method of argument much of its practical force.

The second value of the method, according to Graham (1925), is its stress upon reasoning from the whole situation. It is as a whole that a situation necessitates or invalidates a given conclusion.

> Upon a realization of such belonging-togetherness the natural procedure of argument is based; and in it finds the necessity of its conclusions. Accepting the systematic situation non-contentiously portrayed, the mind must accept its implied part or, turning back upon itself, deny that content which was previously accepted. (327–328)

If correspondences between researcher and audience's observations, and audience's interests exist, a third resultant value of these strategies follows naturally from the two identified by Murphy. Since the strategies consist in the ordered statement of facts, such a method does not depend on an initial statement of, and assumed consensus on, premises and values. The conclusion presented or action advocated seems to flow naturally from the facts that the audience is aware of. Whatever values underlie the argument may be left tacit or unstated in order to seem demanded by the situation. The resulting value of the method is that antagonistic or polarizing appeals to first premises or values prized only by small groups within the audience are avoided. Therefore, the appeals generated by using these strategies are nonantagonistic—they are capable of generating *unified* support when directed toward an otherwise pluralistic public.

Having demonstrated how rhetorical inquiry can inform social scientific inquiry in a powerful and significant way, attention is now directed to observing how social scientific inquiry can inform rhetorical inquiry in a significant and powerful manner.

How Social Scientific Scholarship Can Provide Central and Powerful Solutions to Problems Facing Rhetorical Inquiry

Recall that in the second section of this essay we outlined four serious problems confronting rhetorical scholarship.

First, rhetorical inquiry into public actions must be sure that the interpretive categories for filtering the audience's perceptions of actions are understood by the rhetor and distributed in the audience's minds in such a manner to guide practical action.

Second, rhetorical analysis, especially its dialectic variant, frequently employs essentialistic and/or dialectical filters in the interpretation of problems and experience where proportional filters are more appropriate for the resolution of a rhetorical problem.

Third, rhetorical inquiry frequently employs a tautological propositional logic to resolve problems where a nontautological specification of the relationship between perceptions, terms, and solutions is actually required.

Fourth, because the resolution of significant rhetorical problems requires perceptual filters that are held both by the rhetor and audience, proportional representations of these filters (rather than essentialistic and/or dialectical representations of potential solutions) where the probabilistic consequences of outcomes are correctly evaluated, require a new invention and judgment system to supplement rhetoric's existing invention and judgment system in these cases.

We believe that system is inherent in social scientific inquiry. To illustrate how and why that system can inform rhetorical scholarship in a powerful and constructive manner, let us return to John Gottman's social scientific inquiry into marital conflict and indicate how the invention and judgment system of science resolves the aforementioned problems.

Gottman attempted to describe marital conflict and how it was perceived by couples with as much precision as possible. A laboratory was constructed to facilitate the collection of data. Recall that Gottman (1991) and his colleagues' work involved:

> [Collecting] videotapes of couples interacting in which we also obtained physiological data synchronized to the video time code. In other words, couples came to our lab at the end of the day and they were interviewed to identify a major area of disagreement in their marriage. They were asked to discuss this area and try to come to some resolution. While they talked we videotaped them and simultaneously collected physiological data including their respective heart rates, blood velocity and the amplitude of each quantity of blood that their hearts ejected on each beat, skin conductance and gross motor movement. (4)

In addition, Gottman (1991) obtained:

> Several questionnaires: (1) *A Parallel Lives Scale* (sample item: My partner and I live pretty separate lives); (2) *The*

> *Extent to Which the Husband Does Housework,* a question-
> naire filled out by the wife on the extent to which the hus-
> band did household chores; (3) *Loneliness* (sample item:
> Sometimes I feel so lonely it hurts); (4) *Chronicity of Prob-
> lems,* based on subjective estimates of how long a set of
> issues in the marriage had been problems; (5) *Escalation,*
> which assessed the extent to which the partner's negative
> emotions were perceived as aversive, irrational, unexpected,
> and overwhelming; and (6) *The Avoidance of Conflict,* which
> assesses the extent to which the subject believes that nega-
> tive feelings and problems were best worked out alone rather
> than by talking things over. (4)

The behaviors observed on the videotapes were coded using two observational coding systems. One coded the sequenced verbal interaction,
the other, only nonverbal facial expressions of emotion with the oral
expressions on the videotape turned off. A graphic representation of
Gottman's findings are found in Figure 6.1.

In the core triad of experience, we find the coding of *verbal interaction* into positive and negative statements. A ratio of one positive to
seven negative triggers physiological arousal to the point of flooding.
Nonverbal interactions are likewise coded into positive-to-negative
ratios, which when they reach one to seven, trigger physiological arousal
and flooding. When physiological arousal reaches a heightened range,
flooding ensues. Recall Gottman's (1991) explanation:

> The results from the physiological measures were that:
> Physiological arousal, particularly of the husband, predicted
> the longitudinal deterioration of marital satisfaction.
> Couples whose hearts beat faster, whose blood flowed
> faster, who sweated more during marital interaction or
> even when they were just silent but anticipating marital
> conflict, had marriages that deteriorated in satisfaction over
> the course of three years. Also, couples who were physi-
> ologically calmer had marriages that improved over time.
> The strength of the prediction in this longitudinal study
> was amazing to us. For example, the higher the husband's
> heart rate during interaction, controlling marital satisfac-
> tion at Time One, the greater the deterioration in marital
> satisfaction over three years. The correlation was 0.92.
> This meant that using only physiological data we could
> predict, with over 95% accuracy, which couples' marriages
> would improve and which would deteriorate in the next
> three years. (4)

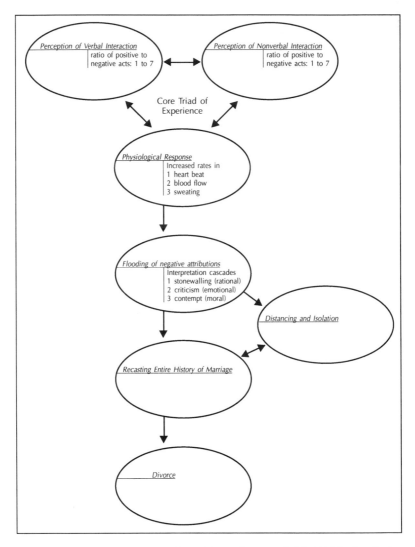

Figure 6.1. *Marital Conflict.* Adapted from Gottman J. M. (1991). *Predicting the longitudinal course of marriages.* Journal of Marriage and Family Therapy 17:3–7.

Recall that the results from one videotaped coding were as follows:

We found the missing link in predicting separation and divorce. Briefly, the results were that marital separation was predicted by the following Time One variables. When the videotapes' sound was turned down and only the faces were observed, couples who were more likely to separate showed more of the following facial expressions: wife's disgust (and this was the strongest correlation in the study, 0.51), husband's fear, husband's miserable smile, and wife's miserable smile. Accompanying these facial expressions were the following behaviors: husbands and wives were more defensive (they made more excuses, denied responsibility more), wives complained and criticized more, husbands disagreed more and both husbands and wives yes-butted more. To predict divorce, one needed to add the husband's stonewalling and the wife's verbal expressions of contempt. (4)

Note how the use of questionnaires represents an attempt to capture the actor's perspective and how the use of ratios proportionalized what would otherwise be considered an oversimplistic, essentialistic, and/or dialectic analysis of marital conflict. The empirical specification of relationship clearly delineates the one-way from two-way flow of influence.

Next Gottman found that when the core triad variables reached certain proportions, flooding took place. This flooding involves three different, yet combinable, interpretation cascades: one that is rational in character and leads to withdrawal or stonewalling, another that is emotional in character and leads to criticism, and one that is moral in character and leads to contempt. These interpretations represent the actor's analysis of the input from the core triad once they hit critical levels. The flooding by these three separate and combinable cascades of interpretation lead to either distancing and isolation or to recasting the entire history of the marriage in negative terms.

The questionnaire's results allowed Gottman to enrich his findings with regard to the husband's loneliness, the wife's contempt, and the husband's stonewalling. Recall Gottman's (1991) summaries of the observed behavioral patterns:

The first stage begins with marital conflict in which the husband becomes very physiologically aroused and stonewalls with his wife. Then, finally, emotionally withdraws from the conflict. Over time, he becomes overwhelmed by his wife's emotions and avoidant of any conflict with her.

The husband's stonewalling is very aversive for the wife and leads to her physiological arousal. She responds by trying to re-engage her husband.

The second stage is marked by the withdrawal of the wife. She expresses criticism and disgust. Their lives become increasingly more parallel and he is fearful. In short, the husband's withdrawal from hot marital interaction is a precursor of the wife's withdrawal. When both withdraw

and are defensive, the marriage is on its way to separation
and divorce. (4)

Gottman has tracked the elements intrinsic to dyadic conflict
from the participant's perspective. His model suggests that an actor
can, based on any one (or all) of the cascades, recast the interpretations of the entire history of marital interaction in negative terms and
terminate the relationship. The moral cascade, for instance, may create sufficient contempt toward the other to reinterpret the history of
the relationship. It may be the rational, the moral, or the emotional
cascade, or it may be all of them together. They each have different
thresholds, however, and science can proportionally inform us as to
what these thresholds are. Gottman also empirically specifies the relationships between these constructs avoiding the limitations of tautological relationships expressed in propositional logic. Finally, note
how the three cascades divided into rational, emotional, and moral
influences correspond to a time-honored foundation of traditional
rhetorical judgments.

Rhetoricians have long recognized the need to locate consensually established criteria and assumptions to serve as common grounds
for evaluating the appropriateness of otherwise debatable claims. Social
scientists address this need by turning to special methodological standards for appraising the appropriateness of claims about social interaction patterns. Those standards are used to assess the empirical strength
of claims and, thereby, to give assurance that those claims address real,
existent features of social interaction patterns and are not idiosyncratic
or mere artifacts of some single interpretive frame of reference.

We contend that the methodological standards of empirical social
scientific inquiry lend special substance to general rhetorical forms of
argumentation. General rhetorical questions and rhetorical argument
forms apply to all argumentation, but social scientific argumentation is
distinctive because it draws its special contents from methodologically
certified empirical sources. These special contents transform general
rhetorical questions into special issues of scientific inquiry and infuse
general rhetorical argument forms with substance appropriate to the
empirical resolution of those special issues.

Social scientific arguments can be distinguished according to the
methodological standards used to assess whether the substance of
argued claims is appropriate to the particular issue under dispute. The
four methodological standards are (1) reliability, (2) validity, (3) direction and strength of relationship, and (4) adequacy. Each yields empirical contents that are specially appropriate for arguments addressed to a
particular problem of social scientific inquiry. Let us return to those
specific problems and discern in detail how these methodological standards furnish general rhetorical argument forms with special empirical

contents that are appropriate for the resolution of each respective kind of fundamental issue of scientific inquiry.

Reliability Standards

The social scientific version of the question of existence (Is it?) is addressed typically with arguments that follow the standard noncontentious rhetorical form of description. As a rhetorical form of argument, description does not often express shareable operational procedures so that others may locate the same interaction pattern. But in social scientific argumentation this is a common application of that rhetorical form.

Social scientists use a reliability criterion to assess the appropriateness of operational descriptions. A reliability criterion requires the researcher to demonstrate that the located social interaction pattern is not merely the outcome of one person's unique interpretation (see Brody, 1992). The researcher must provide evidence that other observers could follow and repeat the operational description and, thereby, locate the same interaction pattern. Accordingly, test and retest data are often needed to show that located interaction patterns are, in fact, operative within a recurring kind of research situation. For example, Gottman and Levenson (1992) argue that the test-retest reliability of his observational coding procedures ranges from .60 to .79.

Validity Standards

The social scientific version of the question of definition (What is it?) is addressed typically with noncontentious arguments that follow the rhetorical form of exposition. Rhetorical expositions do not, as a matter of course, require strict methodological standards for certifying a pivotal term's definition and application during ongoing argumentation. However, social scientific inquiry furnishes special standards for appraising the contents of expositional claims.

Social scientists apply a validity criterion to assess the appropriateness of conceptual expositions. A conception is valid when those who work with different measurement systems or from different theoretical vantage points can still discriminate among the conception's constituent features. Researchers thus often bolster their conceptual expositions with data drawn from factor analysis, cluster analysis, multidimensional scaling, or some other analytic technique. For example, Gottman (1994) cites several studies that employ different operational descriptions for locating interaction patterns. He does so to warrant his use of negative and positive verbal statements and nonverbal cues during this exposition of the concept "flooding of negative attributions."

*Direction and Strength of the Relationships between
Constructs Standards*

The social scientific version of the general rhetorical question of relationship (What is it related to?) is addressed typically with arguments
that follow the noncontentious rhetorical form of narrative. Rhetorical
narratives do not usually incorporate methodological criteria for appraising the exact character of linkages between conceptions that are
woven within a temporal sequence. Social scientific inquiry, however,
furnishes special criteria for evaluating connections among conceptualized interaction patterns that are incorporated within a narrative sequence.

Social scientists apply direction and strength of relationship criteria to assess posited connections between two or more conceptualized
interaction patterns incorporated within a temporal sequence. Researchers must, of course, furnish evidence that posited relationships are not
tautological or multicollinear. They must offer evidence to support the
strength and direction of posited relationships. Moreover, they often
need to provide evidence that distinguishes the relationships' qualities
as (1) one way or reciprocal, (2) necessary or substitutable, (3) sufficient or contingent, and (4) sequential or coextensive.

For example, we have seen how Gottman (1991) provided empirical evidence that the relationship between his proposed sequence of
negative interaction variables and marital separation is one-way, necessary, sufficient, and sequential with the strength of a multiple correlation coefficient of 0.8. Moreover, he adduced evidence that one could
predict with 90 percent accuracy that married couples who followed
that sequence of negative interaction patterns will become separated
after a four-year period.

Adequacy Standards

Finally, the social scientific version of the general rhetorical question
of judgment ("How can we judge?") is addressed typically with
enthymematic forms of argument. Rhetorical enthymemes do not typically evoke special methodological values and evidential tests to constrain judgments of otherwise debatable claims. However, these are the
core standards of empirical social scientific inquiry and, thus, furnish
technical "common grounds" for completing the enthymemes of social
scientific argumentation.

Social scientists apply methodological adequacy criteria to assess
enthymemes about the degree to which a chosen investigative model
can test claims empirically. These models are well-known to social
scientists. Some are more appropriate than others for testing particular
kinds of claims. Researchers therefore develop enthymemes about chosen
methodologies that evoke these often tacit standards for judging their

technical appropriateness in furnishing adequate empirical tests of particular kinds of descriptive, expositional, and narrative claims.

We have already considered some of the leading standards for judging a model's adequacy for testing descriptive, expositional, and narrative claims. Models are appraised comparatively according to the degree that they adequately meet such technical standards as reliability, validity, and relational direction and strength. For example, narrative arguments about relational issues are often accompanied with enthymemes about the degree to which a chosen methodology is adequate for investigating those issues empirically. A variety of models are available for testing the strength and direction of different kinds of relational claims. One could claim that a relation between two conceptualized interaction patterns is one-way, two-way, necessary, substitutable, and so on. Researchers thus make enthymemes to argue that they have chosen the best type of analytical model for testing the strength and direction of relationships. When a judging audience tracks such enthymemes, they are more likely to conclude that the chosen model is more adequate methodologically than available alternatives.

In this section we have argued that standards of social scientific inquiry generate the special contents of rhetorical arguments that are addressed to issues incurred during investigations of social interaction patterns. These standards increase the likelihood that argued claims about those patterns designate real, existent features of social interaction and are not idiosyncratic to the inquirer's chosen frame of reference. If social scientists' arguments do not satisfy those standards, then the claims they adduce literally will lack the requisite contents for empirical resolution of the issues of inquiry. Consequently, their arguments would fail to furnish a reasoned basis for the presence of facts about social interactions.

The special standards of inquiry furnish the unique *scientific* contents for standard rhetorical forms of argument. Accordingly, we have contended:

1. Reliability standards yield contents for rhetorical descriptions that guarantee that the arguer and audience can locate the same patterns of behavior in a systematically repeatable manner.
2. Validity requirements furnish the substance of rhetorical expositions that guarantee that the arguer and audience can classify and discriminate among patterns of social interaction with a shared conceptual vocabulary.
3. Strength and direction tests yield the contents of rhetorical narratives that ensure that the arguer and audience follow the same relational linkages within a sequence of conceptualized interaction patterns.

168 Branislav Kovačić, Donald P. Cushman & Robert C. MacDougall

4. Methodological adequacy criteria yield the substance of enthymematic judgments that ensure the arguer and audience reason from technical grounds in common when appraising the adequacy of chosen models and methods for testing claims empirically.

Reasoned social facts are established when social scientists make methodologically adequate use of models and procedures to work through problems of locating, classifying, and interconnecting recurrent patterns of interaction. The *rhetoric* of reasoned social facts involves making arguments that convince interested social scientists that these fundamental problems of inquiry have been resolved with claims supported by empirical grounds sufficient to warrant claims of social facticity. Such argumentation ultimately links observed recurrent social patterns with theoretical propositions that, to some degree, explain or predict them. When this occurs through convincing argument, we are then furnished with reasoned, scientifically grounded, social facts about human interaction.

Finally, Gottman's social scientific inquiry successfully resolved the three problems raised by traditional rhetorical inquiry by (1) locating the actor's perceptual filters in order to guide an analysis of the problem, (2) proportionalizing rather than essentializing perceptions, and (3) specifying the relationship between perceptions, terms, and solutions in a precise and nontautological manner, and with adherence to the social scientific invention and judgment system outlined earlier in this essay. Finally, note how this method of inquiry can track the impact of the logical, emotional, and ethical cascades with respect to the reinterpretation of the history of an event. This tracking of reflexivity is the very essence of rhetorical persuasion.

Summary

We began with a call for a movement from monologue to dialogue between rhetoric and science. We then put forward the criteria under which such a dialogue could be successful. In this essay we have attempted to meet the first two criteria: (1) the elaboration of a significant and important new rhetorical invention and judgment system to inform science and (2) the elaboration of a significant and important social scientific invention and judgment system to inform rhetoric. We hope such inquiry will lead to the fulfillment of the third criteria: a willingness by some participants from both of the above groups to listen to and learn from the other group and enter constructively into a dialogue on these issues. In short, we invite the constructive extension of this dialog. We seek the voice of both the scientist and the rhetorician in this dialog.

Notes

1. Portions of this section are adapted from D. Cushman and B. Kovačić (1994), The rhetoric of the reasoned scientific fact, 1994 *Argumentation* 8:33–47.

2. Portions of this section are adapted from B. Kovačić, R. MacDougall, and D. Cushman (1996), Prying open the window of opportunity: Some rhetorical and social scientific dynamics to argumentation, *Communication Theory* 6:361–373.

References

Bitzer, Lloyd F. (1959). Aristotle's enthymeme revisited. *Quarterly Journal of Speech* 45:399–408.

Brody, Jane. (1992). To predict divorce, ask 125 questions. *New York Times,* August 11, p. C1.

Cushman, Donald P. (1990). A window of opportunity argument. *Communication Monographs* 57:328–32.

———— and Branislav Kovačić, (1994). The rhetoric of the reasoned social scientific fact. *Argumentation* 8:33–47.

———— and Robert McPhee. (1975). Three strategies of non-contentious argument. Paper Submitted to the Annual Convention of the Speech Communication Association, Houston, Texas.

Duhamel, Albert P. (1949). The function of rhetoric as effective expression. *Journal of the History of Ideas* 10:345–53.

Ehninger, Douglas. (1968). On systems of rhetoric. *Philosophy and Rhetoric* 1:134–44.

Fay, B., and D. Moon. (1972). What would an adequate philosophy of science look like? *Philosophy of Social Science* 7:209–77.

Feyerabend, P. (1974). *Against Method.* London: NLB.

Gottman, John M. (1994). *What Predicts Divorce?* Hillsdale, N.J.: Erlbaum.

————. (1994). What makes marriage work? *Psychology Today* March/April: 38–68.

————. (1993a). A theory of marital dissolution. *Journal of Family Psychology* 7:57–75.

————. (1993b). The roles of conflict engagement, escalation, or avoidance in marital interaction: A longitudinal view of five types of couples. *Journal of Consulting and Clinical Psychology* 61:6–15.

————. (1991). Predicting the Longitudinal Course of Marriages. *Journal of Marriage and Family Therpay* 17:3–7.

————. (1990). How marriages change. In G. R. Patterson (Ed.): *Family Social Interaction.* Hillsdale, N.J.: Erlbaum, 75–101.

———. (1983). How children become friends. *Monographs of the Society for Research in Child Development* 48 (3, Serial No. 201).

———. (1982). Temporal form: Towards a new language for describing relationships. *Journal of Marriage and the Family* 44: 943–62.

———. (1979). *Marital Interaction: Experimental Investigations.* New York: Academic Press.

——— and R. W. Levenson. (1992). Marital processes predictive of later dissolution: Behavior, physiology, and health. *Journal of Personality and Social Psychology* 63:221–33.

——— and A. L. Porterfield. (1981). Communicative competence in the non-verbal behavior of married couples. *Journal of Marriage and the Family* 43:817–24.

———, C. Notarius, F. Gonso, and H. Markman. (1976). *A Couple's Guide to Communication.* Champaign, Ill.: Research Press.

Graham, Gladys M. (1925). Natural procedure in argument. *Quarterly Journal of Speech Education* 11:319–337.

Griffin, W. (1993). Transitions from negative affect during marital interactions: Husband and wife differences. *Journal of Family Psychology* 6(3):230–44.

Kovačić, Branislav, R. MacDougall, and D. P. Cushman. (1996). Prying open the window of opportunity: Some rhetorical and social scientific dynamics to argumentation. *Communication Theory* 6:361–373.

Krokoff, L. (1990). Hidden agendas in marriage. *Communication Research* 17(4):483–97.

———. (1987). The correlates of negative affect in marriage. *Journal of Family Issues* 8(1):111–35.

Kuhn, T. S. (1962). *The Structure of Scientific Revolutions.* Chicago: University of Chicago Press.

Lessnoff, M. (1974). *The Structure of Social Science.* London: George Allen.

Mead, G. H. (1934). *Mind, Self and Society.* Chicago: University of Chicago Press.

Noller, P., and C. Venardos. (1986). Awareness in couples. *Journal of Social and Personal Relationships* 3:31–42.

Popper, K. R. (1959). *The Logic of Scientific Discovery.* New York: Basic Books.

Prelli, L. (1989). *A Rhetoric of Science: Inventing Scientific Discourse.* Columbia: University of South Carolina Press.

———. (1990). Rhetorical logic and the integration of rhetoric and science. *Communication Monographs* 57:315–22.

Rands, M., G. Levinger, and G. Mellinger. (1981). Patterns of conflict resolution and marital satisfaction. *Journal of Family Issues* 2(2):297–321.

Rusbolt, C., D. Johnson, and G. Morrow. (1986). Determinants and consequences of exit, voice, loyalty and neglect: Responses to dissatisfaction in adult romantic involvements. *Human Relations* 39(1):45–63.

Sabatelli, R., R. Buck, and D. Kenny. (1986). A social relations analysis of nonverbal communication accuracy in married couples. *Journal of Personality* 54(3):513–29.

Sillars, A., G. Pike, T. Jones, and M. Murphy. (1984). Communication and understanding in marriage. *Human Communication Research* 10(3)317–30.

Solmsen, F. (1941). The Aristotelian tradition in ancient rhetoric. *American Journal of Philosophy* 62:33–50.

Toulmin, S. E. (1972). *Human Understanding.* Princeton, N.J.: Princeton University Press.

Weber, M. (1964). *The Theory of Social and Economic Organization.* Glencoe, Ill.: The Free Press.

Chapter Seven

Establishing Interdependence in Employee-Owned Democratic Organizations

Teresa M. Harrison

Bureaucratic hierarchy is so fundamental to our everyday notion of organization that many of us can scarcely begin to imagine how an organization could be structured any other way. And yet, cooperative organizations, managed on the basis of democratic principles, have dotted the landscape of organizational life in the United States since early in the history of the nation. According to Rothschild and Whitt (1986), cooperative organizations have appeared in five distinct waves over the course of the last two centuries; their creation has been inspired by socialist, syndicalist, marxist, anarchist, feminist, neocapitalist and other philosophies (Mellor et al., 1988).

The latest wave of cooperative development to which Rothschild and Whitt (1986) refer took place in the 1960s and 1970s; it was led by individuals who rejected traditional bureaucracy and were motivated by ideological principle to construct economic and political alternatives to bureaucratic workplaces. The "alternative" or "collectivist-democratic" organizations they created sought to realize some form of participatory or representative democracy in the workplace through their efforts to create egalitarian conditions in wages, work, decision-making, and face-to-face relationships.

More recently, the 1980s witnessed a new round of democratic organization development in the form of worker buyouts through the creation of certain employee stock ownership plans (ESOPS) (see, e.g., Rosen et al., 1986) and the development of "phoenix" cooperatives (Cornforth et al., 1988; Mellor et al., 1988). These organizations came into existence largely as efforts to save jobs lost from the shutdown, sale, or geographic transfer of a factory or an entire enterprise. In these organizations, the need to create or save jobs has become the impetus for a radical transformation of organizational structure. This has not happened in all buyouts, of course; however, buyouts have been more likely to lead to efforts to develop democratic organizational structures than other forms of employee ownership (Hochner et al., 1988). In these cases, employee-owners turn to democratic forms not because democracy itself is pursued as an objective; instead, democratic structures are used to protect employees' investments by distributing control across multiple employee-owners.

Despite the persistent appearance of democratic organizations over the course of history and in the more recent past, there has been relatively little interest in studying them on the part of organization researchers across the social sciences and virtually none on the part of organizational communication researchers (Pacanowsky, 1988, and Cheney, 1995, are exceptions).[1] Instead, researchers have traditionally tended to assume that bureaucracy is the only form of structure that an organization can assume and, conversely, that organizations must always look like bureaucracies. Furthermore, particular aspects of social life that are intrinsic to bureaucracy have been taken to be inherent features of organizations. One implication of this tendency is that the "subject" has been eliminated systematically from organizational research.

The hallmarks of bureaucracy—fixed and universalistic rules, standardized procedures, distribution of authority and rewards by position, and impersonal social relations—are intended to minimize or eliminate the effects of subjective factors in the administration of organizations (Weber, 1946, 1947). Bureaucracy realizes a type of formal, legal authority that is predicated upon impersonality for its legitimacy, in that individuals occupy certain positions and are owed obedience on the basis of purely rational grounds (i.e., individuals acquire offices by virtue of their technical qualifications, individual identities are separated from the offices they fill, etc.). Bureaucratic authority exists in contrast to traditional authority or charismatic authority, where obedience is owed to particular individuals occupying traditional positions or possessing particular characteristics. By minimizing the influence of individual identities, bureaucracies strive to avoid the arbitrariness and capriciousness of rule typically associated with patrimonial and charismatic authority.

In assuming that organizations should function as bureaucracies, organizational researchers have ignored questions about how other types of structures in organizations might function, for example, organizations designed on the basis of collectivist-democratic features. This is especially harmful at a time when organizations are increasingly experimenting with innovations such as flattening organizational hierarchies and creating autonomous work teams that "democratize" traditional bureaucracies (see, e.g., Lawler, 1986; Passmore, 1988; Whyte, 1991).

Democratic organizations have not historically enjoyed the economic success of bureaucracy, but it is increasingly apparent that the success of bureaucracy may be a historical phenomenon now at an end (Heydebrand, 1989; Peters, 1992). Unfortunately, there is little democratic organizational theory to guide experimentation away from bureaucracy; we simply do not know very much about organizational processes in pure democracies.

Furthermore, the irrelevance of the subjective component has come to function as an unstated assumption as researchers have asked questions about how organizations work. Individual subjectivities are suppressed in most organizational research, which has been more interested in how classes of individuals—such as managers or workers—make decisions, communicate, or are influenced by various organizational factors. Such an assumption is particularly detrimental to the study of democracy in organizations because, as Rothschild and Whitt (1986) point out, collectivist-democratic organizations are characterized by social relations that are antithetical to bureaucracy, such as individuated decisions, personalistic appeals to members for coordinated action, and holistic and personal social relations between members. Many of the decisions made in administering democratic organizations cannot be understood without understanding the particular subjectivities involved.

In this paper I focus on the earliest stages in the development of democratic organizations and argue that the decision to become a member or co-owner of such an organization should be studied through reference to individual subjectivity. The paper begins by describing a conceptual basis for understanding the evolution of democratic interdependence that relies initially upon Weick's (1979) model of collective structure. This model presents a useful framework for understanding *what* kinds of judgments are involved in creating interdependence. However, I suggest that Giddens's (1979, 1984) concepts of system and structure help us to better understand *how* individuals make these judgments. Finally, I present data collected in a field study of individuals working together to create employee-owned democratic organizations, which suggests that participants draw upon structures of ownership and democracy to create interdependence in earliest stages of organizing.

Establishing Interdependence in Democratic Organizations

To ask how democratically structured organizations come into being is to ask how a particular kind of interdependent social relationship is created through communication (Harrison, 1994). Most discussion of the origins of interdependence begins with Weick's model of collective structure and his depiction of the processes by which structure is created. According to this model, interdependence is the outcome of structure; it is the product of recurrent cycles of interlocked behaviors whose effect is to bind elements of a given social entity. For Weick (1979), the term "organizational structure" is synonymous with interlocked behavior cycles: "The structure that determines how an organization acts and how it appears is the same structure that is established by regular patterns of interlocked behaviors" (90).

Although organizational theorists have assumed traditionally that organizations are created when individuals work together to achieve common goals, Weick (1979) argued that the cycles of interlocked behavior comprising the basic building blocks of organizing need not depend on goal-sharing to come into existence. Instead, a cycle of interlocked behavior can emerge when two individuals wish to perform their respective "consummatory" acts and realize that the "instrumental" act of the other individual is needed in order to do so. As Weick (1979) explains, a "mutual equivalence structure" is created when the "ability to perform my consummatory act depends on *someone else* performing an instrumental act. Furthermore, the performance of my instrumental act has the function of eliciting the other's instrumental act. If this pattern holds, and if I keep repeating my instrumental act, then the two of us have organized our strivings into a mutual equivalence structure" (98). Thus, instead of converging upon similar goals, individuals converge upon common means: each participant performs the instrumental act that, sooner or later, will allow the other to perform his or her consummatory act.

Weick (1979) argued that the formation of a mutual equivalence structure is a "basically solitary" activity (102). Having demonstrated that shared goals are not a prerequisite, he suggests that all an individual needs in order to participate in the development of a mutual equivalence structure is to (1) recognize that his or her consummatory activities require instrumental behavior from another (reliance), (2) realize that others will perform their instrumental acts in response to the performance of one's own instrumental act (prediction), and (3) repeatedly perform his or her instrumental act (repetition). However, it is only when *both* individuals (1) have recognized their mutual reliance on one another, (2) can predict the performance of the other's instrumental behavior, and (3) have established a repetitive sequence of behavior that a mutual equivalence structure comprised of interlocked behaviors has been created.

The simplicity and elegance of this model has made it a valuable tool for visualizing how action unfolds in the earliest stages of organizing. However, it is important to recognize that the model offers an abstracted and generic depiction of social action, viewed from the standpoint of an observer who is outside of and thus removed from the context in which real action takes place. Although such a perspective is useful for understanding, the skeletal configuration that constitutes structure, it tells us very little about how particular sequences of action are chosen and how they become constituent elements in a framework that binds real individuals.

An inquiry into the origins of any actual case of interdependence would require that one account for the specific choices that particular individuals make in constructing particular mutual equivalence structures. It would be crucial to understand how particular consummatory actions are selected and how individuals come to recognize the prospects for mutual reliance, that is, the potential for achieving their respective goals through the interlocking of their instrumental acts. Furthermore, while it is a relatively simple matter for the model to acknowledge that mutual prediction is sufficient for the interlocking of instrumental and consummatory acts, an individual's actual ability to predict the future behavior of another requires complex judgments about the other's trustworthiness and reliability as well as the other's capacity to engage in the promised behavior. Trust and reliability play a role in assessing the other's willingness to engage in repetitive cycles, but one must figure in as well the possibility that factors external to the developing structure may prevent others from fulfilling their obligations.

As I have argued elsewhere (Harrison, 1994), Giddens' (1979, 1984) structuration model complements the Weickian model by supplying concepts that enable the theorist to understand the basis upon which decisions of the kind described above might be made. What Weick refers to as patterns of interlocked behavior or structure, Giddens (1984) calls "systems" or "reproduced relations between actors or collectivities, organised as regular social practices" (66). According to Giddens, social systems are not structures; social systems *have* structures, which serve as the basis for the production and reproduction of particular behaviors, in particular sequences, under particular circumstances.

Structure consists of rules and resources that actors draw upon in interaction and that serve as the basis for an actor's selection of subsequent behavior. Rules define what behaviors mean, which behaviors are appropriate, and which are liable to sanction within given situations. Resources, on the other hand, are "vehicles" of power, capabilities over materials and persons, through which actors' intentions and interactional programs are actualized. Actors draw upon rules for knowledge about how to act and they draw upon resources for the power that enables action. Thus structure may be conceived as the stocks of knowledge and abilities that actors use to shape conduct, making interaction possible, meaningful, and legitimate. Structures of signification (modes of discourse, symbolic orders, interpretive schemes), legitimation (an accepted order of rights and obligations), and domination (power over resources and people) represent three types of mutually supportive

structures to which actors may refer in selecting future behavior. Giddens'
(1979, 1984) analysis of strategic conduct centers our attention on how
actors draw upon rules and resources in the constitution of their social
actions.

One can view the process of becoming a member of an organization as engaging in the construction of a mutual equivalence structure
between one individual and the organization writ large. It seems almost
absurd to ask why individuals become members of traditional bureau-
cratically structured organizations since it is readily acknowledged that
becoming a member of such an organization is a predictable route
toward accomplishing individual goals. And when individuals become
members of traditional organizations, there are a variety of tacit assur-
ances, embedded in the familiar structures of bureaucracy, that can be
brought to bear in one's calculations regarding predictability and
repetition.

Bureaucratic organizations typically supply ready-made expectations for a complex network of instrumental behaviors that members
contribute to organized action; these expectations may take the form of
task descriptions for particular organizational positions (structures of
signification), organizational charts (structures of legitimation), standard operating procedures (structures of domination), and other forms
of rules and regulations. In becoming employees of a traditional organization we typically know what particular kinds of employees are
required to do, when they are required to do it, where they are to do it,
how long they must do it, what they may but are not required to do, and
what they may not do. Understandings regarding the instrumental behaviors to be expected from other employees of the organization are
similarly well-defined. Knowledge and capabilities of these kinds are
represented in the structures of signification, legitimation, and domination that comprise bureaucratic hierarchy, most of which are taken for
granted in our organizational society.

However, when we consider the possibility of starting or joining
a new organization, the issues of reliance, prediction, and repetition
acquire renewed salience. The opportunity to cooperate with others in
beginning a new organization enmeshes an individual in a series of
assessments regarding one's own goals, the reliability of others, and the
possibilities for organizational survival and development. But even in
these cases, the familiar structures of bureaucratic hierarchy provide
readily available models for action. They supply guidance to entrepreneurs and their employees about how members should behave, how
relationships should be defined, how interaction should be regulated.

But very little of this kind of guidance is available to those who
choose to become members or co-owners in democratic organizations.
Schools, government, and other community organizations model the
kind of behavior appropriate for "employees" or subordinates within

bureaucracies. But there are few models of appropriate behavior for "owners" or members that interact with each other as equals. Although we all know what democracy is and can readily identify appropriate democratic behaviors within political contexts, there are no well-known models of democracy that relate specifically to a workplace context populated by equals. Indeed, individuals considering the prospect of joining into democratic interdependence must improvise behavior, drawing upon knowledge and capabilities that are far from routinized aspects of experience and in many cases antithetical to the organizational practices that are most familiar.

Thus, inquiry into the origins of employee-owned democratic organizations must attempt to address actors' strategic conduct, i.e., the kind of knowledge and the kind of capabilities potential members or owners draw upon in creating mutual equivalence structures. Focusing on the very earliest stages of creating democratic interdependence, I use Weick's concepts of reliance, predictability, and repetition to understand the kinds of decisions that participants must make initially in creating mutual equivalence structures. To understand how participants make such decisions, I attempt to identify the kind of knowledge and capabilities that participants draw upon in establishing interdependence between participants.

Method

The Research Site

The data presented in this paper are interim results of an ethnographic case study investigation of employee-owned democratic organizations, whose creation and development has been facilitated through the efforts of the Employee Ownership Project (EOP).

The EOP is a private social service organization located in upstate New York that was created in response to the 1984 U.S. Roman Catholic Bishops' pastoral letter on the economy entitled *Economic Justice for All*. One of the principles articulated in the Bishops' letter was the belief that the ability to participate and share an ownership stake in one's own business enterprise is fundamental to the development of greater economic justice and prosperity.

Responding to the Bishops' letter, three local college professors proposed development of a project that would take as its central concern the creation of employee-owned democratically run businesses in the Capital District of New York.[2] The proposal they submitted on behalf of this project was subsequently funded by the Albany Roman Catholic diocese, and the outcome was the creation and staffing of the EOP in 1986, an independent, not-for-profit corporation. The EOP's mission is "to promote economic development and local empowerment through the creation of worker cooperatives (businesses owned and controlled by the employees on a one-person/one-vote basis) and other democratically-managed enterprises" (*EOP Owners' Manual,* 1993, 1–2). Over the past seven years, the EOP has pursued a variety of projects in support of this mission. Staff members have offered seminars on democratization, consulted with existing organizations interested in becoming democratically managed, provided mediation services for existing cooperatives, and worked with individuals who have contacted them with plans to open their own democratically managed businesses.

The EOP has refocused its efforts in the last two years to concentrate on developing "models for neighborhood economic development and empowerment in economically distressed areas" (*EOP Owners' Manual,* 1993, 2). This work has centered upon identifying low-income individuals who are interested in creating and developing their own businesses. Through a variety of outreach efforts EOP is able to establish contact with individuals who express some degree of initial interest in the idea of starting their own businesses. When contact with such an individual is made, EOP staff members typically provide information about the business-related services that they can supply, engage in a brief description of the democratic character of the organizations that they seek to create, and encourage future contact with EOP. This contact can take many forms, such as personal meetings with staff members and/or attendance at a Business Planners class, a biweekly meeting in which basic business skills are taught and guidance is provided to specific individuals regarding efforts to launch their own businesses. The EOP also makes significant attempts to connect individuals with similar interests and complementary skills into joint efforts to start businesses.

Cultivating a Garment Manufacturing Business

Recently the EOP received a Community Development Block Grant funding the creation of a joint project with the Capital District Community Loan Fund in which the two organizations would work together to develop "micro-enterprises."[3] Involvement by the Community Loan Fund has meant that EOP has access to small amounts of capital (approximately $2,000 per project) that can be devoted to enterprise development. The EOP staff decided to concentrate their efforts on growing two specific businesses. One of these projects was guiding the development of a garment manufacturing business whose members so far have been an ethnically diverse group of women.

The staff hoped that the successful development of such a business would provide visible proof of the viability of employee-owned democratic organizations, thus establishing their credibility within the neighborhood. As one EOP staff member put it, residents of low-income communities have been frequent targets of social activists trying to sell them new programs that will "change their lives," and they are justifiably suspicious of any such efforts. The development of a successful garment business owned by low-income individuals was thought to be an important way to showcase the potential of democratic employee-owned organizations.

The EOP staff chose to pursue a garment business because, at the time, they had already identified one interested individual possessing sewing skills, and they ascertained that there were significant possibilities for locating other sewers.[4] Furthermore, the staff themselves could offer technical expertise in this area. Staff members acknowledged that such a business could not compete on a large scale basis with major garment manufacturing enterprises. Instead, the strategy was to create a niche organization, aimed at producing high-quality garments, in relatively small lots, on a short-term basis.

The data presented below are based largely upon interviews conducted with five principal figures involved in the EOP and the garment business project as well as observations of meetings among EOP staff, members of the garment business project, and other individuals who came into contact with the EOP to explore their interest in starting democratic organizations. In addition to extensive interviews of three EOP staff members, I interviewed Betty and Anne,[5] who initially were the individuals principally involved in organizing the garment business. Specifically, I attempted to answer the following questions: (1) What factors play a role in establishing mutual equivalence structures between prospective owners and the EOP staff toward the creation of an employee-owned democratic organization? (2) How do individuals make judgments about potential coparticipants in such an organization?

Data Analysis

The EOP Staff and Members of the Garment Business Project

The EOP office is staffed by four individuals, three of whom are paid, who bring various types of expertise to the organization that can be applied directly to the creation and development of small businesses. Each of these individuals is also motivated by social action concerns that are consistent with the goal of developing employee-owned democratic organizations.

Richard, the executive director of the EOP for the last five years, is a lawyer trained at Howard University with a special interest in employee ownership. He is white, Jewish, in his late thirties, and was born and raised in a nearby city, where he worked as a community organizer. Besides his contact with prospective owners, Richard manages the day-to-day affairs of the EOP including fund-raising and administration. He is responsible for legal issues associated with creating new businesses, which involves everything from drawing up incorporation papers to helping new owners continue to receive government-sponsored medical and financial benefits while they are pioneering their businesses.

Paul is the associate director of the project; he has primary responsibility for community organizing. He is white, Catholic, in his early thirties, and was born and raised in the Capital District. Earlier he worked as a fabric cutter in various garment factories located in the area before moving on to garment work in Boston and Philadelphia, where he became active in the Amalgamated Garment and Textile Workers' Union. Some of the experience that Paul brings to EOP is his work with the union in facilitating a worker buyout of a garment factory in Maine several years ago. Paul works with prospective owners to identify and locate needed resources, such as equipment and financial donations for nascent organizations. He brings to the EOP extensive knowledge of the resources available in the Capital District: individuals with expertise, businesses with equipment to sell or work for hire, and nonprofit organizations with financial and other resources to offer.

Kathryn, a white female in her early thirties, served for several years as a business consultant to the EOP; she recently moved into a half-time paid position (20 hours per week). She received her MBA from a local state university several years ago, a course of study she pursued for the explicit purpose of using business management skills to help grow local businesses in community-based economic development efforts. Her job is to provide business expertise to individuals planning the development of a business, such as skills development, market analysis, and establishing prices for goods and services. She facilitates the Business Planners meetings discussed above and works with prospective owners on a one-to-one basis to help them ascertain the economic viability of the businesses they are considering.

Betty is a 37-year-old white woman, the mother of three children whose ages range from 8 years to 10 months. She has lived in the Capital District and surrounding areas on and off since she was 16. She currently receives public assistance from the state in the form of financial and medical benefits. Although Betty has never worked in a garment factory, she has maintained an active interest in sewing for most of her life. At different points in time, she attended classes at the Fashion Institute of Technology in New York City, worked in fabric stores and retail stores setting up fashion displays, and has taught others how to sew. She found out about the EOP when, in the winter of 1993, she took a course in entrepreneurship offered by the Albany Chamber of Commerce's Entrepreneurial Assistance Program, which she discovered through New York State's Displaced Homemakers Project. As a part of this course, she was brought into contact with the EOP staff, who gave her a book to read about democratic organizations entitled *Putting Democracy to Work* (Adams and Hansen, 1992). She became interested in the idea of starting her own democratically organized garment manufacturing business.

Anne is a 36-year-old black woman, the mother of three children whose ages range from 12 to 5 years old. She has lived in the Capital District for the last 2 1/2 years after having been laid off from her job as a secretary in a neighboring state. She is currently in the process of completing a two-year program of studies at a local community college training as a paralegal worker. While she is attending school, she also receives public assistance from the state in the form of financial and medical benefits. Her hobby is sewing, which she has applied to reupholstering furniture. Anne found out about the garment business project through her sister Marcy at the beginning of the fall and has since become an enthusiastic participant.

*Establishing Interdependence between Participants
and the EOP Staff*

What factors play a role in establishing mutual equivalence structures between prospective owners and the EOP staff toward the creation of an employee-owned democratic organization? That is, how do individuals enter into the initial stages of reliance upon each other that is at the heart of a mutual equivalence structure? Initially, serendipity plays a large role in bringing potential owners into contact with the EOP staff. EOP staff engage in a number of strategies to bring them into proximity with individuals who may be interested in the idea of ownership. Word of mouth plays a role in informing individuals about the existence of the EOP as does contact with other social service agencies in the area. However, once initial contact with the EOP is made, each individual selects himself or herself into future interaction with the EOP staff.

Outreach efforts are successful in producing a small but steady stream of potential owners with whom the EOP begins to work. These are individuals who, to some degree or another, are able to see themselves as possible members of the category "owners." For example, those who first attend the biweekly Business Planners meetings typically come with their ideas for starting a business, and those who have been attending report progress they have made in researching their markets, locating resources, or otherwise carrying out plans for the development of their businesses.

Being able to draw upon the meanings of "ownership" seems to be crucial to continued participation with the EOP. Betty and Anne both report having wanted to own their own businesses well before any contact with the EOP. But these individuals stand in contrast with the many who came into initial contact with the EOP or someone in the garment business project and were uninterested in pursuing the idea of ownership. For example, Betty attempted to recruit unemployed friends and acquaintances to join her in starting the garment business and was surprised to learn that the idea of becoming an owner, as opposed to simply getting a job, seemed to be "beyond their comprehension." Staff member Paul described the reactions of four other women who were initial participants in the early planning of the garment business, all of whom dropped out relatively quickly. One fairly well educated woman said that people involved in the project were "out of their minds" to think that they could start a business of their own. Two others were intimidated by the idea and eventually stopped coming to planning meetings. A fourth was skeptical of the prospects for the business, wanting a job right away, but said that the others could contact her "when you come up with something." In Anne's opinion, there is a fundamental difference between employees and owners:

> some just are satisfied in being an employee. They don't want the responsibilities of a company. They just want to make their money and go home. But other people who are, I guess, ambitious like I guess me, I am, and just want to be able to do a lot of different things because today you got to be flexible.

One major reason why the idea of ownership fails to excite is because of the low expectations that many within the community have for themselves. Paul described the staff's experiences in conducting door-to-door surveys that asked respondents to talk about their ideal job. For many, the ideal job, the job they dream about holding, is typically something that represents very low expectations, such as becoming a home health aide. Others fear that ownership will disrupt their social services, without promising any of the benefits typically associated with employment, such as consistent wages and health insurance. For mothers with children, these are not light considerations.

Betty and Anne have discovered that employment in someone else's organization is never guaranteed. The attractiveness of ownership is at least partially predicated upon the inability of other organizations to supply reliable employment in an uncertain economy. Both of them have experienced relatively recent lay offs and both see ownership as a way to assert control over their lives. Ownership offers Betty something to do even if it may not guarantee wages:

> [Ownership] means that I can get up in the morning and go to my business and know that I still have a job. Even if I don't have the contracts, there's always things to do in your own business. I don't want to have to get up and go into work and then find that I'm fired or I can't go to work because they don't have the work then.

Ownership is one of a series of options that Anne is creating to help secure an income in the future. When asked what she would do if she received an offer of full-time employment at the same time that it looked as if the garment business might take off, she replied:

> well I would have to look in a couple things, like where am I going to get my medical coverage, especially like if I'm off of Social Services and all those benefits I need to secure my family? If [the garment business] could give me that then I probably would go full-time, but I have to keep my foot in the legal arena by doing something at home. . . . I want to be flexible. I want to be able to do a couple of things so that I'm insured of some kind of income.

If being able to participate in the *idea* of ownership brings individuals into initial contact with the EOP staff and other potential co-owners, then being able to engage in rudimentary ownership *behaviors* is required to sustain and develop repetitive cycles of interlocked behavior. Initially, mutual equivalence structures are created between the EOP staff, who wish to create employee-owned businesses, and individuals interested in beginning their own business. EOP staff member Richard distinguished between those who were simply attending Business Planners meetings and those with whom the staff were working actively by describing the development of a cycle of reciprocating moves that emerges between staff and individuals actively organizing businesses. The staff look for prospective owners to make the first move, which they can do by scheduling appointments. The staff reciprocates by providing support in various forms (e.g., suggestions about how to proceed, possibilities for resources, and training in necessary skill development). As individuals follow up on these suggestions or make other proactive gestures, the staff reciprocates by continuing to provide support, thus furthering the cycle of involvement. Although the EOP staff is not always convinced that there is potential in the business ideas that individuals have chosen to pursue, and will provide these assessments where necessary, the staff will continue to work with an individual who continues to take the initiative.

In the beginning stages, the continuing potential of an individual is frequently judged simply on the basis of whether he or she makes and keeps appointments, or at least calls to explain why an appointment was not kept and then schedules another. The staff are aware that there are many contingencies in the lives of the individuals with whom they work—lack of money for gas, sick children, conflicting meetings with Social Services workers—that can prevent a person from arriving on time for meetings or from getting to meetings altogether. Meeting times are scheduled and changed on an extremely fluid basis; an individual may be up to 30 minutes late before staff are willing to acknowledge that he or she may be missing an appointment. Staff frequently pick up individuals and take them to meetings if lack of gas money or transportation prevent an interested person from attending.

However, over time, it becomes increasingly important for the prospective owner to engage in behaviors that further the development of the business. For example, Betty has progressed from attending a course in entrepreneurship, to reading literature about employee-owned democratic businesses, to winning a series of sewing contracts with a local children's clothing store. She has investigated other contract possibilities, searched for sewing equipment to purchase and bought it, and she and her co-owners are now in the process of setting up offices in the neighborhood center in which the EOP maintains offices. Recently she appeared before the social concerns committee of a local Catholic church and convinced them to make an immediate donation of $1000 to her business and a subsequent donation a year later. It should be emphasized that Betty did not identify most of these resources herself; her progress has been sustained because she has followed up systematically on the leads provided to her by the EOP staff. The initiative she has taken in pursuing these leads, however, has been critical to the continuing evolution of interdependence.

Contrast this behavior with that of another potential owner "Sam," who has been attending Business Planners meetings for several months, with the aim of starting his own business making résumés, business cards, flyers, and other documents on his own computer equipment. During this time, Sam has been purchasing computer hardware and software, learning how to operate his equipment, and creating samples. On several occasions, he has distributed the fruits of his experimentation to those attending the planners meeting. However, when staff member Kathryn suggested recently that he might begin to distribute flyers announcing the availability of his services, he responded by stating that it would be damaging to generate too much business too fast and suggested instead that he spend more time learning how to use his software.

Establishing Interdependence between Prospective Owners

How do individuals make judgments about others as potential coparticipants in an employee-owned democratic organization? The EOP is dedicated to creating democratically managed businesses, which means that, although they work initially on helping single individuals to develop business ideas, eventually they want those individuals to join others involved in similar ventures or to recruit others to become co-owners in developing a business. Owners who have progressed far enough inevitably confront the question of whom to work with and the question of how to engage in democratic management.

Although there may well be a point in the development of a business when a specific set of skills are needed, it appears that taking initiative and contributing virtually any skills is important to the development of mutual equivalence structures in the earliest stages of the creation of the business. At this point, there is so much that needs to be done in starting a business that nearly any help, enthusiastically offered, will be taken as an encouraging sign. For example, Betty acknowledges that Anne's sewing skills will eventually need to be improved, but she finds other attractive qualities Anne can contribute:

> [Anne is] a very bright lady. And she's always open to ideas [unintelligible] and she's always willing to help. Like when we sat down and started having this meeting yesterday and she started taking notes, and I said, "Oh, are you prepared to be secretary," and she said, "Yeah you want me to send this letter out this afternoon?" I said, "Oh good, I don't have to do that 'cause I do hate writing letters.

Anne is similarly unconcerned about the sewing skills potential participants might lack, noting that an individual can always learn those skills. What's important to her is that they recruit "serious-minded" people who are not approaching the garment business project as a "temporary" thing. "Or if it is a temporary thing for them, they should be up-front and let us know so that we won't rely on them or expect anything from them."

Although neither Betty or Anne has ever been involved in a democratically managed organization, both claim that the democratic aspect of the business they are starting is one of its central appeals. Betty acknowledges that she could not set up a business by herself; she knows that she lacks the necessary skills to do so. But rather than recruiting partners, for example, it is important for her that the business be democratic because she needs others to contribute the skills required to run the business. Although Anne says that she would probably continue to work in the garment business if she wasn't an owner, the reason she got involved with it was because it was democratic and if it wasn't democratic "maybe I wouldn't put my all and all into it."

Similarly, both are wary of individuals who might restrict their ability to wield democratic control. At an earlier point in the development of the business, Betty was invited to set up a work site on the premises of a store whose owner had been contracting with her for the production of children's clothes. Betty rejected the offer to share space because she feared that she would lose control over her work if she did so. When asked if she would be willing to allow men to join the business, Anne replied that they would be welcome "as long as he wasn't no bang-bang [beats her fists against her chest], 'I'm Tarzan, I'm heading this.' "

Although the democratic aspect is important to them, Betty and Anne are less clear about what democracy will look like in practice. Both are aware that in a democratic organization, everyone will have "a say" in the company in contrast to working in traditional organizations where they have been told what to do. Betty insists that the books will be open, unlike in conventional businesses that may be making a profit but not telling their employees about it. But neither appears to have thought very much about how they might handle disagreements between members. Anne's idea is to

> offer disadvantages and advantages of whatever, of whatever the disagreement is. So we, like, democratically weight out the pros and the cons; OK, what we should do it this way or that way or whatever. . . . Hopefully the person or persons who are disagreeing will come to understand why it should be done a certain way or whatever. I mean put your cards on the table and make a decision about what's going to be best.

Betty believes that a serious disagreement may require some intervention on the part of an outsider. She suggests that calling in an EOP staff member may be the best solution at that point.

Assessing Predictability and Repetition

The most important requirement for the development of an ongoing cooperative arrangement between two individuals is trust—a factor mentioned by both staff and participants. Trust is built incrementally over time and occurs within the context of activities guided by the EOP staff. Participants are keenly attentive to the same cues that EOP staff see as signs of ownership potential: the willingness to attend meetings and/or reschedule those that are missed and the willingness to take some initiative in furthering the development of the business. For example, following one potential co-owner's first (and, to date, only) meeting with the EOP staff and Betty, there was an active discussion regarding this individual's level of interest as indicated by the calls she had made to staff at home and at the office inquiring about meetings and arranging for transportation. Only as an afterthought did Richard raise the point that sooner or later it would be necessary to see how well this individual was able to sew.

In the early stages of the development of the garment business, missed meetings were easily forgiven as long as participants knew that the individual who missed had remembered the meeting and was trying to get there but was delayed or prevented from attending by an unforeseen contingency. But it appears that predictability will become increasingly important to participants as the business continues to evolve. Very recently, the members of the garment business established two regular weekly meeting times when they were expected to confer with each other and with members of the EOP staff. Betty was visibly distressed to find members arriving late to one of these recent meetings and commented that in the future they needed to do a better job of keeping to their schedule.

Predictability involves the short-term ability to assess the likelihood of continued instrumental acts from others; repetition, on the other hand, involves the ability to make assessments of the long-term prospects for continuation of interlocked cycles. Here, participants must evaluate their own abilities as well as their coparticipants. At this stage in the evolution of the garment business, Betty and Anne are actively monitoring and assessing their own capabilities and potentials. Certainly, their ability to present themselves to others as business owners and engage in making purchases and negotiating contracts is important to their ability to maintain confidence in themselves.

But they are also thinking about the ways that they will need to grow in the future. Although they may not now possess all the skills they will need, Anne maintains that the qualities that enable each of the women to engage in parenting are qualities that will be crucial in their ability to become successful business owners.

> Now to me, a parent, especially a single parent like myself, why can't my qualities as a parent, meeting responsibilities, meeting deadlines, making decisions, the same sort of decision-making as that head of that company person there, the same sort. So I feel like parents raising families and stuff they constantly got to make decisions, got to make this, got to change this whatever. Certainly they can also do the same thing with a company, make adjustments, make their deadlines, be responsible and mature, keep it going like a household.

Betty, on the other hand, has been involved in the process long enough to have discovered, through her work, qualities she didn't know she had. Because she has been soliciting and completing contract work for children's clothing that is sold at a fairly expensive store in an upscale shopping center, she has "just discovered that I'm really good. I'm good at what I do." She points out that this has been a relatively recent development:

> No, I didn't know how good I was until I actually started working with [the children's clothing store owner], and I figured, well, she likes my work, I'm sure that other people will. I mean, I guess that working with [the store owner] there's not only self-esteem there, but I know that. . . . She's in a prominent place, you know, the people in [name of shopping center] have big money. [If] my skills are good enough to be down there then I think I can really do this.

Conclusion

Although this garment manufacturing enterprise is still quite young, the data show that participants are engaged in the construction of mutual equivalence structures. In order to achieve their objectives, individuals are creating interdependence by exchanging instrumental acts, first with members of the EOP and later with others who may become co-owners. It is also possible to discern that participants are actively assessing the predictability and repeatability of the mutual equivalence structures that they are constructing. But the data seem to indicate as well that, to understand the nature of the mutual equivalence structures that are under construction, we need to refer to more than just the concepts of reliance, predictability, and repetition. In constructing the very rudimentary social system now under development, participants draw upon two complexes of rules and resources to guide their actions and their interactions with other participants.

The first of these complexes is the structure of ownership. Out of all the individuals that could come to the EOP for assistance, only a handful actually do. What motivates them is their ability to see themselves as potentially able to assume the identity of "owner" as opposed to the identity of "employee." For the women involved in the garment business project, the meaning of this identity is linked to the potential to realize long-held goals and ambitions. The meaning of ownership is also linked to the potential to control their future activities and, to some extent, their financial resources.

An owner is someone who does things, that is, a person who is able to maintain a cycle of interlocked behavior by continuing to act and in so doing, continuing to stimulate the production of others' acts. At these early stages, taking this initiative requires small investments of time and energy and relatively little obligation to other individuals. However, even now, it is apparent that participants are attentive to behaviors on the part of others that can be taken as signs that a similar set of understandings is at work. This is understandable because the stakes will rise quickly and participants are embarking on a risky and uncertain relationship with someone they have only begun to know.

Finally, participants also appear to be assessing the prospects for their own continued development within this identity. Success at the more familiar structure of parenting and success in meeting current challenges are taken to be signs of future abilities. These qualities help to boost participants' confidence, providing a growing foundation for the challenges that lie in the future.

Participants also turn to the structure of democracy for guidance in creating interdependence. That is, participants appear to be knowledgeably engaged in the creation of cycles of reciprocal behavior that will be characterized by democratic, rather than hierarchical, relations of power. Part of this can be seen in participants' willingness to welcome involvement by essentially anyone who has anything to offer. Individuals who are not welcome are those who will prevent participants from exercising control. Participants are willing to share control with other newer participants, and understand that doing so will require that members engage in certain practices, such as allowing everyone to voice their opinions and ensuring that information about the organization will be available to members. They know that individuals will have to try to understand each other in order to resolve disagreements, and they also know that they may need help in getting over rocky periods.

Based upon the analysis to date, participants seem to know more about ownership than they do about practicing democracy in the workplace. This is understandable since our culture provides far more information about entrepreneurs than about how egalitarian practices can be transferred from political contexts to workplace contexts. At this early point, it is probably more useful to know more about how to be an owner than how to be democratic, since so much needs to be done and it is unlikely that members' actions will interfere with each other.

But as the organization grows in members and in workload and individuals become progressively interdependent, as they start to stake their futures on each other, one expects that it will become increasingly important for members to explore with each other what it means to be democratic and what kinds of interlocked behavior cycles one produces in an effort to practice democracy. The EOP staff will no doubt provide information about practices used by other democratic organizations, but it is also highly likely that members may invent some new ones of their own.

The data demonstrate the usefulness of accessing individuals' accounts of their experiences as they come together in the process of developing democratic organizations. Decisions to join traditional organizations are guided by what we are taught about how to behave in and what to expect from bureaucracies. The structures of bureaucracy are familiar and can be taken for granted; they are the results of a double hermeneutic at work, in which the categories of social science research have been appropriated by actors who use them in the routine reproduction of traditional bureaucratic organizations. These structures, lurking unacknowledged in the conceptual background, make the Weickian model's emphasis on reliance, predictability, and repetition appear to be sufficient to account for the development of interlocked behavior cycles.

But decisions to join or create democratic organizations require actors to engage in relatively novel social action. The ethnographic data make it apparent that actors draw upon structures of ownership and democracy rather than bureaucracy in making assessments of each other's potential for interdependence. These structures encompass a range of behaviors, some of which will be quite different from those characteristic of bureaucracy. In the absence of individuals' accounts, it would be impossible to understand what actions are viewed as democratic and what such actions mean to those who perform them.

The ethnographic data also suggest that it may be important to share some goals as individuals join together in creating democratic organizations. Both Betty and Anne stress the need to find others who similarly wish to create and work in a democratic organization. Weick's model, in contrast, minimizes the importance of shared goals, focusing instead on common means as the foundation for the development of interdependence. The model's ability to dispense with shared goals is attractive because it has always been difficult for traditional organizational theory to explain how owners and employees, two classes of individuals who are not likely to share goals, could find it possible to become interdependent. However, bureaucracy may well be one type of organization that does not require shared goals in order to work. Although the data are insufficient to support this conclusion at this time, it seems possible that the development of genuinely democratic organizations may require the genuine commitment of all members to democracy as an endgoal. Only further ethnographic data collection, focusing on the subjective experience of democratic organization members, will allow us to assess the validity of this claim.

Thus, in a strong sense, recovering the subjective aspects of individual experience may be vital to building a theory of democratic organizational communication. But, as traditional organizations move away from bureaucracy by experimenting with novel, democratic arrangements, it may become more generally important to reconsider individual subjectivity. Standard organizational concepts such as supervisor, subordinate, leadership, and management will become obsolete or take on new meanings in organizations structured as autonomous work groups in flat hierarchies that make their own hiring decisions, maintain their own budgets, and gather their own information. What meanings will employees attribute to such new arrangements? What new discourses will be invented to describe the novel organizational designs invented through such experimentation? How will authority be legitimized in work contexts predicated upon equality in group member relationships? Questions such as these can only be answered through careful attention to the experience of individuals transitioning from bureaucracy to whatever their organization will become. Thus, given the new organizations we are building for the future, recovering the subject in organizations may well be an indispensable feature of organizational communication research.

Notes

1. Attendance at a recent one-day conference on organizational democracy sponsored by the Organizational Communication Division of the Speech Communication Association in November, 1994, was substantial enough to indicate that this situation may be changing.
2. This region encompasses the cities of Albany, Schenectady, and Troy and surrounding smaller communities, known collectively as the "Capital District" and representing a population of over 750,000.
3. This term reflects the fact that these businesses are so small, usually consisting of just a couple of members, that they don't even qualify for the label "small business."
4. The cities of Troy and Cohoes in the Capital District and nearby Gloversville and Johnstown have historically been the site of large garment manufacturing concerns. The last large-scale garment factory in Troy shut down in the 1980s.
5. Pseudonyms have been created for all individuals involved in the EOP or sponsored organizations.

References

Adams, F. T., and G. B. Hansen. (1987, 1992). *Putting Democracy to Work: A Practical Guide for Starting Worker-Owned Businesses.* Eugene, Ore.: Hulogos'i.
Cheney, G. (1995). Democracy in the workplace: Theory and practice from the perspective of communication. *Journal of Applied Communication Research, 23,* 167–200.

Cornforth, C., A. Thomas, J. Lewis, and R. Spear. (1988). *Developing Successful Worker Co-operatives*. London: Sage.

EOP Owners' Manual. (Spring, 1993). Who is EOP, Anway? 1-2, 3.

Giddens, A. (1979). *Central Problems in Social Theory*. Berkeley: University of California Press.

———. (1984). *The Constitution of Society*. Berkeley: University of California Press.

Harrison, T. (1994). Communication and interdependence in democratic organizations. In S. Deetz (Ed.): *Communication Yearbook* 17:247–74.

Heydebrand, W. V. (1989). New organizational forms. *Work and Occupations* 16:323–57.

Hochner, A., C. S. Granrose, J. Goode, E. Simon, and E. Appelbaum. (1988). *Job-Saving Strategies: Workers Buyouts and QWL*. W. E. Upjohn Institution for Employment Research.

Lawler, E., III. (1986). *High Involvement Management*. San Francisco: Jossey-Bass.

Mellor, M., J. Hannah, and J. Stirling. (1988). *Worker Cooperatives in Theory and Practice*. Milton Keynes, Great Britain: Open University Press.

Pacanowsky, M. (1988). Communication in empowering organizations. In J. A. Anderson (Ed.): *Communication Yearbook* 11:356–79.

Passmore, W. (1988). *Designing Effective Organizations*. New York: Wiley.

Peters, T. (1992). *Liberation Management*. New York: Knopf.

Rosen, C., K. Klein, and K. Young. (1986). *Employee Ownership in America*. Lexington, Mass.: Lexington.

Rothschild, J., and A. Whitt. (1986). *The Cooperative Workplace*. Cambridge, Great Britain: Cambridge University Press.

Weber, M. (1947). *The Theory of Social and Economic Organization*. (A. M. Henderson and T. Parsons, Trans.) New York: Free Press.

———. (1946). *From Max Weber*. (H. H. Gerth and C. W. Mills, Eds.) New York: Oxford University Press.

Weick, K. (1969, 1979). *The Social Psychology of Organizing*. Reading, Mass.: Addison Wesley.

Whyte, W. F. (1991). *Social Theory for Action: How Individuals and Organizations Learn to Change*. Newbury Park, Calif.: Sage.

Chapter Eight

Transcribing the Body and Materializing the Subject: Women's Victim Narratives in Penalty Phase Testimony

Sara Cobb

> *It is in particular the issue of "entrapment" or trained "incapacity" that concerns me here; the fact that our current ways of sense making prevent us from experiencing and understanding certain aspects of ourselves. . . . I do not think that it is going too far to suggest that there is a "political economy of selfhood" at work here, differently controlling the access to the "development opportunities" people provide to one another.*
>
> —Shotter (1984, 174, 179)

Feminist legal scholars have critiqued criminal trials,[1] particularly rape trials (Bumiller, 1987), on the grounds that they revictimize women, not only by requiring them to reexperience the violence (Bumiller, 1991), but by structuring the communication in ways that reduce women's ability to tell their own story, in their own way (Matoesian, 1993), by forcing them to become objects of violence, dismembered body parts, presenting them as locations where wounds appear and weapons are wielded.[2] Arguing that law constrains, controls, and denies women's subjectivity, feminist scholarship concludes the exclusion of women's experience, coupled with the social construction of women as objects (Eisenstein, 1988), reconstitutes the patriarchal order, the male standard, and women's domination (Matoesian, 1993; Mackinnon, 1983, 1989).[3] Women's objectification is thus a central focus in feminist legal scholarship, at both empirical and theoretical levels.

These arguments are compelling precisely because they reflect the feminist concern over emancipation and domination, freedom and constraint, agency and structure. Women-as-objects are evidence of domination through the absence of their ability to control or impact their context (structure), through the absence of their subjectivity (or the absence of a subjectivity that is not contaminated by structure).

But this focus on objectification itself constrains our notion of power. First, to critique the objectification of women in the courtroom is to proffer a normative model that valorizes subjectivity, yet as Matoesian's (1993) data shows, rape victims are regularly navigating to forestall their construction as subjects, which inevitably functions to lay the groundwork for their culpability as agents in their own victimization.[4] So the subjectivity, indirectly advocated by the feminists, is problematic, if not dangerous, for women victims in the courtroom.[5]

Furthermore, the valorization of subjectivity is part of a formulation of power that equates subject with agency/freedom and object with passivity/domination. However, paradoxically, it is the liberal legal goal of "emancipation" that not only makes constraint/imprisonment possible (to discipline is to take away freedom), it simplifies the relation between agency and structure, reducing our understanding of the recursive/reflexive effects of action in structures. Women do not act within structure, they participate to evolve (through action) the very structures that regulate their action. Thus, power is not only evident in its negative, repressive forms but in its positive form as well—the positive effects of power are visible in the "grid" in which women navigate the construction of themselves as subjects. If we see only objectification (domination) we miss the ways that women enact and evolve the framework for the construction of the "subject" and "object" dichotomy itself.

Second, there is a Cartesianism at the core of the distinction between subjectivity and objectivity that, like the distinction between meaning and action, fails to consider how subjectivity is objective (experience is material, corporal) and, conversely, how objectivity is subjective (the material/corporal is symbolically coded experience). Feldman (1991) writes:

> At first glance, the . . . body-as-object seems at odds with the thesis of subjectification. Yet . . . the body made into . . . artifact by an embodied act of violence is no less a political agent than the author(s) of violence. The very act of violence invests the body with agency. . . . Violence is a mode of transcription; it circulates codes from one . . . surface or agent onto another. Transcription requires agency, both the communicative act of the transcriber and the transcribed "object." (6–7)

From this perspective, the act of testifying is both subjective and objective—it is the symbolic act of inscribing meaning onto the body, the creation of the body-as-object by the subject.[6] Yet the "embodied subject,"[7] or the subject-as-body, is eclipsed in the subject/object dichotomy at the base of the feminist critique. The critique of "objectification" simplifies and mystifies the complexity of the role of the body in the construction of subjectivity.

Third, the categories "subjectivity" and "objectivity" are treated as outcomes and take as given the narrative/discursive processes that produce, valorize, and require subjectivity, as well as its opposite— objectivity; yet it is precisely at the level of the discourse that the distinction between victim/victimizer, between guilt/innocence is produced. As Scarry (1985) and Feldman (1991) have noted, reconstructing violence-as-event requires what McKenna (1992) calls "tracing" the origins, the history, the causality of violence. And this narrative process, in turn, constitutes both the source of the violence, as well as its reception. And in the process, the roles, victim/victimizer and subject/object, are established and stabilized. Because the categories subject/object are central to tracing/stabilizing violence, they are central to law's ability to mark out (condemn) the victimizer and justify law's next move in the story of violence, that is, imprisonment and/or death.

In this way, the subject/object dichotomy in discourse enables the directionality of violence to be stabilized, contributing to the construction of law's privilege, its authority (Goodrich, 1987). For law only traces the violence against the victim and leaves untraced/unmarked/unknown the violence done by law to the "victimizer,"[8] and in this process "covers its tracks" (Sarat and Kearns, 1991), retaining it disciplinary power (Dumm, 1990). From this perspective, this subject/object dichotomy is key to law's ability to regulate *and* authorize violence; it reflexively constitutes a way of knowing that reconstitutes the categories for knowing which *is* the exercise of power in the courtroom. As Foucault (1983) notes, this knowledge/power is:

> a form of power that applies to immediate and everyday life which categorizes the individual, makes him by his own individuality, attaches him to his identity, imposes a truth on him which he must recognize and which others have to recognize in him. It is a form of power that makes individuals subjects. (212)

In other words, the social construction of the individual as individual, as location for personess, as particular, as capable of "reporting" about agency and experience, is the process through which the directionality (historicity) of violence is established, through which power is "exercised" in the courtroom and the disciplinary power of law, reaffirmed.

In summary, the feminist critique of objectification decontextualizes the discursive processes in and through which the directionality of violence is established; it fails to attend to the symbolism of the body and the materialism of the subject, and it valorizes subjectivity and, paradoxically, reconstitutes the distinctions between active/passage (subject/object) that deny the complexity of women's work to navigate the "politics of selfhood." Instead, this paper accents not the repression of women-as-subjects (negative power) but the production of the subject/object relations within which women mark themselves as a self (the positive effects of power).

My analysis seeks to explore the Foucauldian question about how "subjectness" or "personness" is itself constituted. For it is through the construction of the individual-as-subject that the directionality/causality of violence is established, simultaneously enabling (and hiding) the force of law, stabilizing the social/moral difference between victims and victimizers. Through the analysis of four women's testimony of their victimization, in the course of a capital trial, I offer a critical description of parameters regulating the constitution of "individual-as-subject" and its role in the construction of the victimizer as subject/agent.[9] I shall argue that the subject/object dichotomy is the disciplinary apparatus of law and show how, within this apparatus (which includes the attorney/interrogator) there are very specific forms of subjectivity that are constituted. And these forms are critically important to the construction of the accused as victimizer. Ultimately, my goal is to shift the level of analysis away from the critique of objectivism, to a critique of how "subjectness" and "objectness" are themselves constituted. Collectively, attention to these patterns will enable a shift in the figure/ground relation between a focus on the woman as subject/object, to a focus on the nature of the "political economy of selfhood," i.e., the work done to construct the individual as subject.

The Social Construction of the "Individual-as-Subject" and Narrative Process

"Subject," as a category, is a social position in discourse and therefore, is dependent upon the discursive presentation of self as a self, as a source of and location for experience and action (Harre, 1984; Kerby, 1991; Foucault, 1978).[10] Individuals are socially constituted as individuals as they occupy a *unique* place in discourse, distinguished from others either by *their* actions (which establish social roles), i.e., "I/she was walking down the street eating an ice cream"; their reception of *others'* actions, i.e., "and then he hit me/her"; or their experience (their signification of and reflection on the body), i.e., "I/she am/is cold" (and/or their second-order signification of action/experience), i.e., "I can't go out alone now because of what he did." Relative to both action and experience, the location of subject as individual can be done by speaker for speaker, or by speaker for other—in both cases, a unique location for action/experience is established, and the person is constituted as a site for "signifying discourse" (Foucault, 1978).

The actions/experiences that establish the individual-as-subject, as a site for signifying discourse, are themselves situated in narrative structures/processes (Kerby, 1991; Ricoeur, 1984–88) and thus never "free" from their role in the reflexive construction of both content and relational dimensions of communication.[11] The content of the story (actions/plot) recursively impacts the relationships between characters (roles) *and,* at a metalevel, between the speaker and the story (point of view) (Scholes and Kellogg, 1968; Polkinghorne, 1988; Ricoeur, 1981).

"Point of view" is a function of the relation narrators establish with their own story, i.e., the narrative *distance* they construct for themselves as speakers, as (co-)constructors of the speaking event, with the content of the story they are relating (Scholes and Kellogg, 1968).[12] However, point of view does not simply refer, as Harre (1984) points out, to the first- or third-person narrative position; it is more complicated than that. Point of view refers to the *relation* between the saying and the said, the act of constructing a world and the world that is constructed through that process. In other words, point of view is a hermeneutic *process,* not a static state of being. From this perspective, the point of view is an evolving, nonstationery location, impacted both by the content of the story told, as well as that which is done in the *saying of* the story.[13] If this is the case, there are many, if not infinite, points of view, and these cannot be exhausted by the first or third person.

For example, two stories may be told in the first person, but one recounts action as an experience dissonant to self, while the other constructs self as the source of action. In the former case, the speaker signals passivity and loss of control/agency; this is very different from a story in which the speaker depicts self as in control, an agent in the unfolding of a string of events. So even though both stories can be told in the first person, differences in position *within* the story construct differences in point of view, i.e., subject position.

Subject position also varies with respect to the proximity persons construct relative to their own action/experiences. In turn, this proximity is related to the presence of reflection where women create the meaning of the violence, by constructing its consequences in their lives; when reflection is absent, women are simply reporting the violence, without commenting on what it means to them, without referring to or addressing their pain/suffering/feelings. In the former case, they *personalize* the violence by reflecting, at a second-order level, on the significance of the violence; in the latter case, the violence remains *depersonalized,* an aggregate of acts, floating free, unattached to its consequences.

However, whether subjects reflect or report on violence, whether violence remains *personalized* or is *depersonalized,* is, in turn, a function of the interaction with the "confessor," the "examiner," the "interrogator," and in this case, the attorney (Foucault, 1978). As Scarry (1985, 1994) points out, violence destroys discourse, shatters persons' abilities to formulate linear time frames (on which plots depend), and disrupts or mystifies roles (on which character and theme depend). Thus, the return from violence is a return to discourse; because discourse is interactive, the return from pain is a social process, which (historically but perhaps not inevitably) relies on the presence of an "other" whose participation may resemble that of the torturer, the confessor, the examiner, the inquisitor, the therapist.[14] So the attorney in the courtroom plays a central role in the construction of the individual-as-subject, impacting not only the content of the narrative,[15] but the potential for women to reflect on the violence, to signify their pain themselves. Contrary to the feminist critique which argues that attorneys contribute to the objectification of women, I shall argue that attorneys, as inquisitors, enable women's construction as subjects by favoring particular narrative forms that polarize and distinguish victims from victimizers, regulating the proximity women have to their own testimony.

In summary, the social construction of the individual as subject, as a site for signifying discourse is dependent on (1) their (interactive) construction as *source* or *recipient* of the action and (2) the (interactive) construction of violation as *personalized* or *depersonalized.* And on both these dimensions, the attorney and the legal apparatus contribute to shape the context for the construction of subjectivity, both that of the women and that of the accused.[16] Figure 8.1 provides a model for examining the construction of individual as subject.

Using this 2 × 2 model, it is possible to describe how women get created as subjects through their testimony; specifically, we can look at the contours of what is done and what is not done. In Quadrant I, the

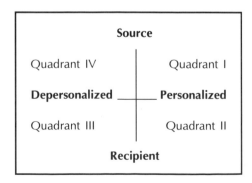

Figure 8.1.

subject is constituted as the *source* of action and as the site for signifying the meaning of the violence through *personalizing* its consequences. In Quadrant II, the subject is constituted as a *recipient* of others' actions, as well as a site for *personalized* violence, signifying violence through reflections on its meaning. In Quadrant III, the subject is constituted as a recipient of others' action, without reflecting on the meaning, but instead reporting or listing the violations—presenting the violence as *depersonalized*. In Quadrant IV, the subject is constituted as a *source* of action and a site for *depersonalized* violence, without reflecting on the meaning of the violence. In each of these quadrants, the attorney/interrogator contributes to the constitution of the subject in and through the nature of the questions that he (in this case) asks, for it is through his questions that the victim has the opportunity to reflect on the meaning of violence or just report on a list of acts aggregated in and through their location on her body.

My analysis involves the application of this model for tracking subject construction to the stories of four women who testified to their violation by Theodore Wrest, during the course of the penalty phase of his capital trial.[17] Wrest was tried and convicted for the murder of Virginia Aceves and Nancy Croom on March 6, 1987. All the women who testified were attacked at different moments of Wrest's life;[18] two were attacked before March 1987, and one, Kimi Hansel, was attacked on the same night that Wrest killed Virginia and Nancy; Shannon Alton was attacked in the days following these murders. These four narratives[19] provide the database[20] for this analysis of the "exercise of power" in the courtroom, which, I have argued, is the constitution of the category of "subject" itself.[21]

The examination of what Foucault calls the "positive effects" of power will hopefully provide a new way to assess and critique the interpellation of women victims in the legal apparatus; I examine each woman's testimony for (1) the distinctive way she constitutes herself as subject, (2) the attorney's role in that process, and (3) the consequences of her particular subjectness on the social construction of the victimizer.

Kimi Hansel: Subject as *Recipient* of *Depersonalized* Violence

Quadrant III

On March 6, 1987, Kimi Hansel, age 23, was assaulted with a knife by a stranger in an alley, narrowly escaping both rape and death. She retells the story of her violation during the course of the penalty phase of the criminal trial of her assailant, Theodore Wrest:[22]

Prosecutor: Something happened as you were walking down that alley?

Ms. Hansel: Yes.

Prosecutor: Can you tell the ladies and gentlemen of the jury in your own words what the next thing was that you realized?

Ms. Hansel: The next thing I realized was I heard someone running really fast, behind me. And I was turning to look, like this, and before I had a chance to look all the way, I felt something hit me really hard—I mean I can't explain how hard—in the middle of my back. And it, like, hit me so hard that I, well, and I'm a big tall girl, so it was like really hard. And all the wind was knocked out of me. And then I heard someone say, "You bitch." And then I was, as I was hit, I tried to protect myself. And I turned like this, and I felt a flurry of motions going out of my body. And I asked as this was happening, I managed to ask, "Why are you doing this?" And I heard him say, "Because I don't give a shit about anything anymore." And then I remember I put my hand up to try to protect my face. And I think I tried to cry for help, but I couldn't really get it out because I was being hit so fast and hard that I didn't, I couldn't speak. And then I fell. I fell to the ground. I hit my head really hard. And I was laying there and it stopped, stopped for a second or stopped for a couple of minutes, I'm not sure how long. And I remember thinking, I remember being really scared and thinking, oh, I'm going to die now. And I could feel everything getting really dark. And so I'm laying there and I see myself bleeding and I am trying to move my body. And I couldn't get away. I was trying to get away. And so I started to cry for help, "Someone help me" and I, I guess he was standing behind me. And he stabbed me again in the head. And then I said, "Okay, I'm dead. I'm dead." And then I went out.

Prosecutor: In other words, you lost consciousness?

Ms. Hansel: I lost consciousness.

Prosecutor: Okay, now what is the next thing that you remember after you lost consciousness?

Ms. Hansel: The next thing I remember is I came to and I was being dragged down the (street)—up towards my apartment.

Prosecutor: Were you on your back being drug or on your stomach?

Ms. Hansel: I was on my back being drug, but I had been on my stomach when I was lying there before.

Prosecutor: You remember the last time you went down, you were on your stomach?

Ms. Hansel: Right.

Prosecutor: And now you're on your back—

Ms. Hansel: Right.

Prosecutor: And someone is dragging you?

Ms. Hansel: Right.

Prosecutor: And what was the next thing that you realized after you realized you were in motion, being drug. Did you feel the hands on your wrists?

Ms. Hansel: Uh-huh.

Prosecutor: Okay.

Ms. Hansel: And then I remember someone telling me to look up at him. He said, "Look up at me." And I looked up. I looked up and I saw his whole face. And I saw that he was wearing a baseball hat backwards and a plaid shirt. And I saw he was smiling. And he said, "You're not going to live long, are you." And I didn't answer. And then he said, "Now I'm going to take you in the bushes and fuck you." And then I felt his body stop, like this, and look. And then he dropped me. And that was it. And the next thing I remember was the ambulance.

Prosecutor: OK you say the next thing you remember is the ambulance. . . . What is it that you remember about the ambulance?

Ms. Hansel: I remember the paramedics came up to me. I was drifting off and all of a sudden this man was asking me all these questions about "Did you have fight with this woman," and all this stuff. And I didn't know there was another lady. And I said, "No."

Prosecutor: Do you remember going to the hospital?

Ms. Hansel: Uh-huh.

Prosecutor: Do you remember being treated by a doctor at the hospital?

Ms. Hansel: Uh-huh. A whole bunch of doctors.

Prosecutor: Do you remember waking up in the hospital that next day? How did you feel?

Ms. Hansel: I was really out of it. I didn't—I couldn't move my body. I can't explain how I felt, because I was not—I was not living in reality. I was not living in a full capacitation of myself. I mean, I was just, I was just so injured that I didn't—you know when you're really injured and you're in shock, it's like, you don't—I don't know how to explain it. I felt awful.

Prosecutor: At some point did you learn that you were going to have to go through some rehabilitation because of the injuries you sustained?

Ms. Hansel: Right.

Prosecutor: When did you find that out?

Ms. Hansel: In the morning. I found out that some of the spinal fluid had leaked from one of the injuries in my neck and it had left me paralyzed on my right side. And my left side was no feeling, no sensation.[23]

Prosecutor: How long did that paralyzation last?

Ms. Hansel: It is still occurring right now. It's been a year and a month. It will probably—it will probably be couple—probably about two years or a year and a half before I'm fully better. And thank God I'm . . .

Prosecutor: You've made a lot of progress?

Ms. Hansel: I've made a lot of progress. I was told that I would never walk again. . . .

Prosecutor: What's it like in physical therapy?

Ms. Hansel: It's hard work. It's hard work. But its also rewarding. But, it's hard.

Prosecutor: Can you see progress?

Ms. Hansel: Yeah, it's great. I'm really fortunate.

Ms. Hansel then is asked to identify Wrest as her assailant, which she does. Her testimony ends there.

Hansel's subjectivity is complex; first, she constructs self as a body violated. She is the recipient of Wrest's blows, marked by the wounds of his knife. Her agency/ability to control either the situation or even her own body is denied through her use of the passive voice "I was hit" as well as through her explicit references to her loss of control, i.e., "I felt a flurry of motions coming out of my body."

Second, Hansel's absent agency is highlighted by her as she describes the acts she intended but could not perform, i.e., "I tried to cry for help . . . I couldn't speak . . . I was trying to get away." Devoid of agency, she describes witnessing her own helplessness, her own impending death, "And I'm laying there and I'm seeing myself bleeding and I am trying to move my body and I couldn't get away." Here her use of the present tense reflects her own momentary location in the past, in the experience; paradoxically, this occurs at the moment of maximal depersonalization—her observation of her own suffering, from outside her own body.

Hansel depersonalizes the violence throughout her testimony in very complex ways. First, while the violence is occurring, she turns to Wrest to ask him the meaning of his acts; so again, there is a double-level construction here in which she reports, as a subject, about her inability to signify the violence, during the violence. Second, although she does discuss the meaning of the violence in terms of its consequence in her life, these terrible injuries that she names are reframed by her and the prosecutor as good "fortune!" In other words, the injuries do not stand as a sign of the terribleness of the violence but are instead constructed through their progressive disappearance as she tells a story of "improvement." At one point she even began to thank God that the effects of the violence were waning!

The attorney contributes to Hansel's depersonalization not only by continually asking her to report rather than reflect on the violence which functions to create a linear plot,[24] but by following her into the story about "progress." In asking her to detail her injuries, which were extreme, he pushed to condense her subjectness into her body, into the sites of violence; and in so doing, he "fractures the body as 'organic,' 'natural,' object" (Feldman, 1991, 7). She "resists" and moves to comment on consequences of those injuries, i.e., "progress," and in this process reconstitutes herself as a site for signifying discourse. She is more than the sum of her injuries.

However, her insistence that she be more than her body (beyond her body as she was during the violence) has curious consequences for the accused, Wrest. If his conviction depends upon his construction as a source (agent) of violence, the direction of violence must be from him, *through* Hansel's body, toward the effects of the violence (its significance). When she constructs herself as "improving," not only are the signs of violence dissipated, but the significance of the violence is connected to God's blessing.[25]

And in this process, Wrest-as-source-of-violence begins to dissolve. The complexity is astounding—Hansel's move to personalize the violence as positive, to characterize it in terms of "progress," destabilizes the subject/object categories on which law depends—Wrest flickers at the boundary of violent subject, his outline as victim of law's terrible disciplinary power becomes momentarily visible, only to have it disappear in his rematerialization as violent subject, in the testimony of the next witness, the emergency room doctor, who recounts in gory detail, the nature of Ms. Hansel's wounds.[26] Ms. Hansel's body, through the act of interrogation, becomes a vehicle for her own subjectification; as her body becomes an unnaturalized and fractured site of signification, site of "adversarial" or contested "transcripts," it becomes a site of meaning, "accelerating the body's subjectification" (Feldman, 1991, 7).[27] In summary, Ms. Hansel constructs herself, in interaction with the prosecutor, as a recipient of action, a site for depersonalized violence; she poses a threat to the directionality of violence as she characterizes her injuries as signs of progress—for if she is not a victim, if there are no negative consequences of the violence, then Wrest's role as victimizer begins to dematerialize.

Mrs. Bolin: Subject as *Source* and Site for *Depersonalized* Violence

Quadrant IV

Mrs. Bolin was attacked by Wrest in her own home when Wrest was about 15 years old. Mrs. Bolin was a teacher in a local public school and knew "Teddy" through contact with him in the neighborhood. In her first-person account, she tells a story of how she overcame her attacker (pp. 1274–80). After recounting that she has just returned home from school, and had noticed that some items were misplaced, Mrs. Bolin recounts the violence itself:[28]

> *Prosecutor:* What happened then (after Teddy appeared in your laundry room where you were standing, with a fireplace shovel raised over his head and said that he was going to kill you)?
>
> *Mrs. Bolin:* I said, "No, you're not." And I reached up and I—well, we were about the same height. And as luck would have it, I guess, for my sake, I had a lot of weight over him at the time. And I reached up and took the shovel in my hand also and I whirled him around.
>
> *Prosecutor:* Was there a reason you did that?
>
> *Mrs. Bolin:* Well, yes there was.
>
> *Prosecutor:* What was the reason?
>
> *Mrs. Bolin:* Well, as I told you a few minutes ago, I had locked this particular door (to the outside), and my back had been to the door and I knew that I couldn't get out that door very easily.
>
> *Prosecutor:* Okay, so you turned him around and put him against the door, is that right?
>
> *Mrs. Bolin:* Right. . . . When I got the shovel away from him, in his right hand he had my butcher knife. . . .
>
> *Prosecutor:* And when you saw him with the knife, would you describe to the jury what the next thing was that happened?
>
> *Mrs. Bolin:* He said, "I'm going to kill you" again. And he started bringing the knife up towards my chest. And I reached up like this and I hit him in the bridge of the nose. And blood went everywhere.
>
> *Prosecutor:* Okay. What happened to the knife?
>
> *Mrs. Bolin:* He dropped the knife.
>
> *Prosecutor:* All right. What did you do then?
>
> *Mrs. Bolin:* I took hold of his jacket. I unlocked the utility room door. I opened the utility room door. I opened the

storm door and told him to get the hell out of my house and
I never wanted to see him again. And he went flying down
the stairs. And that's the last I saw of him. . . .
Prosecutor establishes with Bolin that Wrest had gathered
items from the house that indicated that he intended to
strangle her.
Prosecutor: Now after these events occurred, did you stay
by yourself in the house?
Mrs. Bolin: No, I did not.

Clearly, Mrs. Bolin constructs subject as source of action, not only
saving herself from a violent death, but even reversing the directionality
of violence, breaking Wrest's nose and throwing him out of the house.
It is important to note that there is not one single passive verb construction in Mrs. Bolin's account—she uses exclusively active voice. The
gesture that accompanied her explanation of how she hit him ("and I
reached up like this") is the analogic representation of herself as a
source of action. In addition, her own voice in the story is authoritative
"No, you're not" and telling him "to get the hell out of my house." In
her account of the conversation, she also is explicitly contesting/resisting
the direction of the violence and announces her refusal to be a recipient
of his blows.

However, interestingly, her story does not contain any account of
her suffering; in the minutes when she was in the house, before the
attack, after she noticed that there had been someone in the house, she
does not recount being afraid; after the attack, she does state that her
parents came to stay with her and that she slept elsewhere for a period
of time, moving back into her house accompanied by a friend, because
"Teddy" was on the loose. However, at no time does Mrs. Bolin describe her emotional experience or her suffering.

Again, the prosecutor's questions, as well as the court's constitution of "injury" played an important role. The prosecutor asked questions that construct a linear plot, but they do not allow for the
second-order relection on that story. Thus Mrs. Bolin builds a "behavioral list" of actions but is not able to signify the meaning of those
actions. However, the prosecutor tried, in vain, to introduce testimony
about her "emotional scars" but the defense blocked it, mobilizing the
legal apparatus to constrain Mrs. Bolin from personalizing the violence,
evidence that the law is using her to regulate the category of subject
itself. In this case, it is the wounded emotional subject that is not
permitted to appear:

> *Prosecutor:* As a result of the things that happened to you,
> between you and Mr. Wrest, did you have to alter some of
> the things that you did at school?

Mrs. Bolin: They did not immediately find Teddy. And so the principal advised me to change a lot of my routines. I had to . . .

Defense Attorney (DA): Your Honor, I really think we're getting kind of far afield on this stuff.

Judge: And you're making an objection?

DA: Yes.

Judge: Sustained.

Prosecutor: With regard to anything that happened at the school. Your Honor?

Judge: Yes.

Prosecutor: Did you have to alter the way you lived?

Mrs. Bolin: Yes I did.

Prosecutor: What precautions did you take?

DA: Your Honor, I'm going to make the same objection.

Judge: Sustained.

Prosecutor: I guess no opportunity of me being heard?

Judge: Sure.

Prosecutor: May we approach the side bar?

Judge: Yes:

(At sidebar)

Prosecutor: Basically my position is that the emotional effects of what happened and the impact that it had on her life is certainly relevant on the issue of the aggravated nature of the crime, just as if she had had a physical injury that had stayed with her the rest of her life, which would be admissible. Why is the emotional scar any different than the physical?

Judge: She already said that she was afraid to stay in the house.[29] I think he's objecting to the precautions which the school took, things that, well, go ahead.

DA: I'm objecting to any precautions that the school took and I'm objecting to any change that she made in her own life, because all the cases are really clear that unless something fits one of the categories under 190.3 I think it is, it doesn't come into evidence. Injury fits one of the categories. But what she changed about her life or even any emotional trauma is not listed under 190.3.

After more discussion that repeats the same points, the judge rules that the prosecutor could ask a question regarding the emotional impact of the violence:

Judge: I'm not going to argue . . . I don't think that means we've got to hear a whole bunch about how she locked the

windows every night and all that. She can testify that she was upset but I just don't want to spend a lot of time on how she might have changed all the things she did.
Prosecutor: Mrs. Bolin, without getting into the detail of everything that you did after your confrontation with the defendant that afternoon, did it leave some lasting emotional scars on you that stayed with you for years?
Mrs. Bolin: Yes sir.
Prosecutor: I have no further questions, Your Honor.[30]

I find it very revealing that Mrs. Bolin could not signify her own violation by reflecting on its consequences in her life. First, it is clear that the dichotomy of subject/object has at its core, as I indicated, the mind/body distinction that I have elsewhere argued is requisite to the distinction between physical and emotional violence, a distinction that, in turn, is regularly used in the diminishment of the effects of violence (Cobb, 1991). By forestalling the construction of emotional violence (and Mrs. Bolin as the site of an emotional injury), the Court is forestalling the materialization of the body-as-subject, a category of subjectness that would collide with the subject/object dichotomy that separates mind from body.

But I think Mrs. Bolin presents a particular challenge to the legal apparatus; as a source of violence herself, the court begins to equate her subjectness with that of her attacker. Note the use of the word "confrontation" by the prosecutor to refer to the violence. In her own construction of subject, Mrs. Bolin seems to have ruptured the Court's ability to distinguish between her and Wrest; from this perspective, their unwillingness to allow her to signify her emotional suffering was a move that contributed to the stability of the subject/object dichotomy. Through her account of her action, she had tread too close to agency and she had no wounds through which the prosecutor could construct her as a victim-subject. If the subject comes into being through interrogation/confession as Foucault argues, and the confession is the process of signifying the body, the absence of physical injury dissolved the prosecutor's role as confessor and *de*-celerated the subjectification of Mrs. Bolin, whose subjectness depends upon the "transcription" of the body (Feldman, 1991, 7). Unable to signify her experience or her body, Mrs. Bolin's subjectivity is limited.

In summary, Mrs. Bolin, as an effective and authoritative source of action, threatened to destabilize the victim/victimizer, subject/object dichotomy; the evidence of this lies both in the way the Court blocked her signification of the violence (she could not tell of her pain), as well as in the prosecutor's reconstruction of the violence as "confrontation." How Mrs. Bolin could *not* constitute herself as a subject outlines the parameters of what law permits. Her agency, coupled with the fact that she could not be constructed in and through her physical wounds, clearly posed a threat to the directionality of violence, upon which law's authority to do violence depends. It seems that women may present their self as both source and recipient of action, but extreme agency, without the presence of wounds, threatens the stability of the victim/victimizer distinction because it mystifies the directionality of violence by mutualizing it. In summary, Mrs. Bolin is a source of action and a site for depersonalized violence; she was blocked from personalizing the violence, perhaps because she lacked any physical injury. And in the process, Wrest's construction as a victimizer dematerializes as the violence is mutualized.

Rose Peck: Subject as *Source* and Site for *Personalized* Violence

Quadrant I

Mrs. Peck was attacked by Wrest in her home at 6:25 AM, with her two daughters (age four and eleven) in the house. Her victim narrative constructs her, like Mrs. Bolin, as an agent; however, Mrs. Peck additionally constructs the violence as personal, signifying her injuries and those of her daughters. (1291–301):[31]

> *Prosecutor:* Okay, could you tell the ladies and gentlemen of the jury in your own words what the first thing was that you noticed was unusual?
> *Mrs. Peck:* I was standing at the foot of the bed and all of a sudden I heard a loud screaming and yelling. I heard, "I'm going to kill you and your daughter." And I looked up and there was man, a young man, at that time, running down the hall with a pole in his hand. . . .
> *Prosecutor:* Did he come into the room?
> *Mrs. Peck:* Yes.
> *Prosecutor:* What happened then?
> *Mrs. Peck:* We fought. And I immediately resisted. When I heard that and seen him coming, I knew that was my only chance.
> *Prosecutor:* When you say that you fought, when he came in and he has this pole in his hand and he says that he's going to kill you . . .
> *Mrs. Peck:* And my daughter . . .
> *Prosecutor:* So he comes into the room and he has the pole. Would you describe to the ladies and gentlemen of the jury

what happened with the pole in terms of the battle? Did you ever get hit with it, for instance?

Mrs. Peck: Yes, many times. I grabbed the pole when he came at me with it the first time and tried to, you know, hang on. I was pulled around alot. Sometimes he would get it away and would hit me. I ended up with numerous bruises on my leg by the end of the battle. I had a black eye too.

Prosecutor: Okay, so you're in the room and you're going back and forth, and sometimes you're hanging on to it and sometimes you're not. Is that right?

Mrs. Peck: Yeah.

Prosecutor: How long did this go on?

Mrs. Peck: I think I checked the clock later when we called the police, and it was like, quarter until, or 10 minutes until seven. It was 20, 25 minutes, somewhere around there.

Prosecutor: At some point in time during the struggle, did the defendant say something to you about money?

Mrs. Peck: Yes.

Prosecutor: What did he say?

Mrs. Peck: He said, "I want your money."

Prosecutor: What was going on when he said that?

Mrs. Peck: We were fighting.

Prosecutor: In the bedroom still?

Mrs. Peck: Yes. . . .

Prosecutor: And when he asked you for money, what did you say?

Mrs. Peck: I said, "I only have $5.00. It's on the dresser right over there.

Prosecutor: Did he respond to that at that point?

Mrs. Peck: No.

Prosecutor: What was the next thing that happened when you told him about the money? . . .

Mrs. Peck: Well, just, we went on fighting, you know for a little bit. And finally, he finally told me to—directed me over towards the bed, pushed me back that way. And he said, "Sit down. Sit here." And he was making a motion with his hand, sit here, you know, like stay there. And he started turning when he seen that I was going to sit there. So I thought, oh well, he's going to leave. I'll be quiet and maybe he'll just go on and leave. And he turned and headed for the door to the hall. And the direction he was going towards the door, he was going to where my four year old had stood there in the hall while we were fighting and said, "Quit hitting my Mommy. Leave my Mommy alone." And

she was standing right there. And he wasn't going towards
the side of the door, toward the hall. So I got him from
behind, because he had the pole in his hand. By the time,
by that time, he was at the door. And I was frightened that
he would hurt her and so . . .

Prosecutor: So the struggle started again?

Mrs. Peck: Yeah.

Prosecutor: This time you sort of jumped him from behind?

Mrs. Peck: Uh-huh.

Prosecutor: Could you describe as best you can what happened during the struggle this time?

Mrs. Peck: Well, it was more of the same fighting. And it
was really hard this time. And during that time, he hit me
really hard in the, in the eye, in the left eye. And I had a
black eye. And finally as the, we got to a place that he quit,
and he again asked me where my money was and I said,
"On the dresser." And he took it and he started up the hall.
He got halfway up the hall and turned around and come
back. And I got up. I had sat down on the bed, thinking he
was leaving. And I got up. And he got down in the middle
of the floor, looked around for a little bit, and found a chain
or bracelet or something that he'd lost during the fight. And
then he left. . . .

Prosecutor: Were there other parts of your body which had
also been injured which were not in the sense, physically
visible or covered by clothing?

Mrs. Peck: Yes, after I turned in the police report, I called
them back that afternoon and I had, at the time of the attack, I just had my undergarments on and I had a long
panty-girdle on, so I didn't notice when they photographed
that I had any bruises. And I had a very large bruise about
that size on my left leg, which I had for about two years.
It took two years for it to completely go away. And then in
the last three years, starting in '85, I've had some X-rays,
back X-rays. And I have a twisted spine. It's twisted at the
top and it's twisted at the bottom, both going either way.
And I've got a lot of problems and pain and muscle spasms
and all kinds of stuff that the doctors were not able to find
until they found that.

Prosecutor: And with regard to this incident, would you
say that it had a pretty traumatic effect on your family?

Mrs. Peck: Yes. Immediately afterward, and for some time
thereafter, my children would not let, if I was at home and
I went to my bedroom, or if I was in the bedroom and I

went to the living room, the children would go from room to room with me. They wouldn't be left alone. Somebody had to be with them. They were very scared. They were scared of being in the house. We finally, that happened in February, and finally in May we found a house and purchased it and moved.

Interestingly, Mrs. Peck, like Mrs. Bolin, is a source of action/ violence, working to save her own life and the lives of her daughters. She uses action verbs and active voice, almost exclusively. Only once does she use the passive voice "I was pulled around alot" and even when she constructs herself as the object of Wrest's action ("He hit me really hard in the eye"), she maintains the active voice, and the narrative focus on her "resistance." In this way, even though she describes how she was the recipient of blows, the point of her story is not how she was overcome by violence, but how she struggled not to be overcome by violence.

Like Mrs. Bolin, Mrs. Peck resisted, even becoming the attacker at one point "(getting) him from behind." But there are interesting differences between these two narratives: Mrs. Peck includes an account of her body, referring to her wounds, as well as to the subsequent pain that she suffered as a result of the "fight," and describes the emotional consequences of the attack on her daughter-victims—"they were scared of being in the house,"[32] as well as the pragmatic hardship of needing to find another house and move. Together, through these additions, Mrs. Peck personalizes the violence—she constructs herself as having a subjectivity that is active and reflective; she becomes, through her reflections, a site where violence is signified. But again, the attorney plays an important role in constituting her subjectivity.

First, the prosecutor plays an important role stabilizing Mrs. Peck as *source,* rather than *recipient* of action. He does this by defining the violence as a "struggle," rather than an attack, following Mrs. Peck's initial construction of the attack as a "fight."[33] In addition, the prosecutor, at one point, makes a reflective restatement of Mrs. Peck's story, crystallizing the mutuality of the violence: "Okay, so you're in the room and you are *going back and forth* and sometimes you're hanging onto it (the pole) and sometimes you're not." "Going back and forth" is a construction of the event that consolidates Mrs. Peck's subject as equal participant and fails to acknowledge that when she is not hanging onto the pole, she is being beaten with it.[34]

Second, despite his "denial" of her position as victim, the prosecutor does enable her to reflect, to signify the meaning of the violence on her body, as well as in the lives of her daughters. He asks, "were there other parts of your body which also had been injured that were not in the sense physically visible or covered by clothing?" This question works to construct the injuries as "hidden" and opens the possibility that injuries can be mysterious and unknown, even to Mrs. Peck herself. The personalization of violence (connecting it to a person) can only occur when there are physical injuries/wounds; however, if these are constructed as "hidden," other nonvisible injuries can be signified.

She responds with an account of how the pain has become, over time, a "twisted spine" that even the doctors could not immediately identify. This construction of the injury as "hidden" and capable of transmutation over time then opens the possibility that she can construct the "hidden" nature of her daughters' injuries, which are "emotional," i.e., fear. It is fascinating to note that the same prosecutor, judge, and defense attorney that would not allow Mrs. Bolin to reflect on the "hidden" nature of her injuries, enabled Mrs. Peck to do so.

My explanation is two-fold: first, Mrs. Peck *did* have physical injuries, which were used to lead into the discussion of her nonphysical injuries, whereas Mrs. Bolin did not. Second, the prosecutor's question about the "traumatic effect" of the violence was not only a question about her but a question about the effects on her family. Given that mothers are culturally constructed as conduits of their family's experience, Mrs. Peck's reflection on her family was obligated given the presence of the children in the story—she was the only way for the spectacle of their victimization to appear. Her subjectivity is thus predicated on the representation of the subjectivity of her family, particularly her daughters. In contrast, Mrs. Bolin was asked by the defense attorney to represent the subjectivity of Wrest by means of questions to her about Wrest's mother, questions which implied that Wrest had had a difficult childhood. So in different ways, both women were required to signify self though the subjectification of others. But in one case, this personalized the violence, in the other, it did not.

And the difference is significant for Wrest, for the personalization of violence magnifies its effects (Foucault, 1979)—the closer we are to the screams of the tortured, the more proximate/real the pain. As the pain materializes, so does the presence of the torturer. This is why there is always interrogation in the torture session (Scarry, 1985)—moral absolution for the infliction of pain can only come about if the tortured is constructed, through interrogation, as a *source* of action, having originated his own torture through a prior act of violence. The same historization occurs in the courtroom—Wrest is transformed into a subject, an agent, a source of violence, through the interrogation of the women that materializes their pain, which will, in turn, forestall the construction of law as torturer. In Mrs. Bolin's testimony, pain was not allowed to materialize, and therefore, she was not a vehicle for Wrest's materialization as violent subject, whereas Mrs. Peck's reflection on her injuries and the "hidden" injury to her children, historicized not only the violence that was done to her, but the violence that will be (has been) done to Wrest.[35] In summary, Mrs. Peck constructed herself as a source of action and a site for personalized violence; as subject, she greatly contributed to the stability of the subject/object dichotomy, reflexively through her construction as subject, but perhaps it was Mrs. Alton who, more than the others, materialized Wrest as a violent subject.

Shannon Alton: Subject as "Active" *Recipient* of *Depersonalized* Violence

Variation in Quadrant III

Shannon Alton was attacked by Wrest in May 1987, in her home, after her husband had left for work. Her story offers us an example of both depersonalized violence in a victim narrative, coupled with a paradoxical version of agency: she cooperates in her own victimization (1304–3). Mrs. Alton was in bed, watching the *Today Show* and reading a book:

> **Prosecutor:** You said that he was standing (at the head of your bed pointing a rifle at your head)—where was he standing?
> **Mrs. Alton:** He walked inside the bedroom door, which is at the head of my bed.
> **Prosecutor:** He had a rifle . . .
> **Mrs. Alton:** Yes, sir.
> **Prosecutor:** And do you recall what the first thing that he said or did was?
> **Mrs. Alton:** He said, "I won't hurt you. I just want money."
> **Prosecutor:** Where was the rifle at the time in terms of, was it pointed down or up at you?
> **Mrs. Alton:** At me. . . .
> **Prosecutor:** What was the next thing that was said, if you could just tell us? Was there a series of exchanges, verbal exchanges, back and forth, between you and the defendant?
> **Mrs. Alton:** I told him where I had $200 in my purse downstairs on the kitchen counter. He said that he couldn't just leave me; that he'd have to tie me up. And he went over to the chest of drawers and got a sock and threw it at me and told me to put it in my mouth.
> **Prosecutor:** Did you do that?
> **Mrs. Alton:** Yes sir.
> **Prosecutor:** Okay.

Mrs. Alton: Then he threw another sock and asked me to tie my wrists together. And I couldn't tie my wrists with a small sock.

Prosecutor: Okay.

Mrs. Alton: And I motioned to him that I couldn't.

Prosecutor: By this time, you already had the sock in your mouth?

Mrs. Alton: Yes sir.

Prosecutor: Okay.

Mrs. Alton: He tied the sock on my wrists. He asked me if I'd had a good time in New Orleans a month or so before.

Prosecutor: Had you been in New Orleans a month before?

Mrs. Alton: Yes. And my house was broken into at that time.

Prosecutor: Okay.

Mrs. Alton: He told me that it was my husband's fault; that he'd seen him leave the house to go to work; that he hadn't locked the door to the garage; and that it was all his fault that this was happening. He said that he'd been in my house before when I was home and had taken $10 off the kitchen counter. I don't know what all else he said.

Prosecutor: Did you have a nightgown on at this time?

Mrs. Alton: Yes, sir.

Prosecutor: Were your feet bound in any way?

Mrs. Alton: Not at that time—point. . . .

Prosecutor: After your hands were tied, and after the conversations that you described between—basically unilateral conversations,[36] his statements to you, what was the next thing that happened?

Mrs. Alton: He asked if I had any rope or tape, because he wasn't satisfied with the way I was tied and didn't want to leave me there. And I motioned no. And he asked me if there was any pantyhose. And I motioned no. And he started to get upset, so I motioned, yeah, I knew where they were. And he went in the dressing room where the pantyhose were, and came back out, and then tied my feet.

Prosecutor: When you say you motioned, you were indicating, the jury saw, but the record couldn't, you were indicating with your head moving up and down for positive or back and forth for negative; is that right?

Mrs. Alton: Yeah, and crying.[37]

Prosecutor: So he comes back with the pantyhose and ties your feet; is that correct? . . .

Mrs. Alton: Uh-huh.

Prosecutor: What was the next thing that happened after your feet were tied?

Mrs. Alton: I believe then he went downstairs. . . .

Prosecutor: What was the next thing that happened?

Mrs. Alton: He came right back up and he had a beer in his hand. And again, he made some comment that he wasn't satisfied, that he wanted to make sure that I was more secured. And he looked at the bed, trying to find some way to tie me to the bed. And there was nothing to do that, so he had me get out of bed and hop into my closet, which is off my dressing room, and lie down on the floor.

Prosecutor: So your feet were still tied and your hands were still tied and you hopped . . .

Mrs. Alton: Yes.

Prosecutor: Did he say anything to you at that time?

Mrs. Alton: Not that I can actually recall right off. Not at that time. He did untie my hands and tied them to the back of me. And then he took a belt and tied my feet up to my hands so I was laying on the floor, tied all together. . . .

Prosecutor: Now after you were tied in the fashion that you described to the jury, was anything else said by the defendant at that time?

Mrs. Alton: He said that he wasn't going to hurt me and that he isn't going to rape me, but he was going to go downstairs and that he'd be there for a while and that it would take me a while to get untied and that he would leave before I would be able to get untied. And then he closed the door and left me in the dark. . . .

Prosecutor: What was the next thing that you recall happening?

Mrs. Alton: The door swung open and he was standing there with a butcher knife. And he said he'd changed his mind; that he was there to rape me. . . .

Prosecutor: What was the next thing that he said or did?

Mrs. Alton: He untied my feet and rolled me onto my stomach and pulled my nightgown up. He laid the knife down next to me. And—and then he attempted to have intercourse with me anally, but he wasn't very successful at that. And after awhile, he rolled me onto my back and he—then he raped me vaginally. And I was crying the whole time and he told me to quit crying, to start moaning, which I did. He told me to keep my eyes closed; that this wasn't working out very well; that he was going to ejaculate on my stomach; and to keep my eyes closed. And he did that. Then he pulled my nightgown down and tied my feet back to my hands.

Prosecutor: All right. What was the next thing said or done?

Mrs. Alton: He went into my dressing room, which is right in front of where I was lying, and tucked in his T-shirt and his shirt and got his comb out and combed his hair and took his bandanna out of his pocket. I don't remember what he did with that. Took the money out of his pocket and counted it. He went through the drawers, just a little bit. He came back into the closet and pulled out a jacket that I had hanging in the closet, and put that on. And went back to the mirror and made sure he looked cool, or whatever. He— then he came back into the closet and knelt down beside me and said, "Now what are you going to tell the police?" And I still had the sock in my mouth this whole time. And he said, "You're going to tell them that a six-foot tall black man in a suit with bright green eyes did this." And I motioned to him, for reasons unknown to me, that I had something to say. And he took the sock out. And I told him that black men usually don't have bright green eyes. And he said, "Yeah, you're a pretty smart lady." And he put the sock back into my mouth. And he said, "Pretty lucky too." He says, "I'm going to leave now. It's going to take you a while to get undone." And he closed the door and left. I could hear him walking downstairs. And I heard the garage door open and screen door open. And I heard the door close. And I was instantly out of the ties and crawled to the telephone and called 911.

Mrs. Alton's victim narrative is different from the other three in that she, paradoxically, constructs herself as an agent in her own victimization, describing how she complied with Wrest's commands, all the while using active voice—she is somehow an "active" or *sourcing recipient* of the violence: she helps him tie her, she follows his instructions, hopping into the closet, moaning, instead of crying during the rape. As subject, she is the object of the violence.

Perhaps the most astounding and confusing evidence of her forced agency is when she enacts the relationship Wrest has constituted through force. As torturer, he moves to consolidate how the violence will be seen by others, instructing Mrs. Alton to blame the violence on a "black man with bright green eyes." And she enacts the relation the tortured have with their torturers—she takes his need, his world as hers in the moment she asks him to take the sock out of her mouth. But rather than denote agency or participation, it reveals the completeness of her violation. Her effort to make sense, i.e., "black men don't have green eyes," in a world that is already inverted by violence speaks to her own loss of herself; he has remade her through pain.[38] And she notes in her testimony, she is a stranger to herself (Kristeva, 1991).

While Mrs. Alton does not personalize the violence, i.e., she never reflects on the meaning of the violence nor does she detail her injuries,[39] she does trace the construction of herself as "stranger" by historicizing the violence, by giving it directionality. She consistently reports what he told her to do and she even attributes intention and makes interpretations. So although she does not construct herself as site for signifying her violation, she does signify the actions of Wrest, cementing not only his construction as subject, but his control of her subjectivity.

The construction of the woman-as-subject is critical to the directionality of violence—women become a site for signifying discourse (through the interrogation) and in the process, Wrest becomes the agent of their victimization, their suffering. They trace Wrest's writing on their bodies and in so doing, trace the origin of their violation to him. The prosecutor enables this construction by continually asking questions about what Wrest said, so the behavioral list that is constructed through the prosecutor's linear question ("What happened then") includes Wrest's discourse which functions to materialize him as a site for signification, as a subject.[40] Whereas in the other testimonies, Wrest's subjectivity was constituted through the "transcription" of wounds, here it is constituted without transcription and is, instead, materialized through the historized (progressive) colonization of Alton's subjectivity itself. Attorneys regulate when/if violence is personalized; their reflective questions allow women the opportunity to construct the significance of the violence. However, much of the attorney's role involves the coconstruction of the linear plot itself, and like the medical examiner in Foucault's analysis, he often reserves for himself or the legal apparatus the privilege of interpreting the body-as-transcript in the context of the closing argument. In summary, Mrs. Alton constructed herself, in interaction with the prosecutor, as a sourcing recipient of action and a site for depersonalized violence.

Conclusion

The feminist critique of criminal proceedings, which argues against women's objectification, is an argument for women's emancipation from the patriarchy of law; it equates subjectivity with agency/freedom and objectivity with constraint/domination. I have argued in this paper that this liberal ideology leads to analysis of the negative, repressive forms of power and leaves unchallenged and undescribed the second-order level at which the positive effects of power operate.

At this second-order level, first I have tried to show that the objectification thesis, while it valorizes subjectivity, fails to attend to how law forces the subjectification of women, requires that they become sites for signifying, for meaning-making, and shapes the construction of particular subjectivities, permitting some and evaporating others; as subjects, women are not free agents nor are they dominated as their bodies are symbolized; tracing the positive effects of power, I have tried to show that signifying the body is a practice which constructs the woman as individual-subject. But the nature of that subjectivity, despite its plurality and nonuniformity, is regulated—if we look at the nature of subjectivity that is *not* produced, the positive effects of power are clearly outlined: none of these women construct themselves as *recipient* of *personalized* violence; these women seem only able to construct themselves as recipients of action *if* they depersonalize the violence or, conversely, they are only able to *personalize* the violence when they have been a *source* of action. As a shadow of the subject/object dichotomy, this empty quadrant speaks to the impossibility of signifying violation in the *absence* of physical wounds and in the *presence* of agency.

Second, I have challenged the feminist critique of objectification by arguing that subjectivity is both material and symbolic—it is not a decorporalized state of being in which women are socially constructed as different from or beyond their bodies. The act of interrogation/confession enacted by the prosecutor and the woman giving testimony operates not to objectify women, but on the contrary, it enables women to signify their bodies (as Ms. Hansel did when she framed her injuries as positive signs of growth and healing) and become, through this process, not only a site for the circulation of meaning but a participant in its construction. In this way, the body-as-subject makes possible the construction of woman as object of violence.

And third, I have critiqued the objectification thesis by showing how the subjectivity of violated women is central to the construction of the directionality of violence; unless and until the women's injuries are constructed as such, and there is a causal connection made between the actions of the victimizer and the appearance of those wounds, violence has no origin (it can be reframed as an "accident") and the defendant cannot be constructed as a victimizer; in turn, if he is not a victimizer, law has no authority to imprison or execute. In other words, law's privilege to do violence is dependent upon its ability to stabilize the subject/object relations and distinguish victim from victimizer. Through their testimony, these women become sites of and processes for the production of meaning. And the meaning that is produced impacts the directionality of violence, constituting the authority of law itself.

Attention to the "political economy of selfhood" (1) problematizes the equation of subjectivity with freedom and objectivity with domination, (2) enables the examination of the role of the body in the construction of the subject, and (3) links the subject/object dichotomy to the directionality of violence and law's authority. This focus on the positive effects of power challenges the feminist critique that focuses on the repressive forms of power. If these four women are, indeed, caught up in and simultaneously navigating the subject/object dichotomy, a new concept of "power" must be invoked to speak about the relationship between law and victims,[41] between structure and agency, between constraint and freedom. For it is not the case that women are captured by the courtroom discourse, nor are they "free agents"; rather they are reflecting and constituting the "grid" or "net" of power relations where power is neither uniform nor unilateral (Foucault, 1979). The grid under study in this analysis is the subject/object dichotomy in which women navigate the construction of themselves as subjects; I avoid examining repression (and arguing for freedom) or identifying ideology (and advocating truth). Sidestepping the liberal legal goal (emancipation through truth), this analysis presumes that there is no world that stands outside the effects of power; instead, I have tried to describe the "political economy of selfhood" by attending to the construction of the very categories through which people come to know violence.

Notes

1. The feminist critique of law extends beyond the analysis of criminal trials or rape law and includes complex debates over the nature of "difference" and "gender" itself. See Chamallas (1993), Maher (1992), Minow (1990), Williams (1991), and Young (1990) for the debate about difference, and see Butler (1990) for discussion of the construction of gender as a binary system of representation. While the debates within feminist legal studies are not limited to "objectification," this concept plays a central role in the feminist critique of law.

2. See Kristin Bumiller's (1992) work on "viewing violence"; she asks the reflexive question about who *we* are as viewers in a "field of violence" and suggests that witnesses (in this case, courtroom and community members) are participants in the construction of violence, implicating those that view violence in its production. Her work has forced me to consider the "aesthetics of violence" (Cobb, 1993), and it is out of this consideration to the construction of subjectivity arose, for if we are implicated in the construction of violence, as Bumiller suggests, I would prefer to participate in ways that confirm, rather than deny, women's work to appear themselves as subjects.

3. This argument is challenged by Girard's (1978) account of the semiotics of violence in law; he suggests that the reconstruction of violence is essential to the regulation of violence, that is, persons must

tell the violence in order to establish culpability and deliver punishment. And furthermore, he argues that this telling, from a semiotic perspective, inevitably requires that the victim (either dead or alive) become an object of and a placemarker for the violence. In this way, the subjectivity, the personness, of the victim is sacrificed up unto the account of the violence itself. Girard agrees that the social construction of violence in discourse is accompanied by the objectification of the victim. However, this semiotic perspective, centered also on the distinction between subject and object, is not gender-sensitive but, instead, offers a gender-neural account of the relation between violence and discourse in the criminal trial. Girard is thus also arguing that the objectification of women in the courtroom is inevitable, as it is a function not of culture/gender but of the process of containing violence in discourse.

4. See Wowk's (1984) study of blame allocation in her narrative analysis of a murder confession. She reports that the subject tries to diminish his blame through the sexualization of his victim, which functions to both forestall his construction as victimizer and, in the process, lay the blame for the violence on his victim.

5. Consider Patty Hearst's trial—she was convicted after she was constituted as a subject, an agent of violence, capable of reasoning and knowing the difference between right and wrong. Clearly her construction as subject was precisely what led to the denial of her experience as victim, as passive "kidnapee."

6. I am not suggesting that women are able to write the meaning of their bodies in ways that are consistent with their experience. Law constrains and organizes the parameters of how violence can be storied (Sarat, 1993). I am simply suggesting that the dichotomy in which this process is evaluated or critiqued is not particularly useful.

7. "Embodied subject" constructs the subject *as* a body, as material. It attempts to break the Cartesian dualism between subject/object, a dualism that has separated the physical from the mental, meaning from action (see Kerby, 1991).

8. See Sarat and Kearn's (1991) call for a jurisprudence of violence, which, they argue, should attend to the effects of law's violence on those who are convicted/punished.

9. I am aware that there is a large literature on the role of the attorney in shaping womens' testimony. This research regularly finds that attorneys instrumentally shape women's victim testimony. However, this work, based on conversation analysis, imports a view of power into the analysis of women's testimony that inherently contributes to instantiate the subject/object dichotomy in the courtroom, for these studies either presume a strategic instrumentalism or a structural determinism. In other words, conversational analysis reproduces the tension between emancipation and free will (individualism) and constraint (social structure). This tension then reduces our capacity to witness the

way persons, within the grid of power, navigate their subjectivity. See Hoy's (1986) discussion of this point in his analysis of how Foucault's concept of power differs from more traditional concepts. As examples of conversational analysis in the courtroom, see Atkinson and Drew (1979), Dunstan (1980), and Wodak (1980). For examples of research on the role of gender in courtroom conversation, see West and Zimmerman (1985) as well as West and Garcia (1988). See also Matoesian's (1993) review of conversation analysis, particularly chapter 4. I have chosen not to rely on this research because of the way it obscures its own dependence on the subject/object (freedom/domination) dichotomy.

10. Much has been written about the role of pronoun use to constitute and index persons as persons. However, I am arguing that the construction of the "embodied subject" relies not on linguistic markers (pronouns) but on discourse markers which constitute the materiality of the location for action/experience. Reliance on a linguistic marker such as "I" tends to reconstitute the mind/body distinction that separates the subject (mind) from the body. So while I acknowledge the literature on and attention to the role of pronouns, I would prefer to shift the theoretical grounds to discourse. See Harre's (1984) discussion of the indexical function of the pronoun "I."

11. See Bateson (1972) and Watzlawick et al. (1967) for discussion and explanation of the recursive effects of communication content on relationships.

12. This is a very nonstatic description of identity for it refuses to nominalize the person/self. Instead, it relies on and constructs the notion that the reflexive recognition of the self by self and others is a social phenomenon and therefore much more effectively addressed by a model that examines the social construction of self-as-person. See Shotter (1984) for a good discussion of the person as a social location in discourse.

13. Speech act theory provides a useful vocabulary for discussing the complexity of point of view; the locutionary, illocutionary, and the perlocutionary dimensions can be understood as levels that interact, reflexively, to produce the relationship between the saying and the said, between story content and story process. Together, these dimensions impact not only the social world of the speaker, but they constitute the location of that speaker, as a speaker, in a given social context. See Austin (1962).

14. Foucault (1979) describes the role of the examiner as a process in which the criminal/subject is transformed, through interaction, into an object of state control.

15. There is a large and growing literature on narrative analysis of the courtroom. This work can crudely be divided into two camps: the interactional approach and the semiotic approach. Maynard's (1988)

discussion of plea bargaining is a good example of the former, and Jackson's (1988) discussion of narrative coherence is a good example of the latter. However, I have chosen not to situate this paper in either camp because they do not speak specifically to the social construction of violence. Instead, this paper draws heavily on Robert Cover's (1983) work in which he provides the theoretical frame for his claim that law is jurispathic—it kills off all but the narratives that support its own knowledge/power base.

16. In this paper, I do not address the intersection of race and gender in the social construction of subjectivity, and I am sure this is one of its main flaws, for the sexual economy of subjectivity is certainly related to this intersection (see Wiegman, 1993). However, I would like to do a comparative study (all the women in this study are white) to see how the subject/object categories are different for women of color.

17. This is the part of the trial where the jury decides whether to recommend life imprisonment without the possibility of parole or death.

18. Interestingly, all but one of these women (Mrs. Bolin) had no prior relation to Wrest, so the violence against them cannot be reorganized in relational terms. Mrs. Bolin lived in his neighborhood at the time of the attack, and she knew him and his mother. However, that relationship was not used to "relationalize" the violence but rather to create the specter of Wrest's mother, humanizing him in the process.

19. The order of presentation of these victim narratives is in keeping with the presentation in the trial.

20. The data is the court transcript, and therefore, the information I have is limited. There are no paralinguistic markers and no way to recapture the nonverbals that surely are involved in the construction of subjectivity. For the most part, the conversation has no indication of interruptions or "talk overs." However, as I am not interested in conversation analysis, I do not find the data paltry.

21. I obtained this transcript from the Supreme Court of California (#168358) where Wrest's appeal is filed; the penalty phase comprises Volume IV, pages 859–1469. The names are a matter of public record, as is the transcript, and therefore, I have not changed the names.

22. All of these violence narratives are lifted out of the total testimony provided during this episode of "witnessing." In the interests of brevity and space, I did not present the totality of what they said. In each case, I present their account of the violent episode.

23. The medical discourse contributes to maintain Ms. Hansel's distance from her own wounds, and depersonalizes the violence.

24. He does ask her to comment on how she felt and to describe the nature of the injuries that she still has, which, in effect, allows her to reflect on the consequences of the violence for her; this personalized the violence momentarily. However, the way she signifies it, in her

reflection, disappears the very consequences that the prosecutor is asking her to construct.

25. The Victim Witness Program "understood" Ms. Hansel's discussion of her "progress" as evidence of some personal circumstances in her life that, because they are not in the transcript and are not a matter of record, I cannot provide here. But the fact that they have a theory is evidence to their participation in the construction of her testimony—her voice was no doubt tangled to their interpretations of her voice.

26. The terrible significance of the wounds was materialized in the testimony of the doctor who examined Ms. Hansel in the emergency room. He not only detailed the nature of her extensive injuries but also reconstructed the nature of the weapon through detailing the nature of the wounds.

27. This, in turn, is related to another curious consequence of attorney/victim story construction, namely, that there is very little expressed emotion, much less outrage, on the part of the victims. In my view, this is related to the kinds of questions asked by the prosecutor that do not allow the development of moral themes in the victims' stories; they are hindered from constructing the experience of anger/righteousness and/or they cannot take on the *role* of the victim. Averill's (1986) definition of emotion as a social role suggests that victims cannot construct a social role from which anger or righteousness is appropriate—they are not able to adopt a relational position that affords them the possibility of emotional display.

28. Again, the transcript displayed begins with her account of the violence. While the prosecutor does ask her a series of questions before this segment, they are questions regarding her address, her work/life routines, her previous knowledge of Wrest. These are very didactic questions that Bolin answers perfunctorily. I did not include them because of space considerations.

29. This is a wonderful example of social construction. She did not say she was afraid to stay in the house; she said that she did not stay in the house, and the Judge filled in the narrative blanks.

30. The defense attorney then goes on to cross-examine Mrs. Bolin concerning her knowledge of Wrest's neighborhood and his mother.

31. I debated whether the presence of wounds/injuries automatically constitutes a subject as *recipient* of other's actions and decided that they do not. In my view, wounds that are inflicted while engaged in a "fight" are different than the wounds inflicted when the violence is asymmetrical. In that case, the wounds mark the body as a recipient of other's action. But how bodies are marked is a function of the social construction of violence. Consider, for example, the injuries inflicted on the bodies that were found by the road in Chile, during the repression;

they had horrific wounds from torture sessions, but because the state constructed them as agents in their own wound production (through the interrogation process), they were socially constructed as *sources* of, rather than *recipients* of, violence. However, I would agree with Feldman (1991): the politicized body has wounds that can continually be rewritten precisely because the meaning of wounds can never be fixed, but rather, is exceedingly modal. Since the state could never totally stabilize the meaning of the violence, it paradoxically continually implicated itself as a source of violence, continually trying the stabilize the meaning of the wounds they inflicted. See Cobb (1995) for an analysis of the semiotics of mass arrest in Chile.

32. During this narrative, Mrs. Peck notes that the oldest daughter had not witnessed the attack because she had been hiding in the closet the whole time.

33. The only time Mrs. Peck constructs the violence as an "attack" is when she is describing what is happening when her daughter is yelling "Quit hitting my mommy." This is really the only place in her testimony that the violence she describes has a one-way directionality, one that creates her as the recipient of violence.

34. Here the "depth" of the interrogation is perhaps visible, for certainly this event did not get constructed as a "fight" or "struggle" for the first time here in her testimony. It would be important to follow, to trace, its production back through the layers of sedimented conversation, first with the Victim Witness Advocates and deputy prosecutors, then later in the final stages of her preparation for court. But I do not think that this story was imposed on her by a patriarchal legal system. She has constituted herself as a subject/source within a context in which this subjectivity resonates, that is, her social network. This suggests that we need to see subjectivity, as it is constituted in the courtroom, as related to, as an extension of, the subjectivity as it is constructed in ongoing interactions outside the courtroom.

35. Wrest was sentenced to die and is now on death row, his case on appeal.

36. The prosecutor is clearly working to repair his slip—he has constructed the interactions as "conversation" that normalizes and erases violence. His move to characterize it as "unilateral conversations" is a move to redefine the interaction as violent.

37. The Victim Witness Program told me that she was not crying in the courtroom at this point—she was referring to "crying" as an act proximate to her motioning *in* the violent event.

38. Alves (1985) reports that in politically repressive regimes, successive torture episodes reduce victims' fear and increase their capacity to survive pain. From this perspective, Mrs. Alton has little preparation for her suffering; she had no prior experience with violence, and

she lives in a culture where there is considerable political "order," rather than random and secret state violence. It is interesting to consider how the constitution of the subject is dependent upon the cultural/political of a given locale. Santa Barbara, Calif., where Mrs. Alton resides, is a seaside community where violence is "located" in the Hispanic neighborhoods between gangs. Mrs. Alton lives in one of the wealthiest areas, where all the homes have elaborate security systems.

39. There is no mention of the risk Mrs. Alton had for AIDS or other sexually transmitted diseases. It seems possible that the risk of AIDS could have been used to signify the violation, but the fact that it was not suggests that sexuality may destabilize the directionality of violence, which is an argument central to the critique of rape law. This implicates sexuality in the construction of "subject."

40. There were also references made to what Wrest said in other women's testimonies, but in these cases, his actions were not connected to his words. So, for example, Ms. Hansel reports that he was stabbing her because he did not "give a shit about anything anymore," but that statement does not provide context for the violence, the way Wrest's discourse does in Mrs. Alton's testimony. Thus, his discourse operates differently in Mrs. Alton's testimony than it does in the others.

41. I am very aware that my analysis did not include the subjectification of a dead woman, and in fact, that may be a very different process. So the women/victims to which I am referring are those that are testifying to their own violation.

References

Alves, M. (1985). *State and Opposition in Military Brazil.* Austin: University of Texas Press.

Atkinson, J., and P. Drew. (1979). *Order in Court.* Atlantic Highlands, N.J.: Humanities Press.

Austin, J. (1962). *How to Do Things with Words.* London: Oxford University Press.

Averill, J. (1986). The acquisition of emotions during adulthood. In R. Harre (Ed.): *The Social Construction of Emotions.* Oxford, England: Blackwell, 98–118.

Bateson, G. (1972). *Steps to an Ecology of Mind.* New York: Ballantine.

Bumiller, K. (1987). Rape as a legal symbol: An essay on sexual violence and racism. *University of Miami Law Review* 42(1):75–91.

————. (1991). Fallen angels: The representation of violence against women in legal cultures. In M. Fineman and N. Thomadsen (Eds.): *At the Boundaries of Law: Feminism and Legal Theory.* New York: Routledge.

————. (1992). *Exposure of Desire: The Complications of Viewing in the Field of Violence.* Presented to the Amherst Legal Seminar, November 1992. (Paper on file with the author.)

Butler, J. (1990). *Gender Trouble: Feminism and the Subversion of Identity.* New York: Routledge.

Chamallas, M. (1993). Book review. *Signs* 18(3):678–683.

Cobb, S. (1991). *The Domestication of Violence in Mediation.* Presented to the Amherst Legal Seminar.

————. (1993). Towards an aesthetics of violence: A comment on Feldman's "The formations of violence: The narratives of the body and political terror in Northern Ireland." *Political and Anthropological Review* 16(3):57–60.

————. (1993). Violence invaginated: The semiotics of mass arrest in Chile. *Law and Critique* 4(2):131–54.

Cover, R. (1983). Nomos and narrative. *Harvard Law Review* 97(1):4–68.

Dumm, T. (1990). Fear of law. *Studies in Law, Politics, and Society* 10:29–57.

Dunstan, R. (1980). Context for coercion: Analyzing properties of courtroom questions. *British Journal of Law and Society* 7(1):61–77.

Eisenstein, Z. (1988). *The Female Body and the Law.* Berkeley: University of California Press.

Feldman, A. (1991). *Formations of Violence: The Narrative of the Body and Political Terror in Northern Ireland.* Chicago: University of Chicago Press.

Foucault, M. (1978). *The History of Sexuality, Volume One: An Introduction.* (R. Hurley, Trans.) New York: Pantheon.

————. (1979). *Discipline and Punish: The Birth of the Prison.* New York: Vintage.

————. (1983). Afterword: Subject and power. In H. Dreyfus and P. Rabinow (Eds.): *Michel Foucault: Beyond Structuralism and Hermeneutics.* Chicago: University of Chicago Press.

Girard, R. (1979). *Violence and the Sacred.* (P. Henry, Trans.) Baltimore: Johns Hopkins University Press.

Goodrich, P. (1987). *Legal Discourse: Studies in Linguistics, Rhetoric and Legal Analysis.* New York: St. Martin's Press.

Harre, R. (1984). *Personal Being.* Oxford, England: Blackwell.

Hoy, D. (1986). Power, repression, progress: Foucault, Lukes, and the Frankfurt School. In D. Hoy (Ed.): *Foucault: A Critical Reader.* Oxford, England: Blackwell.

Jackson, B. (1988). *Law, Fact and Narrative Coherence.* Merseyside, England: Deborah Charles Publications.

Kerby, A. (1991). *Narrative and the Self.* Bloomington: Indiana University Press.

Kristeva, J. (1991). *Strangers to Ourselves.* New York: Columbia University Press.

Maher, L. (1992). Punishment and welfare: Crack, cocaine and the regulation of mothers. *Women and Criminal Justice* 3(2):35–70.

Matoesian, G. (1993). *Reproducing Rape: Domination Through Talk in the Courtroom.* Chicago: University of Chicago Press.

Maynard, D. (1988). Narratives and narrative structure in plea bargaining. *Law and Society Review* 22(3):449–81.

McKenna, A. (1992). *Violence and Difference: Girard, Derrida, and Deconstruction.* Chicago: University of Illinois Press.

Mackinnon, C. (1983). Feminism, Marxism, method, and the state: Toward feminist jurisprudence. *Signs* 7(3):515–44.

———. (1989). *Toward a Feminist Theory of the State.* Cambridge, Mass.: Harvard University Press.

Minow, M. (1990). *Making All the Difference: Inclusion, Exclusion, and American Law.* Ithaca, N.Y.: Cornell University Press.

Polkinghorne, D. (1988). *Narrative Knowing and the Human Sciences.* Albany: State University of New York Press.

Ricoeur, P. (1981). *Hermeneutics and the Human Sciences.* (J. B. Thompson, Trans.) Cambridge, England: Cambridge University Press.

———. (1984–88). *Time and Narrative,* vols. 1–3. (K. McLaughlin and D. Pellauer, Trans.) Chicago: University of Chicago Press.

Sarat, A. (1993). Speaking of death: Narratives of violence in capital trials. *Law and Society Review* 27(1):19–58.

———, and T. Kearns. (1991). A journey through forgetting: Toward a jurisprudence of violence. In A. Sarat and T. Kearns (Eds.): *The Fate of Law.* Ann Arbor: University of Michigan Press.

Scarry, E. (1985). *The Body in Pain: The Making and Unmaking of the World.* New York: Oxford University Press.

———. (1994). *Resisting Representation.* New York: Oxford University Press.

Scholes, R., and R. Kellogg. (1968). *The Nature of Narrative.* New York: Oxford University Press.

Shotter, J. (1984). *Social Accountability and Selfhood.* Oxford, England: Basil Blackwell.

Watzlawick, P., J. Beavin, and D. Jackson. (1967). *Pragmatics of Human Communication.* New York: Norton.

West, C., and A. Garcia. (1988). Conversational shift work. *Social Problems* 35(5):551–75.

———, and D. Zimmerman. (1977). Women's place in everyday talk. *Social Problems* 24:521–29.

Wiegman, R. (1993). The anatomy of a lynching. *Journal of the History of Sexuality* 3(3): 445–67.

Williams, P. (1991). *The Alchemy of Race and Rights: Diary of a Law Professor.* Cambridge, Mass.: Harvard University Press.

Wodak, R. (1980). Discourse analysis and courtroom interaction. *Discourse Processes* 3(4):369–80.

Wowk, M. (1984). Blame allocation, sex and gender in a murder interrogation. *Women Studies International Forum* 7(1):75–82.

Young, I. (1990). *Justice and the Politics of Difference.* Princeton, N.J.: Princeton University Press.

Cases

State of California *v* Theodore Wrest. 168358, Cal.S.Ct., Volume IV, pp. 859–1469.

Chapter Nine

Channel Surfing for Rape and Resistance on Court TV

Lynn Comerford

The recent debate over whether or not rape trials should be televised is a critical site of gender construction. However, this debate has been constituted in large part by a dualism that characterizes the televised rape victim as either an active subject or a passive object. In the past ten years the "Cartesian subject" or the "subject of modernity" has been a heated topic of discussion across a range of academic disciplines. The epistemology of modernity finds a clear-cut distinction between a constituting subject and a constituted subject: the constituting subject (the rape victim for those who argue for televised rape trials) is transcendent, rational, and free; the constituted subject (the rape victim for those who are opposed to televised rape trials) is determined and unfree—a social dope. This dichotomous relationship between the two conceptions is reductionist and inadequately addresses the complexity of the issue. I argue in this paper that the subject/object dichotomy serves to mask how rape trials bring together knowledge, power, the control of the body, and the control of space into an integrated and complex technology of discipline. In order to overcome this "subject" (with power) versus "object" (without power) account, I draw upon the work of Michel Foucault and offer an alternative view of power and the human subject.

The Televised Rape Trial Debate

Steven Brill, CEO of court television, has predicted that the effects of televised rape trials will be an "educational windfall for people who watch his channel" (Zoglin, 1991). Brill admits that it is the entertainment value of court television that most appeals to the viewers, but then adds, "it's popular because it's real. . . . It's a combination of C-SPAN and soap operas" (Ansley, 1992). The Court Television Network is a commercial enterprise supported by advertising and justified by the public's fascination with courtroom theatrics for lucrative sponsors. The new cable channel (owned largely by Time Warner) covers some trials live, with play-by-play commentary from legal experts, and others on tape in nightly wrap-up programs. The channel runs on the assumption that with publicity come vital checks and balances of the legal system itself. It also runs on the assumption that agents have the right and ability to view trials freely: if they do not like what they see they can simply turn the channel.

Rape victims are seen as powerful active agents utilizing a fair legal system established to protect them. The effects of televising all court cases provides an umbrella of protection against government excess, or worse, government nonprotection for individuals charged with a crime. The effects of publicity are said to engage the powerful forces of the public's perceptions about rape and to mold and alter those perceptions in positive ways. Rape crisis centers across the country are thought likely to receive more support and understanding because of publicity surrounding rape trials. Hospitals, police departments, and prosecutors around the country may sharpen their investigatory practices because of televised rape trials. The reporting of sexual assault by women may increase because they will see that when guilt is established beyond a reasonable doubt, juries will convict. Men will become aware of the seriousness of rape and the consequences of the crime. Heightened public awareness about rape may lead to special precautions, preventive techniques, and modes of enforcement that may lead to a reduction of rape. Viewers, it is argued, will see the meticulous care taken by judges, defense attorneys, and the prosecution to assure a fair trial and feel confident in their legal system. These myriad effects of televised rape trials, it is argued, are positive and necessary for women to improve their status in society.

This argument in favor of televising rape trials characterizes female rape victims as free subjects courageously and intentionally utilizing the United States legal system designed to protect them. Such subjects are said to be self-willed, knowledgeable agents capable of responding to a horrible assault by legal means. The law on this view is disembodied reason, accepted on its own terms as a neutral arbiter among conflicting interests. It is characterized as a tool to be used by women for their betterment and status transformation.

The opposing position, which argues against televising rape trials, characterizes rape victims as objects inscribed, commodified, and gendered by a legal system designed to sustain female subordination to males. Women, in this view, are treated as objects of "sexuality," where rape is linked to institutionalized conditions of gender inequality. Power as male dominance is found in the social structures of sexuality (Barry, 1979; Brownmiller, 1975; Chodorow, 1978; Dworkin, 1974, 1981; Millet, 1970; Rich, 1980; Russell, 1984), economics (Eisenstein, 1979; Harman, 1981; Rubin, 1976), and law (Brownmiller, 1975; Estrich, 1987; MacKinnon, 1979, 1987, 1989; Matoesian, 1993, 1995; Russell, 1984; Smart, 1989; Warshaw, 1988). The televised rape trial functions as an institutionalized mechanism of social control to keep women in their place and operates in conjunction with male-centered state ideologies to legitimate and conceal inequality. Televised rape trials are thus viewed as state-supported mechanisms for controlling and disempowering women.

Those who do not think rape trials should be televised argue that they have only negative consequences for women in this society. The effects of televising rape trials are "gang-raped" victims. The presence of television cameras turn the rape victim into a sexualized object packaged for a voyeuristic audience. Lynn Marks (Senate Hearing, 1984), for example, is concerned about the effects of a heightened sense of self-consciousness for potential televised rape victims and their willingness to report the crime. In expressing her concern about the effects of televised rape trials for the viewing audience she states:

> I saw a man in a bar interviewed recently on national television news during the time that the New Bedford rape case was being tried. He said that he normally watched the soaps every day, but that now he was getting his thrills from watching that case. . . . Rape is the ultimate invasion of privacy. In some ways, cameras seem like another rape, a gang-rape, since the eyes of so many would be participating in the invasion. (U.S. Senate Hearing, April 24, 1984)

As modern industrial and information societies change, and as women themselves offer resistance to patriarchy, older forms of domination are eroded, but new forms like televised rape trials take their place. The effect of the televised "gang rape," seen in this way, is a way for patriarchy to get more bang for its buck, an automatic public "second rape." What better way for modern patriarchy to silence rape victims than to threaten them with a televised replay of their assault? The effect of televised rape trials is thus the silencing of sexual assault victims.

Rape victims fear that the process they turn to for help actually ends up being manipulative, controlling, and judgmental. Jennifer Barr, a rape victim explains:

> The trial was only equalled by the rape itself. . . . To testify at the trial was the hardest thing I have ever done. . . . I was

forced to relive the rape in front of strangers and my assailant,
and then forced to face a cross examination designed inherently to discredit the witness. . . . If I had had to face TV cameras in that courtroom, being exposed to anyone in the
community at the flick of a dial, I can say with certainty I
would not have testified. (U.S. Senate Hearing, April 24, 1984)

Consistent with this view, televised rape trials objectify rape victims in even more explicit ways. The face of the victim is covered with
either a blue dot or a graphic mirage in an attempt to preserve her
identity, but the result is that her facial expressions are obstructed. The
viewing audience hears the testimony but views a shot of the alleged
victim's chest. In the Senate Hearing entitled "Impact of Media Coverage of Rape Trials," Ronald Pina (a district attorney in Bristol, Mass.)
testified regarding the Big Dan trial:

People, who over a period of three weeks *believed* that they
had watched the entire trial, did so in their living rooms
where they were subject to the normal distractions of tele-
phones ringing, visitors calling, children desiring attention
and errands to run. More importantly, because the victim's
face was never shown she became only a detached accusa-
tory voice, not a human being whose demeanor on the
witness stand during two grueling days could be observed.
The anguish in the face and the remembered terror in her
eyes were never seen. Additionally, most of those who
watched or heard the trials did so in a mental context removed from a thorough understanding of the law. (U.S.
Senate Hearing, April 24, 1984)

In addition to the visual objectification of the rape victim there is
a "written" objectification of her. In the editing room of the court television network, producers type out "summaries" of the person who is
taking the stand. These summaries block the lower third of the television screen. In an analysis of the William Kennedy Smith rape trial, for
example, Comerford (1994) found that the alleged rape victim was six
times more likely to have a "summary" of her statements typed on the
lower third of the screen than the accused, even though she was on the
stand merely twice as long. It is clear that the availability of resistance
modes for the accuser as subject is highly circumscribed since she is
spoken by the court television editor on the bottom third of the screen.
It is the television editor who deems what is important enough to summarize and how it should be summarized. Because the audience does
not see the nonverbal body language of the alleged victim's face and
"hears" what she says summarized on the screen in words that are not

her own, the effect of a televised rape trial becomes a heroic case where resistance to a horrible form of domination is significantly thwarted by virtue of how the subject is allowed to present herself as subject.

Continuing on in this vein Peter Dalgren (1988) and Andrea Press (1991) have emphasized how television reproduces and reinforces the dominant culture. Television production, they argue, is capable of directing audience attention in strategic ways through the technical aspects of film/video production (e.g., lighting, camera shots, and editing). The dominating structure of television production is always able to define the limitations of the testifier. A victim's resistance to sexual assault is thwarted in significant ways by virtue of how the subject is allowed to present herself as subject, even though it is quite possible that the difference in the use of video and audio overlays are not consciously acknowledged by the producer, director, and audience. The subtle mechanisms of rape trial television production keep the real dynamics of the rape trial hidden from the viewing audience. Camera shots, voice-overs, and editing procedures function to silence and objectify rape victims. Thus, an effect of these trials is that even when the rape victim resists modes of domination within the power apparatus by reporting the rape and going through the trial process, the very resources available to her (i.e., a televised rape trial comprised of rules, processes, and techniques) are shaped and defined by those in power (the dominant discourse).

Historical evidence is also provided by supporters of this view, which traces the rise of the rape trial as a spectacle that objectifies women. Anna Clark (1987), for example, has examined the treatment of rape in England in the eighteenth and nineteenth centuries. In the Victorian era, a woman who complained of rape in open court was regarded as immoral and was found to be lewd to herself and to society. Carol Smart (1989) has found that the consequences of the twentieth-century rape trial are not dramatically different. She has argued that through the discourse of rape trials the victims sexuality is socially constructed and questioned. Further, as in the Victorian era, rape trials today can be seen as constructing women as objects for sexual use and that "complaining of rape" is still seen to reflect upon the victim's own reputation rather than that of the rapist. The effect is that televised rape trials are said to constitute women as objects of a socially structured mode of domination in which rape and the fear of rape produce and reproduce patriarchal social organization, sustaining female subordination to male. On this view, women are depicted in televised rape trials as helpless victims in need of patriarchal protection.

Catherine MacKinnon (1989) has observed that women do not want to go to court with cases of rape precisely because "in the flesh in court" women come to embody the standard fantasy of the pleasure of abuse and sexual power: "Court testimony in sexual abuse cases is

live oral pornography" (152). It is not just that the televised rape victim
must repeat the violation in words, MacKinnon explains, nor that they
may be judged to be lying, but that the woman's story gives pleasure
in the way pornography gives pleasure. In addition, she suggests that
the rape victims story also gives instruction. Consider Ronald Pina's
(District Attorney of Bristol, Mass.) statement:

> I think one of the scariest things is that on March 26, 1984,
> this year, I had just finished sentencing the four individuals
> who were found guilty [of the Big Dan's rape in New
> Bedford, MA] and on the same day, in Rhode Island, a 12-
> year-old boy had watched the trial on television; he came
> home from school and tuned in to see what the latest details
> were on the Big Dan's trial; he raped a 10-year-old girl on
> a pool table, or attempted to, based on what he had seen,
> and what he had observed on television. (U.S. Senate Hear-
> ing, April 24, 1984)

Alisa Carse (1995) has agreed, finding that pornography "may reflect
the way we see ourselves as women and men, but it also teaches ways
of seeing and ways of being; it shapes and fosters attitudes, expectations, patterns of desire, of sexual arousal and response, and other overt
behaviors that can result in harm to women—not only physical violence
and forcible sex but also disdainful and dismissive treatment, incompatible with our status as equals." Televised rape trials, interpreted as oral
pornography in this view, function similarly.

   I intend to argue in the remainder of this essay that both positions in the televised rape trial debate are problematic because
both ignore the possibility that multiple discursive formations exist
which constitute the subject in specific ways. Those who are in
support of televised rape trials do not address how they discipline
participants and viewers in specific ways. And those who take the
"objectivized" position and argue that there are only negative consequences to televising rape trials are blind to any possibility for
positive social outcomes to emerge from the participation of rape
victims in televised trials. In this essay, I argue that Michel Foucault
allows us to get beyond the limitations of seeing the televised rape
victim as either an active subject or a passive object because he
argues that we are both. Foucault's work corrects the tendency to
view power as either "bottom-up," (within subjects), or "top-down,"
(within institutions). Since he views power as complex, capillary,
relational, local, unstable, and coming from everywhere, he takes us
well beyond this simplistic binary. Additionally, I will argue that
viewing televised rape trials as having *either* positive *or* negative
effects masks how televised rape trials are in fact locations where

"sex" and "knowledge" merge in unequal power relationships with willing participants.

Foucault's theory encourages an inquiry into the disciplinary practices that encourage or institutionalize specific forms of discourse to reveal the complex nature of power. I problematize both sides of the television rape trial debate for not adequately addressing the law: the "subject" side sees law simply as the victim's friend; the "object" side views law simply as the victim's foe. Again, Foucault's theoretical framework provides a more sophisticated way to analyze how the law operates in the construction of the subjectivity. "Confessions" are elicited, shaped, and judged by "experts," who cultivate and discipline the rape victim. At the same time, Foucault's theory allows us to see how law also provides a forum where rape victims can express their outrage. A Foucauldian analysis can explain how a rape victim can actively resist the sexual assault, albeit with legal resources shaped and defined by those in power.

Specifically, the debate about whether to televise rape trials, which centers on the public's right to known, versus the intrusive and potentially disruptive impact of television coverage on rape trial proceedings and its principal participants does not address the complexity of sexual assault and publicity. Foucault allows us to focus on the role of the body in the operations of power relations in society. Examining the televised rape trials as an effect of specific power relations provides a useful analytical framework to explain how the rape victim as subject is produced through power. The conceptual move from rape to victim as either subject *or* object to both subject *and* object preserves the idea that hidden constraints of power operate on rape victim's lives and the concept of agency and resistance.

The Foucauldian position I adumbrate in the following sections indicates that discursive formations are not separate from their objects but actually *produce* the object about which they speak. Neither of the two sides of the debate show any awareness of the televised trial as a site where identity is fought over in a discursive battle waged actively by the accuser and the power structure and where identity and experience is the outcome rather than the origin of meaning. The term "subject," in a Foucauldian sense designates a social individual. The televised rape victim is a subject in two senses: (1) a subject of her own perceptions who can think and choose as a "free" agent and (2) as one who is subject to the authority of rape law, lawyers, psychiatrists, television editors, and producers.

Power and Discipline in the Televised Rape Trial

Foucault (1978, 92–98) allows the transgression of the simple views of power presented by both the "subject" argument (i.e., the rape victim is an empowered agent) and the "object" argument (i.e., the rape victim is an unempowered object). For Foucault, power is complex, capillary, and relational through which a televised rape trial becomes a complex technology of discipline. Such trials can be viewed as discursively based disciplinary forces that are, in part, responses on the part of power to the struggle between power (rape) and resistance (testifying women). Foucault's theory encourages inquiry into the practices that encourage or institutionalize specific forms of discourse to reveal the complex nature of power and how it is specifically implicated within law, the courtroom trial, and its televised proceedings.

Michel Foucault's (1977a, 1977b, 1978, 1979, 1980, 1982) work focuses on the role of the body in the operation of power relations in society. His idea that sexuality is not innate but rather the effect of specific power relations provides a useful analytical framework to explain how an agent's body is produced through power. The emphasis that Foucault places on the effects of power upon the body results in a depiction of social agents as responding bodies and as individual subjects who may act as autonomous agents, albeit within certain constrained parameters. The conceptual move from rape victim as either subject *or* object, to both subject and object stresses the idea that power operates on the rape victim's bodied existence and the victim's ability to act as an agent of resistance. A Foucauldian treatment of power provides an explanation for how the televised rape victim is at once a subject and object, with the means to resist but only inasmuch as the victim has access to resources shaped and defined by those in power. For Foucault, power is not a thing to be found only in individuals. It is to be found in practices constitutive of rape, rape law, and the televised trial. Power is the artful negotiation of such practices on the part of subjects, as indicated by the possibility of conduct and the possible outcomes of that conduct.

According to Foucault (1978), power relations are "intentional and nonsubjective . . . they are imbued through and through with calculation: there is no power that is exercised without a series of aims and objectives" (95). Foucault (1982) also stresses, however, that "power is exercised only over free subjects, and only insofar as they are free. . . . The relationship between power and freedom's refusal to submit cannot therefore be separated" (221). For Foucault "power is everywhere." Power is found in agents and in social institutions. This redefinition of agency problematizes the subject-versus-object account of the accuser on court television, but allows us to understand how discourses surrounding televised rape trials create subjectivity and simultaneously create subjects that resist.

This Foucauldian alternative to the subject/object binary gives us a more complex account of the testifying rape victim, in that she becomes an active agent participating in her own subjectivity. Judith Butler

(1991) influenced by Foucault, characterizes the subject (a rape victim in this case) as a "site of resignification" and a "permanent possibility of a certain resignifying process" (160). If the referent is recast as the signified, the culturally constructed subject can rewrite the script. The signified subject (rape victim) is capable of resignification.

A Foucauldian account of power explains how televised rape victims are constrained in freedom. Televised rape victims are not mere objects but are subjects who construct themselves and get constructed in and through different institutional processes. The special task here is to isolate the constituent components of the constituted/constituting subject and to analyze the interplay of those components. Foucault provides the conceptual background necessary to examine how cultural practices, like televised rape trials, are intrumental in forming the modern individual as *both* subject and object.

Foucault's work also historicizes how power acts upon and through the human body. Lois McNay (1991) argues that Foucault's placement of the body at the center of this struggle between different power formations changes the historian's methodology: "Historical development is no longer hermeneutically interpreted in terms of meanings it reveals but is understood as a conflict between different power blocks, i.e., permanent warfare" (127). This methodological contribution provides a way of understanding the materiality of the body in more complex ways. The "natural" body or the "rape victim's body" must "be understood as a central tool in the legitimation of specific strategies of oppression" (128). This does not deny the materiality of the body, but a Foucauldian perspective insists that bodies cannot be separated from the cultural practices which inscribe them. Foucault's contribution is a sophisticated methodological approach that emphasizes the body as the place to find and examine the most minute and local social practices, which he claims are linked up with power.

Genealogy is one of Foucault's methodological approaches for locating power; it is, in a word, about examining history's endless play of rituals of power. Judith Butler (1991) points out that Foucault's subject is itself the "effect of a genealogy which is erased at the moment that the subject takes itself as the single origin of its action" (156). Foucault's genealogy examines the subject as a function of discourse, asking "under what conditions and through what forms can an entity like the subject appear in the order of discourse; what position does it occupy; what functions does it exhibit; and what rules does it follow in each type of discourse?" (Foucault, 1977a, 113–38). Following Foucault, where "the relationship of domination . . . is fixed, throughout its history in rituals, in meticulous procedures that impose rights and obligations where humanity only 'advances' from one domination to another" (150), a televised rape trial is a historically produced site of gender production, a place where an examination of the rituals that dominate subjectivity and make "female" subordination to "male" can be described. Because the subject "is constituted in real practices" it is those practices, in this case, the disciplinary practices associated with televised rape trials, that need to be historicized.

The spectacle of televised rape trials resembles Foucault's (1979, 155) description of Jeremy Bentham's Panopticon, i.e., a system of surveillance which captures the essence of the disciplinary society. The periphery of the Panopticon is a circular building in the center of which stands a tower with wide windows that opens onto the inner side of the ring. The peripheral structure is divided into cells that have windows on both sides, one window facing the windows of the tower, the other window facing the outside, allowing the effect of backlighting to make any figure visible within the cell. Foucault states that "all that is needed, then, is to place a supervisor in a central tower and to shut up in each cell a madman, a patient, a condemned man, a worker or a schoolboy" (200–201). Each inmate is alone, shut off from others, but constantly visible from the tower. The effect of this is "to induce in the inmate a state of conscious and permanent visibility that assures the automatic functioning of power; each becomes to himself his own jailer" (201). This "state of conscious and permanent visibility" is a sign that the object of power is not just the disciplinary control of the body, but the disciplinary control of the mind as well. Foucault (1980) admires the beauty of the architectural design of the Panopticon:

> There is no need for arms, physical violence, material con-
> straints. Just a gaze. An inspecting gaze, a gaze where each
> individual under its weight will end by interiorising to the
> point that he is his own overseer, each individual thus ex-
> ercising this surveillance over, and against, himself. A su-
> perb formula: power exercised continuously and for what
> turns out to be a minimal cost. (155)

The television camera in the courtroom has a similar effect. Power becomes visible but unverifiable. "Visible: the inmate will constantly have before his eyes the tall outline of the central tower from which he is spied on. Unverifiable: the inmate must never know whether he is being looked at at any one moment; but he must be sure that he may always be so" (Foucault, 1979, 201). In Foucault's terms, the televised rape trial, like the Panopticon, brings together knowledge, power, the control of the body, and the control of space into an integrated technology of discipline. Televised rape trials organize bodies in space, distribute individuals in relation to one another, create a hierarchical organization, and become an efficient disposition of centers and channels of power. The Panopticon is similar to the court television camera in that it induces in the person on the stand a state of objectivity, a permanent visibility. Those in the courtroom, specifically those on the stand, do not know if the camera is focused on them or not, so they must behave as if surveillance is constant, unending, and total. The power of a television rape trial is continuous, disciplinary, and anonymous. A heightened self-consciousness and sense of malevolence describes how the alleged rape victim feels on the stand during a court trial.

Sandra Bartky (1988) finds that in contemporary patriarchal culture, a panoptical male conoisseur resides within the consciousness of most women: they stand perpetually before his gaze and under his judgment. "Women live in their bodies as seen by another, by an anonymous patriarchal Other" (72). This perpetual self-surveillance and heightened self-consciousness, Bartky argues, are the hallmarks of modern times. She adds that "modern technologies of behavior are oriented toward the production of isolated and self-policing subjects" (80). The self-surveillance does not end with the accuser on the stand but finds its way into audience viewers.

Foucault (1980) believes that there is something in surveillance (i.e., watching rape trials), or more accurately, "in the gaze of those involved in the act of surveillance, which is no stranger to the pleasure of surveillance" (186). But why is watching rape trials pleasurable? Within a Foucauldian view, televising the rape trial is a final step in the constrainment and cultivation of the victim's subjectivity. From the report of the sexual assault to the determination by experts as to whether she has a "case" or not to the process of televised editing that blocks her face and "captures" her testimony in subtitles across the bottom of the television screen, the victim's subjectivity is constrained and cultivated with audiences in mind, the audience of juries and/or a mass audience.

In many respects, twentieth-century American rape-trial television audiences might be regarded as similar to seventeenth-century French audiences who gathered around the public scaffold to witness public torture and execution. Both are public displays of power, and both rely on an audience to demonstrate this power. In seventeenth-century France, the body of the condemned was an essential element in the ceremonial of public punishment. It was the task of the guilty person to face their condemnation and the punishment for the crime they committed in a public ceremony. The body of the condemned was displayed, exhibited, and tortured for an audience that considered the spectacle as an example of the king's power. States Foucault (1979): "The public execution is to be understood not only as a judicial, but also as a political ritual" (47). The king *needed* the public ceremony to demonstrate his power. In a Foucauldian sense, patriarchy *needs* the public ceremony of televised rape trials to demonstrate women's subordination. Physical punishment in the form of rape, accompanied by a discursively based disciplinary apparatus like the televised rape trial, spreads patriarchy deeper into the social fabric.

Confession and Resistance

The cross-examination of the rape victim resembles nothing so much as Foucault's descriptions of the Christian and psychoanalytic "confession," where sex is transformed into (legal) discourse "in which the speaking subject is also the subject of the statement . . . in a ritual that unfolds within a power relationship" (Foucault, 1978, 61). Televised rape trials capture a legal process that cultivates and disciplines the female rape victim and at the same time provides a forum where she can rupture the legal discourse designed to undermine her credibility. Foucault's claim that power/knowledge is always productive rather than merely oppressive blurs the subject/object binary and allows one to theorize the link between the social practice of a televised rape trial and the social meaning given to the body of the rape victim, as well as to identify the points at which the power invested in the identification/ production of "a rape victim" might be reclaimed by the subjectivities that were formed as a result of this legal process. The conceptual move from viewing a televised rape victim as either subject or object, to both subject and object, provides an explanation for how a rape victim can actively resist the sexual assault albeit with legal resources shaped and defined by those in power.

The discourse of rape law, not unlike the Christian confessional, in a Foucauldian sense can be viewed as enticing the rape victim to "confess." Foucault (1980) points out that "there is a multiplication of discourses concerning sex, an institutional incitement to speak about it, a desire on the part of the agencies of power to hear it spoken about, and to cause it to be spoken about, and to cause it to speak through explicit articulation and endlessly accumulated detail" (18–19). A televised rape trial functions similarly to the Christian and psychoanalytic confessionals as a place where power churns everything having to do with sex through the endless mill of speech:

> the nakedness of the questions formulated by the confes-
> sion manuals of the Middle Ages . . . unveiled . . . that de-
> gree of detail which some authors, such as Sanchez or
> Tamburini, had for long time believed indispensable for the
> confession to be complete: description of the respective
> positions of the partners, the postures assumed, gestures,
> places touched, caresses, the precise moment of pleasure—
> an entire painstaking review of the sexual act in its very
> unfolding. (Foucault, 1980, 18–19)

Foucault sees the confession, and especially the confession about one's sexuality, as a central component in the expanding technologies for the discipline and control of bodies, populations, and society itself. In volume 1 of *The History of Sexuality* Foucault focuses on the role of science in the interplay of confession, truth, and power. Foucault challenges the hermeneutic belief in deep meaning by tracing the emergence of sexual confession and relating it to practices of social domination. The "confession" of the televised rape victim is an example of a totalizing practice that produces the accuser as object and subject, and preserves both our objectified and meaning-obsessed society. Foucault argues that with the expansion of science the individual has become an object of knowledge for the first time, both to herself and to others, an object who "confesses" the truth about herself in order to know herself and to be known. The "confession" of the rape victim is a ritual of discourse where the speaking subject is also the subject of the statement. The rape victim's confession is also a ritual that only unfolds within a power relationship for "one does not confess without the presence of a partner who requires the confession, prescribes and appreciates it, and intervenes in order to judge, punish, forgive, and console" (Foucault, 1978, 61).

Alcoff and Gray (1993) observe that Foucault's description of the confessional is always implicated in (both constituting of and constituted by) an unequal, nonreciprocal relation of power. Further, they argue that the explicit goal of the process of confession is always "the normalization of the speaking subject and thus the elimination of any transgressive potential which might exist" (272). In the first volume of *The History of Sexuality* (1978) and *Discipline and Punish* (1979), Foucault describes how the confession places the confessor in juridical/discursive institutions that mandate his or her confession as sociological/scientific data. In the case of rape trials the confessor (female rape victim) often understands the kind of subjectivity and "confession" required, and "invents himself or herself as a subjectivity in accord with the style, explanatory logic, and moral perspective which the listener will deem convincing or sane" (Hengehold, 1994, 96). When the rape victim confesses on the stand the televised rape trial produces the truth about sex: "for us, it is in the confession that truth and sex are joined" (Foucault, 1978, 61).

Like the Christian and psychoanalytic confessional, a rape trial gives power (in the form of psychiatrists, lawyers, and judges) access to heretofore private knowledge. Unlike the Christian and psychoanalytic confessional, the televised rape trial gives the *public* access to heretofore private knowledge. It is by eliciting confessions in the courtroom, where distinctions between consent and nonconsent are interpreted from patriarchal standards, that the viewing public learns what it takes to get a rape conviction. These findings are easily explained because all discourse puts into play a privileged set of viewpoints. Zillah Eisenstein (1988) argues that the challenge to our subjectivity is not done in a search for "objective truth" but rather "is bound to the questioning of truth which seems objective but in fact rests inescapably in discourse" (22). In keeping with Foucault's belief that identity is something that cannot preexist linguistic signification, and that identity is above all a practice, Butler's (1991) emphasis on the formative role of language in self-experience illuminates the category of sex which "functions as a principle of production and regulation at once, the cause of the violation installed as the formative principle of the body's sexuality" (163). With Foucault's analysis, although confessional modes of discourse may appear to give rape victims voice, they give the "experts" the power to determine their interpretation. This includes the defense attorney eliciting information calculated to ruin the credibility of the rape victim on the stand within the dominant discourse's codes of normality.

Hengehold (1994) finds that "while the defendant is undoubtedly on trial for his liberty or life, his 'reasonability' is assumed, which is in contrast to that of the woman testifying against him. It is the speaker in whom a subjectivity is being cultivated and disciplined by the structure of this questioning, and the speaker whose credibility and capacity to be perceived and to perceive herself as a 'reasonable' member of society are at stake" (96). But the expert eliciting the confession will encounter resistance because power is relational. The televised rape trials thus become "mobile and transitory points of resistance, producing cleavages in a society" (Foucault, 1978, 96). A televised rape victim finds her own speaking body to be the site of a rupture in the techniques of knowledge and power. She is at once resisting a horrible form of domination and articulating (although in a highly proscribed way) her anger, outrage, and revolt against sexual assault.

Is it possible that televising rape trials could start new feminist discourses? Hengehold (1994) argues that a Foucauldian analysis of rape leads neither to "desexualization" of the crime nor to the argument that women should avoid bringing their complaints before the law for fear of acquittal. Rather, she contends that "it indicates that a woman's attempt to publicly reassert herself as a rational and powerful speaker in the aftermath of rape may demand the creation of another speaking community (such as the women's movement) besides that which is mediated by law, and that only an alternative (feminist) discourse is capable of analyzing the asymmetrical speech situation within the courtroom" (103–4). Susan Hekman (1991) agrees and argues that "subjectivity is piecemeal, gaps and ambiguities within the interstices of language prevent a uniform determination of subjectivity" (59–60). It is in these gaps and ambiguities in rape law, in testimony, and in video production, where the possibility for both change and resistance can occur.

Rape, according to Foucault's theory, can be understood to be produced and maintained by discursive regimes. Since rape is "sexed" (usually men rape women) the discourses surrounding rape, rape law, and televised rape trials contribute to the definition of gender. Rape trial television productions advertise what counts as rape in this culture and what counts as being a "woman who can be raped" and a "woman who cannot be raped." Hengehold (1994) suggests that when rape is viewed as a disciplinary matrix with both physical and discursive effects, rape can be seen to contribute to the "hysterization" of women: "To view rape purely as a physical assault denies the role that rape might play in the production or maintenance of a particular regime" (94). What counts as "sex" or "rape" or "violence" in rape cases is determined by the discourses of law and psychiatry. In this sense, the televised rape trial functions as a privileged forum to audience members who are participating in shaping the meaning of "sexual difference."

Foucault (1980) writes that "the political question . . . is truth itself" (133). He continues: "Each society has its regime of truth, its 'general politics' of truth: that is, the types of discourses which it accepts and makes function as true; the mechanisms and instances which enable one to distinguish true and false statements, the means by which each is sanctioned; the techniques and procedures accorded value in the acquisition of truth; the status of those who are charged with saying what counts as true" (131). This is particularly poignant in rape law. Butler (1991) affirms that in rape law:

> the politics of violence operate through regulating what will and will not be able to appear as an effect of violence. There is, then, already in this foreclosure a violence at work, a marking off in advance of what will or will not qualify under the signs of "rape" or "government violence," or in the case of states in which twelve separate pieces of empirical evidence are required to establish "rape," what then can be called a governmentally facilitated rape. (162–63)

Televised rape trials can be understood as a patriarchal strategic response to feminist rape law reform. The televised rape trial itself, as an aspect of the phenomenon of rape, is a governmentally facilitated "second rape" for those opposed to it, but what is remarkable is that the rape victim, as accuser, willingly takes center stage and "confesses." The spectacle of the televised rape trial, as a principle of its operating success, constructs the female-as-subject and subdues her by making her "confess." The alleged victim must relive the assault in all its vile detail while answering questions in a cross-examination designed to assault her character. The "political economy" of a will to knowledge, according to Foucault, had an interest in constructing the confession as a difficult extraction in order to invest it with more meaning and power and to intensify its truth and pleasure. The "blue dot" that covers the rape victim's face can be interpreted as preserving her anonymity and investing the confession with more meaning and therefore intensifying the pleasure for the viewing audience. It is not difficult to understand why the confessor's disclosure is pleasurable to hear since it involves "the description of the respective positions of the partners, the postures assumed, gestures, places touched, caresses, the precise moment of pleasure—an entire painstaking review of the sexual act in its very unfolding" (Foucault 1978, 19). The pleasure produced by the confession is increased by the very difficulty of extracting it. The anonymity of the rape victim's confession is required to reinforce the perceived link between sexuality and the "deep, hidden truth" of subjectivity. The expert (lawyer) reveals the "truth" behind the particular sexual assault victim, but he is actually revealing the "truth" behind her "sex."

Foucault's work allows us to see how the rape victim's "confession" unfolds within a power relationship. States Hengehold (1994), "it is the female rape victim, not the accused rapist, who is forced to confess her sexual experience and to explore her sexual motives publicly and in excruciating detail" (96). The "confessing" victim must monitor her behavior because she knows that in order for a conviction to take place her confession must be constructed in such a way that she is a "good woman," because only "good women" can be raped—everyone else is asking for it. Alcoff and Grey (1993) argue that the confession is an "effective mechanism for enhancing the power of its administering experts, subsuming subjectivities under an increasingly hegemonic discourse and diminishing the possibilities for transgression or intervention by individuals within its domain" (260–61). Foucault's theory, I argue, provides a better analysis of televised rape law. The view of law as either the rape victim's friend or foe misses the impact of how law affects the rape victim's subjectivity.

Concluding Remarks

A postmodern feminist position (e.g., Butler 1990, 1991) deconstructs the relatively unified notion of the social subject "woman." However, this does not mean that we should stop investigating the category when it crops up. Linda Nicholson (1994) finds, rather, that "we should understand them in different and more complex terms than we have tended to do, particularly that we should become more attentive to the historicity of any patterns we uncover" (99). This has been the goal of this essay, namely, to make claims about "women" in the particular context of a televised rape trial. This allows us to escape essentializing the term "woman" and examine its construction as a historically specific variable of a televised rape trial in twentieth-century United States culture.

The rituals accompanying rape have expanded their scope from being primarily physical forces to more discursively based, disciplinary forces. Televised rape trials are a discursively based disciplinary force that may be seen as a response on the part of power to the ongoing struggle between power (rape) and resistance (testifying women). Earlier in this essay I asked the rhetorical question, Are there similarities between twentieth-century rape trials in the United States and seventeenth-century French public scaffolds, and I argued that both are examples of power needing publicity. The effect of power's publicity in seventeenth-century France was that "a whole mass of discourses appeared pursuing the same confrontation; the posthumous proclamation of the crimes justified justice, but also glorified the criminal" (Foucault, 1977b, 68). However, by the latter half of the eighteenth century "protests against *public* execution proliferated . . . Very soon the public execution became intolerable" (Foucault, 1977b, 68–73). Will the effects of twentieth-century rape trials result in a glorification of the rapist or will viewers protest against the public trial? I argue that unlike the spectacle of the scaffold in seventeenth-century France, the spectacle of the televised rape trial does not seem to be creating a public uproar over rape, and this may well be because power assures that the audience only sees rape in a way which minimizes the prospect of real resistance on the part of the victim.

There may be a tendency for dominant discourses always to try to silence the speech of nondominant discourses (such as rape-survivor discourse) or, failing this, to channel them into nonthreatening outlets. Alcoff and Grey (1993) point out that there are ways to inhibit a discourse, including through institutionalization (mental hospitals, prisons, reform schools) or denial of public access to listeners. Further, they argue, "dominant discourses can recuperate their hegemonic position even when disruptive speech is not silenced by subsuming it within the framework of the discourse in such a way that it is disempowered and no longer disruptive" (268). I have attempted to show in this essay that this is precisely what televised rape trials do.

In an attempt to move toward a more comprehensive understanding of the relationship between discourse and power, I have argued that Foucault's theoretical work detailing the interdependence of coercion, discipline, and the production of truthful discourse in the exercise of state and social power, provides the basis for a more thoughtful analysis of rape and rape law and the televised rape hearing. This explanatory potential should not be underestimated. It points to our increased capacity to better understand not only how rape victims are objectified by rape law and television production techniques, but how rape victims, simultaneously, use this opportunity to express their anger, despair, and outrage. This ruptures male hegemonic discourses and may ignite new feminist discourses and elevate the critical consciousness of other sexual assault victims or potential sexual assault victims in the viewing audience. Nancy Fraser (1991) argues that "feminists need both deconstruction and reconstruction, destabilization of meaning and projection of utopian hope. . . . We might conceive subjectivity as endowed with critical capacities *and* as culturally constructed" (175). It is with this awareness that Foucault's theory has such appeal as an antidote to the subject/object dichotomy.

References

Alcoff, L., and L. Gray. (1993). Survivor discourse: Transgression or recuperation? *Signs* 18(2):260–90.

Ansley, L. (1992, June 26–28). Majority opinion: Court TV's a hit. *USA Weekend,* p. 16.

Barry, K. (1979). *Female Sexual Slavery.* Englewood Cliffs, N.J.: Prentice Hall.

Bartky, S. (1988). Foucault, femininity, and the modernization of patriarchal power. In I. Diamond and L. Quinby (Eds.): *Feminism and Foucault: Reflections on Resistance.* Boston: Northeastern University Press, 61–86.

Brownmiller, S. (1975). *Against Our Will: Men, Women, and Rape.* New York: Simon and Schuster.

Butler, J. (1990). *Gender Trouble: Feminism and the Subversion of Identity.* New York: Routledge and Kegan Paul.

———. (1991). Contingent foundations: Feminism and the question of 'postmodernism.' *Praxis International* 11(2):152–67.

Carse, A. (1995). Pornography: An uncivil liberty? *Hypatia* 10(1):155–82.

Chodorow, N. (1978). *The Reproduction of Mothering.* Berkeley: University of California Press.

Clark, A. (1987). *Men's Violence: Women's Silence.* London: Pandora.

Comerford, L. (1993). *Raped Again on Court TV: A Closer Look at the William Kennedy-Smith Rape Trial.* Unpublished manuscript, State University of New York at Albany.

Dahlgren, P. (1988). What's the meaning of this? *Media, Culture, and Society* 10:285–301.

Dworkin, A. (1974). *Woman Hating.* New York: Dutton.

———. (1981). *Pornography: Men Possessing Women.* New York: Perigee.

Eisenstein, Z. (1979). *Capitalist Patriarchy and the Case for Socialist Feminism.* New York: Monthly Review Press.

———. (1988). *The Female Body and the Law.* Berkeley: University of California Press.

Estrich, S. (1987). *Real Rape: How the Legal System Victimizes Women Who Say No.* Cambridge, Mass.: Harvard University Press.

Foucault, M. (1977a). What is an author? In D. F. Bouchard (Ed.): *Language, Counter-memory, Practice: Selected Essays and Interviews by Michel Foucault.* Ithaca, N.Y.: Cornell University Press.

———. (1977b). Nietzsche, genealogy, history. In D. F. Bouchard (Ed.): *Language, Counter-memory, Practice: Selected Essays and Interviews by Michel Foucault.* Ithaca, N.Y.: Cornell University Press.

———. (1978). *The History of Sexuality, Volume One: An Introduction.* (R. Hurley, Trans.) New York: Vintage.

———. (1979). *Discipline and Punish: The Birth of the Prison.* New York: Vintage.

———. (1980). *Power/Knowledge: Selected Interviews and Other Writings, 1972–1977.* (C. Gordon, Ed.) New York: Pantheon.

———. (1982). The subject and power. In H. Dreyfus and P. Rabinow: *Michel Foucault: Beyond Structuralism and Hermeneutics.* Chicago: University of Chicago Press, 208–28.

Fraser, N. (1991). False antitheses: A response to Seyly Benhabib and Judith Butler. *Praxis International* 11(2):166–77.

———, and L. Nicholson. (1990). Social criticism without philosophy: An encounter between feminism and postmodernism. In L. Nicholson (Ed.): *Feminism/Postmodernism.* New York: Routledge.

Hartmann, H. (1981). The unhappy marriage of Marxism and feminism. In L. Sargent (Ed.): *Women and Revolution.* Boston: South End Press.

Hekman, S. (1991). Reconstituting the subject: Feminism, modernism, and postmodernism. *Hypatia* 6(2):44–63.

Hengehold, L. (1994). "An immodest proposal": Foucault, hysterization, and the "second rape." *Hypatia* 9(3):88–107.

MacKinnon, C. (1979). *Sexual Harassment of Working Women: A Case of Sex Discrimination.* New Haven, Conn.: Yale University Press.

———. (1987). *Feminism Unmodified.* Cambridge, Mass.: Harvard University Press.

———. (1989). *Toward a Feminist Theory of the State.* Cambridge, Mass.: Harvard University Press.

Matoesian, G. (1993). *Reproducing Rape.* Chicago, Ill.: University of Chicago Press.

———. (1995). "Language, law and society: Policy implications of the Kennedy Smith Rape Trial." *Law and Society* 29(4):669–701.

McNay, L. (1991). The Foucauldian body and the exclusion of experience. *Hypatia* 6(3):125–39.

Millet, K. (1970). *Sexual Politics.* Garden City, N.Y.: Doubleday.

Nicholson, L. (1994). Interpreting gender. *Signs* 29(1):79–105.

Press, A. (1991). *Women Watching Television.* Philadelphia: University of Pennsylvania Press.

Rich, A. (1980). Compulsory heterosexuality and lesbian existence. *Signs* 5:631–60.

Rubin, G. (1976). The traffic in women. In R. Reiter (Ed.): *Toward an Anthropology of Women.* New York: Monthly Review Press.

Russell, D. (1984). *Sexual Exploitation: Rape, Child Sexual Abuse, and Workplace Sexual Harassment.* Beverly Hills, Calif.: Sage.

Smart, C. (1989). *Feminism and the Power of Law.* London: Routledge.

U.S. Senate Hearing (1984, April 24). United States Ninety-Eighth Congress hearing before the Sub-committee on Criminal Law of the Committee on the Judiciary United States. Second session on "Oversight on the effect of publicity on the victims in rape cases and the right of the press to have access to such proceedings."

Warshaw, R. (1988). *I Never Called It Rape.* New York: Harper and Row.

Zoglin, R. (1991, June 17). Justice faces a screen test. *Time,* p. 62.

Insiders in the Body:
Communication, Multiple Personalities, and the Body Politic

Joseph Gemin

Multiple personality disorder (MPD), or dissociative identity disorder as it is clinically referred to, is a psychiatric diagnosis that has perhaps generated more controversy than any other modern psychiatric disorder (North et al., 1993, 23). Drawing on aspects of this controversy, I want to argue that the manifestation of MPD calls for a cultural reading, one that views MPD as a self-referential expression of paradoxical social tensions. Specifically, MPD may be regarded primarily as a socially constructed phenomenon, one that exemplifies a culturally sanctioned form of bodily escape. In fact, the manifestation of this disorder constitutes an example, albeit an anomalous one, of what John Shotter (1989) has referred to as "*already established* ways in which we *must* talk in order to *account* for ourselves" (141). Given my contention, I intend to use aspects of Michel Foucault's (1980, 1982) position on disciplinary technology and Hayden White's (1978) "tropic" orientation to cultural analysis in order to demonstrate the manner in which the discourse on MPD actively creates the phenomenon that it claims to describe scientifically and objectively. Partly as a way of structuring my argument, I have chosen to analyze the MPD phenomenon as manifested in a 1990 rape trial in Wisconsin in which the rape victim herself, Sarah, was diagnosed as having MPD. The choice of context is not accidental: it provides an opportunity to see the expression of a unique psychiatric phenomenon superimposed on a legal context. Both legal and psychiatric discourses can be shown to function symbiotically, shaping the manner in which multiple personalities present themselves through Sarah's talk.

In an effort to transcend "anthropological" investigations of self and other that exist in more scientifically oriented explanations of MPD,

I will outline some issues associated with the MPD controversy, and then move on to use Foucault's position on power as it relates to disciplinary technologies to analyze those features of Sarah's trial germane to the position described above.

The MPD Phenomenon and Its Skeptics

MPD is considered by many experts to be a pathological condition in which two or more selves become manifest in one person, usually as a response to the trauma of childhood abuse (Crabtree, 1985). That is, if an abused child is not able to cope with the anxiety of traumatic experiences, she may attempt to deny them. This attempt to repress memories that will not dissipate results in the unconscious strategy of producing alternative personalities as a coping mechanism. Each personality is given license to express hidden thoughts, feelings, and desires, but now the guilt associated with such secrets is diffused and parceled out as the property of each separate personality. It takes no leap of the imagination to see that such a strategy can offer a useful means of bodily escape, especially since the MPD patient often has no awareness of the thoughts and memories of each personality, or "alter."

What makes MPD controversial as a phenomenon is the body of evidence that suggests it to be, in large part, a *communicatively constituted* disorder, culturally based (Bruner 1990; Hacking, 1991, 1992; Humphrey and Dennett, 1989), surfacing primarily in the United States and a few other western countries (Aldridge-Morris, 1989, 97–109; Fahy et al., 1989; Takahishi, 1990) and, perhaps most noteworthy, increasing at a exponential rate of "epidemic" proportions (Bloor, 1982). Putnam et al. (1986) state that while MPD is "an exceedingly uncommon diagnosis" (285), more cases have been reported within the last five years than in the preceding two centuries. Even the number of personalities an MPD patient can experience has increased, climbing from two or three in 1950s to between 25 and 30 personalities on average by the mid-1980s (Hacking, 1992). Some have questioned MPD's ontological foundations still further. Spanos et al. (1986, 298), for example, claim to have simulated the MPD experience by having students enact some of the symptoms, arguing that MPD itself may be conceptualized as a form of social role enactment.

Skepticism surrounding the existence of MPD is evident in the media's coverage of the Wisconsin rape trial. The *Milwaukee Journal* quotes a journalist's explanation for covering the trial for a London tabloid: "people in England don't believe in things like multiple personalities." ("Lights, Camera," 1990). Even during the trial, the psychiatrist for the defense referred to MPD as "the UFO phenomena [*sic*] of psychiatry," adding, "There's a band of very intense believers who have all the sightings but the rest of us never see any" (State of Wisconsin, 1990, 25). Following such skepticism, a recurrent assertion in this chapter is that Sarah must "objectify" herself in accordance with cultural forms of talk in order to bring to consciousness the multiple personality experience. But what form does this objectification entail? Foucault's work on power as it manifests itself in technologies of the body offers some insight in explaining MPD's historical conditions of existence.

Disciplinary Technology: The Individual as Object and Subject

In practical terms, the "disciplinary technologies" that Foucault describes as both vehicles and effects of power work to appropriate the phenomenal body as a distinct object—a machine that must be scientifically analyzed by being separated into distinct parts. The aim of such partitioning, as Foucault's historical analyses have emphasizes, was originally to forge a docile, obedient body that could be fashioned for administrative ends, much the same way that a successful use of "divide and rule" renders a close-knit group powerless and dependent through the act of separating its knowledge bearings and points of reference. Scientific management (Morgan, 1986, 29–33) epitomizes this "disciplining" of the individual in the group or organizational context: all tasks to be carried out by the individual are broken down into finite, discrete movements and must be conducted and supervised according to a fixed and regimented preset design.

Disciplinary technology is not confined, then, to a treatment of the phenomenal body alone, but also entails the effective organization of individuals in a space: "This machinery works space in a much more flexible and detailed way. It does this first of all on the principle of elementary location or *partitioning*. Each individual has his own place; and each place its individual" (Foucault, 1982, 143). The space surrounding the body, as much as the body itself, has to be organized; this not only facilitates utility but also enhances observation, surveillance, and comparison. In other words, bringing people together collectively, and then distributing, partitioning, and separating them in a predesigned space, facilitates the development of classificatory schemes and normalizing judgments, ways in which people can be individualized and differentiated. It is a strategy, in effect, of differentiation *by* combination. And what is the purpose of implementing such classificatory schema? Anomalies and differences can now be pinpointed and rectified, even if such anomalies are, in reality, only expressions of the system of notation and observation itself. Michael Rose (1989) notes that the act of scientific observation, and the testing techniques accompanying it, serve to 'stabilize' the individual person being perceived, thus constituting a calculable, potentially knowable object for ongoing analysis.

Evidence of the cultural saturation of disciplinary technologies in their various forms has often come from feminist writings on the body-self relationship. Emily Martin, for example, offers a clue as to why disorders associated with the self—like MPD—seem to be experienced mostly by women. Exploring the metaphors that women use to describe their feelings about selfhood during medical examinations and child-birth, Martin (1992) points out that the central image used by women is that "your self is separate from your body" (77), a statement of body-self alienation that she attributes, in part, to the way women's bodies are treated by medical authorities. Similarly, Bartky (1988) in a discussion of women's experience of dieting, discusses the manner in which the "body becomes one's enemy, an alien being bent on thwarting the disciplinary project" (65), setting up a never-ending battle that, ironically, gives rise to a demand for more discipline in order to win the war. Also echoing the "enemy" theme is Susan Bordo's (1988) study of women with anorexia nervosa. According to Bordo, the body, for many anorectic women, is experienced as alien, an *outside* enemy that entraps them and threatens their attempts at control. And yet, "The attempt to subdue the spontaneities of the body in the interests of control only succeeds in constituting them as more alien, and more powerful and thus more needful of control" (93).

The experience of MPD, at least as revealed by Sarah's testimony at the trial, appears to demonstrate a reformulated expression of the recurrent themes that feminist scholars have identified. But in this case, Sarah talks about her body as if were lifeless, merely a shell that houses the various selves contained within. Her body is still considered an alien force, in the sense that it is deemed a separate part of her being, though she certainly does not consider it a threat or an enemy. Instead, the manner in which she discusses her experience of possessing multiple personalities appears to represent, at least in an analogous sense, an internalization of the disciplinary apparatus itself, in which the self and the other(s) are distributed and organized in an enclosed space.

The constitution of the self requires more than the objectification of identity. The subjectivity of the individual person must be constituted also. In the first volume of *The History of Sexuality* (1977), Foucault documents the transformation of the confession, a technology that came into being in its modern form around the seventeenth century and has since infiltrated all sectors of society as a subjectifying practice. Confession is, as we will see in Sarah's case, a practice inextricably linked to judicial decision-making, as well as functioning as the backbone of therapeutic interventions in psychotherapy and clinical psychology. But unlike the objectifying disciplines that work to make the body malleable from without, confession requires a speaking subject: Sarah, in effect, must tell the truth about herself. The key to this kind of technology, then, is the belief that the MPD patient, with the help of therapeutic experts, *can* tell the truth about herself, and that such knowledge may be obtained by techniques unadulterated by power.

Foucault insists that it is the disciplinary practice of confession itself which articulates the very idea of a hidden truth to be found in the MPD confession: both "surface" meaning and "deep" significance of this disorder—terms that typify confessional practices—are themselves expressions of a power/knowledge dialectic, culturally specific and historical in nature. The belief in a deep interpretation uncovered in confession, of the self as a container of dark secrets, creates the need for scientific expertise to find the "deeper" meaning, the truth of the matter. As such, Sarah is forced to defer to an "outside" trained expert, an authoritative *other* who will attempt to decipher the true meaning of her talk, that which lies beyond the realm of the externally visible. Needless to say, such a strategy, motivated by the desire for truth, only gives rise to a state of infinite regress: the more the subject talks, the more scientific examination is mobilized, setting in motion a never-ending, self-referential quest for still more knowledge and, likewise, more confession.

In the analysis to follow, I will argue that the courtroom styles of discourse encourage forms of talk that sanction the production of discrete, either/or categories: a mode of categorization necessary for the social production of "docile bodies." The judicial system, and the psychiatric institution it relies upon, cannot operate without constituting *coherence* in the form of exclusive categories. As such, the MPD patient, Sarah, who, in the face of trauma, wishes to "escape" the confines of her body, does so by somehow expressing the either/or categories that already exist. In effect, she comes to consider her own experience of multiples mechanistically, as though her alters are independent parts functioning in a consistently one-dimensional manner. And, I maintain, she *must* adopt this orientation in order to make her experience tangible and coherent both to herself and others.

In this legal context, questions from the two attorneys function in concert to presuppose the capacity, the possibility, of "telling the truth" about oneself. But in order for Sarah to tell the truth, she must objectify herself as stable, fixed, and consistent in nature. In this way the courtroom demand for truth *produces* the stability and knowability of Sarah. In this sense, Sarah's production of a coherent, orchestrated text may be viewed as both a vehicle and an *effect* of disciplinary technology: a text institutionally demanded and ultimately legitimized by the victim herself. Without such coherence the judicial-psychiatric machine would simply grind to a halt.

Multiple Personalities on Trial

In November 1990, "Sarah," a woman who experts claimed had forty-six different personalities, testified in a Wisconsin courtroom that she had been sexually assaulted by a resident of Oshkosh, Wisconsin. It was alleged that the defendant, Mark Peterson, knowing that Sarah had a mental disorder, and without asking for Sarah's consent, manipulated her by persuading one of her personalities—Jennifer, the "naïve" personality—into having sex with him at a local park. The presiding judge, facing a challenge as to how to proceed with Sarah's testimony since each personality had its own unique set of perceptions and memories, required that each time a different alter manifested itself in Sarah, he or she be separately sworn in. Attorneys for the prosecution (Salzsieder) and defense (Paulus) accordingly addressed their questions to each personality called to testify. These included, among others, Sarah, Jennifer, Franny, and Emily.

The prosecuting attorney outlined the state's case against Peterson before the trial: "We're saying that when he was having sex with Jennifer, the real person wasn't even there" ("Case Hinges," 1990). A newspaper report anticipating the event commented: "Testimony promises to be a debate between psychiatric experts. Even if one of the woman's personalities agreed to have sex, under Wisconsin law a person with a diagnosed mental illness cannot consent to sexual relations" ("Rape Case," 1990). Psychiatric experts were used by both sides to present opinions as to whether Sarah's was a genuine case of MPD. The defendant, Mark Peterson, was initially found guilty of sexual assault (a verdict that was later overturned on a technicality).

Pretrial publicity focused public attention squarely on the nature of Sarah's identity. Were her personalities "just names assigned to different fragments of one personality?" Or were they "separate individuals inhabiting one body?" Did they "have the same rights and status under the law?" And who should "call the shots?" ("Personality Disorder," 1990). The issue of what happened in this case, of who did what and when, took second stage to the implied question, "who *are* you?" Newspaper coverage, in its mission to find the truth about Sarah, paid meticulous attention to her every move, both in and out of the courtroom. Her looks, clothes, and posture; the nonverbal differences of each personality; their linguistic and paralinguistic peculiarities; and the mysterious process of switching from one personality to the other ("Victim Tells," 1990) were all treated as potential signs of a hidden meaning, existing below the visible surface. Journalists described Sarah as she waited outside the courtroom for the verdict, hoping for some signs of truth: "Sarah held hers arms oddly, a stiff angle to the elbows. She appeared in the sober dress of a promising young executive. . . . She wore eyeliner, neatly, on her upper and lower lids. Her hair was combed smooth and straight to her shoulders" ("Rape Case," 1990).

In true disciplinary fashion, such scrupulous surveillance itself created the sense of a mysterious hidden truth to be found. *The Milwaukee Journal* typified newspaper coverage in the days leading up to the trial, continually repeating the central issue, namely, was this a genuine case of MPD? Or was Sarah lying? Darold Treffert, the psychiatrist for the defense, maintained that MPD was a condition fairly easily induced by a psychiatrist while Salzsieder, the defense attorney, argued that his client had no idea that she was mentally ill: "If she appears perfectly normal and we have sexual contact between consenting adults, there is absolutely nothing wrong with it" ("The Twenty-One," 1990). The outcome of this line of thinking was to draw parameters around Sarah— her body and the secret that lay within were to be the center of the judicial gaze.

Media's scrutiny of Sarah's actions and statements, and their use of experts to decipher the truth of such behaviors, was carried over into the courtroom, in practices that appeared quite innocuous on the surface. The courtroom, and the activities contained therein, the adversarial presentation of issues in an a clear either/or manner (either she was telling the truth or lying), reinforced the idea that *the* truth was *capable* of being told—that Sarah *could* tell the truth about herself. Sarah, by telling the "truth," would render herself knowable both to herself and to others. Of course, she would oblige by expressing "the truth" in the only style that the legal context counts as truthful—by re-producing herself as consistent and unambiguous in her testimony.

Joseph Paulus, the prosecuting attorney in the trial, participated in removing such ambiguity by painting a portrait of Sarah that, ironically, intensified the scrutiny of her. Paulus took care to establish a direct and linear causal link between her early childhood trauma and later psychiatric diagnoses. Such a tactic, while it was sensitive to the suffering that his client had experienced, served to decontextualize Sarah's experience from the contexts that gave it meaning, while at the same time solidified the idea that she possessed an ideal core identity, one that, when healthy, would be coherent and empirical. Such a tactic, unavoidable in many ways, nonetheless functioned to center attention squarely on her as the locus of disturbance, and on whatever meanings had been assumed to be contained *within* her. At one point in her testimony, Sarah describes being attacked by Shadow, an alter created to take on some of her "childhood pain." Paulus asks about her feelings during the attack:

A. It was terrifying. I could feel him coming out because of
the rage. I could not control him. I was terrified.
Q. You were not able to intercede and stop it?
A. No. (State of Wisconsin, 594)

Sarah repeatedly discusses her emotions as being out of control,
generated from a space "inside" the body and directed "outward."
Questions and answers serve to situate her as the possessor of these
inner feelings by requiring that she produce an understandable, coherent text. While Paulus, for his part, does his best to speak Sarah's
language, to speak for her and on her terms, it is the psychiatric-
judicial text that they re-produce together: testimony, in the legal
context, functions to objectify her experience in the demand for clarity and consistency:

Q. Emily would be one of the insiders?
A. The six-year-old.
Q. Now with regard to MPD, different personalities within,
have you now been able to identify some of those people?
(586)

There is a genuine effort to meet Sarah on her own terms: Paulus
does not say "one of *your* insiders," but "*the* insiders," echoing Sarah's
vernacular, yet further participating in the objectification of multiple
personalities as empirically contained within her. On a number of occasions, he refers to personalities "within" Sarah, but even then they are
not discussed as if they are "owned" by Sarah, not as part of her being
but as possessions residing in the body.

Nowhere in Sarah's testimony is there any indication that MPD
is something she suffers from, or that it is even experienced as a disorder. Instead, references to MPD are described in terms of its utility.
Testifying as "Franny," one of the alters, under cross-examination by
defense attorney Salzsieder, is asked whether she ever told the defendant that she suffered from an illness:

A. I am not ill, dear.
Q. You are not. Did you ever say that Sarah has a multiple
personality disorder?
A. I said we are multiple, we are many, we share the body.
Q. I understand that, but then my question is, did you ever
say that Sarah has a multiple personality disorder?
A. I am not aware that it is a disorder.
Q. . . . [D]id you say anything else?
A. I said we share the body. There are many among us
inside. (699–700)

Sarah is clear as to the positive role that therapy has played in her life, occasionally referring to her therapists on a first-name basis during the trial. In the following segment of testimony, Paulus questions her as to when she initially discovered her personalities:

> *Q.* Was there some actual communication within your mind within these personalities?
> *A.* At the time I did not know it as communication. I thought I was hearing voices. After the therapist asked them to speak one at the time, I was able to make sense of them; I could understand them. At first they spoke all at once; this was babbling. (597)

This exchange marks the first point in the trial at which it becomes obvious that therapy has had some part to play in Sarah's capacity to experience MPD in the first place. In fact, her testimony for Paulus is clearly divisible into two phases. The first is highlighted by an uncertainty and ambiguity as to what was originally happening to her, while the second phase, corresponding to the time after she was diagnosed as having MPD, is marked by an unusual clarity and coherence: Sarah is able to tell us *exactly* about the nature and function of each personality and the context in which she (or he) presently operates. Therapy, here, can be seen to have first turned Sarah's attention inward and, in so doing, it encouraged Sarah to view herself as an object to be known.

Nowhere is Sarah's clarity of thought and expression more evident than in cross-examination by Salzsieder, whose questions aim to portray Sarah as a fraud. But his attempt to show inconsistencies in her testimony proves fruitless. In fact, the tables are turned at a number of points, at which Salzsieder himself is made to appear incoherent. In one instance, he asks Sarah about her hobby of horseback riding:

> *Q.* Do any of the other inner selves also ride [your horse]?
> *A.* Yes, Gerald.
> *Q.* Anybody else?
> *A.* Not that I know of.
> *Q.* Where is he kept, is he boarded someplace for you?
> *A.* Gerald or the horse? (686–87)

On questioning Sarah about her capacity to retreat inward when another personality takes control, Salzsieder receives a glib response:

> *Q.* You weren't present before coming out, were you?
> *A.* How could I have been present before coming out? (705)

In this last example, Sarah points out the "irrationality" in Salzsieder's questions by adhering to the conventional, western either/ or mindset, that one cannot be in two places at the same time. In so doing, she demonstrates her allegiance to the separateness and exclusivity instigated by disciplinary technology. However, it is a stretch to view such "resistance" to Salzsieder's questioning as in any way subversive. If anything, Sarah's responses would seem to reinforce the very system that facilitates conditions for MPD in the first place; that is, they support discrete and exclusive categories and foster a view of the world that is rendered static, unaltered by ambiguity. So how is Sarah's "interior" life constituted by Sarah herself? How does she talk about her identity and her own body?

In answering a question from Salzsieder as to her correct legal name, Sarah responds that she is Sarah: "that is the name of the body" (667). Sarah's body ("the body") is discussed throughout her testimony as if it is inert, inanimate, simply a casing of sorts. In fact, when she was attacked and injured by a hostile personality, she discusses how the wise personality, Leona, "took the body downstairs" to a neighbor. When Salzsieder, interested in exploring the "peeking" phenomenon that Sarah had earlier described, asks how he would know if someone was peeking at Sarah now, she responds "if you came very close and looked into my eyes, you might sense somebody looking out" (673). The theme of the body as detached from the self, emerges again—and is legitimized—in questions about the ages of the alters:

> *Q.* Am I correct if I understand that Franny is about the age of thirty-two?
> *A.* Yes.
> *Q.* But you Sarah, the body, are only age twenty-seven now?
> *A.* Yes. (668)

Alters are themselves capable of turning back and objectifying the body that houses them. "Franny" recalls thinking that Peterson had tricked her: "I thought he was a gentleman and he tricked me and he did harm to the body" (644). "Sam," formerly the "animal" personality, remembers being in the hospital after the assault: "I was alone. I knew there had been harm done to the body. I felt it" (651). The alter named "Jennifer" recalls telling Peterson during the assault episode not to worry about getting her pregnant: "I can't get pregnant because Sarah [the body] got her tubes tied" (626). Jennifer also recalls that Emily peeked "through the eyes of the body" (627) during the sexual assault, and that she knew Emily was peeking because she could "feel" her. Jennifer's "feeling" was confirmed by Emily who, during her testimony, admits that she occasionally looks in on the behavior of others: "I peek through the eyes of the inside" (632).

It is because Sarah is able to objectify her body, and because she conceives of her alters as *possessible* others, a feat facilitated, interpersonally, in conjunction with therapy, that she is capable of speaking about her "discovering" new, separate, alters. The objectification of body and selves (alters) offers an explanation as to how each personality came into existence: "approximately half of them were made from further splitting after the assault. . . . I hypnotized myself and went in looking to see if they were real. And I got a helluva lot more than I bargained for" (656).

While Sarah refers to herself as "multiple," she is adamant that "None of the insiders are multiple. They are separate entities" (663). Although she considers them as exclusive entities with separate memories, she thinks that the alters may share the same intelligence level since "they all share the same brain" (599). Here then, she again relays a medical understanding of her experiences, constituting herself as the object of medical gaze. During her testimony, she describes the habits and behaviors of a number of the personalities, those she refers to as "insiders." In keeping with her previous statements she initially refers to them not in terms of what she *has,* but what "there is," as though she is talking about outsiders with herself as their carrier. On occasion, when Sarah uses the first-person singular during testimony, she moves to the first-person plural with ease. There is even a palpable consistency in this practice. For example, with regard to her appreciation of Jennifer's naivete: "*We* have tried to preserve this because *I* find it delightful and wonderful" (593). And on the rationale for the production of additional personalities: "I liked them and we needed them" (605).

When questioned as to whether she was at the park for the initial meeting with Peterson, Sarah responds, "I was told some of my personalities were" (603). Sarah, then, can exist as part of a community with the others, yet can also be absent from a physical place attended by her alters. Although she testifies to having discovered the "insiders" within, three new personalities, she maintains, were *created* in direct response to the sexual assault: "Beth was created basically to take all the pain, fears, sensations, memories of the trauma of the rape because Jennifer is not equipped, not built or created to handle that" (655). Noticeably, these additions were either created by, or with the help of, another personality, Leona, who "made Kim to balance out Beth" (655). Leona also created a male bodyguard: "Leona felt he would be necessary and so she created him as well" (655). This is the first instance in the trial in which Sarah indicates a capacity to generate alters for utilitarian purposes, bringing them into being to complement, expeditiously, the alters already in existence. Note that this "creation" is facilitated by the alters themselves, as if new additions function effortlessly to complement those that already exist. Each alter is given a specific, discrete task to perform. And there is no overlap between them. It is as if each has an exclusive place in a grid or apparatus, again inscribing Foucault's (1982) description of a utility-oriented, disciplined space: "Every individual has his own place; and each place its individual" (143).

Despite Sarah's feelings of affection for this community of "friends," the themes of separation and exclusivity do seem highly reminiscent of the docility-utility goal that Foucault describes in relation to disciplinary technologies. Sarah, in her testimony, would seem to have interiorized an odd, though understandable, permutation of the cultural ideal. While this creative capacity on her part suggests a fertile imagination, upon closer inspection, the alters created seem peculiarly one-dimensional and artificial, well in keeping with the way personalities are reified in conventional empiricist-driven communication theories. Although such a modernist view of personalities is socially sanctioned—perhaps because they signify the potential predictability of behavior—they are hardly the stuff of real life. The intrinsic ambiguity of lived experience, the contradictions and paradoxes that define human behavior, are avoided in favor of idealized types that seem quite unrealistic and exaggerated. Nevertheless, descriptions of the "insiders" fall well within conventional parameters. They make sense.

The communication technique of "co-presencing," which Sarah learned from her therapist, is also discussed in trial. Co-presencing enables her "to have a conversation with [her]self while one of them or two or more people or three on [sic] the outside" (600). She is able to co-presence both on the inside and "on the outside verbally" (600). "co-presencing," for Sarah, is distinguishable from "peeking," which is the capacity for one personality to look through the body in order to "spy" on the activities of other personalities.

In this discussion of co-presencing, we see what must amount to one feature that stands out most in Sarah's testimony as indicative the carceral system of disciplinary technology. This is the clear rendition of the space or situatedness of each personality—that each is deemed to exist somewhere inside the body. Ernesto Spinelli's (1989) phenomenological study of self-perception discussed the manner in which, during psychologically compelling situations, a person's conscience is often experienced as temporarily missing. Spinelli, in a manner antithetical to the conventional belief that a core sense of self follows us at all times, contends that "persistent role enactment temporarily created different beings" (89). In Sarah's case, however, personalities were not considered ephemeral but, in accordance with the dominant ideology, were discussed by her as having a livable space somewhere "inside" the body, emerging when called upon and retreating back inside when not in use. Jennifer, one of the alters, is asked whether another personality, Leslie, resides in her:

Q. Leslie is within you.
A. Within me?
Q. Within Sarah, the body?
A. She is in there *somewhere.* (639, emphasis mine)

Sarah, herself, is asked by Paulus to account for where she is when another personality is in control:

Q. Sarah, when something like this is happening and you don't know it is going on, where are you?
A. I am in the dark place.
Q. That's what you call it?
A. Yes.
Q. Can you describe the dark place?
A. It is place of no sensation, no time passing. You can think, you can't do much else. (595–96)

She goes on to explain that when she is in the dark place she has no idea what's going on the "outside" unless "somebody comes in and gets me, one of the insiders, or if I am called out" (596). This notion of having a personality step back "inside" to call another "outside" is a common theme, repeated elsewhere in the testimony of the other alters. The "dark place," too, is mentioned by various alters as contrasted with the "white place," a twilight space of sorts where a personality can peek out onto events, "can hear, smell, and see" (673), but cannot intervene or make things happen. Personalities can be co-present on the inside and on the outside, but they are still separable in space. This is true even on those occasions where one personality is "bumped" (613), pushed to the inside, while another takes control on the outside. All through this testimony the alters are able to draw a clear distinction between others existing inside the body and others, such as Sarah's neighbors, who accompanied her to the park on the first meeting with Peterson.

The Coordinated Production of Meaning

The appearance of rigid inside/outside dichotomies in Sarah's testimony echoes the extant anthropological themes that Foucault's work has attempted to circumvent. Why does Foucault oppose such dichotomies? Because he sees them as co-producing dominant, reified notions of object and subject, central in reinforcing the idea of the knowable subject, one that seeks to escape "outside" to the objective world. By fixing the perceptual gaze squarely on Sarah—by the practice of going "inside" her to find the truth—inside/outside dichotomies are continually reinforced, a move that can only serve to continually depoliticize the "outside."

The nature of Sarah's "interior" and the secrets thought to be contained therein must be seen, then, as a coordinated effort, interpersonally played out by means of the attorneys' questions (objectifying practices), by Sarah's own confessions (subjectifying practices), and through the incorporation of semantic structures of authority, both psychiatric and legal, that all participants in this event relied upon. While Salzsieder tries to present a different, skeptical narrative from Sarah's testimony, his efforts must be seen as operating *together* with the prosecuting attorney's questioning, to help situate Sarah as the *site* and *container* of secrets (mysteries). The overall effect is made possible only by the juxtaposition of these two sides throughout the whole trial. Only in light of the space created by this juxtaposition of seemingly opposed strategies is Sarah thus constituted as an individual with a mind to be known: the object/subject of surveillance.

Having multiple personalities, despite their utility in facilitating a form of bodily escape, is nonetheless an undesirable disorder. The integrated, "normal" personality is represented as a cultural ideal, an identity that Sarah, despite some signs to the contrary, clearly strives to achieve with the help of therapy. However, the therapist, as mentioned in the court transcripts appears at least in some ways, to facilitate the experience of MPD by transforming ambiguous (both/and) thoughts, feelings and actions that were difficult for Sarah to deal with into ambivalent (either/or) experiences. There is considerable irony when we learn that part of Sarah's therapy entails the process of integrating the alters, for this would seem to involve integrating those separated parts that were, themselves, initially brought into existence with the help of the therapist. In this fashion, the therapeutic act of integration itself, despite the appearance of promoting a kind of socially sanctioned and well-intentioned fusion, continues to reify the idea of personalities as *separate* entities, subtly reproducing the very discourse that forms the foundation for MPD to begin with.

My position in this chapter, given the cultural manifestation of this disorder, is that MPD appears to be an ironic *expression* of a culturally acceptable state for identity formation: MPD, in a sense, signifies the rigidity of the limits placed on identity formation. It is a disorder that, in part, magnifies hidden, mechanistic features of our culture, though its fundamental intelligibility, as a disorder, ought to warn us that despite its strange appearance, it does not represent an oppositional, alien manifestation. Unlike other psychiatric disorders, MPD *makes sense to us*—Sarah, throughout the trial, is extraordinarily coherent and understandable: there are no inconsistencies in her testimony. This coherence would seem to suggest that the expression of multiple personalities reveals the reproduction of a culturally valued, *self-referential system* of separations. Although MPD itself is coded by the scientific community as the "abnormal" property of an individual person, qualitatively different and requiring integration, the process of integrating different selves in therapy ensures that the social system which produced the conditions of existence for MPD remains hidden, and thus it is buttressed still further.

On the subject of MPD's political significance, there is a sense in which some media descriptions of Sarah's testimony during the trial had satanic connotations. This should come as no surprise, given that MPD achieved epidemic proportions during the mid-1980s, where women were starting to achieve a modicum of economic independence. Bordo's historical work is insightful in explaining the relationship between pathologies of the self and economic independence. She discusses the pervasiveness of late nineteenth-century images portraying women as "dark, dangerous, and evil" (1988, 107), arguing convincingly that the greater the threat that women were perceived to pose—the more they were seen as gaining independence—the more that pathologies associated with self-body alienation increased, an increase facilitated by the rise of the disciplinary technology of the time. MPD appears to be subject to the same forces. On the other hand, Bordo's political argument does not explain why MPD appears to be so prominently an American phenomenon, nor does it explain the capacity of MPD patients to multiply the number of alters they are able to experience.

To reiterate: I prefer to view multiple personalities as a real experience *and* an ironic *expression* of paradoxical social tensions at a time of increased "functional differentiation" in society (Luhmann, 1990). Rather than engaging in dialogue about the paradoxes that functional differentiation gives rise to—paradoxes that women find themselves experiencing more markedly yet, ironically, are more prohibited from expressing—the MPD patient, with the "help" of therapy, is moved unintentionally in the exact opposite direction. First by producing clearcut, literalized personalities as if they constituted empirical entities, then by using therapy to integrate the alters, again into an either/or world that seems unable to cope with ambiguity. Perhaps this desire to become "normal" by internalizing discrete, literal characteristics offers an (admittedly weak) explanation as to why MPD is so prevalent in North America, relative to other countries. More than most, literality and the pervasive demand for coherence, albeit as vehicles for control of self and other, are most valued here. To some degree, perhaps the manifestation of MPD in the United States is symptomatic of an attempt to step outside this fixed and literalized, scientific world of control.

As mentioned though, the freedom gained from overprecision in an age of paradox can only be short lived, since one has to "step outside" by using the same literalized, categorical schema available in order to do so. Developing multiple personalities is hardly creativity-inaction, since true creative expression usually encompasses paradox and ambiguity. On this point, I agree with James Glass (1993) that the experience of multiple personalities is not a "liberating" one: it does *not* emancipate Sarah from the status quo. Yet the alternative, the integration of separated alters, does not seem much of a solution, either. Far from it. The attempt to "integrate" sets Sarah on a potentially vicious cycle, one that avoids coming to terms with the paradoxes of everyday life, as well as tacitly recreating the foundations for MPD and similar identity disorders in so doing. The expression of MPD is not an imaginative resistance to carceral society, as some postmodernists would have it. On the contrary, it reaffirms it.

Conclusion: Foucault's "Other"

The rationality and coherence that pervaded all of Sarah's testimony not only enhanced public curiosity, it also functioned to legitimize the actions of law and psychiatry, neither of which function well as institutions that sanction ambiguity. To provide Sarah with a coherent text for self-understanding is to reproduce these institutions *at the same time;* they then function as vehicles for their own self-referential reproduction. In summation, for Foucault, understanding the Other is not a question of getting into the mind of the other from "outside." Such an endeavor, for him, suffers from the anthropologism that his work tried to overcome. It assumes that we can free ourselves of power in the pursuit of knowledge, in knowing another. Perhaps it is not an epistemological question, "How can I understand Sarah's mental life?" which ought to be uppermost, then. Rather, a more feasible shift would be one directed toward understanding those concrete practices that separate us, that produce in Sarah the experience of separateness, and that make us imagine that this anthropological endeavor is possible in the first place.

References

Aldridge-Morris, R. (1989). *Multiple Personality: An Exercise in Deception.* London: Erlbaum.
Bartky, S. (1988). Foucault, femininity, and the modernization of patriarchal power. In I. Diamond and L. Quinby (Eds.): *Feminism and Foucault: Reflections on Resistance.* Boston: Northeastern University Press, 61–86.

Bloor, M. (1982). The multiple personality epidemic. *Journal of Nervous and Mental Disease* 170(5):302–4.

Bordo, S. (1988). Anorexia nervosa: Psychopathology as the crystallization of culture. In I. Diamond and L. Quimby (Eds.): *Feminism and Foucault: Reflections on Resistance.* Boston: Northeastern University Press, 87–117.

Bruner, J. (1990). *Acts of Meaning.* Cambridge, Mass.: Harvard University Press.

Case hinges on special protection for the victim (1990, November 4). *Milwaukee Journal,* p. B5.

Crabtree, A. (1985). *Multiple Man: Explorations in Possession and Multiple Personality.* Eastbourne, England: Holt, Rinehart and Winston.

Fahy, T. A., M. Abas, and J. C. Brown. (1989). Multiple personality: A symptom of psychiatric disorder. *British Journal of Psychiatry* 154:99–101.

Foucault, M. (1977). *The History of Sexuality. Volume One: An Introduction.* (R. Hurley, Trans.) New York: Random House.

———. (1980). *Power/Knowledge.* (C. Gordon, Ed. and Trans.) Brighton, England: Harvester Press.

———. (1982). *Discipline and Punish: The Birth of the Prison.* (A. Sheridan, Trans.) Harmondsworth, England: Penguin.

Glass, J. M. (1993). *Shattered Selves.* Ithaca, N.Y.: Cornell University Press.

Hacking, I. (1991). Two souls in one body. *Critical Inquiry* 17:838–67.

———. (1992). Multiple personality disorder and its hosts. *History of the Human Sciences* 5(2):3–31.

Humphrey, N., and D. Dennett. (1989, Spring). Speaking for ourselves: An assessment of multiple personality disorder. *Raritan: A Quarterly Review,* (9), 68–98.

Lights, camera . . . trial (1990, November 9). *Milwaukee Journal,* p. B5.

Luhmann, N. (1990). *Essays on Self-Reference.* New York: Columbia University Press.

Martin, E. (1992). *The Woman in the Body.* Boston: Beacon Press.

Morgan, G. (1986). *Images of Organization.* Beverly Hills, Calif.: Sage.

North, C. S., J. M. Ryall, D. Ricci, and R. D. Wetzel. (1993). *Multiple Personalities, Multiple Disorders.* New York: Oxford University Press.

Personality disorder examined (1990, November 6). *Milwaukee Journal,* p. A1.

Putnam, F. W., J. J. Guroff, E. K. Silberman, L. Barban, and R. M. Post. (1986). The clinical phenomenology of multiple personality disorder: Review of 100 recent cases. *Journal of Clinical Psychiatry* 46(6):285–93.

Rape case unveils story of Sarah and her "insiders" (1990, November 11). *Milwaukee Journal,* p. A29.

Rose, N. (1989). Individualizing psychology. In J. Shotter and K. Gergen (Eds.): *Texts of Identity.* Newbury Park, Calif.: Sage, 119–32.

Shotter, J. (1989). Social accountability and the social construction of 'you.' In J. Shotter and K. Gergen (Eds.): *Texts of Identity.* Newbury Park, Calif.: Sage, 133–51.

Spanos, N. P., J. R. Weekes, E. Menary, and L. D. Bertrand. (1986). Hypnotic interview and age regression procedures in the elicitation of multiple personality symptoms: A simulation study. *Psychiatry* 49:298–311.

Spinelli, E. (1989). *The Interpreted World: An Introduction to Phenomenological Psychology.* Newbury Park, Calif.: Sage.

State of Wisconsin *v* Mark Peterson (1990, November 5–8). Circuit Court BR IV, Oshkosh, WI (90 CF 280).

Takahishi, Y. (1990). Is multiple personality disorder really rare in Japan? *Dissociation* 3(2):57–59.

The twenty-one faces of Sarah. (1990, November 12). *Time,* p. 87.

Victim tells of struggle inside self (1990, November 7). *Milwaukee Journal,* p. A1.

White, H. (1978). *Tropics of Discourse: Essays in Cultural Criticism.* Baltimore: Johns Hopkins University Press.

Chapter Eleven

Defining Occupational Disease: An Archaeology of Medical Knowledge

Alan G. Gross

In a plot that is typical of textbook and official histories, the story of occupational epidemiology has been recounted as the triumph of the medical and public health heroes who put its scientific and institutional foundations in place (Monson, 1990; Selleck and Whittaker, 1962). By turning the mundane present into the culmination of a mythical past, this plot imposes upon events a cultural pattern designed to celebrate rather than illuminate. I have another story to tell, one told more in the spirit of Foucault. It is an archaeology of occupational epidemiology, designed to reveal the complex interrelationships at the root of a disciplinary formation, indebted equally to industrial power and to medical science: without its alliance with industrial power, occupational epidemiology could never have been constituted as a possible area of investigation and source of knowledge; without medical science as a cognitive resource and a set of existing discourse practices, occupational epidemiology would have had no means with which, and no arena in which to exercise its emerging power. Nevertheless, these two alliances tend to work against the Hippocratic ideals of medical practice: insofar as occupational epidemiology serves industrial purposes, it turns workers from human beings into economic resources; insofar as it serves the purposes of medical science, it transforms them from human beings into experimental subjects.

We will see how these transformations explain otherwise unaccountable delays in the progress of occupational epidemiology. Initially, there is a delay in disciplinary formation well past the point of need and the existence of an appropriate scientific model; after disciplinary formation, there are systematic delays in the support of therapeutic and ameliorative measures relative to worker health. In this paper, the sources of these delays will be explored as relationships between industrial power and medical knowledge, especially insofar as these are realized in the contest over the definition of occupational disease.[1]

This paper concludes by linking its analysis of occupational epidemiology closely to issues of social justice. If sick, disabled, and dying workers are to have a voice in their fate, occupational disease cannot be defined solely in terms of medical science; rather, it must be *re*-defined in order to include such factors as workers' general sense of well-being and their life expectancy. At first glance, such inclusions may seem counterintuitive. But as we shall see, the definition of occupational disease is never a matter of the way the world is; it is always a matter of the way human beings decide how the objects and events of the world are to be classified.

Occupational Health Delayed

Illnesses and disabilities connected with manual work have been noted in the medical literature since antiquity; as early as 1700, they were described in comprehensive fashion by Ramazzini. But none of this early work is scientific in our sense; none constitutes occupational epidemiology as a discipline. According to Richard Monson (1990), author of a standard textbook in the field, the ground-breaking effort at creating the discipline of occupational epidemiology was that of John Snow, a practicing mid-nineteenth-century London physician with an interest in the spread of cholera. Snow (1936) is best known for his role in the removal of the handle of the Broad Street pump, whose water was contaminated by the cholera bacillus:

> As soon as I became acquainted with the situation and the extent of this irruption of cholera, I suspected some contamination of the water of the much-frequented street-pump in Broad Street. . . . On proceeding to the spot, I found that nearly all the deaths had taken place within a short distance of the pump. . . . I had an interview with the Board of Guardians of St. James's parish, on the evening of Thursday, 7th September, and represented the above circumstances to them. In consequence of what I said, the handle of the pump was removed on the following day. (38–40)

Monson (1990) regards the ameliorative effect of this event as incidental. The crucial move toward disciplinary foundation was, rather, the provision of a scientific model: "John Snow's contribution to the history of epidemiology," he says, "lies in the *next* steps he took" (6, my emphasis). In one region of London, supplied by two competing water companies, Snow recognized that he had a natural laboratory: "it is obvious that no experiment could have been devised which would more thoroughly test the effect of water supply on the progress of cholera" (75). Snow (1936, 86) found that over time those households supplied by Southwark and Vauxhall had a mortality rate 8½ times those supplied by Lambeth, and over five times the rate of the control, the rest of London. For Monson, then, the crucial factor in disciplinary formation is not that Snow's work led to the prevention of cholera but that prevention was possible only through medicine conceived of as an experimental science. Lives were saved by means of good experimental design: isolation of the independent variable, the water already identified with the spread of cholera, full randomization of the subject population, and a satisfactory control.

Monson (1990) does not attempt to account for the delay between the discovery of an appropriate scientific model and the constitution of a new medical specialty, between the possibility of epidemiological knowledge and the disciplinary formation that would realize that possibility. He merely noes that "between the middle of the 19th century and the middle of the 20th century, epidemiology progressed slowly" (8).

Concerning the need for such a medical specialty there can be no question. Available data amply document the health hazards of the workplace and the poor health of workers from Ramazzini to the present century. In 1927, for example, the *Journal of the American Medical Association* published a study of thirty-nine American enameling workers, twenty-three of whom showed evidence of lead poisoning. Of the thirty-nine, there was "not a single individual who could be given an absolutely 'clean bill of health' " (Leathers and Morgan, 1927, 1109). Most surprising in a population whose average age was twenty-seven, seven men had arteriosclerosis and three suffered from organic heart disease. The relative youth and poor health of those in the dangerous trades in America is documented as well in a 1928 study of 267 hatters: "boys 20 to 21 years old are already so badly poisoned that their hands shake continually, while many of the men who have served longer at the trade cannot even feed themselves" (quoted in Rosner and Markowitz, 1989c, 59).

As a consequence of earning a living in this century, American workers in the dangerous trades were dying at alarming rates. From 1915 to 1918, the number of deaths among Vermont granite cutters from pulmonary tuberculosis was nearly ten times the state average (Winslow, 1925, 970). From 1909 to 1919, in a Connecticut ax factory, the pulmonary tuberculosis death rate of grinders and polishers was eleven times the state average of employed males. This means that being a granite cutter or an ax grinder was as much as sentence of death as being in the battlefield in World War I (*Information*, 385). In each industrial case, the cause of death was the inhalation of silica dust, the cause also in the case of 467 workers building a tunnel for Union Carbide between 1931 and 1933 (Rosner and Markowitz, 1989a, xvi–xvii). British workers were no better off. In the period from 1910 to 1912, British tin miners died from this same disease at a rate fifteen times that of clergymen (Winslow, 1925, 971).

The generalizability of these cases is suggested by the long-term stable correlation between social class and health: the lower your social class, the more likely it is that you will perceive yourself as sick, that you will be sick, and that you will die well before those above you in the social hierarchy (Blaxter, 1990, 6, 61, 66, 235; Rose and Marmot, 1981; Marmot et al., 1984; Marmot and MacDowall, 1986). Indeed, the situation is steadily deteriorating: "For some . . . diseases, there were once higher mortality rates in higher social classes. This is no longer true: there are now no major causes of mortality where death rates are not higher in lower social classes" (Blaster, 1990, 240). Though the causes for these differences are complex and contested, differential occupational risk is undoubtedly among them (Fox and Adelstein, 1978).

The need for medicine to focus on occupational diseases was made the more desperate by the evident powerlessness or indifference of early unions in matters of worker health. All 267 hatters, poisoned by their work, were union members. Unprotected by local membership, they were unprotected also by national affiliation. The Workers' Health Bureau, the union agency that conducted the study and pressed for reform, was active for only eight years, from 1921 to 1928. Though supported by union locals throughout the country, it disappeared because of lack of support at the national level (Rosner and Markowitz, 1989c, 53–63).

Union powerlessness or indifference was complemented by government ineffectuality. A Federal Coal Mine Health and Safety Act was not passed until 1969. Moreover, there persists to the present day a problem of coordination and control: a de facto division between the roles of the Department of Labor and the Public Health Service, agreed to during the New Deal, is concretized in current legislation. Under this legislation, the Public Health Service provides technical expertise, the Department of Labor, the policing function. This division of functions is virtually a formula for inefficient enforcement (Rosner and Markowitz, 1989b, 83–99).

But so long as the immigrant tide flowed, occupational medicine was not needed to insure the health of workers. All trades, and the dangerous trades in particular—mining, asbestos, textiles, paint manufacture—could be readily resupplied from a working class protected only by ineffective state and federal governments and by unions indifferent or powerless to ameliorate worker health.[2] From 1870 to 1930, a policy of open immigration favored industry by creating a steady surplus of labor. From 1890 to 1924, for example, over twenty million immigrants accounted for nearly 35 percent of the population increase. By 1909, in twenty-one leading industries nearly 60 percent were immigrants. As long as a resupply of cheap, docile labor was secure, and union and government neglect guaranteed, it was in industry's interest to ignore, not to explore, the connections between disease and the workplace.

It was not until the pool of immigrant labor had diminished markedly that industry perceived a need for a medical science related to worker health. It is not coincidental that the years between 1930 and 1959, a time when the American Association of Industrial Physicians and Surgeons surged in membership from 315 to 4,000, is also a time when the number of new immigrants, and the cheap labor they supplied, plummeted.[3]

Occupational Health Neglected

Although after 1930 occupational disease was acknowledged in the general case, industry labored to suppress knowledge of its specific instances, to curb or sidetrack research unfavorable to its commercial goals, and to encourage studies that, directly or indirectly, favored corporate purposes. In the crassest of strategies, company physicians simply colluded with industry by misinforming workers concerning their state of health. In 1933, for example, Union Carbide company doctors systematically misled tunnel drillers concerning the mortal dangers of silicosis (Rosner and Markowitz, 1989a, xvi–xvii). Company physicians at Johns Manville behaved similarly concerning the threat of asbestosis. In 1949, Dr. Kenneth W. Smith, Corporate Medical Director, expressed the corporate medical policy in the following confidential memorandum:

> It must be remembered that although these men have the X-ray evidence of asbestosis, they are working today and definitely are not disabled from asbestosis. They have not been told of this diagnosis for it is felt that as long as the man feels well, is happy at home and at work, and his physical condition remains good, nothing should be said. When he becomes disabled or sick, then the diagnosis should be made and the claim submitted by the Company. The fibrosis of this disease is irreversible and permanent so that eventually compensation will be paid to each of these men. But as long as the man is not disabled it is felt that he should not be told of his condition so that he can live and work in peace and the Company can benefit by his many

years of experience. Should the man be told of his condition today there is a very definite possibility that he would become mentally and physically ill, simply through the knowledge that he has asbestosis. (Quoted in Kotelchuck, 1989, 203)[4]

Unfavorable medical research on occupationally related diseases was also curbed or suppressed. The career of Dr. Leroy Gardner illustrates this second strategy. In a typical incident, Gardner was consulted about an outbreak of a lung disease at the Salem, Massachusetts, plant of Sylvania. The possibility existed that the disease was linked to the beryllium used in the manufacture of fluorescent lamps. Two years after the initial outbreak, action had still not been taken. At this point, Gardner was asked by a company representative to review a paper on workplace conditions and beryllium disease at the plant. The representative was disturbed that the paper "gives an indication that this disease may be of occupational origin" (quoted in Zwerdling, 111). Before the company intervened, Gardner had enthusiastically recommended publication; now, in deference to this concern, he suggested that this indication might be omitted. Later, a compromise was discussed, in which the question of occupational origin would be raised, rather than asserted. In the end, the paper was never published (Zwerdling, 103–15).

A third, subtler strategy for harnessing medical research to the corporate interest is illustrated in a research program into lead poisoning under the leadership of Robert Kehoe. Kehoe reached his conclusions through the responsible use of scientific methods and published his results in leading journals with no hint of industry censorship. In 1933, he published a series of papers demonstrating a thesis he maintained throughout his long career. He found that significant traces of lead in normal human beings were expected and harmless, that even abnormally high levels in workers' bodies did not necessarily indicate lead poisoning, that lead would in any case soon reach normal levels when exposure stopped. As a consequence of these findings, he maintained that the manufacture of tetraethyl lead for gasoline was safe. These findings entailed that lead-using industries needed to employ only minimal safety measures on the job, could continue to manufacture and sell leaded gasoline with impunity, and were well-protected from compensation claims.

Kehoe carried out his research from a privileged position. From 1930 to 1958, he was simultaneously a professor at the University of Cincinnati, the Director of the industry-funded Kettering Laboratory of Applied Physiology, and Medical Director of the Ethyl Gasoline Corporation (Graebner, 1989, 142). He made no secret of his connections. Did he act independently, or was it his intent to support the lead-based industries? This question is misleading because it directs attention away from the point of this episode: the indistinguishability between industry goals and the goals of scientific medicine represents a coincidence of purpose that does not *require* collusion or control; networks of power and knowledge have been so constituted as to manufacture this coincidence as a byproduct of their interaction.[5] As Foucault (1990) puts it: "there is no power that is exercised without a series of aims and objectives. But this does not mean that it results from the choice or decision of an individual subject; let us not look for the headquarters that presides over its rationality" (95).

Kehoe protected his patrons, not by doing shabby science, but by carrying out a research program that defined lead poisoning in a manner that was coincident with corporate interests. As we will see in the next section, the epistemic delays naturally coincident with exacting scientific standards, sufficed, together with a shared worldview, virtually to guarantee a delay in ameliorative social action. The corporate effectiveness of this research program is reflected in the persistence of leaded gasoline as a consumer product despite mounting evidence against its use (Hayes, 1992, 269–77). At a Senate hearing as late as 1966, Kehoe could still testify as an expert witness against the need for its elimination (Graebner, 1989, 142).[6]

Occupational Health Defined

Research in occupational epidemiology depends for its credibility on its scientific status, its definition of disease in terms of a definite pathology, a dependent variable causally linked to an independent variable in the workplace. It depends, in Foucault's (1972) words, on the integration of "daily medical practice [and] the laboratory as the site of a discourse that has the same experimental norms as physics, chemistry, or biology" (52). In *The Birth of the Clinic*, Foucault (1975) identifies a central consequence of this phenomenon: the transformation of disease into an entity that must be defined by means of specifying "the point from which [its] pathological organization radiates" (140). From this definition stems a classification of disease based on invariable organic anomalies, a classification in which the "symptoms speak the very language of pathological anatomy" (129, see also 187).[7]

By the second decade of the twentieth century, medical science and the workplace had experienced a parallel integration in the creation of occupational epidemiology. In 1908, Dr. Harry Mock, a founding member of the American Association of Industrial Physicians and Surgeons and its second president, sold his services as an industrial physician to Sears on the basis of the following argument: "here are 15,000 people, men and women, gathered under one roof in a great industry. *This is a great human laboratory.* Think of the opportunity of making

a complete physical examination of all these people. We have been
trained to examine sick or supposedly sick people, but here I could
study average normal workers and could learn what 'normal' as differentiated from 'sick' really is" (Selleck and Whittaker, 1962, 61). Writing nearly two decades later, a leading epidemiologist, Alice Hamilton,
did not share Mock's optimism: "We hope that some way will be found,"
she wrote, "so that . . . animal experiments will precede not follow industrial experiments, and the question [of dangerous work environ-
ments] will be treated as one belonging to the public health from the
outset, not after its importance has been demonstrated on the bodies of
workmen" (quoted in Heifetz, 1989, 173). The mood had changed; the
metaphor had not.

In this reconfiguration of workplace into laboratory, the methodological standards of physics, chemistry, and biology became the
defining attributes of occupational epidemiology: acceptance of a result by the relevant medical community depended absolutely on its
derivation by approved methods. The nature of this dependence is
exemplified by the discovery of the etiology of "radium jaw." In 1924,
a New York surgeon diagnosed this condition in a report to a meeting
of the American Dental Association; its cause was the poisoning of
women who dabbled radioactive paint into watch-dials, having first
sharpened the points of their brushes with their lips and tongues. In
1925, Dr. Frederick Hoffman published an article in the *Journal of the
American Medical Association* making the same diagnosis and suggesting the same etiology.

But none of this amounted to medical knowledge. Hoffman (1925)
is explicit on the point. He interviewed patients, examined x-rays, studied conditions at the plant, and drew conclusions concerning etiology
based on existing knowledge about the effects of radioactivity. But he
is clear that his observations "fall short in dealing with the medical
aspects of the cases under observation and, as indicated, a thorough
diagnosis fully amplified by all necessary instrumental observations is
of the first importance." Only after such an investigation would it be
possible to establish "what agent or group of agents was responsible for
the pathological conditions in question" (964).

In the same year, Hoffman's challenge was taken up by Harrison
Martland and colleagues (1925). Significantly, Martland established his
priority as the discoverer of the cause of "radium jaw" by means of
autopsy:

> The cases described in this paper represent practically a
> hitherto unrecognized form of occupational poisoning. The
> anemias encountered are for the first time actually proved
> to be due to the ingestion of radioactive elements with
> deposition of insoluble, fixed particles in the phagocytic

cells of the sinusoids of the reticulo-endothelial system [spaces or tubes through which blood passes in the spleen, lymph nodes, bone marrow and liver], where they continuously emit irritative rays, which in time produce exhaustion of the adjacent hemapoietic [blood-producing] centers. (1775)

Martland argues by analogy from autopsy results in assured cases to the diagnosis of a "Severe Case in Person Still Living." It is this analogical reasoning that enables him to judge that an asymptomatic individual—ironically, a "healthy case"—is "in grave danger of dying from severe anemia, developing years after [the] original deposition [of radioactive substances] and under conditions in which the *real etiology* must be obscured or never suspected" (1776, my emphasis). This reliance on autopsy accords with Foucault's (1975) observation that medical science privileges not health but death: "a spontaneous *experimental* situation providing access to the very truth of the disease" (143, my emphasis).

But epistemic closure may be delayed even when postmortem results are readily available. The etiology of radium jaw turned out to be relatively simple, a short clear causal chain from occupational hazard to death. But causal chains are seldom so clear-cut. Reviewing a decade of research on byssinosis, researchers comment that "substantial scientific questions remain about the etiology of byssinosis, the mechanism by which cotton dust acts on the lung, and the relationship between acute and chronic stages of the disease" (Wegman et al., 1983, 191). There were numerous historical, cross-sectional, and prospective studies to serve as "compelling epidemiological evidence of chronic airways obstruction arising from long-term occupational exposure to cotton dust" (138). Nonetheless, these studies did not add up to proof (Merchant, 1983, 138). The few corpses examined produced results that failed to satisfy the criterion of medical science: "postmortem examination of the lungs of cotton workers has shown emphysema and airways disease in varying degrees. [But] one recent study . . . asserted that emphysema was not a consequence of cotton dust but of cigarette smoking" (Wegman et al., 1983, 190).

The motive for the delay needed to certify occupational epidemiology as a science is epistemic, not strategic. Nevertheless, epistemic delay can be at odds with worker health; it can serve strategic purposes. In 1933, for example, "a negro of 45 came to [the attention of Robert Kehoe and his associates] as a result of an attack of lead intoxication." In addition to the symptoms of lead poisoning the man had syphilis, swelling and dilation of the aorta, an enlarged heart, and a chronic swelling below the knee in both legs. But "this previously neglected condition was allowed to go untreated until all lead symptoms had disappeared, nor was any treatment given for the lead intoxication, since the subject was in no distress, and since we wished to observe the lead excretion uninfluenced by therapeutic factors" (Kehoe, 1933b, 324–25).

This is not simply a matter of other times, other standards: a quarter-century later, therapeutic and ameliorative delay remain as byproducts of epistemic delay. In 1962, the U.S. Public Health Service and the University of Pittsburgh conducted a study of coke oven workers and respiratory cancer, an investigation in which researchers discovered that the death rate of "nonwhite" coke workers was 22 percent above expectation, and that their death rate from cancer was double that of other steel workers. A standard textbook states without comment that "while the *tentative* judgment was that this was a *causal* association, it was felt that further information should be collected. *The steel workers were followed for 5 additional years*" (Monson, 1990, 237–39, my emphasis).[8]

The delays that high epistemic standards entail are coincident with the economic motive at the bottom of all industrial health decisions, as the history of beryllium disease illustrates. The adverse effects of beryllium on worker health were first reported in the 1930s and 1940s. On the basis of this research, a federal standard of worker exposure was set. In 1980, however, a study showed a continued excess of lung cancer in beryllium workers. No one doubted that beryllium was a carcinogen. Nevertheless, a standard textbook, published in 1990, comments that "the consistency of findings of an excess occurrence of lung cancer among beryllium workers, while *present*, is not *persuasive*. . . . It does not seem *rational* to spend many millions of dollars on the basis of an excess of 2.4 deaths from lung cancer" (Monson, 1990, 240–44, my emphasis). The text pinpoints the nature of the conflict as "the *cost* in human health vs. the *cost* in dollar" (244, my emphasis).

Occupational Health Redefined:
The Voice of the Worker

There is no question that occupational epidemiology is entitled to the credibility it achieves through high epistemic standards. It may be questioned, however, whether therapeutic or ameliorative action in the workplace is advisable only on the condition that the pathological derivation of a particular occupational disease be unequivocally identified. There is a way out of this epistemological bind: the creation of two levels of certainty, one sufficient for science, and another, lesser standard, sufficient for remedial action.[9] Writing about byssinosis in the *American Journal of Public Health*, researchers put the case squarely:

Occupational health is simply public health applied to the work environment. Such an orientation requires serious efforts aimed at preventing and controlling occupational disease, even in the absence of definitive scientific knowledge. Failure to apply this fundamental approach to the hazards of the workplace has contributed to the continuing political, economic, and scientific controversies over byssinosis, a disabling lung disease of cotton mill workers. Poweiful economic interests, reinforced by medical and scientific uncertainty, have delayed and undermined effective measures for the prevention, control of, and compensation for this industrial disease. This, in turn, has resulted in placing the burdens of hazardous employment in the cotton industry on the party least able to bear the weight of public and corporate inaction—the sick worker. (Wegman et al., 1983, 188).[10]

While these researchers support a double epistemological standard advantageous to afflicted workers, they concede nothing to worker control over the conditions of work. In their formulation, it is they, not the workers, who define occupational disease, and determine both the standard for remedial action and for medical certainty. In the literature on occupational disease—whether by scholars of labor, historians of medicine, public health officials, or occupational epidemiologists—the voice of the workers is generally conspicuous by its absence. But in coal mining in the late 1960s, the miners—not the union, not reformers, not politicians, not public health professionals—initiated an insurgency that eventually provided more liberal compensation for black lung disease. The bill that became federal law in 1972 stipulated that no claim to disability could be rejected merely on the basis of a negative x-ray; moreover, after fifteen years in the mines, if miners evidenced *any* evidence of respiratory or pulmonary impairment, they would be presumed to have an occupational disease.[11]

In an article on the history of this legislation from 1968 to 1972, the miner's victory is represented as a temporary triumph of the social over the medical, of the emotional, economic, and political over the clinical and pathological. In effect, the authors endorse the opinion of their Congressional staff informant that this "was a political decision not a medical one" (quoted in Fox and Stone, 1980, 61–62). At first glance, it would appear that the authors and their informant are entirely correct. Surely, fifteen years in the mines is not the equivalent of a disease-causing agent, a bacillus that would leave an unmistakable spoor in autopsy? But the miners knew that the answer to this question depended on whether you were an employer or an employee.

Decisions about occupational disease have always been related to interests; the only difference in this case was that it was the workers' interest that counted.

If you were an employee in the mines,

> at work you are covered with dust. It's in your hair, your clothes and your skin. The rims of your eyes are coated with it. It gets between your teeth and you swallow it. You suck so much of it into your lungs that until you die, you never stop spitting up coal. . . . Slowly you notice that you are getting short of breath when you walk up a hill. On the job, you stop more often to catch your breath. Finally, just walking across the room is an effort. . . . Call it miners' asthma, silicosis, coat workers' pneumoconiosis—they are all dust diseases with the same symptoms. (Quoted in Fox and Sone, 1980, 46)

The power to define in this one instance should not blind us to the limits of the miners' success. From their early insurgency in the coal fields of West Virginia to their successful fight in Washington, the miners would have achieved little were it not for the help of sympathetic legislators, physicians, and news media, competent attorney working for a pittance, Vista volunteers, community organizers and outside funding. Without the deep-seated and general discontent of the miners, it is true, these latter would have achieved nothing. But there is no denying either that the power of the workers was mediated at each step by those willing to defy the interests of the class from which they came.[12]

Moreover, the goals of the miners and of their professional leadership were not the same. Throughout, the primary goal of the miners remained adequate disability compensation, while the primary goal of the professional leadership was social change (Smith, 1987, 161). At first, these goals converged in the joint effort to process successful claims. But the general interest of the rank-and-file extended no farther than their awards. When most of the claims of the now-retired workers had been adjudicated, they lost interest in the movement (178–79); moreover, a new generation of rank-and-file could not be expected to find issues of disability compensation compelling.

The extraordinary power their control over the definition of black lung disease gave the miners can be gauged by the insistence even of their supporters in Congress that the principles animating black lung legislation were not to be generalized: "when Representative Thompson of Georgia attempted to extend the legislation to cover quarry and textile workers, the House supporters of the bill quickly defeated his proposal" (Fox and Stone, 1980, 61). As a consequence of this anxiety, the political situation of workers actually *eroded* as a consequence of the success of black lung legislation. Barth (1987) puts it well:

the program reduced the probability that the federal government will play a significant role in the near future in workers' compensation for occupational disease. Indeed the fact that the efforts to create such a federal presence all failed in the 1970s and 1980s must be attributable in part to the perception that another black lung program, perhaps on a grander scale, would be an expensive blunder. (284)

Social Justice and Scientific Realism

We can tell a story in which we trace an occupational disease like byssinosis as a radiation from its purported source. The story begins with the scatter of minute fibers generated by milling cotton. Then it turns to the role of those fibers in creating respiratory obstructions that lead, in the end, to a shortness of breath so severe that the victim continually gasps for air. But this chronic shortness of breath is at best only a sign of byssinosis, not its conclusive sign; the same holds for any respiratory pathology that might be discovered on autopsy. Before 1930, before occupational epidemiology existed as a well-recognized medical specialty, contests over the connections between specific pathologies and specific occupational diseases lacked discipline-specific forums in which etiological consensus might be achieved, in which byssinosis might be unequivocally identified as byssinosis. After 1930, though such contests were possible, consensus proved elusive. The byssinosis researchers criticized by Wegman et al. (1983) argued that the obstructed airways revealed on autopsy were caused not by cotton fibers but by cigarette smoke. (By their definition, these workers did not die of byssinosis.)

None of these debates can be settled on the basis of the so-called facts. The questions are always: What facts? What do the facts mean? What the facts mean depends, crucially, not on the way the world is but on the model of industrial disease in play. People sicken and die. But science cannot rest content merely with the facts of sickness and death; science is a system of thought that explains and predicts. The ultimate reality of science must be causal; its job must be to explain *why* people get sick and die and, whey they get sick, *when* or *whether* they will recover. In the social struggle to define occupational disease, what is at stake is never only the way the world is; it is always also the interests of particular groups: physicians, workers, employers. A model of occupational disease grounded in pathological anatomy—the biomedical model—is not only the consequence of inferences concerning the causal capacities of matter; it is also the product of social, political, and economic forces.[13]

The biomedical model of industrial disease is deeply entrenched; it informs both our medical and our folk senses of disease (Engel, 1977, 130). But it is fundamentally flawed. Its only acceptable etiologies terminate in anatomical anomalies causally linked to independent variables capable of isolation: cigarette smoking *or* exposure to cotton dust. Moreover, because it depends for its credibility solely on the evidence of pathological anatomy, the biomedical model marginalizes the known effect of states of mind on physical health, and minimalizes more general linkages between disease and ways of life and work.

Alternative models of disease—the biopsychosocial and the ecological—take a more liberal view of causation and broaden the search for causes beyond the physiological. These alternative models are equally plausible, equally "rational." The biopsychosocial model takes into consideration, not only "the patient, but the social context in which he lives, and the complementary system devised by society to deal with the disruptive effects of illness, that is, the physician role and the health care system" (Engel, 1977, 132). Its goal is a revised medical practice in which even grief may be classified as a disease, and bad habits tagged as etiological factors. Although its originator does not contemplate a circumstance in which a patient might be, not simply an informant concerning symptoms, but a player with the power to influence the definition of disease, his concept could easily accommodate such a modification. So modified, the biopsychosocial model would treat the definition of an occupational disease as a consequence of extended negotiations among workers, physicians, public health officials, and industry leaders.

The ecological is another alternative model of disease, one in which the divisions between disease-caused and accident-caused disability disappear to the extent that they have a common origin in unsafe working conditions. In this refiguring, high levels of coal dust and unsafe equipment are equally pathogens (in the root sense of the word, they are potential causes of physiological or physical impairment).[14] In this model, moreover, the line between the workplace and the general environment disappears in medical diagnosis to the extent that it has already disappeared in fact. In the ecological model, we are all victims of the workplace, experimental subjects whose health is being held hostage to the steady deterioration of the environment; we all have a stake in responsible industrialization, not only the workers in the dangerous trades. Do we want to know the effect of ozone on health? For this purpose, America continues a vast network of natural laboratories from the smog-filled Los Angeles to relatively unpolluted Tampa—as of 1981 (Tepper and Avery, 1983, 17).[15]

In its insistence that explanations refer only to the causal capacities of matter, the scientific realism that underlies the biomedical model of disease has worked against the discussion of issues of social justice within biomedicine. It is, of course, not an inevitable consequence of scientific realism that social justice be marginalized. Nevertheless, as a matter of contingent fact, this realism has inhibited the debate by its tendency to regard questions of social justice as irrelevant to biomedicine and, *a fortiori*, irrelevant to the definition of disease. Opening the definition of occupational disease to public debate—a point of view that privileges rhetoric (or discourse)—guarantees a space in which that definition can be considered a matter not for scientists only but for citizens also.[16]

Notes

1. Delays are to be viewed retrospectively only; once disciplines are formed, these will exist as gaps in origin stories told about them. But they exist only as a consequence of the telling of these stories. Delays are not viewed prospectively, as if disciplines were real entities, rather than political and social attempts to stabilize shifting relationships between knowledge and power.

2. High worker turnover in the dangerous trades is suggested by an average age of enamel workers of 27.1 and an average time of employment of thirteen months; in addition, 98 percent of the hatters examined by the Workers' Health Bureau were between 25 and 45 (Leathers and Morgan, 1927; Rosner and Markowitz, 1989c, 57).

3. Industrial neglect of long-term worker health during this period may seem inconsistent with Foucault's (1972) observation that "at the end of the eighteenth century . . . the health of the population became one of the economic norms required by industrial societies" (51). But as long as there was a labor surplus, industrial concern could focus on *current* fitness for employment, and ignore the long-term debilitative effects of byssinosis, silicosis, or asbestosis, diseases whose symptoms might not be evident for years.

4. It should not be assumed that the 1970 passage of the Occupational Safety and Health Act eliminated this industrial strategy. A case of employer duplicity surfaced as late as 1977, seven years after OSHA. As early as 1961, research had been published showing that exposure to dibromochloropropane (DBPC) caused sterility. Despite this knowledge, workers at American Cyanmide who were routinely exposed to this chemical were told that their concerns were unwarranted (Heifetz, 1989, 167–68).

5. Although patterns can be discovered between institutional affiliation and the direction of scientific judgment (Lynn, 1986), it seems unprofitable to try to establish a causal relationship or to assume collusion only on the basis of statistically significant correlations. See

Hayes (1992, 279) for a discussion that highlights the fundamental inconclusiveness of such investigations.

6. Although there was some dissent from his views in his later years, real dissent occurred only after 1971. See Hayes (1992), Matte et al. (1992), and Needleman (1992).

7. These views also conform to more orthodox opinion. Writing in *Science*, George Engel (1977) characterizes contemporary medical diagnosis as follows: "taxonomy progresses from symptoms, to clusters of symptoms, to syndromes, and finally to diseases with specific pathogenesis and pathology. This sequence accurately describes the successful application of the scientific method" (131).

8. Incidentally, these cases also suggest the operation of racial bias.

9. In the cases of phosphorus necrosis, asbestosis, and byssinosis, the need for this double standard is dramatized by international comparisons. In 1898, the level of remedial certainty concerning the cause of phosphorus necrosis was high enough in France to ban the manufacture of white phosphorus matches (Gordon, 1989), but in the United States white phosphorus matches were not taxed out of existence until 1912 (Lee, 1966, 19–21). In Britain, in 1931, the remedial certainty concerning the cause of asbestosis was high enough to make it a compensable disease (Kotelchuck, 1989, 197), but in the United States in the 1980s workers with asbestosis were still attempting to sue Johns-Manville in the face of that company's bankruptcy (Brodeur, 1985); in Britain, by 1983, the remedial certainty concerning byssinosis was high enough to justify legal compensation, while in the United States the disease remained noncompensable (Wegman et al., 1983).

10. In an accompanying article, Merchant (1983) agrees: from existing evidence "it follows . . . that occupationally disabled cotton textile workers must have adequate workers' compensation available to them." (138). In mid-1970, the *New England Journal of Medicine* argued analogously that the "mechanism of action of coal dust on the lungs remains obscure" but that it was "urgently necessary to apply and enforce the safe exposure limits based on information that is already available" (quoted in Fox and Stone, 1980, 45).

11. Fox and Stone, 1980; for actual cases of compensation claims, see 262–75. The 1977 amendments included a class of miners who would be compensated simply on the basis of service in the mine.

12. It is significant that the lengthy quotation that preceded this paragraph—the moving depiction of the miners' plight—comes, not from the mines' themselves, but from the Director of Occupational Health for the United Mine Workers of America. Dr. Isadore Buff, a sympathetic physician, may have been correct in saying: "This movement must come from the miners themselves. The union and the companies have had their chances and done nothing" (quoted in Smith,

1987, 111). But even this statement does not come from a miner. Given the complexity of the problems other workers face in analogous instances, it is difficult to believe that the intervention of professionals can ever be dispensed with.

13. Paradoxically, within occupational epidemiology this theory functions to deny political, social, and economic forces any role in the explanation of disease.

14. I owe this insight to Professor Eric Rothstein of the University of Wisconsin.

15. The notion of testing alternative social arrangements experimentally was first broached by Campbell (1988) and has been extended by Fuller (1996).

16. The work on this paper was supported by the Minnesota Agricultural Experiment Station. I would like to thank Professors Steve Fuller, Eric Rothstein, and Art Walzer for their criticisms of earlier drafts of this paper.

References

Barth, P. S. (1987). *The Tragedy of Black Lung: Federal Compensation for Occupational Disease.* Kalamazoo, Mich.: W. E. Upjohn Institute for Employment Research.

Blaxter, M. (1990). *Health and Lifestyles.* London: Tavistock/Routledge, 1990.

Brodeur, P. (1985). *Outrageous Misconduct: The Asbestos Industry on Trial.* New York: Pantheon.

Campbell, D. T. (1988). *Methodology and Epistemology for Social Science: Selected Papers.* (Samuel Overman, Ed.) Chicago: University of Chicago Press.

Engel, G. L. (1977). The need for a new medical model: A challenge for biomedicine." *Science* 196:129–36.

Foucault, M. (1972). *The Archeology of Knowledge and Discourse on Language.* (A. M. S. Smith, Tr.) New York: Pantheon.

———. (1975). *The Birth of the Clinic: An Archeology of Medical Perception.* (A. M. S. Smith, Tr.) New York: Vintage.

———. (1990). *The History of Sexuality. Volume 1: An Introduction.* (Robert Hurley, Tr.) New York: Vintage.

Fox, A. J., and A. M. Adelstein. (1978). Occupational mortality: Work or way of life? *Journal of Epidemiology and Community Health* 32:73–78.

Fox, D. M., and J. F. Stone. (1980). Black lung: Miners' militancy and medical uncertainty: 1968–1972. *Bulletin of the History of Medicine* 54:43–63.

Fuller, S. (1996). Making science into an experimental society. In W. Dunn (Ed.): *Policy Studies Review Annual: On the Experimenting Society.* New Brunswick, N.J.: Transaction Books.

Gordon, B. (1989). *Phossy Jaw and the French Match Workers: Occupational Health and Women in the Third Republic.* New York: Garland.

Graebner, W. (1989). Hegemony through science: Information engineering and lead toxicology, 1925–1965. In Rosner and Markowitz (Eds.): *Dying.* 140–59.

Hayes, S. P. (1992). The role of values in science and policy: The case of lead. In Needleman (Ed.): *Human Lead Exposure.* 267–83.

Heifetz, R. (1989). Women, lead, and reproductive hazards: defining a new risk. In Rosner and Markowitz (Eds.): *Dying.* 160–73.

Hoffman, F. L. (1925). Radium (mesothorium) necrosis. *Journal of the American Medical Association Almanac, Atlas and Yearbook.* Boston: Houghton, Mifflin, 1994. 85:961–65.

Kehoe, R. A. (1961). *The Metabolism of Lead in Man in Health and Disease.* The Harben Lectures, 1960. Reprinted from the *Journal of the Royal Institute of Public Health and Hygiene*, 1961.

Kehoe, R. A., F. Thamann, and J. Cholak. (1933a). Lead absorption and excretion in certain lead trades. *Journal of Industrial Hygiene* 15:306–19.

———. (1933b). Lead absorption and excretion in relation to the diagnosis of lead poisoning. *Journal of Industrial Hygiene* 15:320–40.

———. (1933c). On the normal absorption and excretion of lead. II. Lead absorption and lead excretion in modern American life. *Journal of Industrial Hygiene* 15:273–88.

Kotelchuck, D. (1989). Asbestos: "Funeral dress of kings"—and others. In Rosner and Markowitz (Eds.): *Dying.* 192–207.

Leathers, W. S., and H. J. Morgan. (1927). The study of lead poisoning in an enameling plant. *Journal of the American Medical Association* 89:1107–13.

Lee, A. R. (1966). The eradication of phossy jaw: a unique development of federal police power. *Historian* 29:1–21.

Levenstein, C., D. Plantamura, and W. Mass. (1989). Labor and byssinosis, 1941–1969. In Rosner and Markowitz (Eds.): *Dying.* 208–23.

Lynn, F. (1986). The interplay of science and values in assessing and regulating environmental risks. *Science, Technology, and Human Values* 9:40–50.

Marmot, M. G., M. J. Shipley, and G. Rose (May 5, 1984). Inequalities in death—specific explanations of a general pattern? *Lancet* 1:1003–6.

Marmot, M. G., and M. E. MacDowall. (August 2, 1986). Mortality decline and widening social inequalities. *Lancet* 2:274–76.

Martland, S. H., P. Conlon, and J. P. Knef. (1925). Some unrecognized dangers in the use and handling of radioactive substances with especial reference to the storage of insoluble products of radium and mesothorium in the reticuloendothelial system. *Journal of the American Medical Association* 85:1769–76.

Matte, T. D., P. J. Landrigan, and E. L. Baker. (1992). Occupational lead exposure. In Needleman (Ed.): *Human Lead Exposure*. 155–68.

Merchant, J. A. (1983). Byssinosis: Progress in prevention. *American Journal of Public Health* 73:137–39.

Monson, R. R. (1990). *Occupational Epidemiology*. 2nd ed. Boca Raton, Fla.: CRC Press.

Needleman, H. L. (Ed.) (1992). *Human Lead Exposure*. Boca Raton, Fla.: CRC Press.

Ramazzini, B. (1700/1940). *De morbis artificium*. Modena. (W. C. Wright, Ed.) Chicago: University of Chicago Press.

Rose, G., and G. Marmot. (1981). Social class and coronary heart disease. *British Heart Journal* 45:13–19.

Rosner, D., and G. Markowitz (Eds.) (1989). *Dying for Work: Workers' Safety and Health in Twentieth-Century America*. Bloomington: Indiana University Press.

Rosner, D., and G. Markowitz. (1989a). Introduction: Workers' health and safety —some historical notes. In Rosner and Markowitz (Eds.): *Dying*. ix– xx.

———. (1989b). Research or advocacy: Federal occupational safety and health policies during the New Deal. In Rosner and Markowitz (Eds.): *Dying*. 83–102.

———. (1989c). Safety and health as a class issue: The Workers' Health Bureau of America during the 1920s. In Rosner and Markowitz (Eds.): *Dying*. 53–64.

Selleck, H. B., and A. H. Whittaker. (1962). *Occupational Health in America*. Detroit: Wayne State University Press.

Smith, B. E. (1987). *Digging Our Own Graves: Coal Miners and the Struggle Over Black Lung*. Philadelphia: Temple University Press.

Snow, J. (1936). *Snow on Cholera*. New York: Commonwealth Fund.

Tepper, J. M., and J. S. Avery. (1983). *The Book of American Cities*. New York: Facts on File Publication.

Wegman, D. H., C. Levenstein, and I. A. Greaves. (1983). Byssinosis: A role for public health in the face of scientific uncertainty. *American Journal of Public Health* 73:188–92.

Winslow, C. E. A. (1925). Factory ventilation and industrial tuberculosis. *Journal of the American Medical Association* 85:968–73.

Zwerdling, C. (1989). "Salem Sarcoid: The Origins of Beryllium Disease." In Rosner and Markowitz (Eds.): *Dying*. 103–18.

Chapter Twelve

Shooting Downwind: Depicting the Radiated Body in Epidemiology and Documentary Photography

Brian C. Taylor

Whether the attempt to render the [nuclear] unthinkable is visual, philosophical, or narrative, the same icon governs the complexities involved: a circle around a point designated zero.
—Schwenger, 1992, 25.

I'm so full of stories I make myself sick.
—"Downwinder" Irma Allen (quoted in Gallagher, 1993, 183)

The American experience of nuclear weapons has been marked by a recurring "problem" with bodies. The U.S. government, potentially, can use nuclear weapons to destroy and contaminate enemy bodies on a massive scale and with unprecedented speed. Presumably, such an act would occur only in defending the nation against an actual or imminent nuclear attack and would destroy that enemy. Several factors conspire, however, to prevent U.S. officials and citizens from fully acknowledging the fate of nuclear bodies. One reason is *denial*: the public mind recoils from the shattering (even if only projected) qualities of full-scale strategic nuclear war. Whole cities would be lost instantly in retaliatory exchanges; regions would slowly follow. Another reason involves *guilt*: America is the only nation ever to have used nuclear weapons offensively against an enemy. Despite public jubilation and relief following the Japanese surrender in 1945, graphic images of Hiroshima and Nagasaki's devastation still continue to evoke sympathy and shame in some viewers. A final reason involves *fear*: the initial postwar U.S. monopoly on nuclear weapons—and the hope of national invulnerability—quickly faded when the former Soviet Union tested its own bomb in 1949. U.S. nuclear strategy subsequently stabilized in the international suicide pact known as "Mutually Assured Destruction." This arrangement formed a context in which recurring U.S. threats of nuclear attack against the Soviet Union evoked for American citizens the likelihood of their own destruction as well. Throughout the Cold War, as a result, recurring images of dead and dying nuclear bodies (for example, of Japanese sailors caught in the radioactive fallout from a 1954 U.S. nuclear test explosion) have created anxiety for those live bodies which may yet join them (Gusterson, 1991).

Because these inflammatory bodies pose problems for nuclear authorities hoping to maintain a consenting and resolute citizenry, particular strategies for their depiction have emerged. Typically, these official strategies efface the integrity of actual and potential nuclear victims as speaking, experiencing, and situated subjects. They are "disappeared" from technical discussions of nuclear weapons effects (Cohn, 1987; Taylor, 1990), and are recoded as objects of euphemistic, impersonal discourses concerned with their prediction and control (for example, as "acceptable losses"). These "pre-emptive" strikes of signification both depict *and* erase nuclear bodies and are required if nation-states hope to legitimate the *literal* destruction of social bodies during nuclear war. As a result, control over the signifying chain surrounding these bodies is highly contested between cultural interests that alternately support and oppose the development of nuclear weapons. The outcome of that struggle holds powerful consequences for the conduct of nuclear policy, and for the viability of nuclear weapons institutions.

In this chapter, I focus on symbolic struggle over the nuclear body conducted during the unstable cultural moment known as the post–Cold War. Currently, U.S. nuclear weapons institutions and their legitimating narratives are in crisis. The disintegration of the former Soviet Union and the worldwide dismantling of nuclear weapons systems have dramatically affected the missions of these institutions. Now without secure funding or official customers, they must promote their value in new ways (for example, by countering new "threats' arising from nuclear proliferation), and must transform their insular and over-specialized cultures (Browne, 1991; Loeb, 1986; Mojatabai, 1986). Americans are meanwhile coming slowly to terms with the scandalous environmental "legacy" left by these institutions: massive amounts of toxic and radioactive waste whose clean-up will cost billions of dollars, and will take thirty years (Russell, 1990). Antinuclear activists, further, are demanding that nuclear weapons institutions account for the opportunity costs of the arms race, and are challenging their rationales for continued operation (Tirman, 1992). Historians and artists are revising cultural mythology regarding the necessity of the bomb in vanquishing a wartime Japanese enemy and its utility in first containing and then bankrupting a Cold War Soviet enemy (Taylor, 1993b; Lebow and Stein, 1994).

As the fiftieth anniversary of Hiroshima approached and passed in 1995, the repressed nuclear body erupted into cultural consciousness with increasing frequency. In December, 1993, U.S. Secretary of Energy Hazel O'Leary admitted that her Department of Energy (DOE) and its predecessor, the Atomic Energy Commission (AEC) had funded and conducted hundreds of radiation experiments on vulnerable human subjects—in some cases without obtaining their informed consent (Makhijani, 1994). The DOE estimates that these experiments, which were conducted over three decades, involved over 16,000 subjects ("Count of Subjects," 1995, August 20). Images of subjects whose circumstances suggest that they are "victims"—including pregnant women, cancer patients, and mentally retarded children—have circulated widely in the popular media, and have created a haunting intertext suggesting violated innocence and official betrayal of public trust (Schneider, 1993b, 1994b). Images of Hiroshima victims, further, have appeared implicitly in a bitter debate over exhibiting the Enola Gay aircraft in the Smithsonian Museum ("Smithsonian Alters Plans," 1994). Increasing evidence of the DOE's historical disregard for public health and safety in favor of weapons production (for example, regarding the secret release of radioactive materials into the environment; Schneider, 1994c) also suggests the unknown extent of *domestic* contaminated bodies.

I focus here on a recently published volume of photographs and interviews that contributes to evolving cultural memory of the nuclear body: Carole Gallagher's (1993) *American Ground Zero: The Secret Nuclear War.* These photographs depict America's nuclear "downwinders"—the groups of workers, soldiers, and civilians who were affected by radioactive fallout from atmospheric and underground nuclear explosions conducted by the AEC and DOE at the Nevada Test Site (NTS) between 1951 and 1992.[1] For several decades, downwinders have claimed that this fallout has contributed to their excessive rates of illness and death and have sought legal redress and federal compensation. They have been opposed in this process by government officials and epidemiologists, who for complex reasons, generally reject claims of a causal relationship between radioactive fallout and downwinder suffering. This rejection, coupled with repeated denials of responsibility from nuclear weapons officials, has compounded the grief of downwinders by denying their experience and by precluding their financial relief.

My goal in this chapter is to examine the downwinder body as a symbolic site of struggle between opposing cultural interests seeking to establish its ethical significance, its biological status, and its commodity-value. This struggle is fierce because the stakes are high: successful prosecution of the downwinders' claims would not only cost the U.S. government a great deal of money but would also undermine the narrative through which it has historically legitimized nuclear operations. Citizens would potentially conclude that, in order to protect them, the nuclear nation-state was willing to kill them. The consequences of this clarified paradox for the future of nuclear weapons institutions would be grave indeed.

My argument is that Gallagher's acclaimed (Day, 1993; Poliski, 1993; Sipchen, 1993) and disturbing photographs form a "reply" to official government epidemiology, whose methods and practices serve to encode the downwinder body as scientific data and to silence its voice.[2] Recoded in documentary photography, however, as a situated and reflective subject, the downwinder body realizes its subversive potential to restore to public consciousness the lunar signified of official discourse: the unacknowledged victims of nuclear weapons development. This "other," yet equally rhetorical body is revisionist in nature, and potentially contributes to a progressive restructuring of nuclear ideologies and institutions (see Nichols, 1993).

In analyzing the relationship between government epidemiology and documentary photography, I draw on three theoretical projects concerned with the rhetoric and ideology of cultural discourses. First, is the interdisciplinary project of "nuclear criticism." Here, I am concerned with relativizing nuclear discourses in order to create a reflective dialogue between hegemonic, technical-military interests, and traditionally marginalized, ethical interests (Shapiro, 1987). Nuclear critics commonly challenge monologic and official claims to nuclear truth by exposing their contingency and by restoring the alternative narratives of history and rationality that they suppress. In this view, Cold War and post–Cold War cultures are "dialogic" zones of fierce activity in which official and unofficial images, stories, and performances contend to produce both the historical and the possible, future "truths" of nuclear weapons for various audiences (Taylor, 1992, 1993a). Both epidemiology and Gallagher's photographs contribute to the hyperreal and "fabulously textual" status of nuclear matters (Derrida, 1984). They circulate "in a play of [nuclear] discourses whose concerns are power, virtue, the ends of society, and the nature of reality" (Smith, 1989, 15).

Secondly, I draw on critical traditions that conceptualize both the rhetoric and ideology of institutional scientific practice (Prelli, 1989; Gross, 1990). Here, I depict government epidemiology as a systematic and professional project seeking to explain and predict the relationship between radioactive fallout and downwinder bodies. While that project is cloaked in powerful myths of objectivity and rationality, its actual practice involves strategic decision-making about formulating problems, selecting data, and arguing their significance within institutionalized rules and conventions for "true" knowledge claims. While these practices are common in scientific communities, I argue that in this particular case they are not politically neutral: here, science and the state interpenetrate. The history of government epidemiology (discussed below) suggests that it has been integrated within a national-security apparatus that has appropriated and inflected its technical rationality to perpetuate the systems of nuclear weapons control (Aronowitz, 1988, 121–145; Rose and Rose, 1976, 24). The subsequent ideology of this politicized science "comes to light less in its false judgments than in . . . its manner of posing problems, its methods, the direction of its research, *and, above all, in what it closes its eyes to*" (Horkheimer, 1989, 56, emphasis mine). Specifically, I argue that the contingencies of epidemiological data and the rigorous criteria for validating claims of association between fallout and downwinder illness appear to have been exploited by some nuclear weapons officials—and by some of the researchers and technicians in their service—to sustain dangerous nuclear operations.[3]

The issue of to what government epidemiology "closes its eyes [and ears]," finally, is addressed by photography theory and criticism. Here, I draw on recent arguments that emphasize the political productivity of photographs *as signification* within particular historical and cultural contexts (see Burgin, 1982). In this view, photographs are both records of events (to which culture routinely attributes indexical facticity) and are also *themselves* symbolic "events" that figure in the ongoing narrativization of reality. One example of this process involves the ways in which cultural interests have appropriated the image of the atomic mushroom cloud to alternately support and criticize patriotic militarism (Hales, 1991; Rosenthal, 1991). Working from this perspective, critics may examine photographs "on the basis of their tendency to either reproduce dominant forms of discourse, which help circulate the existing system of power, authority and exchange, or . . . on the basis of their tendency to provoke critical analysis, to denaturalize what is unproblematically accepted and to offer thereby an avenue for politicizing problematics" (Shapiro, 1988, 130). Recently, critics have described how documentary photographs of the body have functioned historically to serve both disciplinary institutions (e.g., through the police mug shot) and also progressive reform movements (e.g., through images of the poor used in support of federal relief programs [Lalvani, 1993; Sekula, 1989]).

Barthes (1977) has described how denotative and connotative codes operate in the photograph to achieve the effect of "realism"—the impression that an object is being presented as it exists without mediation or distortion. This effect, Barthes argues, functions to secure preferred meanings of the photographic object against alternative readings and to naturalize particular ideological frames. Here, I am concerned with how these codes operate in Gallagher's photographs to construct an unofficial, or *counter*-realism for the downwinder body, one that subverts dominant epidemiological representations in the progressive interests of peace and social justice (see Franklin, 1994). This alternative realism, I emphasize, does not "capture" the true essence of the downwinder body any more than does epidemiology. It represents, however a significant attempt by marginalized interests to relativize and to "play off" the hegemonic "body code" in nuclear culture, and to reconfigure the power relations that are perpetuated through is naturalization (see Solomon-Godeau, 1991). As I will discuss, this attempt is not without its own contingencies. Like epidemiology, Gallagher also reduces complex downwinder history through her selection of particular "emblematic" subjects and stories. In the process, she engages a dilemma inherent to documentary photography: that viewers will identify more with her individual subjects than with her critique of nuclear weapons *institutions*, thereby selecting "privatized melancholy" over political action (Solomon-Godeau, 1991, 217). Gallagher's text is also marked by an aesthetic tension between documentary realism and a reflexive postmodernism that deconstructs the authority of nuclear representation—potentially including her own.

In the following sections, I analyze this discursive conflict by briefly reviewing downwinder history and by discussing the symbolic production of nuclear bodies in government epidemiology and in documentary photography. I conclude by discussing the consequences of symbolic struggle over the downwinder body and the potential value of this form of criticism.

Clouded Secrets, Secret Clouds: Downwinders and the NTS

Downwinder history involves the technologies, ideologies, and practices of everyday life related to the detonation of nuclear weapons at NTS between the years 1950 and 1992 (Ball, 1988; Fradkin, 1989; Titus, 1986). During the most contested period of that history, from 1951 to 1963, U.S. nuclear officials exploded 126 nuclear bombs above ground. These tests displaced tons of highly radioactive dust and debris into the atmosphere, where it traveled aloft for various distances in wind-driven clouds. Contaminated material in these clouds subsequently drifted and rained back to earth, exposing all organic life (grass, cattle, humans) to pathological and genetic danger from ionizing radiation. That radiation assumed the forms of externally penetrating gamma-rays and beta-particles, and also weaker but internally damaging alpha-particles, which were ingested by breathing contaminated dust and by consuming links (such as dairy products) in contaminated food chains.

The three populations most affected by this fallout includes the over 250,000 U.S. military personnel ordered to witness the explosions and to conduct maneuvers on this simulated "atomic battlefield"; the approximately 25,000 residents of mostly rural eastern Nevada, southern Utah, and northern Arizona immediately located in the fallout paths;

and the thousands of NTS workers assigned to drill the underground test shafts, construct the racks housing and nuclear devices, and to retrieve "hot" diagnostic equipment and soil samples following their detonation (Swanson, 1993).

Almost immediately following the commencement of nuclear testing, members of these groups began to experience unusual health conditions such as fatigue, nausea, and skin burns. These symptoms of radiation sickness were followed over a period of years by alarming, unprecedented increases in various cancers (such as childhood leukemia), and in reproductive and immunologic disorders (such as diabetes). Local sheep ranchers lost large portions of their herds to mysterious burns and stillbirths. The intuitive connection made by downwinders between these conditions and their exposure to radioactive fallout was vigorously rejected by AEC officials, who provided bland reassurances about protection of public health and who invoked the warrants of rationality, patriotism, and secrecy to suppress dissent (for example, by characterizing it as "misperception"). AEC professionals also used their technique expertise to intimidate the less formally educated downwinders. Class differences were further exploited by NTS officials in threatening anxious workers with the loss of employment. The downwinder response was also mediated, finally, by the dominant cultural influence of Mormonism in the region. Highly conservative, patriotic, and obedient to authority, Mormon downwinders were actively discouraged by their religious leaders from challenging nuclear officials.

Despite this strong opposition, several downwinders have attempted to obtain relief for their losses in a series of individual and class-action lawsuits seeking to establish governmental negligence and liability in administering the nuclear testing program (Schneider, 1993a). Two patterns have emerged in these cases, decided in both federal district and appellate courts, in which Department of Justice lawyers have (1) invoked immunity for the government under the 1946 Federal Tort Claims Act from prosecution of its "discretionary" policy decisions and their operational implementation and (2) employed sophisticated epidemiological arguments to reject downwinder claims of a causal relationship between low-level radiation exposure (LLRE) and subsequent illness. With important exceptions, such as the 1984 *Allen* ruling in favor of downwinder residents (subsequently overturned on appeal in 1987), these strategies have been mostly successful. Observers attribute the government's ethically questionable tactics in these cases (e.g., its repeated application for continuances during which time plaintiffs sicken and die) to fears that a favorable downwinder ruling would jeopardize the production of nuclear weapons and would subject the government to a series of tort suits.

While downwinders have not been successful in securing favorable rulings or financial compensation from the courts, Congress has recently responded to their plight by enacting two sets of compensation legislation that do not require them to prove that LLRE caused their conditions (Lippman, 1993). The first, established in 1988, directed the Department of Veteran Affairs (DVA) to provide disability benefits to "atomic veterans" who suffer from at least one of thirteen specific cancers. The second, the 1990 Radiation Exposure Compensation Act, created a $200 million fund to pay resident downwinders (a maximum of $50,000) and NTS workers (a maximum of $75,000) suffering from those same cancers. Currently, an average of 15 percent of claims from NTS workers and 56 percent of the claims from resident downwinders have been approved; as of June, 1995, this fund had paid out a total of $172 million on 2,239 claims (Janofsky, 1994; Schneider, 1994a). Related DOE legal fees approached $89 million (U.S. Nuclear Weapons Cost Study Project, 1996).

Recent events suggest, however, that legal struggle between the government and the downwinders will continue (Manning, 1995). Workers and residents in ten states have filed over sixty lawsuits since 1989 to protest the narrowness of the government's qualification criteria and the arbitrariness of its compensation limits. A summary judgment against the DOE in 1989 resulted in payments of $78 million for deflated property values to Fernald, Ohio, residents living near a contaminated uranium processing facility (Lippman, 1993). As these suits progress, the term "downwinder" expands to formally acknowledge the populations historically affected by the geographically dispersed operations of the U.S. nuclear weapons production complex.[4]

"Virtual Inhabitants": The Downwinder Body in Epidemiological Research

Epidemiology is a medical science concerned with determining the nature, causes, extent, and methods of prevention of diseases occurring in groups of organisms (Ball, 1988 102–127). I am concerned here with the practices through which epidemiologists and their superiors have conducted and evaluated both government-funded and "independent" studies of downwinders. These studies have emerged from and circulated within a variety of Cold War organizations, including the DOE and AEC; Department of Defense and its support organization, Defense Nuclear Agency; Centers for Disease Control; National Academy of Sciences (NAS); National Cancer Institute; Public Health Service (PHS); and several universities and medical schools.

In their study of downwinders, epidemiologists attempt to reconstruct the radiation doses they have received and to infer the effects of those doses from reports of subsequent illnesses and deaths. Commonly, this research takes the form of "population studies." These studies ideally compare the occurrence of conditions allegedly caused by radiation in an exposed population to both their normally predicted occurrence and to their occurrence in a similarly constituted but nonexposed "control" population. Knowledge claims in population studies take the form of statistics signifying the probability of "associations" between variables. These associations are rigorously evaluated for their demonstrated strength, consistency, and plausibility.

For a variety of reasons, population studies do not conclusively establish LLRE as a cause of downwinder illnesses and deaths. This is due largely to the contingencies of downwinder phenomena, which inhibit the determination of direct and singular causality (McCalley, 1990). While the health effects of high radiation doses on humans are both immediate and apparent, the cumulative effects of LLRE are not immediately visible, have long latency periods, do not yield evidence of their cause, and are affected by other intervening variables. Mutations in downwinder children, for example, may be influenced by environmental chemical agents or by latent viruses. Lung cancers in NTS workers may be influenced by their cigarette-smoking. Because of these relatively complex, diffused, and remote influences, epidemiologists favor using the term "risk factor" over "cause" to describe variables believed to affect the probability of individuals developing a particular illness (Schaffner, 1991).

While it is generally accepted among epidemiologists that long-term LLRE can potentially cause cancer, their research proceeds from conflicting assumptions about the nature of that risk. At one extreme, the extremely controversial *hormesis* model holds that LLRE may actually *contribute* to human health (Gofman, 1993). The *threshold* model, alternately, holds that below a certain level of exposure, no harmful effects of LLRE on human health are detectable by researchers (McCalley, 1990). Both of these models have historically enabled nuclear officials to defend or raise established levels of "safe" exposure. In contrast, the *linear* (or *no threshold*) model holds that every dose of LLR adds (however slightly) to the risk of developing illness. The most cautious *supraliner* model, finally, holds that prolonged LLRE may in some cases result in higher injury than that from brief high-level exposure (for example, by destroying the monocyte cells that "trigger" the immune system). These latter two models have assisted researchers attempting to argue for decreased levels of "safe" radiation exposure.

In examining the practices of downwinder epidemiology, I am concerned with how scientific researchers and their critics strategically convince audiences that their knowledge-claims are authoritative and credible (see Solomon, 1985). I am also concerned with how their discourse reproduces relations of domination and consent between Cold War authorities and citizens. An example of the first theme would involve researchers' habitual use of official risk standards to evaluate new

298   *Bryan C. Taylor*

claims of association between LLRE and illness. An example of the
second theme would involve instances in which nuclear officials have
rejected more cautious risk estimates based upon the criterion of "operational feasibility"—of whether the revised standards would increase
the cycle-time and financial cost of nuclear weapons production (Fradkin,
1989, 124).

I must emphasize, however, that not *all* epidemiological research
rejects the possibility that fallout has caused downwinder illness: one
analyst finds that nearly two-thirds of independent and government-
funded studies support the existence of a "fairly clear" association
between exposure to fallout and residents' increased incidence of leukemia (Ball, 1988, 124). Other DOE studies have supported associations between LLRE and excess incidence of lymphoma and leukemia
in DOE workers, as well as excess deaths from melanoma, brain cancer,
and berylliosis (Connor, 1990). However, while rejections of such associations do not necessarily suggest a government conspiracy, historical evidence indicates that conflict within the AEC and DOE between
the interests of health and of weapons production—conflict played out
in the production and interpretation of epidemiological data—has strongly
favored weapons.[5] In the words of scientist-critic Robert Alvarez, "the
unwritten but persistent policy of the AEC and . . . [the DOE] has been
to ignore, suppress and publicly deny evidence of hazards. In this pattern, science is not used to focus on problems but to cloud their appearance and allow agency officials to deny their existence" (quoted in
Connor, 1990, 25).

In this light, I turn to features of epidemiology that enable officials to construct claims about the radiated body that potentially sustain
dangerous operations. I offer three analytic "frames" for understanding
epidemiology that focus on: (1) its positivistic qualities, (2) its "metaphorical" and militaristic status, and (3) its "intertextual" construction
of truth claims from other discourses.

The first analytic frame addresses epidemiology's general premises about the reality of the radiated body and about the correct procedures for discovering and representing its truth. Epidemiology, first,
may be characterized as *objective*. It conceptualizes the radiated body
as a phenomenon existing prior to, and independently of, human consciousness, whose essential facticity may be captured and recorded by
detached researchers using quantitative discourses of measurement.
Secondly, epidemiology is *atomistic*. It fragments the body into independently understandable variables such as "age," "received dosage,"
and "illness category" in order to evaluate their relationships. In this
process, researchers *purify* the body of important cultural and historical features in order to codify it as data. Bodies are then *aggregated*,
or joined with other bodies (from whom they would normally be
relatively independent) in artificial categories (e.g., in "experimental"

and "control" groups) based upon their shared possession of traits and conditions.

Collectively, these premises interact to rhetorically structure epidemiological depictions of the body as scientific truth. Recent criticism, however, suggests that this "preferred meaning" suppresses traces of epidemiology's metaphorical and militaristic "unconscious" (Treichler, 1987). Throughout the Cold War, epidemiology has been institutionalized as a form of medical-scientific knowledge with broad unity for the national-security state. The secret Cold War radiation experiments discussed in the introduction to this chapter reveal how nuclear officials have desired knowledge about human radiation effects for a variety of militaristic purposes (beyond the officially stated goal of protecting citizen and worker health). One purpose involves projecting and "curing" the incidence of illness and mortality among U.S. soldiers on nuclear battlefields as variables inhibiting the achievement of military objectives.[6] Another, more "offensive" purpose involves predicting the effectiveness of U.S. radiation weapons designed for use against enemy soldiers and civilian populations. Such weapons, in the words of one AEC official, would "break the will of nations and of peoples by the stimulation of man's primordial fears, those of the unknown, the invisible and the mysterious. . . . No survivor could be certain he was not among the doomed, and so added to every terror of the [postnuclear] moment, thousands would be stricken with a fear of death and the uncertainty of the time of its arrival" (quoted in Makhijani, 1994, 25).

This militarization of epidemiological research within the AEC and DOD is related to a broader, metaphorical transformation in nominally "civilian" postwar epidemiology (Ball, 1994). The Epidemic Intelligence Service of the CDC, for example, was created in 1950 in response to official fears that only organized groups of expert investigators could respond effectively to the threat of Soviet biological warfare. Within the general Cold War climate of permanent emergency, federal epidemiologists appropriated the militaristic rhetoric of surveillance, command, control, communication, and containment (for example, in petitioning Congress for funds) to define and expand their mandate. This conflation of scientific and state interests has led, ironically, to an increasing "invasion" of the body public by medical/professional agents of control poised to identify and to contain illness.

Epidemiology, then, is a discourse that both produces scientific knowledge-claims and reproduces lager ideological discourses. One way to understand this reproduction involves focusing on how epidemiological arguments about downwinders are socially organized and constructed. When this process is scrutinized, its intertextuality and contingency are clarified. These elements qualify the truth-value of epidemiological claims and, in some instances, appear to compromise it. I conclude this section by focusing on five problems that suggest how downwinder epidemiology potentially inhibits the verification of associations.

Problem 1: Dosimetry

Epidemiology is "plagued" by various difficulties in reconstructing radiation doses received by downwinders (Cardis and Esteve, 1991; Stewart, 1990). Official records of nuclear weapons tests do not precisely reflect how much of which combinations of radioactive isotopes were dispersed where or when, or to expose whom (e.g., because test explosions were larger than anticipated and generated their own unpredictable winds). Isotopes are absorbed differently within the body, depending on their chemical form, their route of entry, and their length of retention (Beral et al., 1988). Recording equipment used by AEC monitors in downwind areas was often insensitive, e.g., to alpha-radiation, and used inappropriately. One example involved the routine measurement by monitors of all types of fallout at waist-level, when some types were strongest at ground-level. This practice was probably influenced by the AEC's policy of exclusively measuring external, penetrating radiation and failing until 1958 to study "internal pathways" of ingested radiation. Maps produced from averagings of these readings do not reflect localized "hot spots" of intense fallout. It is also widely believed that AEC employees failed to record data (e.g., by not retrieving and by destroying film badges that were themselves often faulty and only selectively distributed to residents). AEC researchers also lowered dose-estimates by dubiously emphasizing factors such as shielding, weathering of isotopes and internal, biological repair of cells (Fradkin, 1989, 191).[7] Standardized data-collection methods were not used either within a given DOE facility over time or among facilities during any given time period (Olshansky and Williams, 1990). Exposure data for workers, finally, was often originally collected for employment information— and not epidemiological—purposes.

All of these contingencies now affect researchers as they attempt to correct, standardize, and convert various forms of raw data (e.g., the microfiche records of death certificates) into "intermediate" and "analytical data files" that isolate variables to determine their association (Gofman, 1993; Olshansky and Williams, 1990). Knowledge-claims are further mediated as researchers select and use various statistical models and packages, (e.g., those simulating the "transport" of fallout from explosion to the body; Cardis and Esteve, 1991). Overall dosimetry is a slow, laborious, expensive, and ultimately interpretive process conducted by often underfunded and understaffed organizations whose members possess varying agendas and levels of training. While attempts are commonly made to ensure validity in constructing data files, ad hoc decision-making by researchers about specific cases is not unknown, and data are often sufficiently ambiguous to allow for multiple interpretations. Interpretations can also be influenced, finally, by political urgency, as when the NAS released a 1985 study that rebutted the findings of a 1980 CDC study. The CDC study had found over three times the normal rate of leukemia in atomic veterans who witnessed the 1957 "Smoky" test. A 1992 General Accounting Office report discovered that the NAS study—which argued that the cancer mortality rate in the veterans was lower than that of the general population—had included in its survey 15,000 veterans who had not attended atomic tests, and left out 28,000 who had. NAS officials attributed these errors to the incompleteness of records, the inexperience of data-gatherers, and an ambiguous "pressure" to complete the work (Rothstein, 1992).

Problem 2: Dependency on Hiroshima and Nagasaki Phenomena

Epidemiologists frequently extrapolate the effects of LLRE from data about the effects of high-level exposure generated in studies of the 80,000 survivors of Hiroshima and Nagasaki. These nuclear bodies are perhaps the most closely studied in the world, since their evolving, constructed truths shape the official risk estimates and confidence levels against which subsequent claims of association are evaluated (see, e.g., Gilbert et al., 1993).[8] Ongoing studies of their illness and mortality are conducted by the Radiation Effects Research Foundation (RERF), jointly created in 1950 by the U.S. and Japanese governments, and generally indicate that *hibakusha* (literally, "explosion-affected person") cancers occur in direct proportion to their estimated dose received. The findings of these studies are synthesized by the National Research Council to form its authoritative *Biological Effects of Exposure to Low Levels of Ionizing Radiation* (BEIR) report. The recent 1990 BEIR V reversed previous reports to triple its estimate of cancer risk per unit-dose of LLRE (Beardsley, 1990).

As with other databases, however, the facts of these nuclear bodies are highly contested and contingent. Extensive and systematic study of nuclear survivors was not begun until 1950. It is impossible for researchers to recover definitive information about those who died or moved during those five years, and the population now under study is not representative of the immediate survivors. It is generally agreed that this population is more robust (i.e., it survived both the bombings and the traumas of postwar reconstruction), and that it is not possible to establish the exact doses that they received (Griere, 1991). Additionally, researchers are continually bringing new technologies and methodologies to bear in simulating Hiroshima phenomena: their recent findings concerning the relative effects of high-energy gamma rays and low-energy neutrons indicate that previous lower estimates of risk from LLRE may be correct (Broad, 1992). It is not uncommon for the disparity between these successive findings to involve several orders of magnitude, suggesting that while RERF findings are powerful anchors of epidemiology, they are at best inexact. Gofman (1993) reports that RERF researchers have recently reassigned subjects into different aggregates, a controversial practice which prohibits the continuity of analysis by different researchers and which, in this case, generated lower risk-assessments of LLRE. Because of these contingencies, some researchers argue for a new intertextuality: that RERF risk-estimates and effects-extrapolations should be replaced by those generated in a controversial 1977 long-term study of 35,000 DOE workers (a.k.a. the Hanford Study) that supported the association between cumulative LLRE and cancer deaths (Del Tredici, 1987, 138–41; Stewart, 1990).

Problem 3: Strategic Methodological Choice-Making

Claims of LLRE risk can be potentially undermined by researchers and critics who value the following methodological choices:

1. *Counting the incidence of only those cancers known to be directly induced by LLRE and which form the primary cause of death.* Alternately, counting those cancers believed to be *promoted* by LLRE and which form *underlying* causes of death (dependent, of course, on whether such cancers are noted on death certificates) can enhance associations (Gofman, 1993).

2. *Dismissing findings of LLRE risk as "spurious" and "statistically insignificant" based upon the relatively small size of their populations.* Excessive subdivision of data into increasingly smaller cells (e.g., by comparing increases between groups in specific cancers as opposed to overall totals) also decreases the chance of finding significance. Because of the relatively small size of downwinder populations, the validity of claims of LLRE risk ultimately depends on a cumulative number of "small" studies (Cardis and Esteve, 1991).

3. *Selectively focusing studies on rates of mortality (death) and not morbidity (illness).* Morbidity studies involve more complex methodology but are quicker to identify excess incidence of illness, particularly involving cancers with long latency periods. Since some LLRE-related illnesses, further, are curable, mortality studies alone may underestimate the effects of LLRE. Observing exposed populations too briefly following exposure may, similarly, fail to allow for full manifestation and recording of LLRE-related illness (Connor, 1990).

4. *Making invalid comparisons between exposed and con-trol-groups that suppress the significance of increases in the former's morbidity and mortality.* Examples include comparing illness rates in Mormon and DOE worker populations to those in the relatively less healthy general population and subdividing Utahans into residents of "unexposed" Northern regions and "exposed" Southern regions (Archer, 1987).

5. *Emphasizing viral, genetic, lifestyle, and other environ-mental factors as principal or mediating causes for the associations between LLRE and elevated illness,* (as when AEC and PHS officials attributed the death of down-winder sheep to rancher-caused "malnutrition" (Fradkin, 1989).

Problem 4: Institutional Treatment of Researchers

Throughout the Cold War, AEC officials exerted their considerable power to intimidate and discredit researchers whose findings supported claims of LLRE-risk. They did this by pressuring other, less powerful agencies (such as the PHS) to mute "dissident" researchers, by aggressively presenting those researchers with "updated" and "reanalyzed" data that undermined their findings, and finally, by threatening them with loss of funding, employment, and professional reputation unless they agreed to recant their findings and legal testimony (Fradkin, 1989, 200–201). Perhaps the most famous example involves Dr. Thomas Mancuso, project director of the Hanford study, whose funding was cut and data confis-cated following initial publication of findings (Connor, 1990). When such tactics failed to discipline researchers, AEC officials immediately generated counterstudies, critiques, and rebuttals that discredited the validity of controversial findings. Utah Judge Sherman Christensen, who ruled against downwinder sheep ranchers in a 1956 trial largely based on this "scientific" evidence, ruled twenty-five years later that AEC expert witnesses in that case had perpetrated a "fraud upon the court" (Del Tredici, 1987, 148–49).

Problem 5: Institutional Control of Data

This historical conflation of policies and science has, at the least, "pro-voked questions about [the DOE's] credibility as an object purveyor of the science of radiation health" (Olshansky and Williams, 1990, 30). As part of a dramatic cultural shift, the DOE has recently taken steps to reduce these historical "barriers of secrecy and misrepresentation" (McCalley, 1990, 13) by appointing a panel of outside experts to assist in creating and overseeing a central repository of all its health and safety data. This database will be jointly administered by the Department of Health and Human Services and will ideally facilitate independent research. Serious questions remain, however, about the intentions and ability of midlevel, Cold War era, DOE bureaucrats to declassify controversial data and to share control of its resources with a competing federal agency.[9]

To conclude this section, the analytic frames of positivism, militarism, and intertextuality suggest that epidemiological narratives of the radiated body can be constructed to serve particular political interests. These narratives have functioned hegemonically in postwar legal and legislative arenas to reinforce power inequalities between nuclear officials and downwinders. Following the end of the Cold War, a number of discourses have emerged to challenge this hegemony and to question the ethics and rationality underlying U.S. nuclear weapons production. I turn now to the case of documentary photography.

"Signifying Husks":[10] The Downwinder Body in Documentary Photography

Nuclear explosions and their victims have historically been documented by the U.S. government through a positivist and reactionary visual aesthetic. Official photographers of nuclear tests, for example, have construed them primarily as formidable technical "problems" requiring high-speed cameras that parse and transmit blast-wave phenomena before being destroyed (Del Tredici, 1987, 185–87). Public assimilation of the mushroom cloud image has been tightly controlled by the U.S. military within a "coercive economy of meanings" mixing nature worship, patriotism, and religious righteousness in ways that obscure human accountability for nuclear effects on victims' bodies (Hales, 1991). The Japanese survivors of Hiroshima and Nagasaki, further, have been fragmented in clinical photographs that record their burned surfaces and tumorous organs for the purposes of medical research (Gusterson, 1991). Inevitably, this official realism has influenced artistic and documentary representations of nuclear bodies and of the institutions that produce them. Solomon-Godeau (1984), for example, has noted at least two different aesthetics in documentary photography of the DOE weapons complex: one naïve and sentimental that depicts the nuclear threat as an abstract (and thus inevitable) feature of the human condition and another more critical that depicts the specific manifestations of labor, technology, and rationality that have sustained the arms race.

Photographs reflecting these aesthetics denote particular nuclear actors, locations, and events. They also connote the historical relationships that have developed between nuclear bodies and institutions. Their images signify through internal "syntagmatic" codes (such as lighting and composition), and also through external, "paradigmatic" associations with other traditions of documentary photography (such as photographs of persons with AIDS). They variously evaluate the ethics and utility of nuclear weapons institutions and contribute to an "authority of the morbid" (Watney, 1990, 173) that surrounds the radiated body. The second, more politicized aesthetic discussed by Solomon-Godeau (1984), however, also clarifies the operations of power in nuclear hegemony and facilitates its disruption.

Carole Gallagher's (1993) *American Ground Zero* conforms more closely to this second aesthetic and represents the culmination of her decade-long, "anthropological" immersion in the culture of NTS workers, atomic veterans, and downwind residents. In completing this work, the resistance from her subjects and the unremitting tragedy of their suffering tested Gallagher's emotional resources and her technical artistry. The outcome is reflected in the volume's over one hundred mostly black-and-white, high-contrast, full-page photographs of downwinder subjects and landscapes. These images are accompanied by edited personal narratives and interviews with downwinders and by excerpts from a variety of historical documents (such as official AEC memoranda). These visual and discursive codes interact to construct a "different" truth of the downwinder body (see Mitchell, 1994). Unlike government epidemiology, Gallagher clearly intends to convince readers[11] of the liability and negligence of Cold War nuclear officials in injuring downwind groups. She accomplishes this goal by depicting the radiated body as a sensous, situated, and expressive subjectivity. In the process, Gallagher establishes documentary photography as a "counter-realism" that rejects official claims about downwinder illness and death. In discussing this realism, I focus on three themes in Gallagher's text: (1) the downwinder body in pain, (2) the situated nature of the downwinder body, and (3) reflexive and "novelistic" uses of photography that critique the ethics of official nuclear representation. Each of these patterns, I argue, forms a rhetorical strategy that challenges the positivistic realism of epidemiology. These strategies are also ideological, however, and I will attend to the ways in which they depict history for the purposes of political struggle.

The Downwinder Body in Pain

It is important to note that Gallagher's work adopts a strategy that may be described as "moral positivism." This term reflects her commitment to the "ideal of clear seeing" expressed by her model, the famous documentary photographer Dorothea Lange, and her wish to serve as "a blank slate upon which the stories and images [of downwinders] could be written" (xxiii).[12] For Gallagher, this stance recovers what is forgotten and repressed in the narratives of epidemiology: the bodily

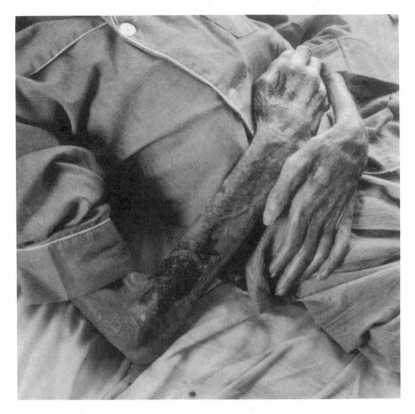

Figure 12.1. *Herman Hagen . . .* From Gallagher, C. (1993), *American Ground Zero: The Secret Nuclear War,* Cambridge, Mass., MIT Press, by permission of the author.

experience of pain and illness that defies language but that also forms the potential for humane community (Scarry, 1985). While epidemiology documents the incidence and rate of downwinder illnesses such as liver cancer and heart disease, Gallagher strives to depict in her images and interviews the forms of experience associated with these conditions: agony, rage, frustration, bitterness, disillusionment, stoicism, dignity, and crippling depression. She records the texture of human extremity: of encountering the lump or mole that signals the onset of disease, and alienation from one's own body; of being slowly and irreversibly consumed by cancer cells; of having one's organs and limbs swell and explode—or alternately, sliced, scraped, and amputated; of losing one's ability to "perform" meaningfully with spouses, children, and coworkers. As a result, readers engage reflective expressions of concrete downwind subjectivity. This engagement clarifies the "cost" and "consequences" of nuclear testing in powerful ways and invites reconsideration of its hegemonic narrative.

Three selected images indicate how Gallagher depicts downwinders in their marginal, liminal states of illness. *"Herman Hagen"* (Figure 12.1) shows the bracketed, faceless torso of a white man wearing pajamas, lying in bed. His arms are thin and wasted; the fingers on his hands are gnarled and elongated, and rest across his pelvis. The skin on his arms is stretched like parchment over wooden dowels. Gallagher's interview with the man's wife reveals that while working at NTS he would—in a display of "unabashed . . . machismo"—dip his arms up to the elbow in radioactive wastewater, and that even now on his deathbed he will not admit that this practice could have caused his bone-marrow cancer: "It was a great living!" (50).

Augusta Peters (Figure 12.2) is a three-quarters shot of an elderly white woman seated in an arm chair located in the living room of her home. Ironically, given his support while President for nuclear testing, a framed photograph of Ronald Reagan sits on the table to her

Figure 12.2. Augusta Peters . . . From Gallagher, C. (1993), *American Ground Zero: The Secret Nuclear War,* Cambridge, Mass., MIT Press, by permission of the author.

left. The woman is smiling faintly (but not with her eyes), and her gaze is directed slightly above and to the left of the camera. She is posed in a sleeveless top which—subversively, given the cultural metonymy of breast-as-femininity—reveals the concavity of her chest. In her interview with Gallagher, Peters describes watching the "beautiful [mushroom] clouds" (172) with her husband while living in Nevada, the collection of their film badges by AEC monitors who offered no feedback about fallout risk, and the trauma of losing both her breasts to cancer: "They've sawed the bone and took everything they could get under the arm, a radical mastectomy. It's been an awful thing. . . . I would die if I could, I'd commit suicide but I'm afraid I'd make a mess out of it and be worse off" (172).

Della Truman, At Rest (Figure 12.3), finally, is a daring, "transgressive" image of the head and torso of an elderly woman posed against the satiny lining of her funeral casket. In her interview with

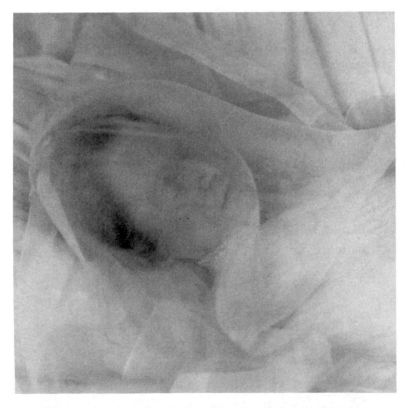

Figure 12.3. *Della Truman, At Rest* . . . From Gallagher, C. (1993), *American Ground Zero: The Secret Nuclear War,* Cambridge, Mass., MIT Press, by permission of the author.

the woman's son, which precedes this image, Gallagher has established that she died of a heart attack related to a thyroid condition likely induced by radiation. Here, the woman wears a white, high-collared lace dress; her body is wrapped in a gauze shroud. Her eyes are closed and her mouth is slightly turned down at the corners. Because of the uncanny power of the dead for the living, the viewer may initially mistake her state for sleep. Gallagher places this image at the end of the volume's lengthy sequence of photographs and interviews with downwind victims and their survivors. Those narratives gather cumulative force, and this particular image forms a shocking climax, a "direct" confrontation with the death that is evoked—spoken *about*—in prior narratives. The photograph's facing page, on which the reader has previously encountered downwinder narratives, is blank. The page is a white emptiness that evokes the radical absence approached by many downwinder bodies in pain, and the silence left in the wake of their passing.

The Situated Downwinder Body

Gallagher's photographs and interviews capitalize on a particular effect of epidemiology's positivism: when downwinder subjects are purified and aggregated in that discourse, they are stripped of their connectedness to their families, neighbors, friends, coworkers, and fellow church members. These different social webs have been affected in at least three ways by nuclear practices. First, symbolically, by AEC officials who rationalized nuclear testing by characterizing downwinders as a "low-use segment of the population" (Gallagher, 1993, xxiii). Secondly, by the actual deaths of their members, which may be caused by nuclear operations. And thirdly (again, symbolically), by epidemiologists and other nuclear officials who fail to preserve these connections as a context for establishing the meaning of those losses. Gallagher's photographs and interviews, subsequently, evoke the integrity of cultural phenomena affected by fallout: *relationships* characterized by love, faith, obligation, and patriotism. These relationships, her work suggests, were the medium through which downwinders maintained their personal, professional, communal, religious, and national identities. LLRE-effects, she suggests, have destroyed the foundations of those identities. Her work also depicts how those identities are situated ideologies that provide downwinders with various folk knowledges and narratives. These narratives have enabled them to alternately reproduce *and* resist hegemonic accounts of nuclear risk.

Again, three sets of images and interviews suggest the range of downwinder embeddedness displayed in Gallagher's work. The first, *Adam and Sarah Haynes* (Figure 12.4) evokes related types of grief and

Figure 12.4. *Adam and Sarah Haynes . . .* From Gallagher, C. (1993), *American Ground Zero: The Secret Nuclear War,* Cambridge, Mass., MIT Press, by permission of the author.

loss suffered by surviving family members of downwinder casualties. This image shows a smiling, middle-aged white woman seated outdoors at a picnic table. She is embraced from behind by a lanky young man who, from their intimacy and resemblance, appears to be her son. Like her, he is smiling directly at the camera, although more shyly; his grasp on her shoulders suggests both protectiveness and dependency.

In the accompanying text, Gallagher and Haynes alternate in narrating the story of Haynes's husband, who was exposed to radiation in his job as a security guard at NTS. Following his death, allegedly from radiation-induced lung cancer, Haynes joined a class-action lawsuit against the government and began to gather official records of her husband's LLRE. In 1985, she was shocked to learn that the DOE denied that her husband had ever been employed at NTS, and then in 1991, that it wanted to exhume his body for an autopsy. This narrative thus depicts three forms of grief: that of a wife forced to watch her husband die slowly and in agony ("Here I see this hulking man shrieking in front of my eyes, I mean literally shrieking" [40]); that of a genetically damaged child, devastated by his father's death ("He always used to call me his trusty sidekick" [40]); and that again of a mother, crippled by her own poverty, heart-disease, and depression, who worries about the future of her asthmatic, learning-disabled son ("There's tears running down my face because I'm out of money now, and I have a child to support, who can't get work" [41]).

The second image/narrative *Al Maxwell* (Figure 12.5), reinforces this theme of family tragedy and extends it by exploring how religious and nuclear interests intersect *within* the family. This image shows a white-haired white man reclining in a raised hospital bed. His head is turned to the left to look knowingly into the face of a young white woman with long dark hair, wearing a surgical gown and clasping his hand with one of her own gloved. The caption confirms what this clasp, their age difference, and their look of mutual devotion suggests: that

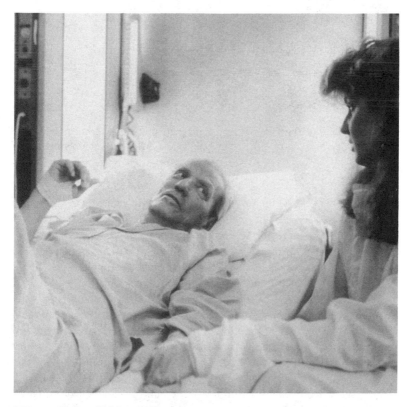

Figure 12.5. *Al Maxwell . . .* From Gallagher, C. (1993), *American Ground Zero: The Secret Nuclear War,* Cambridge, Mass., MIT Press, by permission of the author.

Figure 12.6. *Jay Truman* . . . From Gallagher, C. (1993), *American Ground Zero: The Secret Nuclear War,* Cambridge, Mass., MIT Press, by permission of the author.

they are father and daughter. In the accompanying narrative, Gallagher and Maxwell recreate the near-epic tale of Al Maxwell who, as an American POW, survived the brutal Bataan Death March only to serve as part of a POW clean-up crew in Hiroshima, and then moved back to Utah where he received (along with other family members) additional LLRE from NTS, and died from bone-marrow cancer.

Jackie Maxwell's narration is ambivalent: she is indignant at the injustice of her husband's fate, yet also proudly recounts how he blunted their daughter's anger at the government that apparently contributed to his death by invoking their Mormon beliefs: "Believe me, this country is worth dying for. You may not agree with what's going on, but this Constitution is divinely inspired. It's not administered very well at times" (108). She concludes by recalling her young grandson's consolation offered during Al Maxwell's funeral: "Poppy Al went up to heaven. Now we're happy. Don't nobody cry anymore' (108). While these sentiments are moving, they also suggest with other narratives in the volume how Mormon theology blindly endorses governmental authority, rationalizes governmental corruption as a demonstration of humanity's "fallen" nature, and requires earthly suffering as a confirmation of God's challenge to the faithful to endure. This ideology, Gallagher suggests, renders Mormon downwinders exceptionally vulnerable to nuclear hegemony because it precludes critique of its specific operations and radical, organized action against them.

The third image/narrative, *Jay Truman*, son of Della, discussed above (Figure 12.6) suggests how Mormon and other folk knowledges also functioned during the Cold War to *alert* downwinders to the apparent effects of fallout, and to challenge hegemonic narratives of LLRE risk. In this moody, deep-focus image, a bearded white male sits crosslegged on the bank of a stream at the edge of a cave or tunnel. The viewer's eye is drawn to the figure not only because he is centrally composed but also because he is backlit by stark, blinding sunlight falling on the trees beyond the mouth of the cave. Poised here between light and dark, the figure sits either "trapped" or "safe" in his solitude, contemplating the mossy growth of the cave walls, and of memory.

Truman's narrative speaks to the struggle between official and unofficial knowledges among downwind cultures regarding the relationship between NTS fallout and subsequent illnesses. Specifically, downwinders possessed a variety of intuitive and folk knowledges that clarified the apparent danger posed to them by fallout. Gallagher reports that they read signs of this danger in physical damage apparently caused by fallout to local trees, sheep, cows, horses, crops, and farm equipment. Even as AEC and PHS officials attributed their herd losses to other factors, ranchers confirmed their own suspicions by conducting informal experiments (such as "treating" affected cattle with hay from a nondownwind area). Relatedly, small-town familiarity and the Mormon emphasis on genealogy combined to alert downwinders to the unprecedented excess of cancer in their communities. "Growing up I remember in Enterprise," Truman explains, "I again want to mention that in a small town . . . everybody knows everybody else's business. It was way low in cancer incidence rates from the past that you heard about, and then all of a sudden there was this person and this person and this person [sick]" (312). Mormon downwinders knew, in other words, that they had unusually healthy lifestyles and genes, and were not prone to widespread illness. Truman recounts that this knowledge led him to grow increasingly suspicious of AEC propaganda and to challenge the paradoxical distinction it drew between "safe" fallout from nuclear tests, and the "dirty" fallout from potential Soviet attacks. "We had one guy," Truman recalls, "come in with some AEC nonsense, he was also doing a survival course, the twelve-hour civil-defense instruction course in the high school. He always had a book in front of him, something like *The*

Book of Atomic Facts. I kept asking him questions, like why does [fallout] cause leukemia in the Japanese but not in Americans. He didn't answer the question so I stole his book . . . I knew there was no logic in going to a fallout shelter for [a Soviet] bomb, and something only a hundred miles away we were supposed to go out and roll around in it and watch history being made" (313–14).

Collectively, these narratives and images suggest the interanimating official and unofficial discourses in which downwinders were embedded. Gallagher's work recovers their situated identities from their purification in epidemiological discourse and suggests the ideologies that alternately empowered and constrained downwinders in their apparent oppression by nuclear officials.

Reflexive Use of Photography

In this last section, I turn to the intertextuality and reflexivity of Gallagher's work. As does epidemiology, Gallagher frequently constructs her truth-claims using citations and fragments from prior and "external" texts, including: the political theories of Erasmus and of Frederick Douglass; Dorothea Lange's photographs of Utah Mormons; scenes from the set of the 1988 Hollywood film "Nightbreaker," which reenacts the plight of U.S. atomic veterans; photographs taken by downwinders of approaching fallout clouds; a Lawrence Ferlinghetti poem; letters and memos from AEC officials, and also the Nuremberg Principles. *American Ground Zero* is thus a pastiche that juxtaposes official and unofficial discourses in a "novelistic" manner that often subverts the authority of the former and implicates them in downwinder suffering (Bakhtin, 1981). Within the text of Sarah Haynes's narrative (discussed above), for example, Gallagher includes an official AEC photograph taken of Hayes's husband being tested by an NTS doctor for radiation effects following his work-related exposure to plutonium. The indexical facticity of this image contradicts the DOE's subsequent denial (recorded in the narrative) that the man was employed at NTS.

In this and other uses of photography, Gallagher reflexively comments on the politics of nuclear representation, which saturate downwinder realisms. As a result of using such strategies, however, Gallagher's text is configured within two conflicting aesthetics: a progressive counter-realism, which claims to unearth the historical truth "distorted" by official discourses such as epidemiology, and an ironic postmodernism in which by deconstructing official representations and clichéd iconography, Gallagher ruptures and implicates *her own* realism (as when she repeatedly positions subjects in relation to ominous background features that resemble mushroom and fallout clouds). This tension created in these images has several productive effects: it opens up to scrutiny nuclear weapons phenomena as sedimented sites of discur-

Figure 12.7. *Ken Case* . . . From Gallagher, C. (1993), *American Ground Zero: The Secret Nuclear War,* Cambridge, Mass., MIT Press, by permission of the author.

sive conflict; it confirms the ethical role of representation in constructing their significance, and it motivates a fully active and conscious decoding by viewers. It is also possible, however, that this deconstructive impulse "contaminates" the realism and sympathy that Gallagher has sought to establish for downwinders through her presentation of their bodies and voices.

Two sets of images and interviews suggest the range of Gallagher's reflexive photography. While both images subvert the authority of official texts, they do so with very different tones.

The first image, *Ken Case* (Figure 12.7) is a medium-shot of an older white man wearing glasses and a western-style hat, with a star-shaped badge affixed to his shirt. Posed outdoors against the side of a building, he is holding a framed, official AEC photograph of a brilliant nuclear explosion against his chest. Gallagher's placement of this photograph in the pose suggests a wry commentary on the intertextual relationships between radiation and other, different types of photography.

To trace this intertext, we must first remember that documentary photography is inherently associated with radiation, since it "captures" the spectrum of visible light reflected by its subject. More specifically, x-ray radiation is used by medical authorities in conjunction with photographic technology to diagnose the truth of ill and injured bodies. This technology renders the body's visible exterior invisible, and its invisible interior visible.[13] This phenomenon is a double-edged sword, however: one famous study in the early 1970s concluded that even routine x-rays of pregnant women may pose significant health risks to the developing fetus (Stewart, 1990). Because damaging x-rays are also dispersed by exploding nuclear weapons (and were used in the secret experiments discussed in the introduction to this chapter), they can never be completely separated from connotations of war, violation, and downwinder illness (an association strengthened in Gallagher's text by testimony from atomic veterans, who while viewing the tests through closed eyes, could see the bones in their hands covering their faces). In posing her subject in this fashion, Gallagher is exploiting the amorality and intertextuality of the phenomenon "x-ray." Here, her photograph is a moral pun that presents the AEC image *as-if it were an x-ray plate revealing the irradiated truth of Case's interior.* It uses the image's detonation (nuclear blast) and its connotation (radioactive fallout) to suggest that the relationship established in Case's narrative between his career herding cattle for the AEC across highly dusty and radioactive terrain, and his subsequently fatal cancers, is one of cause. In a wryly humorous way, Gallagher evokes the complex relationships that exit between ethics, photography, radiation, and the downwinder body.

The second photograph displays a recurring motif in Gallagher's text, in which her downwinder subjects offer up images of their deceased loved ones—whom they believe were killed by fallout—for the camera's view. This reflexivity evokes the occult, indexical power of the photograph and wistfully sutures the viewer. These images create a structural analogy between the grieving downwinders that they depict, who cling to the aura of their photograph-tokens, and the viewer, who is urged to similarly identify with the grieving downwinder subject. In this way, Gallagher assumes—and reinforces—the elegiac role played here by her subjects: as they hold up the image of their cherished losses, she holds up for the viewer a subject who has also apparently suffered—and may yet die—from the effects of fallout (some did die during the period between the taking of the photograph and the publication of the volume). As an effect of strategic rhetoric, this identification potentially spurs new thought and progressive action by the viewer toward the apparatus allegedly responsible for these erasures.

Gallagher's *Sherry Millett* (Figure 12.8) is distinctive within this motif because it does not include a live subject holding the image of a dead beloved. Instead, the image is shot looking down on two photo-

Figure 12.8. *Sherry Millett* . . . From Gallagher, C. (1993), *American Ground Zero: The Secret Nuclear War,* Cambridge, Mass., MIT Press, by permission of the author.

graphs and a pamphlet that rest on a white lace mat placed on top of a dark wood table. The photographs show two images of Kay Millett's young daughter, Sherry. The first image shows a smiling, healthy, and deeply dimpled towhead dressed in a striped top with a bow at the collar. This image rests underneath an AEC pamphlet from the 1950s, opened to a cartoon depiction of a cowboy holding a geiger counter (a reference to the many amateur uranium prospectors in the region), and registering surprise at its high readings. The text in this pamphlet instructs downwinders not to be alarmed by such high readings: "Don't let them bother you" (145). The pamphlet in turn rests underneath another, very different image of the girl, now older but bloated and with distorted features. The narrative accompanying these images explains that the girl is suffering in this image from the side effects of the medication prednisone, which she had taken before her death from leukemia to ward off the illnesses affecting her chemotherapy-ravaged immune system.

These photographs and the pamphlet have been formally arranged by Gallagher to connote a certain stone-scissors-paper hierarchy among them. This constructed relationship encapsulates Gallagher's argument about LLRE and downwinder suffering. Here, the "good" photograph of the healthy child is "covered" by the apparently deceitful text, symbolizing the AEC's violation of her health; the text is, in turn, "covered" or trumped by the "bad" photograph of the sick child. This second photograph "comes out on top" in Gallagher's image as the defining consequence and truth of U.S. nuclear testing. In this quasi-narrative sequence, innocence is corrupted by powerful nuclear lies, and is potentially redeemed by the assertion of its tragic loss. Overall, this image reconfirms Gallagher's twin roles as both documentarian and "deconstructive pasticheur" (Solomon-Godeau, 1991, 100), alternately "capturing" the "hidden truth" of downwinder suffering and evoking truth-as-effect by critically juxtaposing discourses within and between images. These strategies are both complementary and competitive and potentially contribute to an ethical mediation by viewers on the discursive manufacture of nuclear culture.

Conclusion: The Epistemology of Fallout

In this chapter, I have contrasted two competing discourses that claim authority over representing the downwinder body. The first, government epidemiology, possesses strict criteria for validating claims of association between LLRE and downwinder illness. It objectifies, atomizes, purifies, and aggregates the downwinder body in order to establish the universal truth conditions of that association. Methodological contingencies and militaristic ideology, however, have mediated epidemiology's relationship to nuclear weapons interests. In contrast to epidemiology, documentary photography combines the indexical quality of the image with the evocative authenticity of personal narrative (Langellier, 1989) to depict the downwinder as an embodied subjectivity. Gallagher's use of these codes activates the cultural ideologies of individualism and of realism; viewers subsequently "see" these subjects in the apparent facticity of their visible, damaged bodies and "hear" them in the pathos of their reflective, mournful voices. This discourse creates not scientific truth but verisimilitude.

As with epidemiology, however, Gallagher's rhetoric is also marked by contingencies. One example involves her strategy of counterassertion, in which she challenges epidemiological reductionism by presenting a series of examples that also—inevitably—reduce complex events. Gallagher's subjects appear to be selected as emblematic of the "suppressed" social history that she wishes to recover. This strategy is potentially undermined, however, by three factors. The first involves potential reader suspicion regarding the omission of conflicting evidence (e.g., of downwinders who discount the potential risk posed by LLRE, *and* whose families and friends appear healthy). The second factor involves reactionary, positivist criticism that formalizes this suspicion and rejects the validity of Gallagher's examples because, in the words of one reviewer, "They are all anecdotal and don't prove anything" (Powers, 1994, 121). Gallagher (1993, 333) anticipates this reaction in the text and includes a consolation from independent epidemiologist John Gofman: "Big Science won't believe any of it, no matter what, but you don't have to worry about that. You're not expected to do a scientific job. You're trying to get their side of the story of what happened the way they saw it. . . . Maybe these people who are telling you these things are closer to the truth than the sanitized stuff I get to see." Additionally, Gallagher defends against the charge of sampling bias by presenting a relatively large number of images and interviews that relentlessly support her claims. The drawback to this rhetoric of quantity is that it may potentially be misread as incompetent (as "too long") or may activate the denial through which postwar subjects commonly defend against critical representations of nuclear risk (as "too depressing") (see Lifton and Falk, 1991). Reviews of the volume suggest that its preferred meaning has in fact been both accommodated (Frick, 1993) and resisted (Powers, 1994) by readers.

The third factor mediating the success of Gallagher's counter-assertion involves a risk that is inherent to progressive documentary realism: that the dominant cultural code of individualism will influence viewers to identify with the pathos of visible subjects, and to deemphasize the "invisible" workings of larger institutions and ideologies that have shaped their fate (Giroux and Simon, 1994). Gallagher compensates for this possibility by presenting the downwinder narratives, which focus reader attention on the specific material practices of nuclear oppression. But while this resonance between the work's visual and verbal dimensions is powerful, it cannot guarantee that readers/viewers will decode the text in the preferred manner.

And finally, as discussed above, there is the question of how tension between Gallagher's two aesthetics affects this reply to epidemiology. This question may potentially be resolved by positing two readings of the relationship between these aesthetics. An orthodox reading, first, may see their relationship as a contradiction or "flaw" that undermines the effectiveness of Gallagher's counter-realism. A postmodernist reading, alternately, reframes this relationship as an exemplary deconstructive strategy. In this second reading, Gallagher has, apparently, destabilized her own text in order to reflexively comment on the ethics of official and "certain" discourses that produce downwinder truth, but that will not admit their own political contingency. In contrast, Gallagher's pastiche creates rhetorical incongruity that clarifies an identity-fiction promoted by epidemiology: that it is somehow above or outside of culture, politics, and history. In this reading, Gallagher successfully negotiates her artistic dilemma, as outlined by Solomon-Godeau (1991): "The problem confronting any genuinely radical cultural production is not simply a matter of transforming existing forms through the insertion of some new politicized content or subject matter, *but rather to intervene on the level of the forms themselves, to disrupt what the forms put in place*" (189, emphasis mine). Gallagher disrupts nuclear certainty, in other words, by formally asserting its opposite.

This chapter, then, has hopefully accomplished three goals. The first is to demonstrate how scientific discourse represents the truth of the cultural Other and is opposed in this process by "unofficial" discourses. While these opposing discourses should also not be misconstrued as transparent truth, they potentially reconfigure the power relations between cultural interests that are encoded in and reproduced through scientific discourse. My second goal has been to demonstrate how this struggle is potentially conducted through the symbolic form of the body, which serves as a cultural resource for legitimating and challenging hegemonic operations (see Taylor, 1993a). This analysis contributes to the growing literature of "body studies" (Balsamo, 1990; Frank, 1990; Turner, 1991) that explore how cultural interests define the body and deploy representations that shape the reflective, expressive, and reproductive potential of cultural subjects. The body subsequently appears as a theoretical space in the relations among institutions and discourses—a contested object of disciplinary knowledges. And finally, I have attempted to explore the productivity of documentary photography in this struggle and to show how its projects are shaped by historical circumstances and cultural milieux. Projects such as Gallagher's "speak" a variety of agendas that influence their content and their popular consumption. Here, Gallagher has placed her text into dialogue with official science in order to resist its objectification and mystification, to reassert the primacy of the juridical (rights-bearing) human, to politicize cultural memory, and to moralize nuclear historiography (Benhabib, 1994). In this case, such a dialogue seems essential to secure justice for the downwinders and to critically engage the post–Cold War transformations of the U.S. nuclear weapons complex. The ways in which that institution remembers and forgets the body will likely affect us all.

Notes

The author thanks Gale Hannigan, Texas A&M University Medical Library staff member, my father, Herbert E. Taylor, and John Tindell, instructor, Texas A&M University Department of Speech Communication, for their valuable assistance with research for this manuscript.

1. This is a somewhat arbitrary delimitation of the multicultural world populations exposed to harmful levels of radiation from nuclear testing. The term has traditionally indicated residents of the western United States affected by U.S. nuclear operations. The United States has also tested nuclear weapons in the Pacific Islands, however, affecting both their indigenous peoples and U.S. military personnel. Combined with fallout generated from testing by the Soviet, British, French, and Chinese governments, and by nuclear accidents such as Chernobyl, this radiation appears sufficient to justify conventional wisdom among many international physicians and activists: "We're all downwinders now." Reports of elevated cancer rates in residents of areas surrounding the former Soviet nuclear test site in Kazakhstan (Yanowitch, 1995) suggest that the discursive struggle depicted here will unfold around the globe in the post–Cold War era.

2. This argument regarding the "dialogic" nature of these discourses is supported by Gallagher's (1993, 333) statements of purpose in the text, and by her allegation in public presentations (Gallagher, 1996) that the U.S. testing program was a "giant experiment" designed to provide officials with data about the biological effects of a limited nuclear war, and by the critical analysis below. Her allegation of a conspiracy is undermined, interestingly enough, by her own informants' reports about the sloppiness and ambivalence of AEC data-collection. One would think that such an experiment would be conducted more carefully. The conspiracy theory, in its defense, offers as evidence the rumors of dual sets of data and findings (with only one circulated for public consumption), and emerging evidence that Nevada was selected by officials as the location for the test site despite their knowledge of the serious health risks that testing would pose to nearby residents (Hilts, 1995). The advantage: Nevada's relatively flat terrain enabled monitors to more easily track the fallout path.

3. For the record, I am neither "blaming" epidemiology for failing to provide standards and data-collection techniques that definitively resolve this conflict nor arguing that an otherwise "pure" science is inherently "corrupted" through a productive relationship with the state. The alleged "purity" of science—the image that its practices exist outside of culture and history—is, of course, a myth. Science inevitably serves particular interests in society (for example, by theorizing physical processes and facilitating the development of particular technologies by corporate interests for use by and on various "consumers"). The question thus becomes *which* political and economic interests will be served and how. In *this particular relationship*, it appears that the nuclear nation-state has strategically directed *some* epidemiological research (for example, through funding awards, peer-review practices, personnel recruitment, and data management) in ways that channel a substantial portion of its productivity toward maintaining nuclear hegemony. The

total productivity of an institution, of course, exceeds any single determination of purpose (see note 5 below).

4. In the summer of 1994, 216 N.T.S. workers suffered a major loss in Nevada's Federal District Court when the judge hearing six representative cases in their lawsuit ruled that there was insufficient evidence to support their claims. The U.S. government also, however, settled during this period a class-action lawsuit brought by 6,000 Fernald, Ohio, workers by agreeing to pay the survivors $15 million in damages for emotional distress (and a yet-to-be-determined amount for medical monitoring) caused by fear of contracting cancer from excessive radiation exposure. Meanwhile, the rapid popularization of Gulf War syndrome (even in the absence of a verified pathogen and of supporting epidemiological research) suggests that "anecdotal" evidence in government-contamination scandals is gaining credibility—at least in media discourse. This discourse both registers and fuels public outrage about the deliberate official cultivation of nuclear, biological, and chemical risks, and about official denial of responsibility for the costs to affected populations. For a related discussion of official censorship of epidemiological research indicating health risks posed to uranium miners, see Proctor (1995).

5. Walker (1994) has analyzed AEC establishment of radiation standards related to commercial nuclear power reactions and argues that the agency used "the best scientific information available at the time . . . in conservative ways in order to provide a large margin of error" (57). That may well be the case. He also details, however, how the AEC was torn between its conflicting mandates of regulating *and* promoting the development of nuclear power, as well as developing and testing nuclear weapons. It would be inaccurate to assume that epidemiological practices related to establishing safe exposure levels for commercial power reactors were necessarily the same as those involved in ascertaining LLRE risk in downwinders—although the research programs were closely related. Instead, I believe that the AEC should be theorized as a complex and loosely coupled system, with various divisions pursuing programs inflected by different priorities and standards. For a related rebuttal of claims concerning health risks from exposure to plutonium, see Wheelwright (1995). Note, however, that the evidence discussed in this article primarily involves nuclear workers, and not downwinders.

6. See "U.S. Tests Drugs for Radiation Nausea," April 27, 1995, in the *Houston Chronicle*. Recently released documents suggest that military leaders ordered soldiers to participate in the tests as "an emotional vaccination" that would help them overcome their "exaggerated fear" of nuclear radiation ("N-Test Rationale Revealed," 1995).

7. Ironically, while underestimating doses may have protected officials in the short run from accusations of negligence, it may have

worked against them in the long run, since subsequent determinations of association between those altered levels and recorded illnesses could suggest that LLRE is *more* risky than previously estimated. The converse practice is for researchers to deliberately *overestimate* exposure, which makes it appear that subsequent illnesses occur at a *lower* rate than would normally be expected for that dosage.

8. See Lindee (1994) for a detailed history of the struggle between Japanese and American scientists over these truth of the bodies.

9. To its credit, the DOE has been vigorous in its efforts to open these files to scrutiny. Fiscal conservatives concerned with cutting the federal budget, however, have recently proposed the elimination of the entire Department of Energy, and the consolidation of its nuclear weapons operations within the Department of Defense. Should this happen, this database would fall under the control of an institution not known for its accountability.

10. Watney, 1990, 183.

11. As a work of photojournalism, Gallagher's text requires both reading and viewing. I use the term "reader" to describe moments of engagement that primarily involve discursive codes, and "viewer" to describe those that primarily involve iconic and indexical codes. This distinction is, of course, artificial: the "actual" experience of interpreting the text involves a dialectical use of these competencies.

12. All subsequent free-standing page numbers in parentheses are for Gallagher (1993).

13. I thank Judith Hamera for this formulation.

Reference

Archer, V. E. (1987). Association of nuclear fallout with leukemia in the United States. *Archives of Environmental Health* 42 (5):263–71.

Aronowitz, S. (1988). *Science as Power: Discourse and Ideology in Modern Society.* Minneapolis: University of Minnesota Press.

Bakhtin, M. M. (1981). *The Dialogic Imagination: Four Essays by M. M. Bakhtin.* (M. Holquist, Ed.) Austin: University of Texas Press.

Ball, H. (1988). *Justice Downwind: America's Atomic Testing Program in the 1950s.* New York: Oxford University Press.

Ball, P. (1994, March). *Centers for Disease Control: Epidemiology as Metaphor.* Paper presented at the "Century's End, Narrative Means" Conference, Interdisciplinary Group for Historical Literary Studies, Texas A&M University.

Balsamo, A. (1990). Reading the body in contemporary culture: An annotated bibliography. *Women and Language* 13:64–85.

Barthes, R. (1977). Rhetoric of the image. (S. Heath, Trans.). In R.

Barthes: *Image-Music-Text*. New York: Hill and Wang, 32–51.

Beardsley, T. (1990, March). New radiation risks prompt calls for tighter controls. *Scientific American* 262 (3):35–36.

Benhabib, S. (1994). Hannah Arendt and the redemptive power of narrative. In L. P. Hinchman and S. K. Hinchman (Eds.): *Hannah Arendt: Critical Essays*. Albany: State University of New York Press, 111–37.

Beral, V., P. Fraser, L. Carpenter, M. Booth, A. Brown, and G. Rose, (1988, September 24). Mortality of employees of the Atomic Weapons Establishment, 1951–1982. *British Medical Journal*, 297:757–70.

Broad, W. J. (1992, October 13). New study questions Hiroshima radiation. *New York Times*, p. C1.

Browne, M. W. (1991, August 3). Atom arms labs defend role in the post-Cold War future. *New York Times*, pp. 1, 22.

Burgin, V. (1982). Introduction. In V. Burgin (Ed.): *Thinking Photography*. London: Macmillan, 1–14.

Cardis, E., and J. Esteve. (1991). Epidemiological designs in radioepidemiological research. *Sozial und Präventivmedizin* 36:279–85.

Cohn, C. (1987). Sex and death in the rational world of defense intellectuals. *Signs* 12:687–718.

Connor, T. (1990, September). Nuclear workers at risk. *Bulletin of the Atomic Scientists*, pp. 24–28.

"Connor of subjects in radiation experiments is raised to 16,000" (1995, August 20). *New York Times*, p. 27.

Day, S. H. (1993, June). The big lie [Review of *American Ground Zero*] *The Progressive* 57:40–43.

Del Tredici, R. (1987). *At Work in the Fields of the Bomb*. New York: Harper and Row.

Derrida, J. (1984). No apocalypse, not now (full speed ahead, seven missiles, seven missives). *Diacritics* 14:20–31.

Fradkin, P. L. (1989). *Fallout: An American Nuclear Tragedy*. Tuscon: University of Arizona Press.

Frank, A. W. (1990). Bringing bodies back in: A decade review. *Theory, Culture and Society* 7:131–62.

Franklin, H. B. (1994). From realism to virtual reality: Images of America's wars. *Georgia Review* 48:47-64.

Frick, T. (1993, July 4). Sweet dreams, Nuclear Regulatory Commission [Review of *American Ground Zero*]. *Los Angeles Times Book Review*, p. 10.

Gallagher, C. (1993). *American Ground Zero: The Secret Nuclear War*. Cambridge Mass.: MIT Press.

———. (1996, February 9). Public lecture at the University of Denver,

Denver, Colo.

Gilbert, E. S., E. Omohundro, J. A. Buchanan, and N. A. Holter. (1993). Mortality of workers at the Hanford site: 1954–1986. *Health Physics* 64 (6):577–90.

Giroux, H. A., and R. I. Simon. (1994). Pedagogy and the critical practice of photography. In H. A. Giroux (Ed.): *Disturbing Pleasures: Learning Popular Culture.* New York: Routledge, 93–105.

Gofman, J. (1993, May). Beware the data diddlers. *Bulletin of the Atomic Scientists*, pp. 40–44.

Griere, R. N. (1991). Knowledge, values and technological decisions: A decision theoretic approach. In D. G. Mayo and R. D. Hollander (Eds.): *Acceptable Evidence: Science and Values in Risk Management.* New York: Oxford University Press, 183–203.

Gross, A. (1990). *The Rhetoric of Science.* Cambridge, Mass.: Harvard University Press.

Gusterson, H. (1991). Nuclear war, the Gulf War and the disappearing body. *Journal of Urban and Cultural Studies* 1:45–56.

Hales, P. B. (1991). The atomic sublime. *American Studies* 32:5–32.

Hilts, P. J. (1995, March 15). Fallout risk near atom tests was known. *New York Times,* p. A23.

Horkheimer, M. (1989). Notes on science and the crisis. In S. E. Bronner and D. M. Kellner (Eds.): *Critical Theory and Society: A Reader.* New York: Routledge, 52–57.

Janofsky, M. (1994, January 11). Cold war chill lingers for those who live near nuclear testing site. *New York Times,* p. A12.

Lalvani, S. (1993). Photography, epistemology and the body. *Cultural Studies* 7 (3):442–65.

Langellier, K. M. (1989). Personal narratives: Perspectives on theory and research. *Text and Performance Quarterly* 4:243–76.

Lebow, N. L., and J. G. Stein. (1994, February). Reagan and the Russians. *Atlantic Monthly*, pp. 35–37.

Lifton, R. J., and R. Falk. (1991). *Indefensible Weapons: The Political and Psychological Case Against Nuclearism.* New York: Basic Books.

Lindee, M. S. (1994). *Suffering Made Real: American Science and the Survivors of Hiroshima.* Chicago: University of Chicago Press.

Lippman, T. W. (1993, June 6). In Utah, angry fallout from nuclear testing. *Washington Post National Weekly Edition*, p. 33.

Loeb, P. (1986). *Nuclear Culture.* Philadelphia: New Society Publishers.

Makhijani, A. (1994, April). Energy enters guilty plea. *Bulletin of the Atomic Scientists*, pp. 18–29.

Manning, M. (1995, January/February). Atomic vets battle time. *Bulle-*

tin of the Atomic Scientists, pp. 54–60.

McCalley, M. (1990, September). "What the fight is all about." *Bulletin of the Atomic Scientists,* pp. 1–14.

Mitchell, W. J. T. (1994). *Picture Theory: Essays on Verbal and Visual Representation.* Chicago: University of Chicago Press.

Mojtabai, A. G (1986). *Blessed Assurance.* Boston: Houghton-Mifflin.

"N-test rationale revealed" (1995, June 2). *Houston Chronicle,* p. A4.

Nichols, B. (1993). "Getting to know you . . . ": Knowledge, power and the body. In M. Renov (Ed.): *Theorizing Documentary.* New York: Routledge, 174–92.

Olshansky, S. J., and R. G. Williams. (1990, September). Culture shock at the weapons complex. *Bulletin of the Atomic Scientists,* pp. 29–33.

Poliski, I. (1993, June). Exposing Americans [Review of *American ground zero*]. *Bulletin of the Atomic Scientists,* pp. 50–51.

Powers, T. (1994, March). Downwinders: Some casualties of the nuclear age. *Atlantic Monthly,* pp. 119–24.

Prelli, L. J. (1989). *A Rhetoric of Science: Inventing Scientific Discourse.* Columbia: University of South Carolina Press.

Proctor, R. N. (1995). Censorship of American uranium mine epidemiology in the 1950's. In M. Garber and R. L. Walkowitz (Eds.). *Secret Agents: The Rosenberg case, McCarthyism and fifties America.* New York: Routledge, 59–76.

Rose, H., and S. Rose. (1976). The incorporation of science. In H. Rose and S. Rose (Eds.): *The Political Economy of Science: Ideology of/in the Natural Sciences.* London: Macmillan, 14–31.

Rosenthal, P. (1991). The nuclear mushroom cloud as cultural image. *American Literary History* 3 (1):63–92.

Rothstein, L. (1992, December). No matter what, says NAS, atomic vets are o.k. *Bulletin of the Atomic Scientists,* pp. 3–4.

Russell, D. (1990). In the shadow of the bomb: Cleaning up after the DOE. *Amicus Journal* 12 (4):18–31.

Scarry, E. (1985). *The Body in Pain: The Making and Unmaking of the World.* New York: Oxford University Press.

Schaffner, K. F. (1991). Causing harm: Epidemiological and physiological concepts of causation. In D. G. Mayo and R. D. Hollander (Eds.): *Acceptable Evidence: Science and Values in Risk Management.* New York: Oxford University Press, 204–17.

Schneider, K. (1993a). Foreward. In C. Gallagher, *American Ground Zero.* Cambridge, Mass.: MIT Press, xv–xix.

———. (1993b, December 16). U.S. spread radioactive fallout in secret Cold War weapon tests. *New York Times,* p. A1.

———. (1994a, January 11). Redressing the harms of the nuclear age may not be cheap. *New York Times,* p. D3.

———. (1994b, March 2). Anguish on both sides in human experiments. *New York Times*, p. A12.

――――. (1994c, April 22). New view of peril from A-plant emissions. *New York Times*, p. A21.

Schwenger, P. (1992). *Letter Bomb: Nuclear Holocaust and the Exploding Word*. Baltimore: Johns Hopkins University Press.

Sekula, A. (1989). The body and the archive. In R. Bolton (Ed.): *The Contest of Meaning: Critical Histories of Photography*. Cambridge, Mass.: MIT Press, 342–89.

Shapiro, M. J. (1987). *Representing World Politics: The Sport/War Intertext—with a Postscript on the Nuclear Question*. Working paper no. 9, First Annual Conference on Discourse, Peace, Security, and International Society, San Diego, University of California Institute of Global Conflict and Cooperation.

――――. (1988). *The Politics of Representation: Writing Practices in Biography, Photography, and Policy Analysis*. Madison: University of Wisconsin Press.

Sipchen, B. (1993, July 18). A hidden holocaust. *Los Angeles Times*, pp. E1–E3.

Smith, J. (1989). *Unthinking the Unthinkable: Nuclear Weapons and Western Culture*. Bloomington: University of Indiana Press.

"Smithsonian alters plan for its exhibit on Hiroshima bomb" (1994, August 30). *New York Times*, p. A17.

Solomon. M. (1985). The rhetoric of dehumanization: An analysis of medical reports of the Tuskegee syphilis project. *Western Journal of Speech Communication* 49:233–47.

Solomon-Godeau, A. (1984). Review of the book *Our Lives, Our Children*. *Exposure* 22 (3):53–56.

――――. (1991). *Photography at the Dock: Essays on Photographic History, Institutions and Practices*. Minneapolis: University of Minnesota Press.

Stewart, A. (1990, September). Low-level radiation: The cancer controversy. *Bulletin of the Atomic Scientists*, pp. 15–18.

Swanson, D. J. (1993, October 31). Failing the test of time. *Albuquerque Journal*, p. B1.

Taylor, B. C. (1990). *Reminiscence of Los Alamos:* Narrative, critical theory and the organizational subject. *Western Journal of Speech Communication* 54:395–419.

――――. (1992). The politics of the nuclear text: Reading Robert Oppenheimer's *Letters and Recollections*. *Quarterly Journal of Speech* 78:429–49.

――――. (1993a). Register of the repressed: Womens' voice and body in the nuclear weapons organization. *Quarterly Journal of Speech* 79:267–85.

――――. (1993b). *Fat Man and Little Boy*: The cinematic representation of interests in the nuclear weapons organization. *Critical Stud-*

ies in Mass Communication 10:367–94.

Tirman, J. (1992). Nuclear decrepitude. *Nuclear Times* 10 (2–3): 21–24.

Titus, A. C (1986). *Bombs in the Backyard: Atomic Testing and American Politics.* Reno: University of Nevada Press.

Treichler, P. A. (1987). AIDS, homophobia and biomedical discourse: An epidemic of signification. *Cultural Studies* 1:263–305.

Turner, B. S. (1991). Recent developments in the theory of the body. In M. Featherstone, M. Hepworth, & B. S. Turner (Eds.): *The Body: Social Process and Cultural Theory.* Newbury Park, Calif.: Sage.

U.S. Nuclear Weapons Cost Study Project (1996, September 30). *50 facts about U.S. nuclear weapons* [On-line], 3. Available: http://www.brook.edu/FP/PROJECTS/NUCWCOST/50.HTML.

"U.S. tests drugs for radiation nausea" (1995, April 27). *Houston Chronicle*, p. 5.

Walker, J. S. (1994). The Atomic Energy Commission and the politics of radiation protection, 1967–1971. *Isis* 85:57–78.

Watney, S. (1990). Photography and AIDS. In C. Squiers (Ed.): *The Critical Image: Essays on Contemporary Photography.* Seattle, Wash.: Bay Press, 173–92.

Wheelwright, J. (1995, April). Atomic overreaction. *Atlantic Monthly*, pp. 26, 28–30, 38.

Yanowitch. L. (1995, October). Cancer soars near test sites. *Rocky Mountain News*, p. A37.

Chapter Thirteen

The Limits of Communication: Lyotard and Levinas on Otherness

Andrew R. Smith

Much communication science has developed out of the work of Shannon and Weaver (1963) and is based on a theory of information processing in which the reduction or elimination of uncertainty and noise are valorized. Noise and uncertainty are Other for any science so conceived. Optimal communication involves an exchange of messages whose values and effects can be specified and analyzed unambiguously according to existing semantic, syntactic, and pragmatic rules of a speech community. Optimal performativity is determined primarily by the efficiency of message exchange—the greatest output for the least amount of input. The greater the uncertainty or noise, the greater the demands (time and energy) on the workings of the system of information exchange—that is, "communication." The larger the system becomes—as in an institutional bureaucracy, for example—the more it demands efficient operations. That which enhances or otherwise reproduces the values of optimal system performativity is rewarded, and the ideal "performer" is one who learns how to need what the system needs (see Lyotard, 1989, 47–64).[1]

As a perusal of recent communication journals reveals quite vividly, most empirical communication research is deemed valuable by the degree to which it produces knowledge that will enhance the efficiency of systems of exchange—whether interpersonal, organizational, or cultural. In addition to explicitly positivistic research that operates according to hypothetico-deductive models, any objectivist or exclusively structuralist project that assumes the existence of an already given context and sets out to discover and represent the dominant (normative or cultural) discursive operations of that context, also potentially serves the interests of a system bent on reducing, eliminating, or forgetting the noise and uncertainty of Otherness (see Lingis, 1994).

A number of communication scholars have argued for quite some time (see Jakobson, 1960; Reusch and Bateson, 1968; Wilden, 1980, Lanigan, 1988, Krippendorf, 1993, Stewart, 1995; cf. Bochner, 1985, Thomas, 1994) that the information exchange model of communication is problematical to the extent it makes a claim of presenting a true picture of communication activity while actually glossing or ignoring the needs, beliefs, feelings, desires, interests, demands, or injustices faced by interlocutors in any event. In contrast to the limitations imposed by a positive science view, these scholars to varying degrees recommend a "human science" approach to communication research that seeks to explicate the "conscious experience" of people living through some event—a consciousness of . . . that is considered to be the minimal unit of meaning in communication (see Lanigan, 1988, 41; 1992, 239). According to this more phenomenological or hermeneutic perspective, messages cannot be abstracted and analyzed unproblematically from an already given context but are formed expressively, evocatively, and often radically by persons whose existential and psychosocial experiences play a dominant role in situating communication in any event that takes place in the heart or at the margins of one sociocultural world or another.

In short, the positivist (Cartesian) view of communication presupposes an "I" (the researcher) who reduces uncertainty about events and subjects by eliminating from consideration perceived extraneous variables or "noise" in the communicative system, thus abstracting the "object" of inquiry out of the vibrant densities and intensities (e.g., existential, cultural, political, historical) of any interlocution, and mapping this reduced object indexically and symbolically through explanatory (cognitive) models for purposes of prediction and control. The phenomenological (human science) view presupposes, rather than the certitude of an Ego that is able to reduce and objectify events and subjects, an "operative intentionality" that becomes "part" of the event or text under scrutiny (temporally, spatially, and bodily) the moment questioning begins. In conjunction with others and *prior to conceptualization*, this "antepredicative" intentionality is constituted and affectively informed by the contingent and malleable densities and intensities of *that which is taken* as an "object" of inquiry (see especially Merleau-Ponty, 1986, xvii–xviii, 137–39).[2] Phenomenology acknowledges that the "essences" of the "object" of inquiry can never be known in themselves but the prereflective affective and imaginative engagement of them guides an inquirer toward, while never totally revealing *in discourse*, that which he or she seeks to understand.

For the purposes of this chapter I am going to accept and elaborate upon the phenomenological critique of positivistic communication science. My interest also, while acknowledging a fealty to the phenomenological tradition, is to question some of its presuppositions, especially with regard to the primacy given to the notions of intentionality, the speaking subject, and intersubjective relations. Drawing principally from the more recent works of Levinas (1991, 1984) and Lyotard (1988, 1991), I wish to take up the following issue: How does prioritizing intentionality in communicative acts—and defining subjectivity according to a speaking subject who constitutes events—and defining subjectivity according to a speaking subject who constitutes events— circumvent the degree to which persons are *subject to* or otherwise *obligated by* Otherness?

The notion of Other defined here concerns something more startling than the empirical "other' of the self-other relation in interlocution and thus may problematize the procedures and results of any form of communication inquiry to the extent that such inquiry does not take the immanence (and possible imminence) of Otherness into account. In the following discussion I offer an overview of Levinas's and Lyotard's respective views of Otherness and consider the consequences these conceptions suggest for communication inquiry. I also take up an apparent contradiction that seems to inhere thematically in these views— that is, how can human beings be subject to (if not determined by) the demands and obligations of Otherness while still being capable of freeing themselves from the shackles of discourse? Or if we follow Levinas's and Lyotard's lead, it would seem that the intentionality of a speaking subject is both operative and inoperative at the same time when faced with the alterity of others. How can this be so?

On Being Subjected to . . .

The idea of *being subject to* comes from Levinas, whose project involves a critical response to the Husserlian ideas of temporality and the subject. A full explication of the issues addressed by Levinas is beyond the scope of this chapter (for discussion see Caputo, 1993, Ziarek, 1989, Drabinski, 1994, Atterton, 1992, Gottlieb, 1994). I will limit myself to an overview of his arguments concerning *responsibility for Otherness in Communication*, in contrast especially to Husserl's notion of self-responsibility in internal time consciousness.[3]

As Lingis (in Levinas, 1991) notes, Levinas develops a phenomenology of Otherness in *Totality and Infinity*, especially with regard to relations between the intentional and the proximate, the sensuous and the signifying, and "the theme of the skin caressed contrasted with the face addressed" (xv). Levinas then assumes these relations in *Otherwise than Being or Beyond Essence* (1991, original publication 1974) as he develops the notion of responsibility, not from the vantage point of a self who intends through a transcendental act, as in Husserl, but as an *ethical relation* understood as being responsible for the Otherness of the other. The Other so conceived (with the upper case *O*) is not thought in terms of the *identity* of the other of the intersubjective relation but as an alterity that summons one's attention and obligation to listen and respond *as an addressee of a demand that is heard through, but not articulated by, the other.* Facing a homeless child afflicted with AIDS might be considered a paradigm case of an alterity that demands, even though the child does not speak the demand and even though the one addressed or *faced* may not know how to adequately respond (see Caputo, 1993).

In this sense, then, *I am first and foremost an addressee who faces demands and obligations*, not an addressor who through some "living present" perceives and appropriates a world of significations and relations. Moreover, as addressee I am not the recipient of a message as in a bit of information that can be heard on the content plane of expression, which is then interpreted and fed back to an addressor who I can see in the present or at least configure in my imagination as being potentially present (as in imagining readers of this essay for example). Rather, I am an addressee of a command, demand, request, or some other "prescription," *the addressor of which cannot be seen or heard in any empirical or scientific sense whatsoever.* The demand heard *through the child* is not spoken by the child, or in a more mundane institutional sense, I might "receive" a group norm ("thou shalt not ...") that proscribes certain conduct even though neither I nor anybody else in or outside of the group has verbally expressed the norm to me or themselves.

The demand implied by the presence of the child, and the demand implied by the tacitly understood group norm, though neither are articulated, have prescriptive or perlocutionary force.[4] To the extent that the demand is linked to moral law, valorizes an ethical relation between self and other but resides beyond the identity of the other, its force of Otherness is infinite and marked by Levinas with the term *"illeity."*[5] Otherness, for Levinas (1991) is a spiritual force whose trace "cannot be tracked down like game by a hunter" (12) but whose enigmatic presence can be felt in the obligation for or responsibility to others. It forms a kind of third party that voices ineffably and absently through a "presence" of others. Without this sense of Otherness, in Levinas's conception, communication becomes corrupt or easily corruptible.[6]

Apart from the pious nature of this conception, a piety that becomes problematical (and this is Lyotard's point) when one considers the godlike force of the "ethical" relations implied by some genres of discourse (including theologies), my interest concerns the way in which Levinas conceives subjectivity and the intersubjective relation as actually formed by Otherness. In what serves as a cogent introduction to the issues of communication addressed in *Otherwise than Being*, Levinas (1984) states:

Subjectivity is not for itself; it is . . . initially for another.
. . . the proximity of the Other is presented as the fact that
the Other is not simply close to me in space, or close like
a parent, but approaches me insofar as I feel myself—insofar as I am—responsible for her. (194)

[T]he intersubjective relation is a non-symmetrical relation. In this sense I am responsible for the Other without
waiting for reciprocity, even if I were to die for it. Reciprocity is her affair. It is precisely insofar as the relationship between the Other and me is not reciprocal that I am
subjected to the Other; and I am "subject" essentially in this
sense (195).

Being subject to is thus not a matter of identity or sameness
("*ipseity*" in Levinas's terms), although Levinas emphasizes that one
must always attempt to *substitute* oneself for the other. Substitution—
imaginatively and affectively putting oneself in the place of another—
is tempered by the inability of ever actually being able to do so
completely, of ever being able to bring the other of the intersubjective
relation into the Same. To the extent that substitution is demanded but
can never be achieved, the self is always "dissembled" by engaging the
other "responsibly." One is displaced both temporally and spatially. He
or she must move away from the familiarity of home, so to speak, and
become *unheimlichkeit*—without a home (see Lyotard, 1988, 171). Such
a dissembling and displacement is precisely what is required for "responsible" communication even though the intensities of such movement cannot be represented or otherwise delimited empirically or
scientifically.

According to Levinas (1991), then, "communication would be
impossible if it should have to begin in the ego, a free subject, to whom
every other would be only a limitation that invites war, domination,
precaution and information" (119). To assume that communication begins
and ends with the ego, the subject who intends, is to valorize the drive
toward certainty when it is precisely the *uncertainty of the other* that
mobilizes communication and creates a kind of obsession to respond
even when no "message" per se has been sent. It is through an embodi-
ment of this uncertainty that one becomes responsible for the other with
no guarantees that this responsibility will be reciprocated. With uncertainty comes risk:

The relationship is also a *resignation* (prior to any decision,
in passivity) *at the risk of misunderstanding* (like in love,
where, unless one does not love with love, one has to resign
oneself to not being loved), *at the risk of lack of and refusal
of communication*. The ego that thematizes is also founded

in the responsibility and substitution. Regarding communication and transcendence one can indeed only speak of the
uncertainty. Communication is an adventure of a subjectivity, different from that which is dominated by the concern
to recover itself, different from that of coinciding in consciousness; it will involve *uncertainty*. It is by virtue of its
eidos possible only in *sacrifice*, which is the approach of
him for which one is responsible (Levinas 1991, 120; emphasis added).

Responsibility for the other *at the risk of misunderstanding and
refusal of communication* is an uncertain adventure that requires resignation and sacrifice. It is a feeling that is anterior even to the pragmatic
conceptualization of the consequences of one's feeling of responsibility.
It is not a duty, whereby the contours of moral action are known in
advance cognitively but an irrevocable call that imprints affectively and
drives one to accommodate according to the terms of the Other. To
accommodate in such a manner is to love asymmetrically, without
expectation of reciprocity, or at the risk of loss of that which one loves.
One is "taken hostage" by the homeless child, by one's parent who is
dying, by the other who is in agony, by the other who refuses love in
return, not because one *should* be taken according to the dictates of an
ethical system but because one has no choice. One is driven bodily to
sacrifice self. When the other who is dying looks at you with her eyes
full of morphine you are irrevocably taken. When you reach and touch
her forehead she relaxes. What you say is not important, but that
you "speak" through the gesture of touching or by saying "it will be
OK" even though you both know it will not be OK, constitutes an
acknowledgement of Otherness, communicates the risk and uncertainty
of substitution, and provides some "relief" of the other's agony. Through
such a gesture or "saying" you are displaced, lose track of time, lose
track even of where or how you are, all projects put on hold. Only a
narcissist—or a technoscientist who says he has done all he can do to
alleviate the pain—would walk away from such a call.

The call is a kind of brute force of the Other that constrains and
affects discourse without being represented in discourse or even presented empirically as that which can be discoursed about. In responding
to this call, one becomes Other even to oneself. The self is sacrificed
through a preconscious bodily act of obligation, transposed temporally
and spatially, and reconstituted communicatively in a state that makes
no "sense" from the perspective of "cognitive" genres of discourse.

Derrida (1991) suggests, in response to *Otherwise than Being or
Beyond Essence*, that receiving and responding to Otherness in the
sacrificial manner described by Levinas is not so much a transgression
in the sense of violating the dictates of a genre of discourse but rather

an interval or interruption that dissembles any "discursive" intentionality (20–22). Even though it cannot be represented in discourse in any
isomorphic way, Otherness continually and irrevocably interrupts
discourse's serial flow. But if this is so, one might ask, how can such
dissembling and displacement be actually known or otherwise shown
except through discourse? And is the interruption that dissembles something Other than what one projects as a certain horizon of meaning or
field of perception that can be indicated or symbolized in one way or
another?

In addressing these questions and the contradictions they portend,
I would like to elaborate through a more commonplace example the
Levinassian case against the phenomenological tradition stemming from
Husserl.

In writing I am expressing myself toward others who are removed
temporally, spatially, and bodily. There is no communication in the
sense that a series of phrases are heard in any sense of immediacy
(except for myself "hearing" my thoughts and feelings *intra*personally
at this very moment), or meanings understood and responded to as in
the immediacy of two people in the same room talking to one another.
But there is a sense of communication in that I imagine the immanent
and imminent presence of certain others whom I expect will read this
work. To the extent that others are "present" for me while writing, even
though they are absent physically and temporally, and to the extent that
I "hear" the demands of their presence and take responsibility for their
views but am unable to ask anything of them in turn, then I am beginning to trace the uncertainty of Otherness that approaches, speaks through
them, and dissembles my writing without them being responsible for it.

From a phenomenological (Husserlian) perspective, these "others" and the demands heard through their altogether "absent" presence
exist on a horizon of my own intentional field, within the spheres of my
own signification, and they themselves can thus be perceived and signified imaginatively without Otherness demanding that I write one thing
or another. A Husserlian would argue that my self-responsibility at this
present time and my intentionality in writing configures the Otherness
of these others without necessarily being taken hostage or otherwise
determined by that. It is my conscious experience of writing and the
retentions and protentions that such writing invokes that make the ad-
vent of my sense of others and Otherness possible, not the other way
around (cf. Langsdorf, 1993).

From the Husserlian position of a synchronic "living present," all
of the preceding ideas about Otherness congeal within me, this author,
this person, this subject who writes and struggles with phrases to make
sense and fulfill a purpose. Does this struggle not presume a certain
autonomy with regard to phrasing? Even though selected others are
present in their absence (for me) and I feel a sense of responsibility or

even fidelity to their interests and teachings, do not these phrases and the ideas and feelings traced through them have a volitional force in my own subjectivity? A force that is presupposed by any reception of Otherness? I am able to write/speak/attend and through this I am able to "reach through a thin layer of time" (Merleau-Ponty 1986, 416)[7] and take on the demands or requests of others and this Otherness. How could it be otherwise?

In the Husserlian living present, then, the significance of the "object of consciousness"—for example, the other in communication—is revealed, not "in itself" as in the metaphysical illusion that an object (or other) "speaks for itself," but *authentically* "for myself." "Consciousness of . . . " in transcendence heightens the significance of the other to the extent that a Self takes it up. At that moment of appropriation "the mode of presentation" of the other changes, and my gaze "turns back on itself . . . changes . . . direction . . . and . . . lifts the veil that separates the ego from its own truth" (Husserl noted in Lyotard 1991, 50–51.)[8] This moment in transcendence is the true state of freedom, in the Husserlian view, since it accomplishes several remarkable feats at once. While remaining "interlaced with the world," the Ego, as concrete constituting subject, becomes "fully aware of itself" in the synthesis of a series of *nows*, which, in turn, allow for a recognition of the Other in his or her authenticity (Thao, quoted in Lyotard 1991, 51). This transcendental moment is an *origin* that subsumes the "diachrony of the Other." Lyotard notes, however, that

> [i]t can be understood that the now is the permanent point of origin for the ecstasis [ek-stasis] of time. This will be the "modern" version of temporalization, the one that prevails in Augustine and Husserl: a constituting time, the "living present," in the charge of a transcendental subject, and a constituted, diachronic time on the side of the object, the diegetic referent. In which time, though, shall the synthesis of transcendental and empirical time take place? This synthesis must nevertheless take place, if it is true that the now never escapes diachrony. (1988, Aristotle Notice, p. 73)

Indeed, the now (a person's, society's, or culture's "living present;" synchrony) never does escape diachrony (objects and others with unique histories and practices that infringe upon the interrupt the "now"), and this is Levinas's point. To receive and respond to the force and import of Otherness, then, one "stay[s] with the extreme situation of a diachronic thought" (Levinas, 1991, 7) and hence sacrifices what perhaps "should" be the case but is not. Especially when faced with an other who is in existential crisis—who, for example, suffers terror, starvation, torture, oppression, or some other form of injustice—one's own "living present" and its associated projects suffer an irrevocable dissolution. The other simply cannot be synthesized into my synchronic (or ecstatic) moment. And yet this other summons my attention and respect, takes me hostage, encourages me to put myself in her place, and in so doing I am displaced—not in her synchronic moment—but in a time that is neither hers nor my own as they had been previously assumed or imagined. To the extent that the "I" is dissembled and displaced, embodies uncertainty and possible refusal, then that "I" is capable of perhaps "saying" something of significance rather than simply repeating what has already been said or what might be expected to have been said according to preconceived models or hypotheses. Again, such a "saying" requires that the "I" is *first and foremost an addressee who is responding to a call.*

In writing, then, I am being influenced by an Otherness that is, indeed, received through an intentional field but does not originate cognitively from my position as an addressor of "messages" and is not expressed concretely by empirical others. Further, Otherness in the Levinassian sense involves a sensibility that is not merely a matter of how others have influenced or are imaginatively influencing my thought at this very moment of writing, but a sensibility that is *responsible for their responsibility (their damages, agonies, uncertainties, fallibilities, vulnerabilities, and so on) without them being responsible for me or my writing.* Out of such a metaresponsibility comes this "saying" that is "preoriginal" or preontological in that it does not have an origin in the signified content of expression formed in particular phrases or messages but precedes and interrupts even that level of "message exchange." Such a "saying" does not have an origin in particular beings but is "otherwise" from even the conception of Being or beings, otherwise even from the rules of language—indeterminate, enigmatic, disruptive, thought at a distance but more proximate than even the lines on this page.

Any such "saying" remains diachronic—that is, it cannot be synthesized wholly or even partially in the form of indexical or symbolic relations of a (synchronic) living present. A discursive analysis of the statement, "It will be OK," which one makes to one's dying mother, says nothing about the sense of being taken by Otherness at that singular time and place. Though the significance of that utterance may reside on some horizon of one's perceptual field, within the sphere of one's signifying acts, and reflect a network of intentionalities, it cannot be grasped in its density nor indicated by conventional signs of demonstration. There is about such significance something uncertain and compelling, something that interrupts the mundanity of one's everyday discourse, makes one hesitate, dissembles thought, and leaves one grasping and gaping at that which one can never appropriate and fully understand.

I am seeking in this writing to articulate the force of significance that comes from answering the call of Otherness. I want to define its contours, but I cannot do so adequately. I fail at every attempt, and so this discourse becomes a kind of fiction-writing. Some readers of this essay may complain, "What is this Otherness and this 'saying'? You have failed to demonstrate its existence." And by its very conditions, it must be so. "Then how can you even conceive this Otherness that is taking you from the comforts of your 'home'?" I do not "know," yet the recognition of its reality and force keeps me writing, keeps me not at home (*unheimlichkeit*), works against the grain of any depiction of a true account, is interminable, and generates a condition of perpetual and often agonizing movement which, as Lyotard (1988) puts it,

> gathers within itself the contradictory relation between ego and other. In acceding to the request[s] I go out far away from my home, as a hostage, without ever taking up habitation with you, nor ever being your guest, since you have no residence, but I also thereby fulfill my calling, which is to be at home no longer. . . . The true understood as appropriation of the other, even if it is done through some "graphism," is false. (171)

Again, in acceding to the demands or requests of Otherness and becoming *unheimlichkeit*, one is displaced not simply in terms of the implied spatial relations of being in one place or another—as is the case with the hypostatized "field" of the ethnographer, for example. One is, moreover, displaced in time, placed up against a different past or different future than what one may have thought would have been otherwise. In being responsible even for the other's responsibility in the intersubjective relation, diachrony—the *forces* of the past (especially that which tends toward the forgotten) and the future (possibilities and consequences imagined and unimaginable)—that elude concrete representation in discourse, has primacy over the "living present" of synchrony, whether conceived positivistically or phenomenologically.

Toward the Communicable

Thus far, I have attempted to show, following Levinas primarily, how being responsible even for the responsibility of the Other requires that one be taken hostage, situated first and foremost as an addressee, rendered *unheimlichkeit*, and faced with the radicality of diachronic time that problematizes any "consciousness of . . ." in the Husserlian sense. The resulting dissembling of self produces the possibility of a "saying" whose significance is not tied to already established genres of discourse that seek to explain the other, or even necessarily to the discursive structures and functions of what is actually said. Being subject to Otherness in the Levinassian sense, then, does not silence a person or determine what is to be said but actually gives a person the capacity to speak in such a way that a difference is made, even though what is actually said may be fictional, phatic, or otherwise insignificant from a communication science point of view. As Lingis (1994) notes,

> You have to say something—something that language cannot say, something that is not in the resources of common discourse to be able to say, and something that is, in the end, inessential. It is the saying that is imperative: your hand extended to the one who is departing, the light of your eyes meeting the eyes of the other that are turned to where there is nothing to see, and the warmth of your voice brought to her as her own breath gives way. This situation is not only the end of language—the last moment when all we have to say to one another ends in the silence and death of the one to whom it has to be said and in the speechlessness and sobs of the one who has come to say something. It is also the beginning, the beginning of communication. (114)

By facing and being receptive to Otherness, I find that I am free to speak in a way that is not predetermined, free to invent new idioms to express what is enshrouded in silence. This is possible, in Lyotard's terms, only to the extent that I am "passible to" the "communicability" of that which is donated affectively (in Levinassian sense) but resists being communicated cognitively (in scientific, economic, or technological senses). In being "passible to" the uncertainties and risks of Otherness, Lyotard argues, a *sensus communis* is possible based on an aesthetic feeling that is "universally communicable." Scientific method, or any epistemology determined largely by the rules of a cognitive genre of discourse, cannot account for this sense of communicability since science requires the "reality" of a referent to be empirically demarcated and verified through processes of ostension (Q.E.D. or Q.E.I.). There are, however, many ideas and experiences that cannot be ostensively demonstrated, such as the ideas of freedom, nation, value, and the feeling of being terrorized or otherwise damaged or wronged: "There exist no procedures instituted to establish or refute [these realities] in the cognitive sense. That is why they give rise to differends" (Lyotard, 1988, 36; see also 28, 61, and Kant Notice 4, p. 161).

Indeed, it would appear that many cognitive genres of discourse—especially the economic and technoscientific—gloss or obscure and certainty are not be-holden to communicability. Consider the images of bombing in the Persian Gulf War—do the fascinated viewers of the flashes of light gain a sense of what it is like to have hundreds of pin-sized shards of metal implanted in one's flesh? One might counter that the fascinating images of starvation in Somalia, for example, generated an international response—but what of hunger in Somalia now? It is being forgotten. Or consider the insipid representation of "others" (the homeless, disabled, disfranchised, and so on) in much positivistically oriented research—do researchers or readers develop a sense of what it is like to be damaged and then restricted with regard to speaking or acting in a way that will expiate or otherwise relieve the damages? Such research ultimately—though not "intentionally"—contributes to the spectacle-ization of injustices that attracts momentary (synchronic) fascination but is then forgotten.

But how does one engage or present communicability or its lack? How is one passible to It? How does one develop a capability for living through or otherwise facing the sublimity of spectacles without being silenced or losing his or her life? These are the principal questions posed by postmodernity for any prudent "communication" inquirer who is receptive to being addressed by them. I will take them up by first clarifying Lyotard's development of the notion of passibility, which he takes from Kant's *Critique of Judgment*:[9]

> Passibility as the possibility of experiencing (*pathos*) pre-supposes a donation. If we are in a state of passibility, it's that something is happening to us, and when this passibility has a fundamental status, the donation itself is something fundamental, originary. What happens to us is not at all something we have first controlled, programmed, grasped by a concept [*Begriff*]. Or else, if what we are passible to has first been plotted conceptually, how can it *seize us*? How can it test us if we already know, or if we can know— of what, with what, for what, it is done? Or else, if such a feeling, in the very radical sense that Kant tries to give this term, takes place, it must be admitted that what happens to us disconcerts us. (1991, 110–11)[10]

Passibility understood as *pathos* is a transitive state—one is al-ways *passible to* some presentation—and this transitivity of feeling is *universally communicable*. Any person is capable of being taken (*pa-thos*) by beauty, for example, even though each may have received some "thing" differently when the attempt is made to reproduce that feeling conceptually on the content level of expression. Since any con-ceptual communication between interlocutors presupposes that some-thing in common has been received, then some form of communicability has already taken place. How can I articulate a concept of something that I have not already been passible to? It is impossible. Echoing

Levinas, then, Lyotard argues that such communicability is not "merely a subjective presence" but "as a demand and not as a fact, precisely because it is assumed to be originary, *ontological*, eludes communicational activity, which is not a receptiveness but something which is managed, which is done" (1991, 109).

In his discussion of communicability Lyotard sets up the problem of "spectacle-ization" by first discussing how one is "passible to" works of art (broadly conceived) or that which is donated to us through a certain engagement of beauty, grace, elegance, grandeur, dignity perhaps, and so on. A receptiveness to this Otherness (which befalls us in Levinassian sense) configures a possible "community of feeling" that is "anterior to all communication and pragmatics. The cutting out of intersubjective relations has not yet happened and there would be an assenting, a unanimity possible and capable of being demanded, with an order which cannot 'yet' be that of argumentation between rational and speaking subjects" (Lyotard 1991, 110).

In contrast especially to Habermas,[11] Lyotard argues that such an "aesthetic" passage is of a different order than that which might link through communicative praxis ethical, political, and cognitive universes of discourse. "Passibility" is better conceived as a receptiveness required when responding to the "demand" of a work of art or the "call" of some Other. Rather than establishing a synthesis in communicative action, then, Lyotard seeks to depict how "passibility" can obligate one to the demands of Others prior to any communication exchange. This attentiveness changes the stakes of the political, he argues, as well as the ethical and the cognitive. Not that "passages" in Habermas's sense are not possible, but they are better conceived as linkages of part to part that change with each new reception of an event, not totalities that hold power over time and hence determine criteria for judgment in ever more rigorous (scientific) ways.

The scientific enterprise, especially the technoscience associated with the "little ideology of communication" (Lyotard, 1991, 116), not only ignores communicability (which is nonempirical, alogical, nonrational, and so on) it actually contributes to its obliteration, in Lyotard's view, and this is "our current fate." The valorization of schemata as models that link isomorphically the sensible with the conceptual lays the groundwork for such obliteration. The result is that forms (of Otherness) which may have otherwise presented themselves for our contemplation, either recede (are forgotten) or are never actually presented, which leaves a kind of void in space and time—that is, there is no im-mediate communicability whatsoever (Lyotard, 1991, 112–13). In its place is the spectacle—the servile, the contemptible, the wretched, the abject. Lyotard (1991), following Kant, argues that such spectacles produce a *feeling of the sublime*,

which exceed[s] any real presentation of a form, in other
words, where what is signified is the superiority of our
power of freedom *vis-à-vis* the one manifested in the spectacle itself. In singling out the sublime, Kant places the
accent on something directly related to the problem of space
and time. The free-floating forms which aroused the feeling
of the beautiful come to be lacking. In a certain way the
question of the sublime is closely linked to what Heidegger
calls the retreat of Being, retreat of donation. For Heidegger,
the welcome accorded something sensory, in other words
some meaning embodied in the here-and-now before any
concept, no longer has place and moment. This retreat signifies our current fate. (113)

If we accept this line of thinking, then most communication science, to the extent that it ignores or even "obliterates" communicability,
potentially contributes to the perpetuation, if not the production, of
spectacles. Injustices, rather than being ameliorated, are actually proliferated. Differends, rather than producing new idioms that might express
a wrong, are circumscribed by a language of representational truth.

To return to the questions posed previously, then, what are the
options for those interested in a philosophy of "communication" that
does not contribute to the retreat of Being, the production of spectacles,
and the perpetuation of injustices? What is there to say or do for the
inquirer who faces the sublimity of a spectacle and wishes to respond
to it other than by signifying his or her own freedom with regard to it?
What can the inquirer say or do who wishes to represent even the
beauty and dignity of a *sensus communis*? In addressing these questions, and concluding this essay, I will return to the notion of possibility.

To be possible is not to be passive, but neither is it to be active
in the sense assumed in communication activity or interactivity, the
demand for which "instead proves that there should be more intervention, and that we are thus through with aesthetic feeling" (Lyotard,
1991, 116). Not to be through with aesthetic feeling means that where
there is a *sensus communis* as I have outlined it here, one would ask not
simply what, how, or why that which is presented is present, but contemplate its "modality of reception" and the "obligatory belonging" that
constitutes the community of feeling associated with this reception. In
this *sensus*, contemplation is not a "devalorized passivity," nor is it
characterized by re-actions dictated by a genre of discourse that is eager
to explain or explicate the communicability according to the terms of
message exchange (see Lyotard, 1991, 117–18). Rather, contemplation
of communicability presupposes that the one contemplating is already
a part of the *sensus communis* instantiated by the feeling. One knows
one is part of such a community by first asking the question "Is it

happening?" If it is not "destined for you, there is no way to feel it. You are touched, you will only know this afterwards" (Lyotard, 1991, 118).

To avoid the legitimation or perpetuation of spectacles, a so-called "communication" inquirer might inquire in the manner suggested by avant-garde artists. These latter not only belong to a *sensus communis* receptive to Otherness and paint reception but are dedicated also to facing formlessness—the sublimity of the spectacle left in the wake of the retreat of Being. In the agonies and injustices of that silence they give it space and time (Lyotard, 1991, 115; see also 1989a; Lyotard and Thebaud, 1989) by bearing witness and "painting" inventively tones of grief that might adequately, albeit experimentally, disclose the differend marked by that feeling. This requires a dissembling of themselves, a displacement in "present" time, an uncertain expenditure. The expressive rules of such an expenditure are neither known beforehand nor already constituted ready to be discovered.

How does one face the "ontological melancholy" of such a spectacle and find anything to say or to paint, let alone potentially contribute to any reinvigoration of communicability? By what rules or methods does one face an abyss where Otherness is receding and attempt to constitute a world? And how does one imagine the results or consequences of such an expenditure through which there may be nothing to gain and perhaps everything to lose? The response to these questions may sound glib: One suffers the agonies of such a "facing" and makes up the rules as one goes, or in Lyotard's terms, one "generate[s] occurrences before knowing the rules of this generativity" (Lyotard, 1991, 72). And one does so with little or no concern for *determining* these rules, especially for future applications or interventions with other singular spectacles. One certainly does not attempt to gain time or to control the spectacle in accordance with the dictates of an institutional bureaucracy or the information theoretic science of communication. Rather, one loses time in facing such an abyss, then finds oneself in a different order of time being questioned by the spectacle itself, the uncertainties and risks of which produce considerable fear and trembling but also, potentially, some form of "relief"—both existential and aesthetic.

Let me emphasize this point: Whether receiving the event of Otherness and becoming obligated to belong to a *sensus communis*, or facing the spectacle that is bereft of any donation of Otherness, one must learn *to stay put and be questioned by it* if one hopes to make a difference with regard to "our current fate" (see Lyotard 1991, 74). One must learn to appreciate that the other bereft of Otherness has become radically Other in turn—miserable, contemptible, enigmatic, and all too easily forgotten. To paint the radicality of this picture, to provide some "relief," to find pertinent idioms for expressing the damages or wrongs disclosed in the wake of any "retreat of Being," one must be anchored in the "immediate 'passion' of what happens" (Lyotard, 1991, 118) and give up one's freedom with respect to controlling what is witnessed. With such expenditure, anything is possible, including death.

Concluding Remarks

With regard to the stakes of this interrogation of Otherness for the science of communication, let me say this: If messages and their exchanges are derived not from an intentional intersubjective relation but, as Lyotard suggests, from a more inarticulate and nonempirical "communicability" of feeling and obligation that results from being subjected to phrases and Otherness, then the scientific study of messages and exchanges would be derivative and even superfluous to the extent that it does not (or cannot, according to its own methods of validation) take such communicability into account.

Moreover, and more reproving, communication inquiry that ignores Otherness and insists that the only true object of research is that which can be empirically or logically delimited—and in such insistence refuses to reflect critically on the interests it serves—then such inquiry and the interventions it recommends would be in constant danger of contributing directly to an obliteration of "communicability" and the perpetuation of spectacles. The "results" of such inquiry, other than legitimating the marginality of abject Others, would involve little more than playing out the stakes determined or the truth conditions implied by the genre of scientific discourse it serves, which is a discourse that ignores or forgets the historical and political forces that interrupt and dissemble the events it wants so eagerly to delimit for purposes of prediction, intervention, and publication.

With regard to phenomenology in the Husserlian tradition, rather than a intentional subject or quasi-objectivist science that takes up events and texts, a "saying" in Levinassian sense would be possible only with a recognition of how the event takes up subjects and throws them into history, mythology, religion, experiment, or a politics that is not necessarily their own. For Levinas, "saying" suggests that a subject has been displaced in the extreme by diachrony, by an Otherness traced in a past and future that cannot be known essentially through signs. In "saying," the radical presence of the past and future undermine a binding to identity and essences that might be perceived to hold over time, at least if the perceiver is a communication inquirer who seeks stasis better to (ostensibly) know and control the other. Once such a stasis is legitimated, however, and the identity of the knower is known—whether as authority, method, or tradition—then one worldview takes precedence over others, a worldview that purports to *knowing*. This, in the Levinassian scheme of things, is delusion and, from Lyotard's point of view, a travesty.

To embody the radical approach to communication inquiry that Levinas and Lyotard recommend, one must restore the presence of diachrony "in the extreme." To interrogate, then, one must first feel the passion invoked by being an addressee of a call; one must feel irrevocably compelled to respond, and one must find oneself asking the question, "Is it happening?" Sitting with this question—whether faced with the engaging aesthetic of a *sensus communis* or the sublime horror of a spectacle—invokes the limits, if not the treason, of "communication."

Notes

1. Lyotard (1988) states the problem of the information theoretic view of communication as follows: "Communication is the exchange of messages, exchange the communication of goods. The instances of communication like those of exchange are definable only in terms of property and propriety [*propriété*]: the propriety of information analogous to the propriety of uses. And just as the flow of uses can be controlled, so can the flow of information. As a perverse use is repressed, a dangerous bit of information is banned. As a need is diverted and motivation created, an addressor is led to say something other than what he or she was going to say. The problem of language, thus posited in terms of communication, leads to that of the needs and beliefs of interlocutors. The linguist becomes an expert before the communication arbitration board. The essential problem he or she has to regulate is that of sense as a unit of exchange independent of the needs and beliefs of interlocutors" (20). References to Lyotard's *The Differend: Phrases in Dispute* are to paragraph numbers rather than pages. However, references to his "Notices" in the text of *The differend* will be to the particular Notice and page number.

2. Merleau-Ponty (1986) emphasizes that movement toward consciousness of some event or other always involves a bodily motility that inhabits space and time in a preobjective or preindicative operation. Thus "operative intentionality" is distinguished from intellection or an "intentionality of act" in the same sense that "I can" or "I am able to" (which implies movement toward) are distinguished from the Cartesian "I think" (which implies stasis). For a technical elaboration of this argument that draws extensively on research with patients who suffer from apraxia and other bodily "disorders," see Merleau-Ponty (1986, chapter 3), Sacks (1987), and Kristeva (1984). More explicitly in terms of interpersonal communication, see Lanigan (1988): "The ability of human communicators to switch back and forth between speaking and listening, to do both simultaneously, to remove the spatially real into memory, or project the conceptually real into memory, or project the conceptually real into time as future expectation—all suggest the way

in which communication is an object of consciousness and not the mere announcement of purpose" (24–25).

3. See Caputo (1993) for a fuller discussion of Levinas's influence on Derrida and Lyotard, especially. For a recent exposition of Levinas's notions of responsibility and Otherness in terms of community, see Lingis (1994). For a critique of Husserl with regard to the primacy of speech in the constitution and signification of phenomena, see Derrida (1973). For a presentation of the influence of Husserl's theory of signs in communication theory and research, see Lanigan (1988) and Smith (1993).

4. In the performative sense defined by Austin (1962): "it indicates that the issuing of the utterance is the performing of an action—it is not normally thought of as just saying something" (6–7). And "With performative utterances are contrasted, for example, 'constative' utterances: to issue a statement. To issue a performative utterance is, for example, to make a bet" (62). Constatives are associated with truth conditions, performatives with obligations—a bet, a promise, and so on. Lyotard (1988) takes Austin one step further: the phrase "The meeting is called to order" is not performative because its addressor is the chairperson of the meeting. The addressor is the chairperson of the meeting to the extent that the phrase in question is performative. The equation chairmanship-performativity is independent of the context. If the phrase is performative and the addressor is not the chairperson, he or she becomes the chairperson; if it is not performative and the addressor is the chairperson, he or she ceases to be the chairperson (142; see also 205 for a discussion of the relation between the normative and the performative; and Levinas Notice, section 1).

5. "Illeity lies outside the 'thou' and the thematization of objects. A neologism formed with *il* (he) or *ille*, it indicates a way of concerning me without entering into conjunction with me. To be sure, we have to indicate the element in which this *concerning* occurs. If the relationship with illeity were a relationship of consciousness, "he" would designate a theme, as the "thou" in Buber's I-thou relations does, probably—for Buber has never brought out in a positive way the spiritual element in which the I-thou relationship is produced. The illeity in the beyond-being is the fact that its coming toward me is a departure, that which makes this departure, this diachrony, be more than a term of negative theology, is my responsibility for the others" (Levinas, 1991, 12–13).

6. Again, I do not wish to delve too far into the theological portent of the Levinassian position. Rather, I refer the reader to the ways in which Caputo (1993), Derrida (1991), and Lyotard (1988) appropriate and critique his work. I will say that the ethical relation of Otherness is a crucial dimension of deconstructionist and postmodern theory, as developed by Derrida and Lyotard, that is often bypassed by

critics and commentators in philosophy, literature, communication, and other fields. See Caputo (1993), especially, for an accessible presentation and critique of Levinas's influence on deconstruction.

7. In revising Husserl's notions of retention and protention, Merleau-Ponty (1986) states: "[The intentionalities] do not run from a central I, but from my perceptual field itself, so to speak, which draws along in its wake its own horizon of retentions, and bites into the future with its protentions. I do not pass through a series of instances of now, the images of which I preserve and which, placed end to end, make a line. With the arrival of every moment, its predecessor undergoes a change: I still have it in hand and it is still there, but already it is sinking away below the level of presents; in order to retain it, I need to reach through a thin layer of time" (416; see also Lyotard, 1991).

8. I am drawing here from Lyotard's (1990) first work on phenomenology, originally published in 1954. His views have changed radically since then, evident especially in *the Differend*. For discussions of Lyotard's relationship to phenomenology, hermeneutics, and deconstruction, see Gasche (1979), Descombes (1980), Bennington (1988), Ormiston (1990), Caputo (1993), and Smith (1994).

9. For further discussion of Lyotard's take on Kant, see the four Kant Notices in Lyotard (1988, 61, 118, 130, 161). See also Lyotard's (1994) lectures on Kant translated as *Lessons on the Analytic of the Sublime*, which focuses on sections 23-29 of Kant's *Critique of Judgment*. For the linkage to Levinas's notion of Otherness, see Lyotard (1988) and Surber (1994). For critical discussions see Piche (1993), Drolet (1994), and Ingram (1988).

10. Much of the ensuing discussion is taken from chapter 8 in Lyotard's (1991) collection of essays entitled *The Inhuman*. Related discussion can be found in chapters 1 and 5.

11. In *The Postmodern Condition*, Lyotard (1989) takes issue with Habermas's defense of modernity as a project of the Enlightenment. Habermas, Lyotard suggests, wishes to reinstate the aesthetic as that which could reunify (conceptually and consensually) the "splintering of culture and its separation from concrete existence" (72). One's task, in Habermas's view, is to find ways of using aesthetics as a language game that investigates a "living historical situation" and in so doing "bridge the gap between cognitive, ethical, and political discourses . . . opening the way to a unity of experience" (72). Such a project, in Lyotard's view, is problematical to the extent that new unities of experience (as Habermas conceives them) reduce the rich gestural, emotional, and otherwise bodily nuances of experience to rationally constituted "passages." Such "passages" are posterior rather than anterior to conceptual communication as Lyotard is defining it.

In contrast, Habermas argues that aesthetic communication is not reductionistic but a way of illuminating the unities of an event or events.

Rationality practiced as an aesthetic sensibility allows (phenomenologically but not transcendentally) for contingent and fallible constructions that take up the normative expectations, cognitive processes, and political orientations of people in "living historical situations." Habermas suggests that an aesthetics taken *from* the world (rather than to it) defines communicative pragmatics and, as such, is self-critical and on guard against exclusions and damages of all kinds and degrees.

For further elaboration see especially Habermas (1985, 1986) and Lyotard (1988, 1989a). See also Rorty (1985), Benhabib (1992), and Descombes (1993).

References

Atterton, P. (1992, Spring). Levinas and the language of peace: A response to Derrida. *Philosophy Today*, pp. 59–70.

Austin, J. (1962). *How to do things with words*. London: Oxford University Press.

Benhabib, S. (1992). *Situating the Self*. New York: Routledge.

Benjamin, A. (1989). *The Lyotard Reader*. Cambridge, Mass. Basil Blackwell.

Bennington, G. (1988). *Lyotard: Writing the Event*. New York: Columbia University Press.

Bochner, A. (1985). Perspectives on inquiry: Representation, conversation, and reflection. In M. Knapp (Ed.): *Handbook of Interpersonal Communication*. Beverly Hills, Calif.: Sage.

Caputo, J. D. (1993). *Against Ethics: Contributions to a Poetics of Obligation with Constant Reference to Deconstruction*. Bloomington: Indiana University Press.

Dalton, S. (1994, Fall). Lyotard's peregrination: Three (and-a-half) responses to the call for justice. *Philosophy Today*, pp. 227–42.

Derrida, J. (1973). *Speech and Phenomena: And Other Essays on Husserl's Theory of Signs*. (D. A. Allison, Trans.) Evanston, Ill.: Northwestern University Press.

———. (1991). At this very moment in the work here I am. In R. Bernasconi and S. Critchley (Eds.): *Re-reading Levinas*. Bloomington: Indiana University Press.

Descombes, V. (1989). *Modern French Philosophy*. (L. Scott-Fox and J. M. Harding, Trans.) Cambridge, England: Cambridge University Press.

———. (1993). *The Barometer of Modern Reason: On the Philosophies of Current Events*. New York: Oxford University Press.

Drabinski, J. E. (1994, Summer). The status of the transcendental in Levinas' thought. *Philosophy Today*, pp. 149–58.

Drolet, M. (1994). The wild and the sublime: Lyotard's postmodern politics. *Political Studies* 42:259–73.

Gasche, R. (1979). Deconstruction as criticism. *Glyphe* 6:177–216.

Gottlieb, R. S. (1994, Summer). Ethics and trauma: Levinas, feminism, and deep ecology. *Cross Currents*, pp. 222–40.

Habermas, J. (1985). Questions and counterquestions. In R. Bernstein (Ed.): *Habermas and Modernity.* Cambridge, Mass.: MIT Press.

———. (1986). *Autonomy and Solidarity: Interviews with Jürgen Habermas.* (P. Dews, Ed.) New York: Verso.

Ingram, D. (1988). The postmodern Kantianism of Arendt and Lyotard. *Review of Metaphysics* 42:51–77.

Jakobson, R. (1960). Closing statement: Linguistics and poetics. In R. E. Innis (Ed.): *Semiotics: An Introductory Anthology.* Bloomington: Indiana University Press.

Krippendorff, K. (1993). The past of communication's hoped-for future. *Journal of Communication* 3:34–44.

Kristeva, J. (1984). *Revolution in Poetic Language.* (M. Waler, Trans.) New York: Columbia University Press.

Langsdorf, L. (1993). Words of others and sightings/citings/sitings of self. In I. Angus and L. Langsdorf (Eds.): *The Critical Turn: Rhetoric and Philosophy in Postmodern Discourse.* Carbondale: Southern Illinois University Press.

Lanigan, R. L. (1988). *Phenomenology of Communication: Merleau Ponty's Thematics in Communication and Semiology.* Pittsburgh, Pa.: Dusquesne University Press.

———. (1992). *The Human Science of Communicology.* Pittsburgh, Pa.: Dusquesne University Press.

Lecercle, J-J. (1992, Winter). Three-way games. *Philosophy Today*, pp. 336–50.

Levinas, E. (1984). Ethics and infinity. *Cross Current* 34:191–203.

———. (1991) *Otherwise than Being or Beyond Essence.* (A. Lingis, Trans.) Boston: Kluwer.

Lingis, A. (1994). *The Community of Those Who Have Nothing in Common.* Bloomington: Indiana University Press.

Lyotard, J-F. (1988). *The Differend: Phrases in Dispute.* (G. Van Den Abbeele, Trans.) Minneapolis: University of Minnesota Press.

———. (1989). *The Postmodern Condition: A Report on Knowledge.* (G. Bennington and B. Massumi, Trans.) Minneapolis: University of Minnesota Press.

———. (1990). *Phenomenology.* (B. Beakley, Trans.) Albany: State University of New York Press.

———. (1991). *The Inhuman.* (G. Bennington and R. Bowlby, Trans.) Stanford, Calif.: Stanford University Press.

———. (1994). *Lessons on the Analytic of the Sublime.* Stanford, Calif.: Stanford University Press.

——— and J-L. Thebaud. (1985). *Just Gaming.* (W. Godzich, Trans.) Minneapolis: University of Minnesota Press.

350   *Andrew R. Smith*

Merleau-Ponty, M. (1964). *Signs.* (R. C. McLeary, Trans.) Evanston, Ill.: Northwestern University Press.

———. (1968). *The Visible and the Invisible.* (A. Lingis, Trans.) Evanston, Ill.: Northwestern University Press.

———. (1986). *Phenomenology of Perception.* (C. Smith, Trans.) Atlantic Highlands, N.J.: Humanities Press.

Ormiston, G. L. (1990). Foreword. In the midst . . . multiplicities . . . always beginnings: An introduction to Lyotard's phenomenological episodes. In J-F Lyotard: *Phenomenology.* New York: Columbia University Press.

Piche, C. (1993). The philosopher-artist: A note on Lyotard's reading of Kant. *Research in Phenomenology* 22:152–60.

Readings, B. (1992, Winter). Pseudoethica epidemica: How pagans talk to the gods. *Philosophy Today,* pp. 377–88.

Reusch, J., and G. Bateson. (1968). *Communication and the Special Matrix of Psychiatry.* New York: Norton.

Rorty, R. (1985) Habermas and Lyotard on postmodernity. In R. Bernstein (Ed.): *Habermas and Modernity.* Cambridge, Mass.: MIT Press.

Sacks, O. (1987). *The Man Who Mistook His Wife for a Hat.* New York: Harper and Row.

Shannon, C. E., and W. Weaver. (1963). *The Mathematical Theory of Communication.* Urbana: University of Illinois Press.

Smith, A. R. (1993). Phenomenology of intercultural communication. In P. Blossner, E. Shimomisse, L. Embree, and H. Kojima (Eds.): *Japanese and Western Phenomenology.* Boston: Kluwer.

———. (1994). Phrasing, linking, judging: Communication and critical phenomenology. *Human Studies* 18 (1):139–61.

———. (1996). Simple signs, intermediate events: Lyotard on sophists and semiotics. In J. Stewart (Ed.): *Beyond the Symbol Model.* Albany: State University of New York Press.

——— and L. Shyles. (1994). On ethnocentric truth and pragmatic justice. In L. Langsdorf and A. R. Smith (Eds.): *Recovering Pragmatism's Voice: The Classical Tradition, Rorty, and the Philosophy of Communication.* Albany: State University of New York Press.

Stewart, J. (1986). Speech and human being: A complement to semiotics. *Quarterly Journal of Speech* 72 (1):55–73.

———. (1991). A postmodern look at traditional communication postulates. *Western Journal of Speech Communication* 55:354–79.

———. (1995). *Language as Articulate Contact: Toward a Post-Semiotic Philosophy of Communication.* Albany: State University of New York Press.

Surber, J. P. (1994, Fall). Kant, Levinas, and the thought of the "other." *Philosophy Today,* pp. 294–316.

Thomas, S. (1994). Artifactual study in the analysis of culture. *Communication Research* 21 (6):683–97.

Wilden, A. (1980). *System and Structure: Essays in Communication and Exchange.* London: Tavistock Publications.

Ziarek, K. (1989). Semantics of proximity: language and the other in the philosophy of Emmanuel Levinas. *Research in Phenomenology* 19:213–47.

Transgressing Discourses, the Voice of Other, and Kant's Foggy Island of Truth

Gary P. Radford

> *We have now not merely explored the territory of pure under-*
> *standing, and carefully surveyed every part of it, but have also*
> *measured its extent, and assigned everything in it its rightful*
> *place. This domain is an island, enclosed by nature itself*
> *within unalterable limits. It is the land of truth—enchanting*
> *name!—surrounded by a wide and stormy ocean, the native*
> *home of illusion, where many a fog bank and many a swiftly*
> *melting iceberg give the deceptive appearance of farther*
> *shores, deluding the adventurous seafarer ever anew with*
> *empty hopes, and engaging him in enterprises which he can*
> *never abandon and yet is unable to carry to completion*
>
> —Kant, 1781/1929, 257

Immanuel Kant's island, enclosed by "nature itself," represents in many ways the ideal of the dominant rationalistic discourses presented in this volume: that place where each part has been "carefully surveyed," "measured," and "assigned its rightful place." Kant calls this domain the "land of truth," where knowledge becomes truth when it is combined with the certainty of a priori categories. But, as Kant (1781/1929) points out, this island is a smaller part of a wider domain, "a wide and stormy ocean, the native home of illusion" (257). The fog banks and melting icebergs of this ocean give the appearance of further shores offering further certainty, knowledge, and truth. Yet, for Kant, the journey to these imaginary shores can result only in enterprises that, once begun, can never be completed. This is the domain of the Other: that place of "rudimentary, imperfect, unequal, emergent knowledge" (Foucault, 1973, 319).

The metaphor of the island of truth in the ocean of illusion is useful in summarizing some major themes that have arisen from the collection of works in this volume. These chapters have strongly suggested that the sands of the "island of truth" are not as stable as Kant idealized; that those sands are, and always have been, shifting; and that the fog banks which Kant saw on the horizon have now rolled over the land. The line between truth and illusion, self and Other, has been shown to shift like the continual movements of the tides upon the shoreline.

This volume has explored the nature of this new fog-laden terrain and taken as its focus that movement between rationalistic discourses and the voices of Other. It has not embarked on a direct critique of these discourses per se but rather a "problematization" (see Foucault, 1984a, 1985) of those matrices of forces that makes such discourses possible, useful, and powerful. The goal has not been to refute the so-called dominant accounts but to historicize them and examine the social functions that such accounts play in the context of practices. These problematizations have been enabled by articulating the voice of Other as one that both resists and interacts with a dominant account. These voices include Bryan Taylor's articulation of the voice of the "downwinders" through documentary photography, Joseph Gemin's articulation of the voice(s) of the rape victim categorized as having a "multiple personality disorder," Teresa Harrison's articulation of the voices of workers dealing with the practices of a democratic organization, and John Shotter's dialogical academic.

These characterizations owe much to the work of Michel Foucault and his influence is present in many of the chapters including those by Gross, Radford, Comerford, Cobb, Shotter, and Gemin. This body of work represents a transgression of Kant's island metaphor and the Enlightenment desire to chart the boundaries of "true" and certain knowledge; what Descartes (1641/1984) termed "clear and distinct perceptions." As Foucault (1973) describes, Descartes's project was concerned with "revealing thought as the most general of all thoughts we term error or illusion, thereby rendering them harmless" (324). The Enlightenment philosopher would then be free to "return to them, to explain them, and then to provide a method of guarding against them" (324). In modern thought, so-called "error and illusion" has returned in the form of the "unthought" (Foucault, 1973, 320): "dim mechanisms, faceless determinations, a whole landscape of shadow that has been termed, directly or indirectly, the unconscious" (320). But such a landscape, reminiscent of Kant's ocean, is not a terrain to be conquered and brought into the light of truth and certainty. It is the "dark half" of Stephen King's (1989) novel; the shadow thrown by positive knowledge which changes shape and dimension as thought moves toward or away from it. This, for Foucault (1973), is the Other:

Man has not been able to describe himself as a configuration in the *episteme* without thought at the same time discovering, both in itself and outside itself, at its borders yet also in its very warp and woof, an element of darkness, an apparently inert density in which it is embedded, an unthought which it contains entirely, yet in which it is also caught. The unthought (whatever name we give it) is not lodged in man like a shrivelled-up nature or a stratified history; it is, in relation to man, the Other: the Other that is not only a brother but a twin, born, not of man, nor in man, but beside him and at the same time, in an identical newness, in an unavoidable duality. (326)

William James (1962) describes a similar "Other" in his essay, "The Sentiment of Rationality." Let it be supposed that the fog on Kant's island of truth has been cleared by whatever means, and that the world is seen and known with a perfect clarity. A sea wall has been erected between the island and the ocean and, as James pictures the scene, "no otherness being left to annoy us, we should sit down at peace" (156). There would be no more questions to ask about the universe, no "further considerations to spin" (156). Upon reflection on this scene, James concludes that such a state of affairs is impossible and, like Foucault, sees the voice of Other as being omnipresent with respect to all claims to positive knowledge, no matter how complete. James (1962) writes:

Our mind is so welded to the process of seeing an *other* beside every datum of its experience, then when the notion of an absolute datum is presented to it, it goes through its usual procedure and remains pointing at the void beyond, as it in that lay further matter for contemplation. In short, it spins for itself the further positive consideration of a nonentity enveloping the being of its datum; and as that leads nowhere, back recoils the thought toward its datum again. (157)

There is no natural bridge between nonentity and this datum, and the thought "stands oscillating to and fro" (157), asking, Why was there anything but nonentity? Why this universal entity and not another? Indeed, for James, it is just when the attempt to fuse the manifold into a single totality has been most successful, when the conception of the universe as a unique fact is nearest its perfection, that "the craving for further explanation, the ontological wonder-sickness, arises in its extremest form" (157). Thus, "when all things have been unified to the supreme degree, the notion of a possible other than the actual may still haunt our imagination and prey upon our system" (157).

The chapters in this volume have made clear that the voice of Other speaks *beside* and not *because* of the dominant discourses of rationality. Foucault's metaphor of the Other as a twin bound in an unavoidable duality and James's metaphor of the constant oscillation between a datum and its Other both reflect the foundational concern of this collection. The problematic addressed by the contributors to this volume is not simply the description of how dominant discourses attempt to capture, categorize, and limit the voice of Other but to articulate an awareness that the voice of Other is a significant and often legitimate partner in a conversation. The consideration of the voices of science and Other in terms of a *dialogue* can potentially provide an orientation for the description of the means by which certain knowledge claims and genres come to be considered objective while others cannot. It foregrounds the recognition that all knowledge is constituted in sites of struggle in which some knowledge claims achieve the status of objectivity through the marginalization of competing voices, and not to its privileged access to an autonomous realm of truth. Further, the claim to objectivity must be made though the suppression of the site of struggle through which it is constituted and must work to maintain a situation in which the use of terms such as "truth," "objectivity," and "discovery" are considered self-evident and unproblematic. As Foucault (1972) argues: "only one truth appears before our eyes: wealth, fertility, and sweet strength in all its insidious universality. In contrast, we are unaware of the prodigious machinery of the will to truth, with its vocation of exclusion" (220).

The collection of chapters in this volume has explicitly reclaimed the notion of struggle in the constitution of knowledge by addressing the question of how the self-evidence of particular knowledge claims is produced and how such practices must operate to suppress their own contingency with respect to the practices of communication communities. By considering knowledge in terms of its status as discourse and communicative practice, an alternative set of issues has been raised in which an object of knowledge is considered in terms of the conditions which make possible its appearance as discourse, and the role which that discourse object plays with respect to its system of discourse objects. This perspective attempts a transgression of the limits that dominant discourses must take for granted in order to be considered objective, and through which it maintains the self-evidence of its cultural authority. Krippendorff (1993) remarks that "the revolution that this new understanding of reality can set in motion could be of a Copernican magnitude" (40) since "the epistemology of this new constructivism challenges the privileged role of disembodied knowledge and reveals its complicity in the emergence of hierarchical forms of social and political authority and its attendant requirement of submission" (40).

This transgression of limits allows one to see knowledge in terms of its possibilities rather than its referents. It reinstates the site of struggle as a key element in the formation of systems of knowledge claims and the objects of knowledge which are produced within them. Foucault (1984b) refers to this philosophical ethos as a "limit-attitude" (45); a view that must move beyond the outside-inside alternative in order to be at the frontiers. Foucault (1984b) writes:

> Criticism indeed consists of analyzing and reflecting upon limits. But if the Kantian question was that of knowing what limits knowledge has to renounce transgressing, it seems to me that the critical question today has to be turned back into a positive one: in what is given to us as universal, necessary, obligatory, what place is occupied by whatever is singular, contingent, and the product of arbitrary constraints? The point, in brief, is to transform the critique conducted in the form of necessary limitation into a practical critique that takes the form of a possible transgression. (45)

Is a genuine understanding of the voice of Other ever possible? The answer is positive, if one is prepared to accept a framework of articulation and interpretation that is constituted in a dialogue between a dominant discourse and the voice of Other. Foucault (1973) writes that "one cannot discover the unthought, or at least move towards it, without immediately bringing the unthought nearer to itself—or even, perhaps, without pushing it further away" (327). For Foucault (1973), man's own being is constituted and deployed in "the distance between them" (327). Transgressing discourses, *both* in terms of transgressing existing dominant discursive forms *and* in speaking discourses that transgress, is an orientation that views a dominant discourse and the voice of the Other as conversational partners, in which the discourse produced between them has the capacity to create new forms of knowledge and knowing. It is also a call for a fundamental movement in the manner in which truth and knowledge is approached. The shift advocated here is from an ethically uninvolved, disinterested, instrumental, ahistorical, and retrospective orientation to the taking of a practical, ethically involved, and historically concerned limit-attitude. The goal is not to lay foundations upon Kant's island of truth where a universal and formal version of the world is waiting to be articulated with complete certainty. It is to develop a sense of living involvement with that island's further development in which debate, struggle, creative imagination, and the voices of Other can and will shape the possibilities of what could come to be in the future. In Foucault's (1984b) words, transgressing discourses is all about giving "new impetus, as far and wide as possible, to the undefined work of freedom" (46).

References

Descartes, R. (1984). Meditations on first philosophy. In J. Cottingham, R. Stoothoff, and D. Murdoch (Eds. and Trans.): *The Philosophical Writings of Descartes, Vol. 2.* New York: Cambridge University Press. (Originally published 1641).

Foucault, M. (1972). The discourse on language. In M. Foucault: *The Archaeology of Knowledge.* (A. M. Sheridan Smith, Trans.) New York: Pantheon.

————. (1973). *The Order of Things: An Archaeology of the Human Sciences.* New York: Vintage.

————. (1984a). Polemics, politics, and problematizations: An interview with Michel Foucault (L. Davis, Trans.). In P. Rabinow (Ed.): *The Foucault Reader.* New York: Pantheon, 381–90.

————. (1984b). What is enlightenment? (C. Porter, Trans.). In P. Rabinow (Ed.): *The Foucault Reader.* New York: Pantheon, 32–50.

————. (1985). *The Use of Pleasure. The History of Sexuality. Vol. 2.* (R. Hurley, Trans.) New York: Vintage.

James, W. (1962). The sentiment of rationality. In W. Barrett and H. D. Aiken (Eds.): *Philosophy in the Twentieth Century.* Vol. 1. New York: Random House, 152–78.

Kant, I. (1929). *Critique of Pure Reason.* (N. Kemp Smith, Trans.) New York: St. Martin's Press. (Originally published 1781).

King, S. (1989). *The Dark Half.* New York: Viking.

Krippendorff, K. (1993). The past of communication's hoped-for future. *Journal of Communication* 43 (3):34–44.

Contributors

Sara Cobb is Associate Dean at the Fielding Institute in Santa Barbara, California.

Lynn Comerford teaches Communication at the University of San Diego and is completing her dissertation in the interdisciplinary Sociology/Communication Ph.D. Program at the State University of New York at Albany.

Donald P. Cushman is a Professor of Communication at the State University of New York at Albany. He is the author or coauthor of 120 chapters in books or articles in journals. He has written, cowritten, or edited ten books including *High-Speed Management: Organizational Communication in the Twenty-First Century* (with S. King, SUNY Press, 1995) and is the coeditor of the SUNY Press book series on Human Communication Processes.

Joseph Gemin is an Assistant Professor of Communication at the University of Wisconsin at Oshkosh. He is specifically interested in the social construction of identity and dialectical or paradoxical approaches to interpersonal communication. He is currently writing a book on the cultural reproduction of self-help identities.

Alan G. Gross is a Professor of Rhetoric at the University of Minnesota–Twin Cities. He is the author of *The Rhetoric of Science* (Harvard University Press, 2nd ed. 1996) and the senior editor of *Rhetorical Hermeneutics: The Art of Interpretation in the Age of Science* (SUNY Press, 1996) and of *Rereading Aristotle's* Rhetoric (University of Chicago Press, forthcoming). He is currently working on a rhetorical history of scientific communication.

Teresa M. Harrison is an Associate Professor of Communication in the Department of Language, Literature, and Communication at Rensselaer Polytechnic Institute. Her research and teaching focuses on organizational communication, communication theory, and computer-mediated communication. She is coeditor of the recently published anthology *Computer Networking and Scholarly Communication in the Twenty-First Century* (SUNY Press).

Michael Huspek is an Associate Professor of Communication and Director of the Communication Program at the California State University at San Marcos. He is interested in the role of discourse in maintaining and transforming relationships between dominant and subordinate cultures. His most recent work focuses on communicative reproduction and resistance among such groups as industrial workers, prison inmates, and urban street gangs, and appears in the *British Journal of Sociology, Communication Theory*, and *Journal of Pragmatics*. He is currently completing a book-length manuscript provisionally entitled *Dueling Codes, Oppositional Cultures*.

Branislav Kovačić is an Assistant Professor of Communication at the University of Hartford. He was formerly a journalist and magazine editor in Yugoslavia. He has written journal articles and book chapters on organizational communication, mental health and communication, and the rhetoric of the social sciences. He is currently working on a number of books addressing communication and transformations in the public sector, emerging theories of communication, and benchmarking and organizational communication.

Klaus Krippendorff is a Professor of Communication at the Annenberg School for Communication at the University of Pennsylvania. He is the author of *Information Theory* (1986) and *Content Analysis: An Introduction to its Methodology* (1980), which has been translated into four non-English languages. He is the editor of *Communication and Control in Society* (1979) and coeditor of *The Analysis of Communication Content* (1967). He has made numerous contributions to communication theory, cybernetics, design theory, and methodology. Much of his current research explores social constructions of reality, particularly emphasizing the role of language and discourse, human-centered theories of communication, cybernetic epistemology/hermeneutics, and liberating vocabularies in the social sciences.

Lenore Langsdorf is a Professor of Speech Communication at the Southern Illinois University at Carbondale. Her research and teaching areas are philosophy of communication, hermeneutic phenomenology, Deweyean pragmatism, and argumentation, cultural, and rhetorical theory. She is the co-editor, with Andrew Smith, of *Recovering Pragmatism's Voice: The Classical Tradition, Rorty, and the Philosophy of Communication* (SUNY Press, 1995).

Robert C. MacDougall is a doctoral student in the Department of Communication at the State University of New York at Albany. His research interests include organizational communication and social/ political philosophy. He is currently writing a book on the methods of argumentation in social science and philosophy.

Gary P. Radford is an Associate Professor of Communication at the William Paterson College of New Jersey. His research interests include the insertion of the works of Michel Foucault into the discursive structures of contemporary communication theory, library science, and cognitive psychology. He is currently writing a book provisionally entitled *A Genealogy of the Threshold.*

John Shotter is a Professor of Interpersonal Relations in the Department of Communication at the University of New Hampshire. He is the author of *Images of Man in Psychological Research* (Methuen, 1975), *Human Action and Its Psychological Investigation* (with Alan Gauld, Routledge, 1977), *Social Accountability and Selfhood* (Blackwell, 1984), *Cultural Politics of Everyday Life: Social Constructionism, Rhetoric, and Knowing of the Third Kind* (Open University, 1993), and *Conversational Realities: The Construction of Life Through Language* (Sage, 1993). He is also coeditor, with Kenneth J. Gergen, of *Texts of Identity* (Sage, 1989) and, with Ian Parker, of *Deconstructing Social Psychology* (Routledge, 1990). In 1990–91, he was the Cornell Distinguished Visiting Professor in Psychology at Swarthmore College, Philadelphia, and currently is a fellow in The Center for the Humanities at the University of New Hampshire.

Andrew R. Smith is an Associate Professor of Speech and Communication Studies at the Edinboro University of Pennsylvania. His research interests include the philosophy of language and intercultural communication. He is coeditor and a contributor to *Recovering Pragmatism's Voice: The Classical Tradition, Rorty, and the Philosophy of Communication* (SUNY Press, 1995) and has recently published two articles on the phenomenology of sexual harassment in the journal *Human Studies.*

Bryan C. Taylor is an Associate Professor of Communication at the University of Colorado at Boulder. His research interests include critical theory, cultural studies, and interpretive methods. His recent publications have appeared in the *Quarterly Journal of Speech, Critical Studies in Mass Communication, Journal of Contemporary Ethnography,* and *American Literary History.* He is currently working on a book about cultural representations of nuclear history.

─────────────Subject and Citation Index

Gary P. Radford

This index was created using the NEPHIS (Nested Phrase Indexing System) developed by Timothy C. Craven (see Anderson, J. D. & Radford, G. P., 1988; Craven, 1986) as implemented in the IOTA (Information Organization through Textual Analysis) textual database management system developed by James D. Anderson (see Anderson, 1988). In addition to subjects per se, all persons cited by the authors of the chapters in this book have been indexed, not only by the names of the cited authors, but also by the subjects related to the citation. Thus, these citing authors may be found not only under their names, but also under the subjects they discuss.

References

Anderson, J. D. (1988). IOTA: Information Organization based on Textual Analysis. In S. S. Intner & J. A. Hannigan (Eds.), *The Library Microcomputer Environment: Management Issues.* Phoenix, AZ: Oryx Press.
Anderson, J. D. & Radford, G. P. (1988). Back of the book indexing with the Nested Phrase Indexing System (NEPHIS). *The Indexer* 16(2): 79-84.
Craven, T. C. (1986). *String Indexing.* Orlando, FL: Academic Press.